In *The Roman Law Tradition* an international team of distinguished legal scholars explore the various ways in which Roman law has affected and continues to affect patterns of legal decision-making throughout the world. Roman law began as the local law of a small Italian city. It grew to dominate the legal relationships of the Mediterranean basin for the first five hundred years of our era. The revival of its study in the mediaeval universities led to its influencing the subsequent development of the legal system of western Europe and thereafter those parts of the rest of the world colonised from Europe. Roman legal ideas penetrated procedure as well as the substance of law and assisted the process of harmonisation and codification of local customary laws. Techniques of legal reasoning which first emerge in Rome continue in daily use. Roman law was also of immense significance in the emergence of modern political thought.

Few scholars have written as widely and influentially on the Roman legal tradition as Peter Stein, former Regius Professor of Civil Law in the University of Cambridge. As a tribute to and continuation of his work, the present volume brings together twelve studies, ranging in time from republican Rome to the European Court of Human Rights, which together provide an emphatic endorsement of the continued importance and vitality of that tradition.

The Roman Law Tradition

The Roman Law Tradition

Edited by

A. D. E. Lewis
University College London

and

D. J. Ibbetson
Magdalen College, Oxford

CAMBRIDGE
UNIVERSITY PRESS

Published by the Press Syndicate of the University of Cambridge
The Pitt Building, Trumpington Street, Cambridge CB2 1RP
40 West 20th Street, New York, NY 10011–4211, USA
10 Stamford Road, Oakleigh, Melbourne, 3166, Australia

© Cambridge University Press, 1994

First published 1994

Printed in Great Britain at the University Press, Cambridge

A catalogue record for this book is available from the British Library

Library of Congress cataloguing in publication data
The Roman law tradition / edited by A. D. E. Lewis and D. J. Ibbetson.
   p.   cm.
ISBN 0 521 44199 4 (hardback)
1. Roman law. I. Lewis, A. D. E. II. Ibbetson, D. J. (David J.)
KJA147.R66 1994
340.5'4 – dc20   93–24746   CIP

ISBN 0 521 44199 4 hardback

Contents

List of contributors	*page* ix
Foreword: Peter Stein, Regius Professor of Civil Law in the University of Cambridge, 1968–1993	xi
List of abbreviations	xii
1 The Roman law tradition DAVID IBBETSON AND ANDREW LEWIS	1
2 Labeo and the fraudulent slave ALAN RODGER	15
3 Doing and causing to be done PETER BIRKS	32
4 The danger of definition: *contrectatio* and appropriation DAVID IBBETSON	54
5 Going to the fair – Jacques de Révigny on possession WILLIAM M. GORDON	73
6 Bembo giureconsulto? MICHAEL H. CRAWFORD	98
7 Gentilis and the *interpretatio duplex* J. L. BARTON	104
8 *Ius gentium* in the practice of the Court of Admiralty around 1600 ALAIN WIJFFELS	119
9 Stair's title 'Of Liberty and Servitude' JOHN D. FORD	135
10 The *actio communi dividundo* in Roman and Scots law GEOFFREY MACCORMACK	159

11 Sale and transfer of title in Roman and Scots law DAVID JOHNSTON	182
12 'What Marcellus says is against you': Roman law and Common law ANDREW LEWIS	199
13 *Audi et alteram partem*: a limit to judicial activity DAAN ASSER	209
Index of sources	224
Index of names and subjects	229

Contributors

DAAN ASSER is Advocate General at the Supreme Court of the Netherlands and Professor of Civil Procedure at the Catholic University of Nijmegen.

J. L. BARTON is All Souls Reader in Roman Law in the University of Oxford and a Fellow of Merton College.

PETER BIRKS, FBA, is Regius Professor of Civil Law in the University of Oxford.

MICHAEL H. CRAWFORD, FBA, is Professor of Ancient History in the University of London.

JOHN D. FORD is a Research Fellow of Gonville and Caius College, Cambridge.

WILLIAM M. GORDON is Douglas Professor of Civil Law at the University of Glasgow.

DAVID IBBETSON is a Fellow and Tutor in Law at Magdalen College, Oxford.

DAVID JOHNSTON, an advocate at the Scots Bar, succeeds Peter Stein in the Regius Chair of Civil Law in the University of Cambridge in October 1993.

ANDREW LEWIS is Senior Lecturer in Laws at University College London

GEOFFREY MACCORMACK is Professor of Jurisprudence at the University of Aberdeen.

ALAN RODGER, The Rt Hon. Lord Rodger of Earlsferry, QC, is the Lord Advocate.

ALAIN WIJFFELS is Professor of Legal History at the Universities of Leiden and Louvain-la-Neuve and formerly a Research Fellow at Churchill College, Cambridge.

Foreword: Peter Stein, Regius Professor of Civil Law in the University of Cambridge, 1968–1993

> Bracton got his Roman law from the Glossators, Hale from the Humanists and Austin from the Pandectists. In each case the English writer was affected by the form and tendency of his source. Bracton found a legal grammar with which he was able to build up a picture of English law in substantive rather than procedural terms. Hale found an account of the parallel development of law and society from a primitive to a sophisticated system. Austin found the categories and tools of analysis with which to test the scientific quality of the law against an external standard.

This passage from his inaugural lecture as Regius Professor of Civil Law in Cambridge, *Roman Law and English Jurisprudence Yesterday and Today* (Cambridge, 1969), witnesses to the depth and range of Peter Stein's scholarship. He has made major contributions to jurisprudence and its history, and he is a master of the western European legal tradition and its Roman foundation.

His writings have ranged across the whole field of the Roman legal tradition: the substantive Roman law and its reflection in modern legal systems, both Common law and civilian, from Scotland to San Marino; the resurgence of Roman law in the twelfth and thirteenth centuries, and legal humanism in the sixteenth; the basic forms of legal reasoning and modes of legal analysis; Roman legal ideas and their pervasive influence on political philosophy.

Few scholars command more affection and admiration, and few have done more to illuminate not only Roman law as it was in its first life but also the huge contribution of the Roman law library to both the principal legal families in modern Europe. His long and immensely fruitful tenure of the Cambridge chair has also brought many to depend on his permanent availability as a leader and defender of a particular view of the law and legal education, as requiring, indispensably, an historical foundation.

PETER BIRKS

Regius Professor of Civil Law,
University of Oxford

Abbreviations

A.C.	Law Reports, Appeal Cases
All E.R.	All England Law Reports
B. & Ald.	Barnewall and Alderson's Reports
B. &. C.	Barnewall and Cresswell's Reports
B.G.B.	Bürgerliches Gesetzbuch (German Civil Code)
B.I.D.R.	Bulletino dell'Instituto di Diritto Romano
B. & S.	Best and Smith's Reports
Bing.	Bingham's Reports
Bulstr.	Bulstrode's Reports
Burr.	Burrow's Reports
C.	Codex Justinianus
C.B.	Common Bench Reports
C.L.J.	Cambridge Law Journal
C.L.P.	Current Legal Problems
Cmnd.	Command Paper
Co.Rep.	Coke's Reports
Coll.	Collatio Legum Mosaicarum et Romanarum
Const.	Constitutio(n)
Cr.App.Rep.	Criminal Appeal Reports
Crim.L.R.	Criminal Law Review
Cro.Eliz.	Croke's Reports of the time of Elizabeth I
D.	Digesta or Dunlop's Court of Session Cases
F.	Faculty Decisions, Court of Session
FIRA	Fontes Iuris Romani Antejustiniani (ed. S. Riccobono *et alii*, 2nd edn (Florence, 1968))
G. or Gaius	The Institutes of Gaius
Gl.	Gloss(a)
H.t.	Hoc titulo
J.Inst.	Justinian's Institutes
Kel.	Sir John Kelyng's Reports
L.Q.R.	Law Quarterly Review
Lib.Ass.	Liber Assisarum

Lord Raym.	Lord Raymond's Reports
M.	Morison's Dictionary of Decisions
M. & W.	Meeson and Welsby's Reports
Mod.	Modern Reports
O.J.L.S.	Oxford Journal of Legal Studies
P.R.O.	Public Record Office
P.S.	Pauli Sententiae
Q.B.	Law Reports, Queen's Bench Division
R.	Rettie, Crawford and Melville, Court of Session Cases
R. &. R.	Russell and Ryan's Crown Cases Reserved
S.	Shaw's Session Cases, first series
S.C.	Session Cases
S.D.H.I.	Studia et Documenta Historiae et Iuris
S.L.T.	Scots Law Times Reports
Salk.	Salkeld's Reports
Stra.	Strange's Reports
T.R.	Term Reports
T.v.R.	Tijdschrift voor Rechtsgeschiednis
Tab.	Twelve Tables
W.Bl.	William Blackstone's Reports
W.L.R.	Weekly Law Reports
Wils.	Wilson's King's Bench Reports
Y.B.	Year Book
Z.S.S.	Zeitschrift der Savigny-Stiftung für Rechtsgeschichte: römanistische Abteilung

1 The Roman law tradition

David Ibbetson and Andrew Lewis

Roman law was first the local law of a small central Italian city-state.[1] As the political boundaries of that state expanded, so did its law, until by the early centuries of our era its influence was widespread over and beyond the Mediterranean basin. Important evidence revealing the application of Roman law at local level has recently been dug up in southern Spain; the Roman lawyer and administrator Papinian is said to have been at the northern British capital York assisting the Emperor in dispensing justice in AD 208; and papyri from Egypt and the Arabian desert indicate the extent of penetration of Roman legal notions even in areas of strong local traditions. Conveyances written on wood in Transylvania testify to a near-obsessive desire to comply with metropolitan standards.

The Roman legal tradition was characterised not so much by its substantive rules as by its intellectual methodology. Between about 100 BC and AD 250 the Roman jurists developed techniques of analogical and deductive reasoning which produced a jurisprudence of enormous refinement and sophistication.[2] When the Emperor Justinian caused the substantial extracts from the writings of these classical jurists to be collected together in the early sixth century AD, he ensured the survival of their thought into subsequent ages. His Digest remains the finest monument of any legal culture.

---

[1] Studies of the history of Roman law are legion. The most recent comprehensive survey is F. Wieacker, *Römische Rechtsgeschichte*, vol. I (Berlin, 1988, continuing). A useful survey in English is the edition of H. F. Jolowicz's *Historical Introduction to the Study of Roman Law* by B. Nicholas (Cambridge, 1972), which was originally written to complement W. W. Buckland's *Textbook of Roman Law from Augustus to Justinian*, now in its third edition, by Peter Stein (Cambridge, 1963). There are numerous studies of the mediaeval development of Roman law in the collection *Ius Romanum Medii Aevi* (Milan, 1961–), which have full bibliographical references, and the ways in which Roman law came to influence western philosophy are well charted by J. M. Kelly, *A Short History of Western Legal Theory* (Oxford, 1992). Peter Stein's own contributions have spanned the whole field. Many of his essays are collected together in *The Character and Influence of the Roman Civil Law* (London, 1988); see too his *Regulae Iuris* (Edinburgh, 1966) and *The Teaching of Roman Law in England Around 1200* (London, 1990).

[2] For discussion of the jurists' techniques of interpretation, see Alan Rodger, 'Labeo and the Fraudulent Slave', below, pp. 15–31.

As the political fortunes of the Roman state waned, so did its direct legal influences. Nevertheless, albeit in Greek dress, it continued to apply within the limits of the Eastern Empire until the fall of Constantinople in 1453. During this long period it succeeded in directly influencing the legal traditions of neighbouring states. For example, its penetration into Slavic territories is well recognised, while significant parts of the Islamic law which developed after 661 have recently been traced to Roman roots.

The western successor states of the fifth and sixth centuries continued an administrative pattern modelled on that of the previous local Roman government, and this involved a commitment to Roman law, applied side-by-side with Germanic custom. Unsurprisingly, the law codes of these Germanic states reveal some infiltration of Roman legal ideas, though these survivals became progressively more corrupt. Still, the Christian Church continued to keep alive Roman ideas and solutions, even in such unpromising territory as Anglo-Saxon England, and the most fundamental ideas of Roman law were sustained in scholarly environments familiar with such works as Isidore of Seville's *Etymologia*.

The revival of the Roman law tradition stemmed from the concurrence of two conditions. First was the intellectual renaissance of the eleventh and twelfth centuries. While there may have been a continuous, if sparse, acquaintance with the Institutes, Code and Novels of Justinian from the time of their promulgation in the sixth century, there is no trace of the most important of the Justinianic tetralogy, the Digest, until the eleventh century, when two copies come to light. One, now known as the *Littera Pisana* or *Fiorentina* from the two Italian cities which successively preserved it, was a copy made within a generation of the original production. The other, known since Mommsen as the *Codex Secundus*, disappeared in the mediaeval period, though its contents were preserved in very many copies. All mediaeval scholarship was based on this text; the Florentine, treated almost as a sacred relic, was little studied before the Renaissance. The pattern of appearance of the *Codex Secundus* strongly suggests that it emerged into a strongly Lombardic legal world, perhaps into the well-known Lombard law school at Padua, though our earliest reliable evidence of its study fixes it in Bologna. Here there developed in the early twelfth century a strong scholarly tradition around Irnerius, and his pupils, the so-called Four Doctors: Hugo, Martinus, Bulgarus and Jacobus.

This intellectual resurgence provided no more than the launching-pad for the revival of Roman law. Setting it off were the political circumstances of the dispute between Pope and Emperor known as the Investiture Crisis, the question by whom and at what moment bishops and lesser clergy were to be invested with the symbols of their sacred and secular functions. The heat of this dispute lasted between 1075 and 1122, and for a long period both the imperial and papal powers encouraged their supporters to seek for any and every argument to support their cause. Amongst the sources culled for this purpose were the written remains of Roman law preserved in the Digest, Code and Institutes of Justinian. Foremost amongst the scholars who applied this learning to the new political uses was the imperial apologist Peter Crassus. Significantly, Crassus was a citizen of Ravenna, the Byzantine capital of reconquered Italy; here the Roman traditions were most obviously retained, and it may be surmised that it was here that Justinian's texts had been preserved.

The first century of scholarly work on the Roman texts was largely devoted to teasing out the meanings of the very heterogeneous opinions and materials contained in Justinian's Corpus Iuris Civilis. Four generations of students link Irnerius, through the Four Doctors, their students Rogerius, Placentinus, Pillius and the student of these in turn, Johannes Bassianus, with Azo and Accursius in the early thirteenth century.[3] Whilst these teachers produced a great variety of literature in their exploration of the understanding of their texts, they are chiefly remembered (and were in due course execrated) for their glosses to the text. Accursius found fame and notoriety as the compiler of the fullest and most widely diffused gloss, known as the Great Gloss or *glossa ordinaria*, which eventually found its way into the standard manuscript tradition and ultimately into the printed editions of the Corpus Iuris.

Later generations criticised the glossators for their narrow-minded literalness and absence of a wider cultural context, but the very narrowness imposed upon them by their task gave them an unrivalled knowledge of the Roman law texts on which their successors could build. Moreover, it is as well to remember that the Bolognese school did not come into being as a research institute, but as a teaching institution for immediate practical need: it needs to be constantly re-emphasised that Roman law at this time was not a dry university subject, but a matter of everyday utility throughout Europe. The law school at Bologna became the centre for the scholarly study of the Roman law texts, and all who wished to advance themselves in literate employment outside the church obtained their training there. The link between law and public administration which remains strong in the continental European tradition began here.

This first wave of reception of Roman law into the European legal tradition had many, intertwined, aspects. Three principal lines stand out. Most obvious is the infiltration of Roman law into written texts; behind this lies a widespread acceptance of Roman law as a subsidiary source of

---

[3] See further William M. Gordon, 'Going to the Fair – Jacques de Révigny on Possession', below, pp. 73–97.

law, filling in the gaps left by customary law; and finally there is the general adoption of the refined Roman techniques of legal reasoning.

As the general rate of literacy increased, there was a consequent rise in the respect accorded to written text and a tendency to reduce law into writing. Roman law provided both a technical vocabulary and a conceptual structure with which local customary law could be explicated. By so affecting the way in which law was conceived and expressed, Roman ideas profoundly influenced – one might say determined – the course of European legal history. This is most visible in the writings of legal commentators; in England, for example, the debt of Glanvill in the twelfth century and that of Bracton in the thirteenth to Roman law are strikingly obvious: whole sections from the latter are copied directly from Justinian's Institutes or the commentaries of Azo, and even those sections apparently most English can be shown to have close connexion with the classical Roman texts. Less obviously, but no less significantly, as local customary law came to be committed to writing there was an infiltration of Roman ideas. Sometimes this might have been conscious and deliberate, as in those Italian city-states whose pro-imperial ideology had caused them to treat Roman law as properly a part of their own customary law. Sometimes, however, it was less conscious, the product of relying on university-trained lawyers to prepare the written text: hence – to select only a sample of geographically distinct examples – there are Roman characteristics in the earliest written Norwegian code, the *Gulathingslov*, in a substantial number of English and Irish borough custumals, and in the majority of the French *Coutumes* of the thirteenth century. Even more, there was huge Roman influence on legislation, both national (the Spanish *Siete Partidas* and the French *Etablissements* of Louis IX, for example) and local. Urban codes were particularly influential in bringing about a diffusion of Roman ideas: the German laws of Lübeck and Magdeburg were widely adopted throughout central and eastern Europe, and the Spanish *Fuero Real* through much of Spain.

The use which had been made of the Roman legal texts in the Investiture controversy gave Roman law a status as essentially a supranational body of legal principles. In the hands of the Spanish scholastics of the sixteenth century and Grotius and his followers in the seventeenth and eighteenth, they were to form the base of an elaborate system of Natural law, an idealised system to which national laws might aspire. While the glossators and commentators similarly treated them as an ideal, they saw them as having a more practical revelance, supplementing the patchwork of local and national laws when these did not give any definitive answer to questions. There developed a widespread practice of academic lawyers giving *consilia* – opinions – to courts on disputed points of law. In some places university-trained lawyers had more direct input into legal practice; in the multi-member parlements of France, for example, they ensured a place for Roman law solutions despite both local and regal opposition to it. Judges operating outside their own immediate region, such as the *podestà* imported into Italian city-states, inclined towards judgments which could be supported by appeal to the written texts of Roman law when local custom was lacking or uncertain, if only to minimise the risk that they might themselves fall foul of the rule which provided that they should be personally liable for a litigant's loss if they gave a wrong judgment. All of these had the effect of providing a common substructure to the laws of continental Europe, wherever the influence of the professors had been pronounced, underpinning the common heritage of the written texts.

Just as importantly, the activities of the mediaeval Roman lawyers had ensured the survival of the rigorous analytical method of the classical jurists. Treating the Corpus Iuris as an authoritative text, they attempted to harmonise the arguments found there; while this essentially quixotic task ultimately led to much criticism, it did require the development of increasingly refined techniques of analysis. Moreover, because of the work of the academic lawyers called on to apply Roman law in the courts, these techniques which had been developed within the universities became a ubiquitous feature of European legal practice.

This general infiltration of Roman legal ideas and practices in the thirteenth and fourteenth centuries can be regarded as the first wave of the reception of Roman law. It marked, most crucially, the absorption of the methodological aspects of the Roman tradition into mediaeval Europe, and thence into the modern world.

The second wave of the reception of Roman legal ideas occurred in the sixteenth century. At an academic level, this was a product of the humanist scholars' perception of antiquity, an important dimension of which was provided by Roman legal sources. Exploration of the juristic texts transmitted from the Middle Ages, alongside recently recovered inscriptional evidence, led Antonio Agustín, Alciatus and their contemporaries to the earliest understandings of the historical dimension of Roman law.[4] It was on the basis of these explanations that later generations of Roman law scholars like Cujas (1522–90) and Donellus (d. 1591), working in northern Europe, were able to establish more critical and reliable editions of the basic texts.

As well as this academic aspect there was, most notably in Germany, a practical side to the second wave of reception. At the beginning of the

---

[4] See Michael H. Crawford, 'Bembo giureconsulto?', below, pp. 98–103.

sixteenth century there was a large range of local customary jurisdictions, reflecting Germany's notorious political fragmentation. In 1495 the remodelled imperial Supreme Court, the Reichskammergericht, adopted a written procedure. This written procedure was modelled on that found in the ecclesiastical courts, akin to that of the late Roman legal sources (as the common term 'Romano-canonical' implies). Moreover, just as the ecclesiastical practitioners had naturally looked to Roman law for solutions to substantive legal problems, so too the Reichskammergericht applied the 'common law of the Empire', i.e. the Roman Empire, which naturally meant Roman law. While the ground had been prepared to some extent by the Roman ideas present in the urban codes of the thirteenth century, it was only in the sixteenth that there was any wholesale or conscious Romanisation of German law. The direct importance of this was at first limited as large portions of the Empire were in practice privileged from its jurisdiction, but under its influence the independent princes began in the course of the century to remodel their own high courts along the same lines. It was not, however, until it became general practice to give reasons for decisions and to report these that Roman law scholarship and the practice of the courts came together.

Elsewhere in Europe, too, this second wave of the reception of the Roman legal tradition was significant. The humanist scholars of the fifteenth and sixteenth centuries had introduced a more historical criticism of the Roman texts, associated with a weakening of the belief in the Roman texts as revealing a near-authoritative supranational law. There was, in consequence, a greater influence on the harmonisation of Roman law with national and local laws. Paramount in this regard was Hugo Grotius' *Introduction to the Jurisprudence of Holland* (*Inleidinge tot de Hollandsche Rechtsgeleertheyd*), published in 1631. Writing in the vernacular rather than in Latin, he laid down the foundations of Roman-Dutch law which could be built on by his successors Vinnius, van Leeuwen, Voet and Noodt. A similar harmonisation was brought about in France by the works of Coquille and Dumoulin, for example, and in parts of Germany by Ulrich Zasius. But even where there was a move away from the traditional reverence for the Roman text, there was no such departure from the ideals of the Roman legal method: the practical dominance of reasoning by deduction and analogy was so deeply embedded that it was easily detachable from its roots in the writings of the Roman jurists.

This harmonisation of Roman law and customary laws reached its peak with the codification movement in continental Europe, beginning with the Prussian Code of 1794. Most important of these codes by far was the French *Code civil*, dating back to 1804, in part at least because it was widely adopted in other countries. The heavy Roman influence – stemming from the pre-existing Roman substrate as well as from the university training of their draftsmen and of those writers such as Pothier on whom the draftsmen relied – is visible in all of these codes. At the same time, though, they introduced a formal diversity into the Romanised systems. Although as a matter of history it could be recognised that French law and German law, for example, had common roots in Roman law, as a matter of legal practice they were clearly distinct systems. No longer were the learned opinions of the professors of Roman law of any direct relevance to the determination of disputes in the courts; no longer was legal practice anchored on the rock of a common legal culture.

While legal humanism had its part to play in the balancing of Roman law and customary law, the older methods of textual analysis continued to play their part too. Such analytical jurisprudence reached its high point in the writings of the Spanish neo-scholastics such as Molina and Covarruvias in the sixteenth century. Their writings, and the shorter but no less profound works of Grotius, provided the base for two separate traditions of considerable importance. Most notable was the growth of international law; the influence of Grotius' *De Iure Belli ac Pacis* was of paramount importance in the formulation of this common law of nations, but behind lay a tradition of writers and practitioners including Oxford's Regius Professor of Civil Law, Alberico Gentili (1552–1608).[5]

The second tradition flowing from the *De Iure Belli ac Pacis* was that of secular Natural law. St Thomas Aquinas, writing in the thirteenth century, had laid down a firm framework of Natural law, but this was strongly anchored in the theology of the Roman Catholic Church. This was hardly congenial to the post-Reformation Protestants, and still less so to the thinkers of the Enlightenment. Basing themselves firmly on a perception of human reason, such writers as Wolff and Thomasius expanded Grotius' systematic analysis into an all-embracing framework of ideal law. The paternity of the substantial categories of Roman law is transparent, as is the theoretical rooting of their position in the implicit belief of the mediaeval civil lawyers that Roman law represented a universally valid supranational system of legal principles. The close parallel between this form of Natural law and Roman law is clearly shown by the ease with which the ideas of the Natural lawyers flowed into the writings of the German Pandectists, culminating with Windscheid's very influential *Lehrbuch des Pandektenrechts* in 1862.

Though it may not be so easily visible, Roman influence was none the less important in shaping the legal consciousness away from the principal

---

[5] See J. L. Barton, 'Gentilis and the *Interpretatio Duplex*', below, pp. 104–18.

centres of Roman law studies in continental Europe. In Scotland, for example, local customary and feudal law were dominant in the mediaeval period, though these owed much more to the Anglo-Norman influence introduced in the twelfth century than to native Celtic tradition. The constant interference of the more powerful state of England in its affairs, coupled with its less favourable commercial and agricultural base, prevented the emergence of a strong central government. Reforms and development of the judicature in the sixteenth century led to the introduction of Romano-canonical procedures into Scottish courts, which led in turn, as elsewhere, to the adoption of substantive Roman solutions.[6] The first universities had been founded in Scotland in the course of the fifteenth century, but they seem not to have flourished, and it became the recognised practice for young Scots lawyers to travel to the continent for their legal education. This ensured that there was a steady supply of lawyers versed in the latest civilian scholarship to staff the Scottish courts. No system of instruction in local law existed to maintain the defences against the Roman encroachment; so much so that when the Faculty of Advocates, who controlled admission to legal practice before the courts, reformed their admission procedures in 1610 to include an examination, a considerable part was devoted to Roman law. As happened elsewhere in Europe, though, the tension between Roman law and customary law was satisfactorily resolved, though in the case of Scotland this did not lead to any written code. The proximity and continued influence of the avowedly non-Roman English legal system, and the survival of a strong native feudal tradition, led to the establishment of a distinctly Scottish legal tradition founded on the institutional writings of the seventeenth and eighteenth centuries.[7]

England provides another variation on the theme of the infiltration of the Roman legal tradition into European legal culture. While there may have been some limited acquaintance with Roman legal ideas in the Anglo-Saxon period, it is not until the middle of the twelfth century that we begin to find evidence of detailed study of the Roman texts. At this time there was no gulf between the study and practice of law in England and the rest of Europe; and, as happened elsewhere in Europe, Roman ideas filtered into the English legal consciousness principally through written commentaries (Glanvill in the late twelfth century, Bracton in the mid thirteenth). Yet, again as occurred elsewhere, there may have been a

---

[6] For examples of the parallels between Roman law and Scots law, see David Johnston, 'Sale and the Transfer of Title in Roman and Scots Law', below, pp. 182–98, and Geoffrey MacCormack, 'The *Actio Communi Dividundo* in Roman and Scots Law', below, pp. 159–81.
[7] See John D. Ford, 'Stair's Title "Of Liberty and Servitude"'. below, pp. 135–58.

more direct influence on actual legislation. The creation of new proprietary remedies closely resembling the possessory interdicts of the Romans in the middle of the twelfth century has been considered by many scholars to indicate both knowledge of the Roman law and perhaps conscious borrowing from it. And when in the fourteenth century the royal courts articulate the custom of the realm that an innkeeper should be strictly liable for the loss of his guest's goods, it is not easy to avoid the conclusion that at some stage in the past the quasi-delictual liability of the Roman *caupo* had found its way into accepted English practice.

This strong Roman influence on the Common law did not last beyond the end of the thirteenth century. Until the sixteenth century, English legal history is largely the story of the development of remedies based on indigenous procedures. There was little, if any, room for the use of Roman learning in such a context, and the vitality and apparent sufficiency of the local procedures prevented for some time the development of Romano-canonical alternatives in secular contexts. Moreover, the strong position of Roman law in continental universities was not mirrored in England, where its study was intermittently forbidden; advanced legal study (and education) in England took place in the Inns of Court rather than the universities, and was the study of the Common law rather than the Roman, of local procedure rather than general substance. Behind this, too, lay a strongly held ideological commitment to the insularity of the Common law and its separateness from the Civil law, which was seen to be at the base of continental systems. Those courts which did operate according to Civil law procedures – the ecclesiastical courts, the university courts of Oxford and Cambridge, and the Court of Admiralty[8] – were marginalised by the courts of Common law notwithstanding their importance in practice. A potentially greater channel for the infiltration of Roman procedures and substantive law was the Court of Chancery, which crystallised in the late fourteenth century, whose procedure was never forced into the rigorous straitjacket of the Common law, and whose judges – the masters – had frequently received a university education. Even here, though, there is little real evidence of the direct borrowing of Roman legal ideas.

The strength of the belief in the insularity of the Common law has protected it from wholesale supersession by Roman legal ideas. Nevertheless, from the later Middle Ages there have been several pulses of infiltration of Roman law into Common law. The first, rather ragged, movement occurred in the sixteenth and early seventeenth centuries. Most obviously there was a revival of the study of Bracton and of the use of his

---
[8] See Alain Wijffels, '*Ius Gentium* in the Practice of the Court of Admiralty around 1600', below, pp. 119–34.

text in Common law contexts in the wake of its printing in 1560; since Bracton had been a judge, the work attributed to him could be cited freely without any fear of being accused of trying to import Romanism into England. Less obviously, but more importantly, English lawyers seem to have had an increasing familiarity with the Roman texts. It was not merely that humanists like Thomas More were closely in touch with the principal currents in contemporary European culture, or even that scholarly lawyers at the end of the century – Thomas Egerton and Francis Bacon, for example – are known to have studied the Digest; the dearth of easily comprehensible texts on English law meant that reliance was increasingly placed on the basic literature of Roman law. Justinian's Institutes were widely recommended as an introductory legal text, and John Cowell transparently based his *Institutiones Iuris Anglicani* on them; the introduction to such a severely practical book as William West's *Symbolaeography* is a crude, and unacknowledged, translation of a contemporary civilian text.[9] A second pulse, briefer but sharper in its focus, occurred around 1700, when the Roman ideas contained in Bracton and in the seventeenth-century Natural lawyers' writings enjoyed a brief vogue. The best-known product of this movement is the adoption by the Common law of the Roman rules relating to the standard of care demanded of bailees; but it can hardly be coincidental that much of the articulation of the Common law of torts at this time closely followed the lines laid down by the Roman jurists.[10] After a period of relative quiescence, the Roman texts move into the light again in the first half of the nineteenth century.[11] Ambiguities in the law of contract were resolved by reference to Roman law, often mediated through the works of Pothier; the law of easements was transformed from a cumbersome mediaeval structure (itself with a Roman base imported from Bracton) into one more in keeping with an urbanised society by direct borrowings from Roman and contemporary civilian texts. It may be that each of these pulses should be regarded as no more than a brief fashion; but each time the fashion died out, it left its legacy in the form of rules embedded in English law.

In terms of substantive rules, one legacy of Roman law has been a considerable measure of uniformity throughout the legal systems of western Europe, stretching beyond this area into regions which adopted European-based codes. Most obviously, the Roman conceptual categories underpin both the structure of modern codified Civil law systems

---

[9] We are grateful to Peter Stein for bringing this to our attention some years ago.
[10] See Peter Birks, 'Doing and Causing to be Done', below, pp. 32–53.
[11] See Andrew Lewis, '"What Marcellus Says is Against You": Roman law and Common law', below, pp. 199–208.

and the structure of the contemporary uncodified Common law. The institutional division of the law into persons, things and actions, with the law of things further subdivided into property and obligations, is so familiar to students of the modern law that it is hard to recognise it for what it is, as an invention of the Roman jurists.

At a more abstract level the Roman law tradition embodies not merely this common core of rules, but a common way of thinking about law. In the perception of the Roman jurists law was a discrete field of knowledge, conceptually disembedded from the society in which it operated, yet very much a part of the heritage of that society. Legal learning was artificial learning; and lawyers were a distinct body of experts who had – or who claimed to have – mastered this learning. The post-Roman western legal tradition is underpinned by an identical commitment to the discreteness of law and to the professionalisation of lawyers. There is an enormous gulf between this conception and the more integrated social conception, where law is essentially indistinct from custom and practice, and where the nearest approach to a lawyer is the tribal elder who is perceived as remembering and articulating this custom.

Treating law as a system of rules separate from social practice, the Roman jurists were forced to develop new forms of reasoning to enable them to identify valid rules. Following the model of the grammarians they used arguments of analogy and contrariety in order to demonstrate the essential similarity or dissimilarity of a new case to an established one, and developed techniques of induction and deduction in order to generate abstract principles from concrete cases and then to reason outwards from these principles to new situations, though invariably tempering these results with a sense of pragmatism. These techniques – not always coupled with pragmatism, it must be said – were used to great effect by the mediaeval jurists in their attempts to harmonise the apparently conflicting texts of the Justinianic corpus. Although the onset of humanism, with its stress on the accurate interpretation of texts, to a large degree undermined this particular form of very close legal analysis and exegesis, the essential principles of legal reasoning survived among both academic and practical lawyers.

In the contemporary legal world their presence is most clearly marked in those states whose law has not undergone comprehensive codification, and where there has remained a strong commitment to the positivist thesis that law is a discrete field of rules and principles. Despite their denunciation as a sham by a range of legal theorists, the Roman jurists' techniques clearly continue to underpin the grammar of the modern Common law. Judges still use arguments by analogy identical to those used by the Roman jurists in order to distinguish one case from another;

and the same basic methods of induction and deduction enable the courts to generate principles and definitions from a set of specific cases and then to apply them to new situations.[12]

The same principles of reasoning form a part of the lawyers' armoury in codified legal systems too. In some places, such as Germany, they have remained powerful tools; in France their importance has been to some extent eroded in the twentieth century as a result of the increasing practical recognition of the quasi-legislative function of the judge, while in places like Switzerland the Code itself expressly authorises the judiciary to take into account extra-legal factors in order to mould the law to changing circumstances. Such a freedom to depart from previous practice, releasing judges from the shackles of strict legal reasoning, has inevitably diminished the centrality of formal canons of legal thinking. Even in these states, though, the Roman law method has been fully integrated into the whole structure of legal thought, and the widening of the scope of judicial discretion has done nothing to disturb the duality of legislation and interpretation which has characterised the post-Roman legal tradition.

The influence of Roman law has not been confined to purely legal contexts; it has had a profound influence on the development of western political theory.

Roman ideas lie at the basis of the mediaeval theory of the state. Already in the twelfth century, as has been seen, one significant reason for the revival of study of the Digest was its political utility in the hands of imperial apologists like Peter Crassus, who were able to cull from its texts support for a theocratic, absolutist conception of the state: 'quod principi placuit, legis habet vigorem' and 'princeps legibus solutus'. The prince himself is beyond the reach of the law; his will has the force of law. Such notions of regal supremacy were subsequently upheld at the start of the sixteenth century by Zasius and Budé, in Germany and France respectively; a century later English writers like John Cowell, who openly argued for the adoption of Roman legal categories as a means of imposing some structure on the mass of the Common law, were vilified for attempting to import such absolutist doctrines into England.

On the other hand, a more 'democratic', conciliarist position was advanced by such writers as Azo and Hugolinus, stressing the origin of the prince's authority in the people's concession of authority – a concession which might in some circumstances be withdrawn. This approach is to be found, for example, in Bracton, and appears to have been the dominant one in the Middle Ages. Aquinas drew from the fact that the prince

[12] For an example, see David Ibbetson, 'The Danger of Definition: *Contrectatio* and Appropriation', below, pp. 54–72.

was said to be above the law the conclusion that this was because he could not in fact be brought before a court, but went on to argue that this in no way relieved him from the duty of voluntary obedience to its demands, citing in support a rescript of Theodosius from the Code: 'It is a saying worthy of the majesty of the ruler, if the prince professes himself bound by the laws; for even our own authority depends on that of the law.' These ideas, coupled with ideas drawn from the Roman civil law, formed the base of the social contractarianism that came to dominate political thinking in the seventeenth century, and whose influence is still strongly felt in twentieth-century political theory.

A second feature of modern thought whose source can be traced back into the Roman texts is the idea of the Law of Nations, its name taken from the Latin *ius gentium* (the term commonly used before Bentham invented the phrase 'International Law'). International law has its roots in two principles. First was the realisation that nation-states had independent legal capacity or, to put it in Baldus' terms, 'The King is emperor in his kingdom', with all the legislative capacity and political independence of the Roman Emperor. The second principle, articulated by William of Ockham in the context of arguments seeking to limit the universalist claims of the Pope or Emperor, was of the equality of these states. The Roman notion of *ius gentium* was an attempt to express the apparent universality of legal ideas observed by the Romans in the legal systems of other peoples. In the hands of some sixteenth-century writers expressing the interests of the inhabitants of the newly discovered American continent, it came to signal the relationship between groups or nations, limiting the exploitation of the New by the Old World. Nations came to be seen as entities with legal rights and obligations, and their relationships with other nations were subjected to regulation in treatises like Gentili's *De Legationibus*, treating of the duties of ambassadors, and *De Iure Belli*, on war. Channelled through Grotius' *De Iure Belli ac Pacis*, these ideas have formed the basis of the theory and practice of international law, the most substantial flowering of the Roman legal tradition in the twentieth century.

Equally important in the twentieth century has been the revival and growth of theories of natural, or fundamental, rights. Some credit is due to William of Ockham, for his use of the subjective sense of *ius*, but again it was Grotius who laid down the essential groundwork for this in his *Introduction to the Jurisprudence of Holland*. Here Grotius expounded a national legal system based upon ideas of private rights; at many points his arguments are underpinned by concepts drawn straight from the Roman texts, as in the derivation of the modes of acquisition of property from the law of nature. It has been shown that his work (together with that of Samuel Pufendorf) lies behind Thomas Hobbes and John Locke, linking the ideas of private property and individual civic rights developed by the political theorists of the seventeenth and eighteenth centuries firmly into the Roman legal tradition. In the same way the basic moral values which form the classical principles of natural justice, the maxims *audi alteram partem* and *nemo iudex in causa sua*, form a part of this tradition, mediated through the Natural law writings of Grotius and his successors.[13]

The Roman law tradition has produced many and varied effects on the legal and intellectual map of the world. Its influences upon the legal systems of western Europe resulted in the age of colonialism in its being spread from Holland to South Africa, Sri Lanka and Indonesia; from France to Quebec, Louisiana and francophone Africa; and from Spain to Texas, South America and the Philippines. Post-colonial export of the tradition has been most marked in Japan and Turkey, though China has also been influenced to a certain extent. Everywhere it has had an influence through the western tradition of political thought. Codification and the influence of subsequent legal orders has modified but not fundamentally altered the importance of this living cultural tradition, so that it remains to the present day the most widely flung and all-pervasive legal tradition, challenged only by the economic competitiveness of the Anglo-American Common law. The maintenance of critical scholarly study of the roots and consequences of the tradition would scarcely need justification in an age more imaginative and less materialistic than our own. Those who have contributed to this volume hope thereby to have furthered each in his way the exposition of the Roman Law Tradition so fruitfully explored by its dedicatee.

---

[13] For the former of these maxims, see Daan Asser, '*Audi et Alteram Partem*: A Limit to Judicial Activity', below, pp. 209–23.

2   Labeo and the fraudulent slave

Alan Rodger

'Every age should be the mistress of its own law.'[1] Altmeister Maitland learned this lesson from Germany, and Peter Stein, who has illuminated the history of legal developments in many lands and at different periods, has passed that same lesson on to us.[2] The message from Cambridge is surely correct – provided, of course, the new mistress does not too readily believe that in her salad days all her judgments are better than the mature reflections of her predecessors. Yet even a suitably cautious age will find that some things must simply be fashioned afresh. The assessment of damages under the *lex Aquilia* is an obvious example. Confronted with unacceptable penal elements and retrospective calculations, legal practitioners soon devised their own schemes, while leaving the Roman rules to be the playthings of generations of legal scholars and historians.[3]

Happily the playthings of Romanists do not wear out quickly, and the Roman rules are studied to this day. But when the original doctrine is discarded in this way, the texts can be particularly difficult to interpret. Since we have all been brought up in a system with different assumptions, we tend to look at the texts through spectacles which are coloured by those assumptions. Even the most conscientious legal historian will find it hard to see a problem as the Roman jurists would have seen it. I have chosen to discuss a text on the *lex Aquilia* whose interpretation illustrates these problems in an acute form.

D.9.2.23.4 (Ulpian, 18 *ad edictum*). Sed et si servus qui magnas fraudes in meis rationibus commiserat fuerit occisus, de quo quaestionem habere destinaveram, ut fraudium participes eruerentur, rectissime Labeo scribit tanti aestimandum, quanti mea intererat fraudes servi per eum commissas detegi, non quanti noxa eius servi valeat.

---

[1] F. W. Maitland, 'The Making of the German Civil Code', in *The Collected Papers of Frederic William Maitland*, vol. III, ed. H. A. L. Fisher (Cambridge, 1911), 474, 487.
[2] P. Stein, 'Continental Influences on English Legal Thought', in *The Character and Influence of the Roman Civil Law* (London and Ronceverte, 1988), 209, 229.
[3] See, for example, H. Coing, *Europäisches Privatrecht*, vol. I (Munich, 1985), 510; R. Zimmermann, *The Law of Obligations* (Cape Town, Wetton and Johannesburg, 1990), 1019.

On the other hand, in the case of killing a slave who had committed great embezzlements in running my affairs and whom I had resolved to examine by torture in order to drag out the names of his accomplices in dishonesty, Labeo writes very rightly that he must be valued according to my interest in detecting the frauds he had committed and not according to the value of the harm he had done.[4]

Scholars[5] agree that the opinion of Labeo in this text is an early illustration of the process by which the measure of damages under chapter 1 was expanded beyond the value of the slave himself to include the loss suffered by the individual plaintiff as a result of the slave's death. But, if that much is agreed, modern writers remain divided about the exact scope of Labeo's decision. We begin by looking at their views.

Existing interpretations

The facts stated in the text are quickly summarised. A slave who had falsified his owner's accounts was killed just when his owner was intending to have him tortured to uncover the names of his accomplices. Labeo says that in the Aquilian action the owner can recover his interest in detecting the frauds committed by the slave ('quanti mea intererat fraudes servi per eum commissas detegi') rather than what the *noxa* of the slave would be worth.

Parts of the text are unsatisfactory. Beseler[6] rightly sees that the opening words ('sed et si') are an inappropriate link with the preceding sentence – presumably a sign that material has been cut out. The most glaring defect perhaps is that 'servi' and 'per eum commissas' cannot both have occurred side by side in the original. Mommsen[7] deletes 'servi' while Lenel[8] removes 'per eum commissas'. Subject to what is said below,[9] for our purposes it does not particularly matter which solution is adopted, since the point being made in the text would remain the same: the measure of value is related to detecting the frauds of the slave who has been killed. The last clause beginning 'non quanti' is generally regarded as very obscure. Beseler[10] and others delete it. In the final section of this chapter I

---

[4] C. F. Kolbert (trans.), *Justinian, The Digest of Roman Law. Theft, Rapine, Damage and Insult* (Harmondsworth: Penguin, 1979), 83.
[5] For literature see Zimmermann, *The Law of Obligations*, 971 n. 125; D. Medicus, *Id Quod Interest* (Cologne and Graz, 1962), 241 n. 34; *Index Interpolationum*.
[6] G. Beseler, 'Romanistische Studien: Zur Sachbewertung nach dem aquilischen Recht' (1930) 50 Z.S.S. 18, 25 at 27; earlier, 'Einzelne Stellen' (1922) 43 Z.S.S. 535, 540. M. Kaser, *Quanti Ea Res Est* (Munich, 1935), 174 n. 26 follows Beseler's later, more radical, attack. P. Voci, *Risarcimento e pena privata nel diritto romano classico* (Milan, 1939), 72 drily observes that the text does not have the defects which Beseler and Kaser wish to find in it.
[7] *Stereotype Digest, ad loc.*
[8] O. Lenel, *Palingenesia Iuris Civilis*, vol. II (Leipzig, 1889), 526 n. 1.
[9] Text accompanying n. 45.   [10] 50 Z.S.S. 27.

hope to show that it is substantially genuine, but for the moment we can concentrate on the previous clause, which gives us the measure of damages which Labeo adopted.

The facts of the problem as set out in the text refer to the plaintiff's intention to torture the slave in order to discover the identity of his accomplices. So scholars tend to treat the text as though Labeo must have directed his assessment of damages to that possibility. In other words they treat the text as if Labeo assessed the plaintiff's damages by reference to what the plaintiff might have found out if the slave had not been killed and he had been able to question him. For instance, Professor Ankum says that according to Labeo the defendant must pay the plaintiff's interest 'à ce que soient découvertes au moyen de lui les fraudes de mon esclave (et de ses complices)'.[11] It is sufficient to notice that under cover of brackets Ankum has smuggled in a reference to the slave's accomplices, who do not appear in the Latin text. Medicus,[12] who would like to interpret the text in a similar fashion, presumably sees the difficulty of straining the meaning of the Latin in this way and simply says that this part of the text is not in order. In other words he says that the original classical decision has been obscured, perhaps by being abridged.

Beseler eventually concluded that the discussion in the text is probably almost completely spurious, since, by including an element of value peculiar to the plaintiff, it did not conform to his theory that under chapter 1 a plaintiff could recover only the highest value which the slave would have had for any owner in the last year.[13] Beseler's general thesis has not found favour, and his radical approach to this text has not been followed.[14] Instead, later writers have rightly pointed out that the text gives us at best a truncated version of the original discussion in which the differing views of various jurists would have been canvassed. Perhaps because he feels that the opinion attributed to Labeo would have been too radical for a jurist of his time, Medicus[15] suggests that in the original text he may have held the opposite opinion. Even although such false attributions are known to occur, there seems little reason to follow the approach of Medicus.

The underlying reason why modern scholars are uneasy with the text is that the plaintiff's claim for damages appears to run up against a difficulty which has puzzled lawyers since the time of the glossators. The plaintiff was about to have the slave tortured in order to discover the

[11] H. Ankum, 'L'*Actio de pauperie* et l'*actio legis Aquiliae* dans le droit romain classique', in *Studi in onore di Cesare Sanfilippo*, vol. II (Milan, 1982), 11, 49 n. 82.
[12] *Id Quod Interest*, 241 n. 36.   [13] 50 Z.S.S. 27.
[14] See, for example, Th. J. Gerke, 'Geschichtliche Entwicklung der Bemessung der Ansprüche aus der "Lex Aquilia"' (1957) 23 S.D.H.I. 61.
[15] *Id Quod Interest*, 242.

names of his accomplices. He would then, it is assumed, have sued the accomplices or, if they too were slaves, their owners in some kind of action to recover what he had lost because of their fraud. So in the Aquilian action he would sue for a sum representing what he might have been able to recover in those actions. Now even if you approach the problem in this way and even if you assume that the plaintiff knows the sum which he lost through the fraud, his claim seems to face an insuperable objection. In order to demonstrate his loss from the death of his slave, the plaintiff would have to show what names the torture would have revealed and so what actions he would have brought and what damages he would have won. But if he could prove this in an Aquilian action, then equally he could prove the same matters in proceedings against the accomplices or their owners, and so he should still be able to sue them for the frauds in spite of his slave being killed. On that basis he has lost nothing, and should be able to recover nothing, under this head. Yet, it is said, Labeo awards the plaintiff damages for loss.

This insoluble riddle confronts any scholar who maintains that Labeo favoured awarding damages to the plaintiff on the basis of his lost opportunity to sue the accomplices. But Beseler,[16] who realises that the text does not actually say this, states the position accurately when he says that the 'problem posed' in the text (*Problemstellung*) contains what he regards as a vicious circle. He rightly does not suggest that the vicious circle is found in Labeo's answer. What Labeo's answer actually says is that Labeo measured the plaintiff's recovery by reference to what it was worth to him to have the slave's frauds detected. That is to say, Labeo looked to the discovery of the frauds of the dead slave and not to any discoveries about the accomplices. Moreover, despite what Medicus and the others say, Labeo does not even mention the sum of which the plaintiff has been defrauded. His reasoning is quite different. Of course, Beseler thinks the reasoning is nonsense, but this does not matter for now. The important thing is that it is the problem and not Labeo's answer which seems to give rise to the logical impasse. As we shall see in due course, Labeo's answer is really directed at a slightly different point.

It is none the less useful to look more closely at the route by which modern scholars try to escape from their self-imposed logical dilemma. We may take Medicus' treatment as typical since it has found favour with subsequent writers. Medicus says[17] – perhaps correctly, perhaps incorrectly – that we can assume that the plaintiff knew how much he had lost through the frauds. What he did not know was the identity of his slave's accomplices. Had he been able to find this out, the argument runs, he

---

[16] 50 Z.S.S. 27.   [17] *Id Quod Interest*, 241.

would have been able to sue the accomplices and recover his loss – in an *actio furti* according to Wolff,[18] in an *actio doli* according to Ankum.[19] Of course, for various reasons the plaintiff might not have discovered any accomplices. For instance, the slave might not have spoken up under torture – older writers get round this difficulty by saying that in the light of experience with torture the jurist assumed that the slave would not have been able to withstand the pain of the rack.[20] Even if the slave had named an accomplice, the accomplice might have been another of the slaves of the plaintiff himself or he might not have been worth suing. One can easily devise circumstances in which the plaintiff would have lost nothing under this head through the death of his slave. But, says Medicus, Labeo or Ulpian argued that the defendant should not be able to take advantage of any difficulty which such arguments posed for the plaintiff in establishing his loss, precisely because that very difficulty was caused by the defendant's wrongful act. So, on this view, the jurist allows the plaintiff to recover his loss from the frauds even though he cannot actually prove that by killing the slave the defendant deprived him of any real prospect of recovering that loss from anyone else.

Not surprisingly, perhaps, Ankum[21] characterises this supposed approach of Labeo as 'audacious'. At all events it is difficult to accept, not least because, as we have seen, it does not fit at all with the wording of the text, especially on the measure of recovery. But in substance also this interpretation is very problematic. Its proponents are really saying that Labeo swept aside the usual requirements and allowed the plaintiff to recover a loss which he could not prove. Of course, as a legal innovator[22] Labeo might have suspended all the usual rules, but there is no sign of anything similar in other damages texts.

Value and loss

None of the solutions proposed up till now is satisfactory,[23] and in fact the text has been misinterpreted. To understand it we must recall the basic

---

[18] H. J. Wolff, *Beiträge zur Rechtsgeschichte Altgriechenlands und des hellenistisch-römischen Aegypten* (Weimar, 1962), 276 n. 7 (1936).
[19] *Studi Sanfilippo*, vol. II, 49–50.
[20] For example, A. Pernice, *Zur Lehre von der Sachbeschädigungen nach römischem Rechte* (Weimar, 1867), 242–3.
[21] *Studi Sanfilippo*, vol. II, 50 n. 85.
[22] D.1.2.2.47 (Pomponius, *Liber Singularis Enchiridii*).
[23] C. H. Monro, *Digest IX.2 Lex Aquilia* (Cambridge, 1928), 28 argues that 'perhaps' the defendant deliberately kills the slave to prevent him revealing his accomplices. Unfortunately there is not a hint of that in the text. Cf. J. B. Thayer, *Lex Aquilia, On Gifts between Husband and Wife* (Cambridge, MA, 1929), 80–1.

facts about a plaintiff's claim under chapter 1.[24] In Institutes 3.212 Gaius tells us that in an action under chapter 1 you do not only estimate the worth of the *corpus*, but you also take into account the additional loss which the owner suffers through the death of the slave. The loss caused by the death is therefore regarded as separate from the value of the slave. As one of his examples of this separate loss Gaius mentions the owner whose slave has been instituted heir under someone's will but is killed before he enters the estate. The owner loses the estate and can recover not only the value of the slave but in addition this loss which has been caused by the slave being killed. Justinian explains that the inclusion of such losses was due to the interpretation of the jurists rather than to the wording of the statute itself.[25] Gaius does not mention the calculation of the highest value of the slave ('quanti in eo anno plurimi ea res fuit') until Institutes 3.214. It is this calculation, rather than the assessment of loss, which is sometimes said to lead to the owner recovering more than the slave was worth at the time of his death. This is still reflected in the treatment in Justinian's Institutes.[26]

So a plaintiff's claim may comprise two elements: the highest value of the slave in the previous year and the loss which the owner suffers as a result of the slave being killed. As long as the notion of value is confined to the market value of the slave, the two ideas are obviously very different. But if the idea of value is widened so as to include value to the plaintiff himself, rather than simply market value, the line between them becomes blurred. In particular both the idea of the value of the slave to the actual plaintiff and the idea of the loss caused to the actual plaintiff by the killing of his slave will tend to be thought of as the interest of the plaintiff in not having his slave killed. Yet, as his Institutes show, the two elements in fact remained distinct even in the time of Justinian. The reason must have been that, whereas you could recover the highest value of the slave in the last year, even if you had not actually lost all of that value, you could recover only those consequential losses which you had actually suffered. So it would matter into which category any element was placed. If, for instance, the jurists had said that an inheritance formed part of the value of a slave, then the slave's owner would have been entitled to recover the value of the slave, including the value of the inheritance, even if the owner had not actually lost the inheritance.[27] But, as we saw, Gaius 3.212 makes it plain that an inheritance was not included in the slave's value and the plaintiff could claim for the loss of the inheritance only if he had actually lost it because of the slave being killed.

---

[24] Gerke, 23 S.D.H.I. 61 contains a very full citation and discussion of the literature on the matter.

[25] J.Inst. 4.3.10.   [26] J.Inst. 4.3.9.   [27] Cf. Beseler, 50 Z.S.S. 25f.

If we now return to 23.4 we find that it is the remains of part of Ulpian's commentary on what elements made up the highest value of a slave for this purpose. The context of the text in the Digest, to which we now turn, makes this clear.

The context

The principal objection to all the existing interpretations of the text is that they really ignore its context in the Digest. Of course, Wolff[28] remarks that the paragraph comes in the middle of decisions which are based on something other than the pure value of the object, and Zimmermann[29] says that 23.4 shows the practical consequences of adopting the principle stated by Ulpian in 21.2: 'hoc iure utimur, ut eius quod interest fiat aestimatio'. But while that may be the wider setting of our passage, the immediate context is much more narrowly drawn.

H.t. 23.4 comes from a group of texts which deal in some detail with the provision in chapter 1 that the plaintiff is entitled to recover the slave's highest value in the last year.[30] The discussion begins at 23.3 with a statement of the rule, apparently culled from Julian. Beseler[31] rightly remarks that we hardly need Julian to tell us the rule since it is in the statute, but this reference may have been part of Julian's reasoning for the decision in the example of a valuable slave artist whose thumb had been cut off at some time during the year before he was killed. His owner recovers the slave's highest value – his value before his thumb was cut off. Then follows our text, which is in its turn followed in 23.5 by the case of a slave who became vicious during the year before his death – the plaintiff recovers the value of the slave before his character changed for the worse. Finally in 23.6 we are told that all the advantages which made the slave more valuable during the year are to be added to his value.

Even if we allow for the possibility of some interpolation,[32] the general position seems to be clear. Our text occurs in a section of commentary where Ulpian is writing about cases in which the value of the slave is to be calculated by reference to a particular time during the preceding year when he had a higher value than at other times. Our text must raise the same kind of issue.

It is astonishing to notice just how consistently this aspect of 23.4 has been ignored by writers. Going back no further than Voet, we find that,

---

[28] *Beiträge*, 276 n. 7.   [29] *The Law of Obligations*, 971–2.
[30] A. Rodger, 'Damages for the Loss of an Inheritance', in *Daube Noster*, ed. W. A. J. Watson (Edinburgh and London, 1974), 289, 297 n. 40 at 299. Some of the conclusions in that essay need to be revised.
[31] 50 Z.S.S. 27.   [32] *Index Interpolationum* and *Supplementum, ad hos locos*.

when he states the rule that the value was to be calculated by reference to the highest value in the last year, he refers to 23.3, 23.5 and 23.6, but jumps over 23.4 in silence.[33] We find exactly the same phenomenon in Windscheid,[34] and more recently, for instance, in Jolowicz[35] and Lawson.[36] None of the writers try to explain why 23.4 occurs at this point if they are interpreting it correctly and if, as they seem to think, it has nothing to do with the subject-matter of the surrounding texts. Only Beseler's radical view[37] that 23.4 is a marginal gloss could even begin to account for the phenomenon of the text occurring here, and even he would have to explain why the gloss was written at this point in the first place.

The exact place of 23.4 in this stretch of Ulpian's commentary is therefore the single most important clue to its proper interpretation and it points to the fact that the text concerns the assessment of the highest value of the slave in the past year. In h.t. 23.3–23.6 all Ulpian's remarks are directed specifically at the calculation of the highest value of the slave. He mentions factors in the slave himself which affect his value. So in 23.3 the value of a slave who is an artist is increased by this talent which he possesses, but apparently assessing that value would not always be straightforward. Presumably, some other skills at least, for example musical ability, would have been thought to increase a slave's value. In 23.5 Ulpian mentions a slave of good character who becomes vicious. The slave's character affects his value, but again complications are being envisaged. When we look at 23.4 in the context of these texts, we see that here also Ulpian is considering whether the plaintiff should be entitled to recover an element in the slave's value which would have been of value to his owner. The element in question is the information which he possessed. That is the real significance of the text, and it has been somewhat overlooked by scholars who have concentrated instead on the supposed illogicality of Labeo's decision.

Certain forms of knowledge must frequently have been relevant to a slave's value. The talent of an artist will often be a combination of skill and knowledge which he has been taught. The slave who teaches Greek

[33] J. Voet, *Commentarius ad Pandectas* (Lugduni Batavorum, 1698), 9.2.4.

[34] B. Windscheid, *Lehrbuch des Pandektenrechts*, 9th edn by Th. Kipp (Frankfurt-on-Main, 1906), vol. II, 455 n. 20.

[35] H. F. Jolowicz, 'The Original Scope of the *Lex Aquilia* and the Question of Damages' (1922) 38 L.Q.R. 220, 227–8. The article as a whole had the misfortune to suffer the honour of a magisterial review by Lenel: (1922) 43 Z.S.S. 575.

[36] F. H. Lawson, *Negligence in the Civil Law* (Oxford, 1950), 59 n. 2 and 140, note to Gaius 3.214; F. Lawson and B. Markesinis, *Tortious Liability for Unintentional Harm in the Common Law and the Civil Law*, vol. I (Cambridge, 1982), 4 n. 25 at 189 and 35 n. 244 at 197.

[37] See in particular Ankum, *Studi Sanfilippo*, vol. II, 47f.

will be valued for his knowledge of the language as well as for any skill he has in imparting it to his pupils. The doctor will be valued for his medical knowledge as well as for his skill in tending his patients. H.t. 23.4 takes the argument a significant step further, since in these other cases the slave's knowledge would be of use to any purchaser and so would be reflected in his value on the market. Here, on the other hand, Ulpian is discussing the slave's knowledge of his accomplices in a fraud – knowledge which would be of use, and hence of value, only to his owner who had been defrauded. The extent to which such personal elements should be allowed in calculating the value of a slave under chapter 1 seems to have been the subject of discussion among the jurists. While in h.t. 33 *pr.* (Paul, 2 *ad Plautium*) Paul quotes an opinion from Sextus Pedius, who seems to have held that nothing other than the ordinary value of any object should be recovered, that narrow view of Sextus Pedius did not go unchallenged, since in h.t. 22 *pr.* (Paul, 22 *ad edictum*) and h.t. 55 (Paul, 22 *quaestionum*) we find indications that the judge should take account of the value of a slave to the individual plaintiff. H.t. 23.4 is simply another facet of that general discussion, and Ulpian is concerned with the problem of the value of knowledge which the slave possessed and which would be of interest principally at least to his owner. Since the idea that a slave's value could be increased by this kind of knowledge may seem strange at first sight, it is worth noting that, even on the existing interpretation of the text, scholars like Medicus contemplate that a claim could lie for knowledge which the slave had, since they argue that the plaintiff can recover for the loss which he suffers through not being able to extract that knowledge by torturing the slave. But the context indicates that Ulpian regarded the slave's knowledge of the events surrounding the frauds as having a possible bearing on the value of the slave himself; he did not treat the loss of that knowledge as a separate loss which the plaintiff suffered as a result of the death of the slave. We must therefore follow Ulpian and consider whether any part of the slave's knowledge of the frauds could be said to increase his value to his owner.

Information about accomplices

When we say that under chapter 1 the plaintiff is entitled to recover the highest value of his slave in the last year,[38] we mean that in practice in an action a plaintiff will try to establish what the highest value of his slave was during that time. When he does this, as is shown by the example of the artist whose thumb had been cut off, the plaintiff will not necessarily be

---

[38] 50 Z.S.S. 27.

saying that he lost all of that highest value. So in this respect he will not be trying to establish his 'loss' in the same way as a plaintiff would in a modern system. Once he has established the highest value, the plaintiff can point to the terms of chapter 1 and say that he should be awarded that amount – plus any loss which he has suffered through his slave being killed. He will, moreover, resist any suggestion that he should recover less than the slave's highest value, simply because he has actually lost rather less.

We saw above that 23.4 deals with the highest value of the slave. It follows that it concerns an owner who would have been trying to establish his highest value in the last year; he would not have been trying to establish what he had lost through his slave being killed. The owner would therefore have argued that immediately before his death the slave was particularly valuable to him, because under torture he would have revealed the name of his accomplices and the owner could have obtained some recompense from them. Put shortly, the plaintiff was arguing that the value of the slave was increased because of certain knowledge which he had.

In one way the owner was on strong ground: just before the slave was killed, his owner would indeed have thought that his value was increased because of this factor and might well have acted on that assumption. So, for instance, if someone had offered to buy the slave for the going rate in the market, his owner would presumably have refused to sell him, on the basis that he wanted to discover who had been his accomplices in the fraud. If the slave had lived long enough to be tortured, then the owner's belief that he was more valuable on this account might well have been proved correct. But in fact, precisely because he was killed, with the benefit of hindsight we can see that the owner was wrong. The slave was worth nothing more to his owner on account of any knowledge which he had about his accomplices, since he took that knowledge with him to the grave without revealing it.

The importance of the distinction can be seen if we change the facts of the case a little. Suppose that the slave had indeed been tortured and had revealed accomplices from whom his owner had then got back some of the proceeds of the fraud. Within the next twelve months the slave is killed and his owner brings an action under chapter 1. In this case also the plaintiff would have argued that during the last year the highest value of his slave included the value of his knowledge of his accomplices. But on these facts the plaintiff could establish that this knowledge had actually made the slave more valuable to him at one stage by pointing to the sum which he received from the accomplices as a result of torturing the slave. If we think only in terms of the highest value of the slave, then it seems that in this example the plaintiff would have succeeded in his claim. The difference between the cases is that in this example the slave was indeed more valuable to the plaintiff because of his knowledge, whereas in h.t. 23.4, although his owner could not see this at the time, the slave was not in fact more valuable, because he was going to be killed before anyone could find out what he knew. In assessing the slave's highest value, the judge looks back, perhaps from the time of his decision, but at least from the moment when the slave has been killed, and uses hindsight to determine what the value of the slave was at any particular period, in the light of events which have occurred since that time. This is what Ulpian means when he tells us of the slave in 23.2 that 'retrorsum quanti plurimi fuit inspicitur'.[39]

This second example is also useful in highlighting the difference between an approach based on the highest value of the slave in the last year and our modern concept of damages as compensation for loss. We have difficulty in accepting that under the *lex Aquilia* the slave's owner could claim a sum which includes money which he has already obtained from the slave's accomplices. Yet if you once concede that the slave's value can include his value as a source of information, the rest follows: that will be the slave's highest value and the plaintiff can claim that value under chapter 1. To avoid that result, you would need to invoke a further principle, viz. that the plaintiff must make allowances for any element in the value which he has not actually lost. In other words you would have to adopt an approach which had moved away from concentrating on the highest value of the slave to the plaintiff and towards focusing on what loss the plaintiff had suffered as a result of the death of the slave.

But the two approaches are very different and, while the jurists may have moved towards an actual assessment of loss, that development appears to have been a slow and uneven process, especially in chapter 1 cases.[40] It has often been pointed out[41] that there is no general statement in the sources that the highest value was to be reduced; and the general view among scholars is that no reductions were made under chapter 1.[42] In other words once the judge determined what the highest value to the particular plaintiff was, that sum should be awarded. Indeed we know from Gaius and elsewhere that from time to time a plaintiff would receive more than he had actually lost.[43] Awarding the plaintiff an amount which

---

[39] See Rodger, *Daube Noster*, 297. I would now argue more strongly that the clause is classical.

[40] D. Daube, 'On the Use of the Term *Damnum*', in *Collected Studies in Roman Law*, vol. I, ed. D. Cohen and D. Simon (Frankfurt-on-Main, 1991), 279, 328.

[41] Beseler by contrast simply assumes the existence of such a principle introduced apparently by juristic interpretation: 50 Z.S.S. 26.

[42] For example Kaser, *Quanti Ea Res Est*, 176f.; Medicus, *Id Quod Interest*, 243f.

[43] Gaius 3.214; J.Inst. 4.3.9. and 4.6.19.

included the value of sums which he had already recovered would simply be a more extreme example of the anomalies which could arise. The anomalies are perhaps more disturbing to us today than they would have been to Roman jurists, for whom the penal element in delictual actions was not at all strange.

If we now go back to h.t. 23.4, we are in a better position to appreciate the kind of discussion which would have occurred at this point. It seems likely that Ulpian would have mentioned a case similar to that of the slave who had been killed after he had revealed the names of his accomplices. Ulpian may well have reported the views of jurists who thought that in such circumstances the plaintiff was entitled to claim a value for his slave which included the value of the information given by the slave even though this might mean that the plaintiff was over-compensated. Equally there may have been others who felt that by their time the notion of *interesse* had developed to such an extent that the plaintiff should not be allowed to claim the value of the knowledge if indeed he had actually lost less than that sum. As a refinement on that case Ulpian would have introduced the problem which is narrated in 23.4, where the slave is killed before he can be tortured. Here again the plaintiff would have argued that the highest value of the slave included something for the value of his knowledge. The defendant would presumably have replied that on these facts he should not have to pay anything for this element. Again there may have been discussion among the jurists about what the correct approach should be, but it seems likely that the predominant view would have been against the plaintiff. Looking at the matter in retrospect, the judge should reject the argument that the value to the plaintiff of his slave had been increased by the slave's knowledge about his accomplices, since in fact as a result of his death that knowledge had proved to be of no value to the plaintiff.

Information about the slave's frauds

But even though the piece of text which is now h.t. 23.4 may have formed part of such a discussion, it is equally certain that Labeo's answer as recorded is not formulated in any of the ways which we have just outlined. We must therefore explore the matter a little further. Unfortunately the facts of the case are not stated very clearly. For instance, the text does not tell us when the frauds were committed or when they were discovered. The date of the frauds is probably not important, but the date when they were discovered is significant. Even though the text is silent, it gives the impression at least that the frauds had been detected not long before the slave's death. After all, the plaintiff had been about to try to discover who

Labeo and the fraudulent slave

else had been involved, and it would be surprising if he had left that inquiry for over a year after his original discovery. We are doing no great violence to the text if we assume that the frauds had been detected within the year preceding the slave's death.

In assessing the value of the slave, Labeo attached importance to the discovery that he had committed frauds. Indeed, to judge from the text, he linked the measure of recovery to it: 'quanti mea intererat fraudes servi per eum commissas detegi'. We can therefore proceed on the basis that Labeo is somehow or other prepared to increase the value of the slave by a sum representing the plaintiff's interest in detecting his frauds. Since both the slave's role in the frauds and the frauds themselves had already been discovered before his death, an assessment of the slave's value based on the discovery of those frauds would refer back to an earlier point in the year.

At first sight it seems perverse to suggest that the discovery of the frauds could somehow or other increase the slave's value. After all, in reality, the discovery that a slave had been falsifying his master's accounts would immediately reduce his market value. If, for instance, his owner wished to sell the slave, he would need to tell prospective purchasers what the slave had done.[44] This would make him less attractive and so lower his price. But that factor would not necessarily matter in a claim for damages for the slave's death. Under chapter 1 any such reduction in the slave's value might have been disregarded if he were killed within a year, since his owner was entitled to recover the slave's highest value, i.e. his value before the frauds were uncovered. But even here we must be cautious, since, if the frauds had occurred some time before, the defendant could well argue to some effect that uncovering them simply showed that the slave had been a crook and as such worthless throughout the year. None the less the jurists would still have to decide whether the discovery of the frauds pointed to some other element which should be included in the slave's value.

The only guide to Labeo's decision can be what the text actually says, and since it links the value of the slave and the discovery of the frauds, we may not be too rash if we assume that Labeo's reasoning must also have been based on a link between the slave and the discovery of the frauds. Especially in the light of the discussion in the previous section of this chapter, the most obvious link would be that the slave was somehow or other responsible for the frauds being discovered. This link does not actually appear in the text itself, although some scholars, for example Ankum,[45] might be prepared to interpret 'per eum' and 'detegi' together

---

[44] See O. Lenel, *Das Edictum Perpetuum*, 3rd edn (Leipzig, 1927), 555.
[45] *Studi Sanfilippo*, vol. II, 49f., especially at n. 82.

so as to make it say that the frauds were uncovered through the slave. This is to strain the existing text but it is conceivable that the rather unsatisfactory Latin at this point ('servi per eum commissas') has come about because of the compilers abbreviating an original in which Ulpian had explained that the plaintiff discovered the frauds through the slave. Most obviously the frauds might have come to light because the slave decided to confess – though in that event he might have been expected to reveal who his accomplices had been. Or else some act of the slave might have alerted his owner, and then, whether under torture or not, he admitted what he had done.

We can therefore usefully identify three factual situations, although elements of more than one could be combined in a particular problem:

Case 1 A slave is killed just when his owner is about to torture him to try to discover who his accomplices were in a fraud.
Case 2 A slave is killed after he has been tortured and has told his owner who his accomplices were in a fraud.
Case 3 A slave is killed after he has told his owner that he had been committing fraud on his owner.

It is suggested that in 23.4 Labeo was asked to consider a problem of the following kind. During the year before a slave was killed, his owner had discovered through him that he had committed various frauds and, just before he was killed, the owner was intending to torture him to find out who his accomplices had been. What was the value of the slave to the plaintiff for the purposes of chapter 1? The problem is a combination of case 3 and case 1. For the reasons given in the previous section, on the case 1 point Labeo would have held that the slave's value was not increased by the slave's knowledge about his accomplices. But in answering the question Labeo made an additional point. He observed – and we can probably assume that he was the first to do so[46] – that at one stage the slave's value to the plaintiff had in fact been increased by his knowledge of his own frauds and that the plaintiff was therefore entitled to recover, as part of the slave's value, what it was worth to him to discover those frauds.

Labeo's decision is really based on the same principle as the decision in case 2, where the slave had in fact been tortured and had revealed the names of the accomplices. Just as in that case at one stage the value of the slave to his owner included the value of the information which he revealed about his accomplices, so here on the case 3 point Labeo saw that at one

---

[46] To this extent correctly: A. A. Schiller, 'Trade Secrets and the Roman Law', in *Studi in onore di Salvatore Riccobono*, vol. IV (Palermo, 1936), 98 n. 145.

stage the value of the slave to his owner had included the value of the information which he had revealed about his own frauds. The fact that in case 2 the slave has been tortured and has revealed information about his accomplices' actings whereas in case 3 he has spoken without torture and has revealed information about his own actings can make no difference to the underlying legal position – as Labeo spotted and as Ulpian or the compilers acknowledged by saying that he 'rectissime scribit'. Labeo was really saying that if the judge looked back over the year, he could see that, at any time after the slave had committed the frauds and before he revealed them, he was carrying about in his head this information which was of value to his owner. If the slave eventually revealed that information, then the judge could see that the information in the slave's head had been of value to his owner and so it had actually formed part of the slave's overall value to his owner.

None the less case 3 does differ subtly from case 2, and Labeo's decision is properly regarded as breaking new ground. In case 2 the owner knows or at least correctly believes that his slave has the information; in case 3, on the other hand, the owner is not aware at the time that the slave has the information, since, of course, the existence of this information does not come to light unless the slave actually speaks about the frauds. Indeed the information forms part of his value to his owner only if the slave reveals it. So in case 3 we have a situation where at one point in the year, after the slave has committed the frauds but before he reveals them, his actual value to his owner is higher than the owner realises at the time.

We can also compare this claim in case 3 with the claim in case 1 for the knowledge which the slave has, but which he does not reveal because he is killed. In case 3 the slave is in actual fact more valuable to the owner because of knowledge about the frauds which the owner does not realise the slave has until he speaks up. By contrast in case 1 the owner knows, or rightly believes, that the slave has certain knowledge and therefore considers that he is more valuable to him. But in actual fact the slave is not more valuable on this account, since he will be killed before the knowledge can be extracted from him. Doubtless a variant of case 1 may have been discussed. Suppose that the slave has committed frauds and intends to reveal them, but before he can do so, someone else tells his owner. The slave is then killed. In such a case it would seem that a judge looking back would hold that the slave's information never in fact formed any part of his value, because in the event the owner discovered the frauds from another source. A judge making a retrospective assessment of value has plenty of opportunities to indulge a taste for dramatic irony.

It is also important to notice that a reference to the decision of Labeo on the case 3 point would have fitted well into this particular part of

Ulpian's commentary. As we saw, in the segments which the compilers have selected Ulpian is mentioning cases where the slave's value for the purposes of the assessment under chapter 1 is not his value at the time he was killed but his value at some other time during the year. On Labeo's approach to case 3 the slave's value to his owner would include his knowledge about the frauds, and his role in them, only up to the moment when he revealed what had happened. Once the frauds are known to his owner, the slave's knowledge of them and of his role in them ceases to be any part of his value to his owner. It follows that, where the slave is killed after he has admitted the frauds, that knowledge does not form part of his value to his owner at the time of his death.

Labeo is prepared to include the value of this information in the value of the slave, but he is careful to say that the value of the claim is the value of discovering the frauds. Again this is something which is concealed in the usual interpretation of the text, which maintains that the sum to be recovered is the sum of which the plaintiff was defrauded. Labeo's version is much less crude than this modern formulation, and, what is more important, it makes excellent sense. He realises that, if the discovery of the fraud had not led to any money or property being recovered by the plaintiff, then the discovery as such had not in fact been worth anything to the plaintiff. Suppose the slave had told the plaintiff about the frauds. The plaintiff would then have been able to investigate them and discover what he had lost. He might have found, for instance, that the slave had taken 10,000 sesterces by falsifying the accounts, In itself that discovery would not be worth anything to the plaintiff at least as far as past frauds (*fraudes ... commissas*) are concerned – though it might have prevented any further depredations. After all, the owner is no better off just because he has discovered that he has lost 10,000 sesterces and that the slave has spent that sum on riotous living. On the other hand the discovery would lead to a positive financial return if, for instance, the plaintiff then searched the slave's quarters and found 5,000 of the missing 10,000 sesterces hidden under his bed. Then one could say that discovering the slave's frauds had been worth 5,000 sesterces to the plaintiff. Labeo therefore thought that in such a case the slave's value included this element and the plaintiff should be allowed to recover it in the Aquilian action.

This is precisely the distinction which is being made in the text if we read the account of Labeo's decision as a whole, including the part at the end of the text in the clause 'non quanti noxa eius servi valeat'. No particular criticism has been directed at the grammar or language of the clause. Scholars have just been unable to fathom what it means, because they have not understood the point which Labeo was considering. We can adopt the straightforward translation of Kolbert, which gives *noxa* its well-established meaning and treats it as referring to the wrong[47] committed by the slave. Labeo is then saying that the true measure of the slave's value includes the interest of the plaintiff in uncovering the slave's delict ('quanti mea intererat fraudes servi per eum commissas detegi') rather than the value of the slave's delict itself ('non quanti noxa eius servi valeat'). In other words the plaintiff cannot simply add to the slave's value the sum which the slave took; but the plaintiff can argue that his value should include the amount which the plaintiff got back as a result of what the slave had told him.

Of course, the result of giving the plaintiff even this additional amount would be that he would be rather over-compensated, since in the example given above he would already have recovered the 5,000 sesterces and would obtain a corresponding sum of 5,000 sesterces in the Aquilian action. As we saw when discussing case 2, that is not in itself a reason for thinking that Labeo could not have held this view. On the other hand such an approach to the plaintiff's claim in a delictual action has not commended itself to later ages – and this may help to explain why Labeo's view, which was so appreciated by Ulpian, has been so misunderstood and disparaged by more modern jurists.[48]

---

[47] E. Seckel, *Heumanns Handlexikon zu den Quellen des römischen Rechts*, 9th edn (Jena, 1907), s.v. *noxa* 1.

[48] I am grateful to Professor Peter Birks and Dr David Johnston for their comments on an earlier draft. Professor Birks in particular allowed me to bombard him with letters and made time for me to come and discuss the matter with him at short notice. After this essay was in the press I received, by the courtesy of the author, G. Valditara, *Superamento dell'destinatio rei nella valutazione del danno aquiliano ed estensione della tutela ai non domini* (Milan, 1992). The author's explanation of 23.4 differs from mine, but he does recognise the need to interpret the text within the context of 23.3 and 23.5. See, for example, at 170.

3 Doing and causing to be done

Peter Birks

Why did both the Roman and the English law of civil wrongs adopt, and override, causal tests which were embarrassingly, even absurdly, restrictive? This paper, a token in recognition of a debt to Peter Stein, suggests an answer. Harm-verbs in the active voice drove the law into a causal corner. A system which imposes liability on a person who does (damages, injures, wounds, breaks, spills) will be forced to define doing narrowly and will have to supplement the liability for doing with another for causing to be done (be damaged, injured, wounded, broken, spilled). This effect becomes stronger as the harm-verb is tied more closely to physical damage. It is stronger for 'break' than 'harm' itself.[1] Defendants will compel the law to look for the act of breaking. The image of a person doing that act cannot admit much intervention between the defendant's bodily movements and the thing broken.

The seeming absurdities have nothing to do with competitions between concepts of liability different from our own, much less with the pursuit of different socio-economic goals.[2] Litigation was caught up in the implications of the words in which it happened to be conducted. The modern law school, with the help of procedural reforms, is able to debate ideas detached from actional forms. When it looks at the past, it must learn to

---

[1] German law appears to have escaped this difficulty despite the use of an active harm-verb in the dominant text, namely 823 I B.G.B.: 'A person who wilfully or negligently injures the life, body, health, freedom, property, or other right of another contrary to law is bound to compensate him for any damage arising therefrom.' The operative words in German are 'Wer ... das Leben ... eines anderen widerrechtlich verletzt'. Discussion: R. Zimmermann, *The Law of Obligations: Roman Foundations of the Civilian Tradition* (Cape Town, 1990), 977, 989; B. S. Markesinis, *The German Law of Torts* (2nd edn, Oxford, 1990), 10, 50ff. The escape from the problem may be put down partly to luck, partly to the departure from the image of a physical act effected by the introduction of non-physical interests as the object of the verb and, in association with such abstract objects, to the non-physical range of *verletzen* ('injure').

[2] For a modern version, seeking to revise others of the same kind, see David Kretzmer, 'Transformation of Tort Liability in the Nineteenth Century: The Visible Hand' (1984) 4 O.J.L.S. 46. For Kretzmer the present subject-matter represents a shift from liability based on the defendant's generation of a risk which the plaintiff could not avoid to a liability based on the defendant's duty to avert a loss likely to be suffered by the plaintiff.

read the semantic constraints imposed by forms of action precisely as constraints, not as evidence of a different mind-set. However, this shortening of the chain of causation was not thrust upon the law by particular words, only by the choice of harm-verbs in the simple active voice. The Roman story in relation to killing slaves and livestock, for example, cannot be explained as turning on the choice of the word *occidere*; it would have worked out in the same way if the draftsman had chosen *interficere* or *necare*.[3] So much has been written of killing that it is helpful to concentrate on something different. This paper chooses burning. This is only a matter of focus. 'Burning' represents all active harm-verbs, and 'causing to be burned' exemplifies all bringing about of damage. The first section below sets the scene; the second seeks to explain it.

Burning and causing to be burned

It is convenient to have a recurrent point of reference. The events of *Hughes* v. *Lord Advocate*[4] suit well. Post Office workers had left lighted paraffin lamps to mark an open manhole down which they had been working. The manhole remained open, covered by a small tent. Two young boys, the pursuer and his friend, began to play with the lamps. The pursuer entered the tent and let one of the lamps drop down the hole. The paraffin vaporised and exploded. The pursuer was horribly burned. On these facts a liability based on the proposition that the workmen burned the boy could never have attached. The pursuer was indeed burned, but the question was whether that consequence could be attributed to the defenders at all: could it be said that they had caused him to be burned? The freak explosion was not foreseeable. That children would play with the lamps and burn themselves was foreseeable. The Post Office was held liable. In the words of Lord Pearce: 'When an accident is of a different type and kind from anything that a defender could have foreseen he is not liable for it. But to demand too great precision in the test of foreseeability would be unfair to the pursuer since the facets of misadventure are innumerable.'[5]

In Roman law the *Hughes* facts would have fallen within the delict of wrongful loss, dominated by the *lex Aquilia*, but they would have had to

---

[3] The meanings of these words are further discussed below, nn. 57–9 and text thereto.
[4] [1963] A.C. 837.
[5] *Ibid.*, at 857. Contrast *Doughty* v. *Turner Manufacturing Co. Ltd.* [1964] 1 Q.B. 518 (explosion in boiling liquid qualitatively different from splash); *Tremaine* v. *Pike* [1969] 3 All E.R. 1303 (Weil's disease through rat's urine qualitatively different from other rat contamination).

be litigated through an *actio in factum*, not through the statutory action.[6] This would have been true even against the immediate wrongdoers, the negligent workmen. There are two reasons. First, the statutory action lay only to an owner who had suffered loss from wrongful damage to a thing owned. The young pursuer who was burned was not owned, nor did he own his limbs.[7] For our present purposes, this is not interesting and no more will be said about it. Secondly, the direct action lay only where the injury or damage, here the burning, had been inflicted by bodily force (*corpore*).[8] These negligent workers had left behind the lighted lamps. The injury arose because the pursuer himself dropped one down the manhole, so that it broke and exploded. The workers had not, by any stretch of the imagination, burned the pursuer by the application of bodily force. They had not shoved torches in his face or thrown burning coals at him. Nor had they even set fire to the place in which the pursuer was.[9]

In the eighteenth century the action of trespass was very similarly restricted. It could only be brought for direct or immediate damage. For injuries and damage brought about indirectly the victim had to have recourse to an action on the case, not for burning but for causing to be burned: why had he 'so negligently and improvidently kept his fire that (the house had been burned down)'?[10] The choice between the general action and the action on the case was often difficult. In *Scott* v. *Shepherd*,[11] the plaintiff had lost the sight of one eye when a firework exploded in his face. He brought an action of trespass, not case, against the defendant, who had tossed the lighted squib into a crowded place. This divided the judges. It is useful to have in full the special case subject to which the verdict was given:

---

[6] The action under the *lex* is properly known as the *actio directa*; in order to reduce confusion in a context in which it is necessary to use 'direct' of causation it will be referred to throughout this chapter as the 'statutory' action.

[7] Roland Wittmann, *Die Körperverletzung an Freien im klassischen römischen Recht* (Munich, 1972), 43–6 and, on D.9.2.13 *pr.* (Ulpian, 18 *ad edictum*), 76–82. It is of no materiality to this paper to decide whether the supplementary action on the case apparently given by Ulpian to a free man *sui iuris* in respect of injuries to himself is classical or (which seems unlikely) a Justinianic interpolation. Transplants and other scientific developments now put *nemo dominus membrorum suorum* in doubt: P. Matthews, 'Whose Body? People as Property' (1983) 36 C.L.P. 193; further: I. Kennedy and A. Grubb, *Medical Law: Text and Materials* (London, 1989), 1000–22.

[8] It is only Gaius, followed by Justinian's Institutes, who uses the generalised *corpore* test: see G.3.219 (cf. J.Inst. 4.3.16, and nn. 48 and 49 below, with text thereto).

[9] D.9.2.27.6–8 (Ulpian, 18 *ad edictum*). Cf. Coll. 12.7. In D.9.2.30.3 (Paul, 22 *ad edictum*) it seems certain that Paul's comments must be directed only to the fault element of the defendant's liability; he did not mean that a direct action could lie for a wind-driven fire in the countryside.

[10] See below, example in text to n. 68.   [11] (1773) 2 W.Bl. 892.

On the evening of the fair-day at Milborne Port, October 28, 1770, the defendant threw a lighted squib, made of gunpowder, etc., from the street into the market-house, which is a covered building supported by arches and enclosed at one end, but open at the other and both the sides, where a large concourse of people were assembled; which lighted squib, so thrown by the defendant, fell upon the standing of one Yates, who sold gingerbread, etc. That one Willis instantly, and to prevent injury to himself and the said wares of the said Yates, took up the said lighted squib from off of the said standing and then threw it across the said market-house, where it fell upon another standing there of one Ryal, who sold the same sort of wares, who, instantly, to save his own goods from being injured, took up the said lighted squib from off the said standing, and then threw it to another part of the said market-house, and in so throwing it struck the plaintiff, then in the said market-house, in the face therewith, and, the combustible matter then bursting, put out one of the plaintiff's eyes.

No classical Roman jurist would have persuaded himself that the injury to the plaintiff's eye had been done by the bodily force of the defendant. The plaintiff would indubitably have been driven to an *actio in factum*. Blackstone, J. thought the same for English law. He held that the plaintiff's action of trespass must fail. He should have brought an action on the case. 'He took the settled distinction to be that, where the injury is immediate, an action of trespass will lie; where it is only consequential, it must be an action on the case.'[12] Applying this, he concluded:

The original act was as against Yates a trespass; not as against Ryal or Scott. The tortious act was complete when the squib lay at rest upon Yates's stall ... But Shepherd, I think, is not answerable in an action of trespass and assault for the mischief done by the squib in the new motion impressed upon it and the new direction given it by either Willis or Ryal, who both were free agents and acted upon their own judgment ... Here the instrument of mischief was at rest till a new impetus and a new direction were given to it, not once only, but by two successive rational agents ... I give no opinion whether Case would lie against Shepherd for the consequential damage, though, as at present advised, I think upon the circumstances that it would. But I think that in strictness of law, Trespass would lie against Ryal, the immediate actor in this unhappy business. Both he and Willis have exceeded the bounds of self-defence and not used sufficient circumspection in removing the danger from themselves.[13]

---

[12] (1773) 2 W.Bl. 892, 894.
[13] *Ibid.*, 895–6. As one might expect, the doctrine of this passage closely follows what Blackstone had already said in the *Commentaries*. See 3 *Commentaries* (Oxford, 1768), 122–3 and 208. Roman law, especially J.Inst. 4.3, is here clearly very near the surface, though his only explicit citation is of 4.3.6–7, which is about fault, not causation. For 'the settled distinction' the *Commentaries* cite 11 Mod. 180 (*Bourden* v. *Alloway* (1708), in which Bain, *arg.*, attempting to drive the plaintiff from case to trespass, said, apparently with the approval in principle of the court, 'The true difference is this; Trespass is where there is an immediate injury; Case, where the injury is collateral') and Lord Raym. 1402 with Stra. 635 (the famous statements of Raymond, C. J. and Fortescue, J. in *Reynolds* v. *Clarke* (1725)).

However, Blackstone, J. found himself in a minority of one. Though we dare to assert that no Roman jurist could have aligned himself with them, the majority judgments serve as a reminder that among all lawyers, Roman or English, a test based on words such as 'immediacy' or 'directness' or 'bodily force' will inevitably have elicited disagreements, especially when the merits pulled strongly in one direction. Thus, De Grey, C. J. expressly said, 'I agree with my Brother Blackstone as to the principles he has laid down, but not in his application of those principles to the present case.'[14] And he went on to say that in his view the injury was the immediate product of the force set in motion by Shepherd:

I look on all that was done subsequent to the original throwing as a continuation of the first force and first act, which will continue till the squib was spent by bursting ... The new direction and new force flow out of the first force, and are not a new trespass ... It has been urged that the intervention of a free agent will make a difference: but I do not consider Willis and Ryal as free agents in the present case, but acting under a compulsive necessity for their own safety and self-preservation.[15]

Plaintiffs were put in real difficulty by the need to bring the correct form of action. By natural reason causing to be burned includes burning. An action on the case might therefore be thought to lie on all facts. There was, however, a routine obstacle to that simple solution. It consisted in the subsidiarity of actions on the case. In the fifteenth and sixteenth centuries the structure and stability of the Common law were thought to require that the first-generation general actions be given primacy, so that an action on the case was excluded if a general action lay. This doctrine had largely been given up well before the eighteenth century,[16] but it mustered a late burst of energy in relation to trespass. Natural reason was ultimately allowed to prevail. In *Williams* v. *Holland* in 1833 it was held that a plaintiff could bring an action on the case even if the injury had been inflicted directly, so that trespass was also available:[17] 'where the injury is occasioned by the carelessness and negligence of the defendant, the plaintiff is at liberty to bring an action on the case, notwithstanding

---

[14] *Ibid.*, 899.   [15] *Ibid.*, 899–900.
[16] S. F. C. Milsom, *Historical Foundations of the Common Law* (2nd edn, London, 1981), 339–50, 366–79, 392–400; J. H. Baker, *Introduction to English Legal History* (3rd edn, London, 1990), 389–95, 413–19, 445–51, 480–3. Landmark cases: Case/Debt, *Slade* v. *Morley* (1602) 4 Co.Rep. 92 and [1971] C.L.J. 51, on which see D. Ibbetson, 'Sixteenth Century Contract Law: *Slade's Case* in Context' (1984) 4 O.J.L.S. 294; Case/Detinue: *Eason* v. *Newman* (1596) Cro.Eliz. 495, *Isack* v. *Clarke* (1614) 1 Rolle Rep. 126; Case/Nuisance: *Cantrel* v. *Churche* (1601) Cro.Eliz. 845.
[17] (1833) 10 Bing. 112. In the judgment Tindal, C. J. justly says the work had been done eight years earlier in *Moreton* v. *Hordern* (1825) 4 B.& C. 223.

the act is immediate, so long as it is not a wilful act'.[18] The rise of the tort of negligence dates from that decision, a century before *Donoghue* v. *Stevenson*.[19] Doing damage was displaced by (negligently) causing damage to be done.

In Roman law, once the formulary system disappeared in the third century AD, the distinction between the statutory action under the *lex Aquilia* and the supplementary actions on the case became conceptual, not formal. The plaintiff no longer had to choose a set of words which would tie his claim unequivocally to one or the other, but he would still conceive of his claim as arising either under the statute or in the periphery which would once have been covered by actions on the case. Nothing then prevented the plaintiff from arguing in the alternative, that the defendant was liable either as under the *lex* or as under the praetorian actions on the case. However, while the formulary system lasted, the plaintiff could not bring a statutory action where his facts would only support an action on the case. If he brought the statutory action, he would have to show that the defendant did the harm *corpore suo*. Doing, after all, does not include the other forms of causing to be done. What about the other way around? Did the Romans apply the rule of *Williams* v. *Holland* before the abolition of their forms of action, with the effect of allowing a plaintiff to bring an *actio in factum* even where he might have brought the statutory action? Though it would cost him whatever marginal advantages the statutory action had to offer, an action on the case would relieve the plaintiff of the burden of establishing corporeal causation. In other words, the defendant would be deprived of the opportunity of exploiting the mysteries of direct causation in order to challenge the form of action. The texts do not allow a definite answer, but it seems likely that the *Williams* v. *Holland* position was taken.[20] Even in English law successful challenges this way round, to actions on the case rather than to trespass, were extremely rare.[21]

---

[18] (1833) 10 Bing. 112, 117–18, *per* Tindal, C. J. Further: M. J. Prichard, 'Trespass, Case and the Rule in *Williams* v. *Holland*' [1964] C.L.J. 234.

[19] [1932] A.C. 562.

[20] This is all the more likely if, as Barton argues, the jurists were hostile to the statutory action because of the *lis crescens* rule which probably did not apply to the praetorian extensions: J. L. Barton, 'The *Lex Aquilia* and Decretal Actions', in W. A. J. Watson (ed.), *Daube Noster* (Edinburgh, 1974), 15, 22–4 (though on the view taken here Barton is wrong to suggest that the words of the *lex* did not dictate the *corpore suo* test: see further n. 45 and text thereto).

[21] *Savignac* v. *Roome* (1794) 6 T.R. 125 was said in *Williams* v. *Holland* (1833) 10 Bing. 112, 116 to have been wrongly brought in case only because of procedural limitations on what a court could do on a special demurrer with an allegation of 'furious' driving (*ibid.*).

The restricted range of active harm-verbs

In Roman law liability for wrongful loss turned on the words of the *lex Aquilia*. The details of the text of the *lex* are notoriously controversial, and we can omit all that is not immediately relevant to the present discussion. It is certain that the *lex* said, using the active voice, that the defendant must have killed, burned, broken, burst – the verbs were *occidere, urere, frangere, rumpere*.[22] The statute thus confronted jurisprudence with this question: when can it be said of a man that he has killed, burned, broken or burst? The *lex* also required that the deed be done wrongfully (*iniuria*), but that requirement was never interpreted to mean that he must have acted intentionally – Aquilian liability included unintentional harm, which was indeed the usual case.[23] This matters, because it bars one possible answer to our question.

It would have been tempting to say that a man burns when, having formed the intention that a thing should be damaged by fire, he executes that intention by bringing that damage about. The Philistines, for example, were sure that they knew who had burned up their fields, even though Samson had used an ingeniously indirect method of causing their crops to be burned up. He had tied torches to the tails of one hundred and fifty pairs of foxes,

And when he had set the brands on fire, he let them go into the standing corn of the Philistines, and burnt up both the shocks, and also the standing corn, with the vineyards and olives. Then the Philistines said, Who hath done this? And they answered, Samson, the son in law of the Timnite, because he had taken his wife, and given her to his companion. And the Philistines came up, and burnt her and her father with fire.[24]

The basis of the finding that Samson had burned the crops, and of the horrible revenge, is his intent to bring about that result, coupled with action, however indirect, which successfully achieved his intended goal. That approach was not open under the *lex Aquilia*, certainly not from the moment at which it was decided that 'I did not mean to do it' was no defence. The question set for courts by defendants anxious to get off was, 'When can it be said of a man that he, not having intended to burn, has burned?' A double answer might have been a possibility, one limb for

---

[22] A convenient review of arguments as to the text of the principal chapters of the *lex* is: J. A. Crook, '*Lex Aquilia*' (1984) 62 *Athenaeum* 67.
[23] Gaius 3.211; D.9.2.5.1.
[24] Judges 15.5–6 (Authorised Version). Verse 3, which looks interesting, mistranslates the Hebrew: see M. Black and H. H. Rowley (eds.), *Peake's Commentary* (London, 1962, repr. 1982), 313 *ad loc.*, where reference is also made to a parallel at the Roman Cerealia.

Doing and causing to be done 39

intentional burning, the other for unintentional cases. There is no sign of that in the developed law.[25]

It is interesting that in the delict *iniuria* we find no requirement of corporeal causation. Part of the reason must lie in the intentionality of that delict, part in the immateriality of the interest conceived in developed law to be protected, the integrity of the personality, not the body.[26] However, equally important is the fact that in cases of physical *iniuriae* no text relevant to the edictal action required that what the victim suffered be described by a harm-verb used in the active voice. The model formula used the passive: 'Whereas Aulus Agerius was struck on the cheek ... for as much as on that account it shall seem fair and good that Numerius Negidius should be condemned, etc.'[27] These words would reach the case both of a Numerius who struck and a Numerius who acted as decoy so that another could strike.[28] If the ellipsis concealed the words 'by Numerius Negidius' the passive would be neutralised, since 'by' has equivalent effect. Lenel thought that 'a Numerio Negidio' must have been included.[29] One dissents with hesitation from an unequivocal opinion of the master. But these additional words are not necessary and are not warranted by any text.

When can it be said, without reference to intention, that a defendant has damaged or injured? I knock your slave into the river. He is a poor swimmer and not blessed with Horatius' strength. Everyone sees him struggling towards the bank, but he tires and goes under. I was careless, but my submission will be that I did not kill him. He was killed by the river, or by his own weakness as a swimmer.[30] I step into the road without looking. A carriage swerves to avoid me and hits your innocent slave on the other side of the road, breaking his leg. Again, perhaps I was careless, but surely you will not say that I broke his leg? The leg was broken by the carriage which ran over him. Show me the act of breaking. I am not a

---

[25] D.9.2.39 (Pomponius 17 *ad Quintum Mucium*) may reveal, in the word *consulto*, that early on a jurist might allow intent to filter into the question whether the defendant had done the harm.

[26] Compare life, freedom, health in 823 I B.G.B., n. 1 above.

[27] O. Lenel, *Das Edictum Perpetuum* (3rd edn, Leipzig, 1927), 398–9.

[28] D.47.10.11 *pr.* (Ulpian, 57 *ad edictum*). Cf. the Aquilian case for which Ofilius prescribed one of the earliest actions on the case, D.9.2.9.3 (Ulpian, 18 *ad edictum*), text to n. 51 below.

[29] He thought the formula would have spelled out both 'by Numerius Negidius' and, in the alternative, 'caused to be struck through the *dolus* of Numerius Negidius': *Edictum Perpetuum*, 398. The passive *demonstratio* without reference to NN suffices to leave the liability for the event to be considered in the *intentio*, focusing on *videbitur*.

[30] The texts' conclusion for the statutory action on these facts suggests a distinction overruled between the case of one who went straight under or broke his neck on hitting the water and the one who was seen to struggle only to be overcome: Celsus D.9.2.9.7 (Ulpian, 28 *ad edictum*); Gaius 3.219; J.Inst. 4.4.16.

breaker. There is no ready answer to this form of argument. Deprived of the criterion of intent, it is difficult to see how any lawyer could formulate a test other than in terms of bodily energy and motion: a defendant kills, burns, etc., when he supplies the kinetic energy which brings about the effect in question. And such a test would by nature be embarrassingly narrow, clearly revealing the bad consequences of the original choice of the active voice. Even as the test began to crystallise, defendants would be armed with the means of winning against the merits, creating an imperative need for a supplementary action against those who, though they had not wrongfully burned the crops, had wrongfully caused the crops to be burned.

It is not in the nature of legal authority to jump in one bound to a clear formulation of the answer to such a difficult problem. What seems to have happened is that by individual rulings the jurists pushed at the limits of the central image of a person damaging a thing,[31] as, for instance, by including damage inflicted by throwing something hard or sharp at the thing[32] or the thing at something hard or sharp,[33] by rubbing, pouring in or injecting harmful drugs,[34] by pouring things not water-resistant into muddy water,[35] or watery mud into such things,[36] by knocking an object from a height to the damage of something or someone below,[37] by letting slip a load with the same effect,[38] or by allowing a vehicle to slip down a hill crushing people below.[39] The case-law picture extended, of course, to examples on the other side of the line, such as offering poison for the victim to take,[40] frightening a horse which threw the victim down,[41] sending a slave up a tree or down a well, so that he fell to his death,[42] or watching the wind carrying your fire to a neighbour's farm.[43] It has been suggested that after the end of the Republic the case-law began to narrow the limits of the statutory action.[44] That would certainly be an understandable response to the difficulty of handling the defendant's argument

---

[31] This activity of building up illustrations from a core about which all persons would agree is well conveyed by N. Andrews, '*Occidere* and the *Lex Aquilia*' (1987) 46 C.L. J. 315.
[32] D.9.2.9.4 (Ulpian, 18 *ad edictum*).
[33] D.9.2.7.7 (Ulpian, 18 *ad edictum*) – the slave dashed against the rock.
[34] D.9.2.9.1 (Ulpian, 18 *ad edictum*).   [35] D.9.2.27.19 (Ulpian, 18 *ad edictum*)
[36] D.9.2.27.20 (Ulpian, 18 *ad edictum*), where the messy nature of *harena* shows that 'ut difficilis separatio sit' is a mistaken gloss.
[37] D.9.2.31 (Paul, 10 *ad Sabinum*).   [38] D.9.2.7.2 (Ulpian, 18 *ad edictum*).
[39] D.9.2.52.2 (Alfenus, 2 *digestorum*).
[40] D.9.2.7.6 and 9 *pr*. (Ulpian, 18 *ad edictum*).   [41] D.9.2.9.3 (Ulpian, 18 *ad edictum*).
[42] Gaius 3.219; D.11.3.3.1 (Ulpian, 23 *ad edictum*) with D.11.3.4 (Paul, 19 *ad edictum*).
[43] Coll. 12.7.4–6 (Ulpian, 18 *ad edictum*).
[44] W. A. J. Watson, *The Law of Obligations in the Later Roman Republic* (Oxford, 1965) 243; W. A. J. Watson, 'D 7.1.13.2 (Ulpian 18 *ad Sabinum*): The Lex Aquilia and Decretal Actions' (1966) 17 Iura 174.

that he had not done the killing, burning, and so on,[45] but the evidence of a stricter case-law is not secure.[46]

A single test of doing is the culmination. The notion that the damage must have been done by the defendant *corpore suo*, still only foreshadowed in Julian,[47] is achieved by Gaius in the next generation, in the mid second century AD.[48] The articulation of the distinction, but without the *corpore* test or anything like it, seems to appear in the legal texts with Celsus, at the beginning of the second century.[49] But the difference must have been articulately understood much earlier. Nörr shows that the distinction between doing and causing was expressed in non-legal texts in the Republic and argues that it was already expressly present in the *lex Cornelia de sicariis*.[50] Whether or not it was actually in that *lex*, it is unlikely that the republican jurists were unable to articulate it.

At the end of the Republic Ofilius concluded in favour of an *actio in factum* for the case in which the defendant had excited a horse with the effect that its rider, the plaintiff's slave, was precipitated into a river and thus met his death. This is the earliest documented *actio in factum*, except the one from which, in the same text, Ofilius himself analogises: the defendant lured the plaintiff's slave into an ambush and another dispatched him.[51] Nörr must be right in saying that Ofilius cannot but have understood and been able to articulate the difference between killing and furnishing the cause of death.[52] It would have been impossible to keep the statutory action and the *actio in factum* in play without being able to

---

[45] Watson suggests in 17 Iura 174, also *Failures of the Legal Imagination* (Edinburgh, 1988), 43, that the words of the *lex* did not require the narrow view and that the narrowing was the result of a deliberate policy to restrict the statutory action. That is not right; it underestimates the extent to which first the active harm-verbs and then the logic of the case-law which they provoked armed the defendant with an unanswerable technical defence. Cf. Barton, '*Lex Aquilia* and Decretal Actions' 22–3: the 'perversity' of the juristic test of causation cannot be explained by any words in the *lex* itself.

[46] It is, in particular, unsafe to build much on a literal interpretation of Proculus in D.9.2.7.3 (one who pushes another into the victim), since we do not know what facts he was addressing, and the narrowest understanding of his words is not consistent with his position in D.9.2.11.5 (one who irritates a dog which then bites the victim) and, possibly, D.9.2.11 *pr.* (one kicks a ball which hits a barber's arm when he is shaving the victim).

[47] D.9.2.51 *pr.* (Julian, 86 *digestorum*). [48] Gaius 3.219.

[49] D.9.2.7.6 (Ulpian, 18 *ad edictum*): 'Celsus says that a crucial question is whether he killed or supplied the cause of death, in that a person who has supplied the cause of death is liable, not to the Aquilian action, but to an *actio in factum*.'

[50] D. Nörr, *Causa Mortis* (Munich, 1986), 15–24, 101–21. An outline of the evidence and findings is: '*Causam Mortis Praebere*', in N. MacCormick and P. Birks (eds.), *The Legal Mind* (Oxford, 1986), 204–17.

[51] D.9.2.9.3, cf. D.9.2.11.1 (Ulpian 18 *ad edictum*). Watson, *Obligations*, 244 and 281, thinks that Servius Sulpicius, whose pupil Ofilius was, allowed the action on the case given in D.9.1.1.7 in the case of damage done by a horse in pain against the person who caused the pain.

[52] Nörr, *Causa Mortis*, 141.

express that difference. On the other hand there is no reason to suppose that Ofilius could have ventured the generalisation that the limits of doing were defined by the defendant's bodily force. More probably, the *actio in factum* simply began as a necessary recourse to meet the case in which the jurist found himself obliged to accept, without any stable test of the matter, that the harm-verb could not be satisfied – the defendant should answer for the damage but could not on any view be said to have done the killing, burning, breaking, and so on. The ambush is one good example, the *Hughes* facts another. The case-law on both sides of the line then continued to build up. In the end the *corpore* test was proposed as the key to all the illustrations.

That pattern of development seems to explain the evidence in the texts. However, although it is also compatible with almost all of Professor Nörr's study of the concepts and language of indirect causation, it differs very markedly from his account in one crucial respect. The view propounded with great learning and sensitivity by Nörr is very much more dependent on the words of the *lex* itself and, in particular, on the word used for killing in the first chapter, *occidere*. On the view advanced above it would not have made any difference at all if the word used for killing had been, say, *necare* or *interficere* so long only as the verb appeared in the active voice, thus creating a condition of liability that the defendant must have killed: if any one shall have wrongfully killed another's slave or four-footed beast, etc. However, Professor Nörr's view is that the first chapter was about an event specific to the word *occidere*, narrower than killing. It was about killing-by-striking, which is what *occidere* originally meant.[53] When it was chosen by Aquilius, or taken over by him from an earlier statute, *occidere* will necessarily have brought its killing-by-striking meaning into the *lex*.[54]

There are a number of difficulties with this theory. The first is that we know that the *veteres*, the republican jurists, dealt vigorously with a literalist interpretation of a different aspect of another chapter of the *lex*. The argument was that chapter 3 in using the verbs *urere, frangere, rumpere* had intended to deal only with three types of damage. This had nothing to do with the defendant's side of the matter. It was concerned not with the doing but with what was done. Literally, the plaintiff must have suffered a disaster of a particular description, loss from something *ustum, fractum* or *ruptum*. But Ulpian tells us that almost all the old jurists rejected this view and held, taking the widest possible meaning of *rumpere*, that the chapter covered all kinds of spoiling.[55] It was enough to

[53] Nörr, *Causa Mortis*, 4–9. See further below, text to nn. 57–9 and text thereto.
[54] Nörr, *Causa Mortis*, 121–4, 135–8.
[55] D.9.2.27.13 (Ulpian, 18 *ad edictum*).

bring the plaintiff *prima facie* within the *lex* if the disaster which he had suffered was loss arising from a *res corrupta*, something spoiled. In view of this dynamic attitude to the triplet in chapter 3, it is difficult to believe that the old jurists would have had much time for an argument based simply on the narrowest possible meaning of the word *occidere*. Less violence would have been done to *occidere* by the assertion that it was a general word for killing than to *rumpere* by treating it as though it were *corrumpere*.

Next, Gaius tells us unambiguously that the requirement of corporeal causation was common to both chapter 1 and chapter 3.[56] Hence, if the requirement was grounded in the literal meaning of *occidere*, we have to believe, not only that the jurists sustained the argument for that literal meaning, but also that they carried it over to verbs to which it was entirely alien. *Urere, frangere* and *rumpere* do not in themselves contain any hint of a narrow meaning linked to striking or bodily force. It might be objected that *occidere* was also relevant under chapter 3 and could, so to say, have infected the other verbs, as in the killing of birds and bees and wild beasts (non-*pecudes*). But the answer to that is that, under chapter 3, there was no need to conduct the debate in terms of any particular killing-verb, for in the terms of the *lex* a killed goose was just another *res rupta*. So, though killing was sometimes a chapter 3 event, *occidere* was not itself any more in play than *interficere* or *necare*. The application of the *corpore* test to all statutory actions, not just to those of chapter 1, thus strongly suggests that the narrow causal test is rooted in the general problems of the active voice, not in specific shades of meaning to be discovered in the verbs chosen to describe the damage.

The third objection is that the specially narrow meaning of *occidere* is nowhere evidenced outside the law. The etymology, from *caedere*, does not in itself indicate a powerfully restricted meaning, any more than its survival in other compounds such as the Latin *homicidium* and the English 'homicide' serves to reveal their scope at any period of their use. Julian's appeal to that etymology is much more likely to have been made in support *ex post* of the narrow Aquilian interpretation than as the reason for that narrow interpretation:

D.9.2.51 *pr.* (Julian, 86 *digestorum*)
In ordinary speech a person is said to have killed (*occidisse*) however he has brought about the cause of death; but under the *lex Aquilia* a person is only held to be liable when he has furnished the cause of death by the application of force and so to say with his hand (*adhibita vi et quasi manu*), the interpretation of the

[56] Gaius 3.219: 'The conclusion was also reached that the statutory action lies only where someone causes loss by his bodily force. Where people cause loss in other ways actions are given based on the policy of the statute.'

word evidently being taken from the words for smiting and slaughter (*a caedendo et caede*).

This passage rather carefully abstains from a direct assertion '*occidere* means, or once meant, killing-by-striking'. It asserts that the word has no natural restriction to particular kinds of killing. It then invokes the etymology in support of the restrictive Aquilian understanding of the word. That etymology is drawn from Valerius Flaccus via Festus, who says that opinions differ as to whether *occidere* and *necare* should be distinguished, on the ground that the one comes *a caedendo* and happens *ictu*, the other *sine ictu*.[57] Etymology is a guide to nuance, not to usage. There is no indication that the etymology reflected an originally narrow usage, and the *quidam* who favoured the narrow view of *occidere* need only be the lawyers driven to it by the fact of its having been employed in the active voice in the *lex Aquilia*. Exactly the same can be said of Labeo's definition from his exposition of the *SC. Silanianum* (AD 10), which, with its brutal provisions for the household of an owner murdered by a slave, required a restrictive construction.[58]

Literary sources suggest that *occidere* was always a very general word for killing. Professor Nörr himself admits that already in Plautus the word is used to denote killings other than by striking, as, for example, by starvation. The word had already broken out of its killing-by-striking meaning by, he thinks, a metaphorical extension: it was used when a writer wanted to personify hunger or poison as attacking its victim as a murderer attacks with a knife.[59] In this way the narrow and specific sense which supposedly gripped the *lex Aquilia* has to be pushed back into the dark period before Plautus. More room is made for it by casting doubt even on the 287 BC *terminus post quem* which most scholars accept and by supposing that the word may have been carried over from earlier *leges*.[60] In other words the text of the *lex* itself has to be advanced to the earliest

---

[57] The example instanced is Numa's law relating to a person killed by lightning (*fulmine occisus*): Festus 178, see FIRA, vol. I, 13 n. 2: 'Occisum a necato distingui quidam, quod alterum a "caedendo" atque ictu fieri dicunt, alterum sine ictu. Itaque in Numae Pompilii regis legibus scriptum esse: "Si hominem fulmen occisit, ne supra genua tollito", et alibi: "Homo si fulmine occisus est, ei iusta nulla fieri oportet."'

[58] D.29.5.1.17 (Ulpian, 50 *ad edictum*): 'Occisorum appellatione eos contineri Labeo scribit, qui per vim aut caedem sunt interfecti, ut puta iugulatum strangulatum praecipitatumve saxo vel fuste vel lapide percussum vel quo alio telo necatum.' Stein rightly points out that Labeo adopted a narrow definition of *occidere*, which is different from inheriting one from the past: P. Stein, 'School Attitudes to the Law of Delicts', *Studi in onore di Arnaldo Biscardi*, vol. II (Milan, 1982), 281, 288. And Zimmermann, *Law of Obligations*, 978, correctly observes that Labeo himself did not require force or violence in the Aquilian context but only physical doing, as is proved by D.9.2.9 *pr*.-1 (Ulpian, 18 *ad edictum*) – application of harmful drugs *manibus*.

[59] Nörr, *Causa Mortis*, 7–8.   [60] *Ibid.*, 127–8.

Doing and causing to be done 45

possible date, to accommodate the hypothesis that, when the statute was enacted, *occidere* meant killing-by-striking.

The one secure fact which we know about the date of the *lex* is that it had been passed before the jurist Brutus died, since he gave an opinion on its scope. That means that it must have been passed by about 125 BC.[61] Though most scholars do place it earlier, a case every bit as strong can be made for a date after the third Punic war, late in the 140s.[62] In short the *lex* may anyhow have been passed after Plautus; even if it was passed before Plautus, there is no hard evidence that *occidere* ever meant killing-by-striking.

This touches very little of Professor Nörr's account of the concepts and language of causation in the ancient world. It only substitutes the general problems of the active voice as the agent effecting the consequences which he derives from a rigidly narrow original sense of *occidere*, and it eliminates the question why the draftsman should have chosen or adopted that narrow word. If what is said here is correct, nobody ever chose restrictive terminology. All that happened was that the draftsman happened to express the conditions of liability using the harm-verbs in the simple active voice. Room was thus left for ingenious arguments, often but not always against the merits; and those arguments drove the lawyers to say what facts would satisfy those active verbs and to recommend actions on the case where liability needed to be extended to those who had brought about harm but had not harmed. Actions on the case were given by the praetor. And, after a long period in which the matter lay in case-law illustration, the distinction between the statutory action and the actions on the case was generalised or summed up in the test of bodily force: the statutory action lay where the defendant had done the harm *corpore suo*, by his bodily force.

Let us underline two aspects of this story which turn out to be interlinked. First, the period of development to the mature position is very long. Even taking the latest possible date of the *lex Aquilia*, three centuries elapse between it and Gaius' '*corpore*' test. Secondly, supplementation precedes crystallisation of the difference between doing and causing to be done. The Roman development passes through these three phases: (1) before the time of Servius Sulpicius[63] the statutory action

---

[61] Brutus was praetor in c. 140, possibly curule aedile in 146. The date of his death is not known. See R. A. Bauman, *Lawyers in Republican Politics* (Munich, 1983), 240. Brutus' opinion was that a blow which brought on an abortion counted as a *rumpere* within chapter 3: D.9.2.27.22.

[62] See P. Birks, 'Wrongful Loss by Co-Promisees' (1994) 22 Index 184.

[63] For the role of Servius (praetor 65 BC, d. 43 BC) in the development of the law, see P. Stein, 'The Place of Servius Sulpicius Rufus in the Development of Roman Legal Science', *Festschrift für Franz Wieacker zum 70. Geburtstag* (Göttingen, 1979), 175–84.

stood alone, with no supplementation by *actiones in factum*; (2) supplementation began, as, for instance, against one who led a slave to an ambush to be killed by another, or frightened a horse which bolted and killed its rider,[64] for these were fact situations in which the defendant needed to be liable but no reasonable man could say of him that he had done the harm, only that he caused it to be done; (3) first by illustration and then by abstract generalisation the law mapped the frontier between the statutory action and the *actio in factum*. But this sequence contains a mystery. Why should it be more pressing to locate the frontier at stage 3, when it had become a line between available actions, than at stage 1, when it marked, if it could be found, the limit of liability? The answer must be that at stage 1 the system, younger and less able to formulate and insist on difficult artificialities, relied on mechanisms of evasion and postponement. These are more clearly visible in the English story.

In English law the two species of liability, for doing and causing to be done, also co-existed before anybody drew a precise line between them.[65] In trespass the plaintiff affirmed that the defendant had with force and arms and against the king's peace done some harm: 'Thomas Weaver brought trespass against George Ward, and counted that on 18 October 1614 in the parish of Mary-le-Bow, London, with force and arms (namely with swords, clubs and knives), the defendant beat, wounded and ill-treated the plaintiff so that his life was despaired of, against the king's peace.'[66] Again: 'One Henry T. brought his writ of trespass against a woman, and supposed by his writ that she had burnt his house in G, with force and arms.'[67]

By contrast, the supplementary action on the case typically alleged that, within the context of a given duty, the defendant had so negligently conducted himself as to cause the plaintiff to be harmed. For example:

---

[64] Text to n. 51 above.

[65] The *lex Aquilia*, by its very words, created and defined a liability in terms of active harm-verbs. In England no superior text required that trespass be so defined, though nearly every writ of trespass did use an active harm-verb, and those that in the earlier period did not severely strained the words *vi et armis et contra pacem*. See Baker's comments on the action for knowingly keeping a dangerous animal: J. H. Baker, *Spelman's Reports*, vol. 2 (1977) 94 Selden Soc. 228–9. Note also *Reynoldes v. Clarke* (1615), in J. H. Baker and S. F. C. Milsom, *Sources of English Legal History* (London, 1986), 307. Similarly, the directness test aside, no superior rule actually required a writ on the case to be framed in the 'causing to be done form', although, if it were not, the defendant was likely to seek some advantage from characterising the writ as trespass: cf. *The Farrier's Case* (1372) Y.B. Trin. 46 Edw.III, fol. 19, pl. 19, in Baker and Milsom, *Sources*, 341; *Jason v. Norton* (1653) Style 398, Baker and Milsom, *Sources*, 353.

[66] *Weaver v. Ward* (1616) Hobart 134, extract from the record in Baker and Milsom, *Sources*, 331.

[67] *Anon.* (1374) Y.B. Mich. 48 Edw.III, fol. 25, pl. 8, printed in Baker and Milsom, *Sources*, 304; cf. 320.

If William Beaulieu [shall make you secure of pursuing his claim], put [by gage and safe pledges] Roger Finglam [that he be before our justices of the Bench, etc. to show] why, whereas according to the law and custom of our realm of England until now obtaining everyone in the same realm should keep and is bound to keep his fire safely and securely so that no damage befall any of his neighbours in any wise through his fire, the aforesaid Roger kept his fire at Carlyon so negligently that for want of due keeping of the aforesaid fire the goods and chattels of the selfsame William to the value of £40 (being in the houses there) and the aforesaid houses were then and there burned by the fire, to the damage of the selfsame William etc.[68]

As we saw in the first part of this paper, it was not until the early eighteenth century that challenges by the defendant to the form of action, usually maintaining that a plaintiff who had brought trespass should have brought case, compelled the courts to articulate a test in terms of the elusive notion of 'directness' or 'immediacy'.[69] That might be said to be the equivalent of Gaius' enunciation of the test of bodily force. Trespass was thus crippled by the same inconveniently restrictive causal test as had cut back the Aquilian action. But liability as a whole was not so restricted, since supplementation, as at Rome, had preceded definition: 'he harmed' (trespass) had been extended by 'he caused harm to be done' (case). This supplementation had happened in two stages, indeed in two long-separated generations.

Until the late seventeenth or early eighteenth century, there was no secure action on the case which could operate as a general supplement to trespass. Early supplementation, going back to the end of the fourteenth century, provided actions on the case for special instances of causing to be done, most obviously for negligently causing damage to happen within the context of a contractual or near-contractual relationship. Apart from these examples, with *assumpsit*-based duties, there were some others, as, for instance, the action on the case for fire exemplified above, where the duty was alleged to rest on a custom of the realm.[70] This limited supplementation must have taken some pressure off trespass.[71] However, if we think of trespass as making liable anyone at all who wrongfully did damage, it remained true that there was no similarly general action on the case with the potential for making anyone at all liable who wrongfully caused damage to be done. The gap thus left was less pronounced than it

[68] *Beaulieu v. Finglam* (1401) Y.B. Pas. 2 Hen.IV, fol. 18, pl. 6, printed in Baker and Milson, *Sources*, 557; cf. 559, 565.
[69] M. J. Prichard, '*Scott v. Shepherd* (1773) and the Emergence of the Tort of Negligence', Selden Society Lecture for 1973 (London, 1976), 15.
[70] Above, text to n. 68.
[71] Outside the relationship cases, cases which could not be fitted within trespass would not have been common, especially in the days before the concept of 'directness' was insisted upon. See Baker, *Introduction*, 463.

might have been; it was undoubtedly reduced in size by keeping the limits of trespass – the 'he did it' claim – unexplored, the black box phenomenon discussed immediately below.

Pronounced or not, that was the gap that began to be filled in the late seventeenth century. Actions on the case were then brought, and escaped challenge, which alleged or assumed an omnipresent duty to take care not to cause damage to be done. A good example, much abbreviated in the skeleton which follows, is provided by *Browne* v. *Davis* (1706):[72]

whereas William [Browne] ... was possessed of a certain flat-bottomed boat ... and ... John Davis ... his barge so negligently, carelessly and unskilfully managed and steered, that the said barge, for want of good and sufficient care and management ... in and upon the said boat of the said William ... then and there fell foul, and the said boat broke and sank.

The full potential of this kind of claim, assuming a general duty of care, was openly and officially realised only through the great cases of *Williams* v. *Holland*[73] and *Donoghue* v. *Stevenson*.[74] But as soon as such claims could safely be advanced,[75] the general supplementation of trespass became a tactical reality for every individual plaintiff, in the sense that for the first time it was possible for any plaintiff troubled by possible limitations on trespass to contemplate turning instead to an action on the case, without having to ask himself whether he fitted within the special circumstances and relationships which had previously hedged that alternative about. Moreover, as we have seen,[76] this general action on the case for injury and damage had, as in Rome, the potential for handling even facts within the range of trespass itself. As in Rome after Servius Sulpicius in the late Republic,[77] the definition of a trespass became a question about the choosing between two available actions, the younger of which, unless inhibited by a doctrine of subsidiarity, was capable of gobbling up all the work done by the older.

The matter would have come more quickly to the boil but for keeping

---

[72] C. H. S. Fifoot, *History and Sources of the Common Law* (London, 1949), 180; Baker and Milsom, *Sources*, 575. The example is taken from *John Lilly: A Collection of Modern Entries*, 3rd edn (London, 1758), 38, and W. Bohun, *Declarations and Pleadings* (London, 1733), 211. Baker and Milsom, *Sources*, say that such actions were available against masters of ships from at least 1664.
[73] (1833) 10 Bing. 112, text to n. 18 above.   [74] [1932] A.C. 562.
[75] For pre-eighteenth-century forerunners, see Baker, *Spelman's Reports*, vol. II, *291*; Baker and Milsom, *Sources*, 567–74; Prichard, '*Scott* v. *Shepherd*', 16ff.
[76] Above, text between n. 18 and n. 20.
[77] N. 51 above and text thereto, where it is observed that Ofilius was following a model. 'After Servius' is an approximation, since we cannot be sure that it was he who first approved actions on the case to supplement Aquilian liability under the statutory action. We know only that Servius' pupil Ofilius found such actions, or one such action, in place.

Doing and causing to be done 49

the question of liability in a black box, the jury at *nisi prius*.[78] The jury was unlikely to be sympathetic to technical arguments against the merits. If it thought that you had negligently caused the defendant's leg to be broken, it would not respond to your attempt to insist that liability was only for breaking. Furthermore – a peculiarity of the English story – wide disparities between stereotyped allegations and the real facts revealed in evidence were routine: no jury would expect to hear the formal allegations proved to the letter, and the court would not afterwards look for disparities 'with eagle's eyes'.[79]

In Rome there was also a black box, not a jury but, in most cases, a single *iudex* who gave no reasons for his decision. We must presume that he too absorbed technicalities and, in effect, postponed their resolution. However, the Roman *iudex* was a somewhat less efficient mechanism for suppressing nice questions. Being highly educated and bearing a responsibility which was not shared with others, he was more vulnerable to ingenious argument. Also, in England before the eighteenth century there were few means of bringing the real facts before the eyes of legal authority, the court itself.[80] In Rome, by contrast, litigants could arm themselves with *responsa* from jurists and seek thereby to constrain the judge.

In some cases English defendants did try to take the matter out of the black box by entering a special plea. The courts did not co-operate. On the contrary, they allowed the vigilant plaintiff an opportunity to win on a technicality of his own: the defendant should have taken the general issue. In *Gibbons* v. *Pepper* (1695)[81] the action was trespass for assaulting, beating and wounding, in the usual form. The defendant's special plea was that the horse he had been riding took fright and ran off out of control, running down the plaintiff. It was the horse that ran down the plaintiff, not the defendant, and, further, the defendant was not to blame for it. The court took the view that this matter should have

[78] The role of the jury, and other modes of decision such as compurgation, in obviating the need for scientific rules is central to Milsom's picture of legal development: Milsom, *Historical Foundations*, esp. 38–52, 263–5. The metaphor of the black box is Frier's: B. W. Frier, *The Rise of the Roman Jurists* (Princeton, 1985), 230.

[79] Where a surgeon and apothecary sought to resist an action on the case brought by a patient, the Common Pleas took this view: 'But then it is said that the defendants ought to have been charged as trespassers *vi et armis*; the court will not look with eagle's eyes to see whether the evidence applies exactly or not to the case, when they see that the plaintiff has obtained a verdict for such damages as he deserves, they will establish such verdict if it be possible', *Slater* v. *Baker* (1767) 2 Wils. 359, 362, relied upon in *Scott* v. *Shepherd* (1773) 2 W.Bl. 892, 894 *per* Nares, J. (who, taking advantage of *oratio obliqua*, helpfully adds a 'but' after 'case'). Cf., instancing cases of battery, Baker, *Introduction*, 456.

[80] Prichard, '*Scott* v. *Shepherd*', 14–15.

[81] (1695) 1 Lord Raym. 38, 2 Salk. 638; 4 Mod. 405: extracts printed with the record in Baker and Milsom, *Sources*, 335–7.

been given in evidence under the general issue, thus essentially insisting that it be kept as an issue of fact for the jury and as such kept in the black box:

> For if I ride upon a horse and John Style whips the horse so that he runs away with me and runs over any other person, he who whipped the horse is guilty of the battery, and not me. But if I, by spurring, was the cause of the accident, then I am guilty. In the same manner, if A takes the hand of B and with it strikes C, A is the trespasser and not B.[82]

Gibbons v. *Pepper* thus shows the law resisting pressure to disentangle the causal question from the general issue. Had the defendant not tried a special plea, he would have argued to the jury, under the general issue, that (a) it was the horse which did the injury, not him, and (b) it was not his fault that the horse bolted. Baker speaks of the law's consistent failure to separate issues of causation from issues of fault.[83] The reason why the causation issues never appear to have been taken separately is probably that only when mixed with assertions of blamelessness would they have enough moral weight to encourage a defendant even to try a special plea. In all other cases such matter was completely hidden from the law, lost in the arguments on evidence to the jury.

Nevertheless, it cannot be pretended that there are no elements of unsolved mystery as to how the jury could so long be used to evade and postpone the separate consideration of the causal questions. The Yearbooks show that early defendants were well able to challenge the allegations of force and arms and breach of the peace.[84] These allegations thus lost their natural force and became decorative words of court. You could not hope to escape liability by showing that you had not in fact used weapons or other violence. When these words had been denatured, there remained the harm-verbs. The conventional counts still said, discounting the decorative words, that the defendant had beaten, burned, and so on. It is not obvious why defendants should have had difficulty in taking the causal points inherent in the verbs, and some seem to have done so. In 1353, for example, a plaintiff brought trespass for killing a horse, and the defendant answered that he had taken it damage feasant, that it was so wild that he had had to tie it up, and that, being tied up, it later struggled

---

[82] (1695) 1 Lord Raym. 38. Note that Ofilius would have made the one who whipped the horse liable in an action on the case. In the other example, likewise, Proculus (unless he was actually thinking of facts in which B added motion of his own) would have given an *actio in factum* against A: D.9.2.7.3 (Ulpian, 19 *ad edictum*); see n. 46 above. It does not follow, however, that the test applied is not the Roman test. We have already seen that the same test can be applied differently by different people. See text from n. 13 above.
[83] Baker, *Spelman's Reports*, vol. II, 222–4; cf. Milsom, *Historical Foundations*, 296–300.
[84] Milsom, *Historical Foundations*, 289–92; Baker and Milsom, *Sources*, 297–307.

so much that it strangled itself.[85] The argument having gone off on another point, the plaintiff succeeded. But, seeing the distinction between killing and furnishing the cause of death so close to the surface, we have to admit that we have not found the full explanation why these questions were suppressed till the eighteenth century.

In 1368 a defendant to trespass for burning with force and arms was found not guilty after a jury had found specially that the fire had started suddenly in the defendant's house without his knowledge and had spread to the plaintiff's house.[86] It seems likely that he had pleaded, as in the next four cases of alleged burning with force and arms, that he had not done the burning (which was in addition accidental). In *Richard Tucker* v. *Philip and Eve Smith* (1359) the defendants said, 'the house of the said Philip [the defendant] which was neighbouring on the house of the same Richard caught fire by mischance and was burned down so that the fire therefrom being blown by the wind to the aforesaid house of the aforesaid Richard came down on that house and thus it was burned by mischance, etc.'.[87] This is a plea that the forces of fire and wind did the burning, not the plaintiff, mixed with insinuations of guiltlessness. In *Joan Havent* v. *Richard Ward* (1364) the defendant said, 'And as for the burning timber etc. ... a fire broke out in the houses of the adjacent neighbours from an accidental cause and thus burned the aforesaid timber ... without this, that the same Richard burned the aforesaid timber as the same Joan above complains.'[88]

In *William Cook* v. *William Hasard* (1387) the defendant said that he was the plaintiff's servant ordered to light a badly built oven: 'And so he, as servant of the aforesaid William Cook and by his order, put fire into the aforesaid oven in order to heat the oven. And the fire suddenly came out from the back of the oven, the same William Hasard being entirely unaware of this, through various holes and cracks ... and burned the goods and chattels and houses aforesaid.'[89] This put the matter down to the force of fire itself. In *John Ellis* v. *Nicholas Angwin* (1390) the defendant said, 'And as for the burning the houses, etc. ... on the aforesaid Friday, unknown to the same Nicholas and against his will, a fire suddenly arose by mischance in the houses of the same Nicholas and burned down his houses there so that on account of a great gust of wind the fire spread rapidly to the houses of the said John, and thus by

---

[85] *Anon.* (1353) Y.B. 27 Lib.Ass. pl. 64, printed in Baker and Milsom, *Sources*, 312–13; cf. 304 and 320, where a purely causal point might have been taken, as between burning and causing to be burned.
[86] *Anon.* (1368) Y.B. 42 Lib.Ass. pl. 9 (Essex Assizes), Baker and Milsom, *Sources*, 321.
[87] *Select Cases of Trespass from the King's Courts 1307–1329*, ed. M. S. Arnold (1987) 103 Selden Society 402.
[88] *Ibid.*, 402.   [89] *Ibid.*, 404–5.

mischance and against the will of the same Nicholas the harm befell the same John in this behalf; without this, that he burned the aforesaid houses as the aforesaid John by his writ and count supposes.'[90] Here the conflagration of which the plaintiff complains is again attributed to the wind, and misfortune; the defendant did not do the burning and, in addition, the defendant was not to blame for the force which did do it.

These all seem to be cases in which the defendant plainly denies a 'you burned' claim by saying that, though the burning happened, he did not burn, and, not surprisingly, he adds that the disaster happened *contra voluntatem suam* or words to that effect. By that addition the point ceases to be technical and unmeritorious. Nevertheless, the addition should not obscure the fact that these defendants were primarily saying that they did not do the burning. Fire, having a tendency to proceed with and without the aid of the wind, is particularly apt to provoke that answer.

In fact the making of such answers directed to the act of burning seems to have demonstrated the imperative need for supplementation of the 'he burned the house' claim by a claim on the other pattern, 'he negligently caused the house to be burned'. Fire was one case where trespass was fully supplemented by case before the end of the fourteenth century. There were actions on the case alleging a general duty to keep fire safe based directly on the custom of the realm.[91] Later there was even a second species of action on the case for fire which dispensed with the custom of the realm and simply assumed a general duty of care,[92] in the same way as does the collision example from *Browne* v. *Davis* above.[93] This, therefore, is one area in which we should have expected to find early attempts to draw the line between burning and causing to be burned. We do not. The supplementation was seemingly too successful. There was no embattled defence of the 'he burned' claim and hence no attempt to define its proper sphere.

This evidence deepens the mystery why for the next three hundred years defendants in other forms of trespass did not succeed in taking the causal question out of the general issue. It is not quite sufficient to say simply that the law was so: the question whether you had done the harm had to be considered before the jury under a general plea of not guilty. Whatever the answer may be, the eighteenth century saw both a general supplementation of trespass by case and an increase in litigation about loss arising from injury and damage, chiefly because of better roads and more traffic.[94] At the same time there was an improvement in the procedural mechanisms for bringing the real facts before the court. Through reserva-

---

[90] *Ibid.*, 405.   [91] See the example in the text to n. 68 above.
[92] Baker, *Spelman's Reports*, vol. II, *230*, opining that the custom of the realm version required the fire to have been lit deliberately.
[93] Text to n. 72 above.   [94] Baker, *Introduction*, 466–7.

tions of points of law arising on the evidence and by taking special verdicts reciting the facts which happened rather than the conclusion to be drawn from them, it became possible to compel the court to examine the legal inferences supported by the real facts as opposed to the facts conventionally recited in the plaintiff's count.[95] When the facts were at last looked at by analytically minded jurists instead of lay juries, the distinction between doing and causing to be done necessarily crystallised along the same line as it had at Rome.

Conclusion

What are we left with? A liability which extends beyond intentional harm and is expressed by a harm-verb in the active voice – a person is liable if he kills a cow, burns a house, breaks a vase, and so on – will send the law down a cul-de-sac. The blindness of the alley may long remain concealed if the system resolutely insists on treating the question whether the defendant killed, burned, broke, etc. as an issue of fact, not to be mediated by any test. Defendants will want a test. If juristic authority once accepts the challenge, that test is bound to be inconveniently narrow. Such verbs require the damage to be the defendant's act. Some version of Gaius' 'bodily force' will have to be adopted. There is no other possibility.

The narrow test cannot be adopted without at the same time being supplemented, since, though it will solve the problem of the active harm-verb, it will contribute nothing to the larger problem of the ultimate reach of liability. Supplementation is almost bound to begin before the inconveniently narrow test crystallises. The reason is that, long before the limitations of 'he killed, burned, broke, etc.' are fully explored, it will be obvious that some defendants ought to pay who manifestly cannot be reached as doers of those deeds, not even with the help of a well-meaning and inscrutable tribunal of fact.

In the end the law's way out of the cul-de-sac is likely to be, not only general supplementation of the liability based on the active harm-verbs, but permission to plaintiffs to use the supplementary action for all cases. Since wrongfully causing to be harmed naturally includes all wrongful harming, the supplementary action has only to be given its head. The original preference is thus in effect reversed: 'if he burned the house' gives way to 'if he caused the house to be burned'. At that point the system must finally confront the real problems of remote causation, as opposed to the semantic impediments put in the way by harm-verbs in the active voice.

---

[95] Prichard, '*Scott* v. *Shepherd*', 15, points to the eighteenth-century development of the practice of reserving points of law arising on the evidence, a device 'which ensured that any reasonable point of law arising on the facts could be brought back to Westminster if the trial judge so decided'.

4 The danger of definition: *contrectatio* and appropriation

David Ibbetson

A recurrent subject of Peter Stein's writings has been the development of legal reasoning from the Roman world to the modern.[1] This paper, offered as a mark of gratitude and respect to a teacher who led many a fledgeling law student on the path towards an understanding of what legal thinking is about, takes as its subject one of the problems of definition in law, the tension set up when the legal definition of an institution gets too far removed from its popular conception. 'Omnis definitio in iure civili periculosa est; parum est enim ut non subverti potest.'[2] Nowhere is this warning more necessary than in the law of wrongs, whether it be the Romans' law of delict or the English law of crimes, for it is here that the legal definition is most strongly (and continually) brought up against the popular perception of wrongful conduct.

Sometimes the problem is simply one of language. The legal definition of rape in English law, for example, is non-consensual intercourse with a woman by a man who knows that there is a risk that she may not be consenting or who is indifferent to whether or not she is consenting;[3] English language, though, has no word in common usage to denote non-consensual sexual intercourse in circumstances where the man did

---

[1] See in particular *Regulae Iuris* (Edinburgh, 1966). Among his many articles: 'The Digest Title, *De Diversis Regulis Iuris Antiqui*, and the General Principles of Law', in R. A. Newman (ed.), *Essays in Jurisprudence in Honor of Roscoe Pound* (Indianapolis, 1962), 1 (reprinted in *The Character and Influence of the Roman Civil Law* (London, 1988), 53); 'Justice Cardozo, Marcus Terentius Varro and the Roman Juristic Process' (1967) 2 Irish Jurist 367; 'The Relations between Grammar and Law in the Early Principate: The Beginnings of Analogy', in *La Critica del testo, Atti del II congresso internazionale della Società Italiana di Storia del Diritto* (Florence, 1971), 75; 'The Two Schools of Roman Jurists in the Early Roman Principate' [1972B] Cambridge Law Journal 8; 'The Development of the Notion of *Naturalis Ratio*', in W. A. J. Watson (ed.), *Daube Noster* (Edinburgh, 1974), 305; 'Sabino contra Labeone: due tipi di pensiero giuridico romano' (1977) 19 B.I.D.R. 55; 'Logic and Experience in Roman and Common Law' (1979) 59 Boston University Law Review 437 (reprinted in *Character and Influence of Roman Civil Law*, 37).
[2] D.50.17.202 (Javolenus, 11 *Epistularum*); see Stein, *Regulae Iuris*, 70.
[3] Sexual Offences (Amendment) Act 1976 s. 1; *Director of Public Prosecutions* v. *Morgan* [1976] A.C. 182; *Satnam* (1983) 78 Cr.App.Rep. 149. See S. Gardner, 'Reckless and Inconsiderate Rape' [1991] Criminal Law Review 172.

genuinely believe that the woman was consenting.[4] In popular parlance such a situation is rape; in law it is not.

Sometimes a problem can be caused when the overlay of the legal definition on the popular conception is close but not exact. The offence of burglary is defined (*inter alia*) as theft committed by a person who has entered a building as a trespasser,[5] a definition fairly close to the popular usage of the word. But what if property is stolen by a person who has a general permission to enter? In *Jones and Smith*[6] it was argued that such a person (in this case the son of the family, who had entered his parents' home with an accomplice in the dead of night and stolen their television set) could not in law be a trespasser and hence could not be guilty of burglary.[7] The legal point is difficult, yet his conduct in breaking into a house at night and stealing clearly fell four-square within the ordinary conception of burglary: that, presumably, was why he was charged with burglary rather than simply with theft, of which he was clearly guilty. When faced with such potentially inconvenient results flowing from the use of technical legal terms, the courts have a propensity to avoid them by asserting that civil law concepts should have no part to play in the criminal law;[8] but it may be more accurate to see the conflict not so much as between criminal law and civil law as between technical legal definitions and untechnical popular conceptions.

Sometimes, however, there can develop a more substantial disjunction between a legal definition of a wrong and its underlying conception. This is peculiarly marked in the case of theft, where both classical Roman law and modern English law reveal a very broad approach to the construction of legal liability. In both systems the original notion of theft involves a removal of another's property;[9] in both systems the physical act of theft comes to be defined as no more than an interference with another's property, a *contrectatio* in Roman law, an 'appropriation' in English law; but, in opposition to this definition, in both systems the idea of taking remains at the heart of the conception of theft. In Roman law the

---

[4] The overtones of the word 'rape' have caused some jurisdictions to replace it with an offence of 'criminal sexual conduct' or the like. See J. Temkin, *Rape and the Legal Process* (London, 1987), 118–19.
[5] Theft Act 1968 s. 9(1) (b).   [6] [1976] 1 W.L.R. 672.
[7] The argument was rejected on the facts of the case. For criticism, see G. L. Williams, *Textbook of Criminal Law* (2nd edn, London, 1983), 812–14.
[8] J. C. Smith, 'Civil Law Concepts in the Criminal Law' [1972B] Cambridge Law Journal 197.
[9] Other legal systems generally show the same starting-point: G. P. Fletcher, *Rethinking Criminal Law* (Boston, 1978), 3–29. We may see Roman law as typical of early Indo-European systems: C. Watkins, 'Studies in Indo-European Legal Language, Institutions and Mythology', in G. Cardona (ed.), *Indo-European and Indo-Europeans* (Philadelphia, 1970), 321, 334–45.

distinction between the two levels remained more or less visible, for while the physical act required ground liability for *furtum* was a simple *contrectatio*, the mental state of the wrongdoer could be specified as an *animus furandi*,[10] an intention to steal, which clearly involved more than an intention to handle. In English law the distinction is less easily visible, for the mental element, the *mens rea*, is more precisely defined as 'an intention permanently to deprive' the other of his property; in consequence there is no place for a general 'intention to steal' and no idea of stealing clearly distinct from the idea of appropriating.

Taking and interfering

The early Roman conception of *furtum* as taking[11] seems to have survived until towards the end of the Republic. For Sabinus it was sufficient that there had been an improper interference – *adtrectatio*[12] – and later jurists refer commonly to *contrectatio*, which seems to mean the same thing.[13] The shift had probably begun to occur before the time of Sabinus: the fact that jurists of the generation or so before him dealt with problems of touching suggests that the move away from the older conception had already begun by the middle of the first century BC.[14] There may have been a number of reasons for this move. In part it may have been because of a desire to impose liability on unsuccessful thieves, which could not be achieved directly in a system whose criminal law was still limited and contained no theory of attempts.[15] In part it might have been because of the need to deal with the situation where *furtum* was committed by a depositee or similar person already in possession of another's property.[16] More generally there may have been difficulties with the whole idea of *furtum manifestum*; could a person caught in the act of carrying away goods and prevented from so doing be treated as a

---

[10] Infra, n. 44.
[11] D. Daube, 'Furtum Proprium and Furtum Improprium' (1937) 6 Cambridge Law Journal 217; B. Albanese, 'La nozione del *furtum* fino a Nerazio' (1953) 23 *Annali Palermo*, 1; J. A. C. Thomas, 'Contrectatio, Complicity, and Furtum' (1962) 13 Iura 70, 87 n. 51; W. A. J. Watson, *The Law of Obligations in the Later Roman Republic* (Oxford, 1965), 220. The contrary approach of P. Huvelin, *Etudes sur le furtum* (Lyons, 1915) cannot be supported.
[12] *Noctes Atticae* 11.18.20, 21, 23.
[13] W. W. Buckland, 'Contrectatio' (1941) 57 L.Q.R. 467, 469.
[14] D.47.2.21 *pr*. (Ulpian, 40 *ad Sabinum*), citing Trebatius and Ofilius. See too D.41.1.5.1 (Gaius, 2 *Rerum Cottidianarum*), based on a substrate of Trebatius (Albanese, 23 *Annali Palermo* 84ff.); the stress on the mental element points to an attenuation of the physical element of the delict.
[15] Buckland (1941) 57 L.Q.R. 468 (citing Mommsen).
[16] G. D. MacCormack, 'Definitions: *Furtum* and *Contrectatio*' [1977] Acta Juridica 129, 132–4.

thief at all? Similarly, the provision of the Twelve Tables excusing the killing of a nocturnal thief would have looked rather hollow if it could be argued that the person killed could not have been a thief unless he had succeeded in carrying off the goods. A single feature lies behind each of these possible reasons: the later republican jurists' increasing concern with accuracy of definition.[17]

The classical Roman lawyers, then, adopted a definition of *furtum* as a *contractatio rei fraudulosa*, adding an additional mental element that it must have been *lucri faciendi gratia*.[18] *Contrectatio* itself, with its overtones of improper touching,[19] was treated as meaning any wrongful handling of (or interference with) a thing belonging to another. Yet this definition did not displace the basic conception of *furtum* as involving the actual removal of property; the most common word used to describe the act of stealing is *subripere*, with *contrectare* normally being used to designate the interference with goods which have been stolen already[20] or simply to underline the minimal condition for liability.[21] The focus on removal remained easily visible through the word's etymology – the derivation from *ferre* and *auferre* is clearly the most plausible of those suggested by Paul[22] – and Aulus Gellius hints at the common belief of his time that *furtum* requires a carrying off.[23] The definition of *furtum* as *contrectatio* was therefore established as something different from its underlying conception, and many of the problems of the law can be seen as stemming from the tension set up between these two levels.

The same development and the same tension are visible in modern English law. The early English law of larceny, like the Roman, required an asportation.[24] Even by the seventeenth century it had been established that, although asportation required that the goods be moved, they did not

---

[17] Stein, *Regulae Iuris*, 26–48; and, with particular reference to the development of the law of theft, 'School Attitudes in the Law of Delicts', in *Studi in onore di Arnaldo Biscardi*, vol. II (Milan, 1982), 281–7.
[18] D.47.2.1.3 (Paul, 39 *ad edictum*). In his Institutes (4.1.1) Justinian adopts the same definition, though omitting *lucri faciendi gratia*.
[19] D. Pugsley, 'Contrectatio' (1980) 15 Irish Jurist 341 (reprinted in *Americans are Aliens* (Exeter, 1989), 89).
[20] D.47.2.17.1 (Ulpian, 39 *ad Sabinum*); D.47.2.52.27 (Ulpian, 37 *ad edictum*); D.47.2.61 (Africanus, 7 *Quaestionum*); D.47.2.67.1 (Paul, 7 *ad Plautium*).
[21] D.47.2.52.19 (Ulpian, 37 *ad edictum*); D.47.2.66 (Ulpian, 1 *ad edictum aedilium curulium*); D.47.2.22 *pr.*, 1 (Paul, 9 *ad Sabinum*). Similar in force are D.47.2.20.1 (Paul, 9 *ad Sabinum*) and D.47.2.56 (Ulpian, 3 *Disputationum*), in both of which the word is used explicitly by way of contrast to a verb connoting carrying off.
[22] D.47.2.1 *pr.* (Paul, 39 *ad edictum*).
[23] *Noctes Atticae* 11.18.13. Cf. G.3.195: 'Furtum autem fit non solum cum quis intercipiendi causa rem alienam amovet, sed generaliter cum quis rem alienam invito domino contrectat.' That Gaius thinks this worth saying strongly suggests that he recognised the need to disabuse his audience of the belief. See Thomas (1962) 13 Iura 87 n. 51.
[24] J. H. Baker, *Introduction to English Legal History* (3rd edn, London, 1990), 605–6.

have to be removed very far; in *Simson*[25] it was held that taking goods from a chest and putting them on the floor nearby was sufficient to ground a conviction. Nevertheless, this requirement that there be some movement of the thing survived and was put on a statutory basis in the Larceny Act of 1916;[26] as one commentator described the law, 'The test seems to be: Has every atom left the place in which that particular atom was before?'[27] The shift towards a yet more broad definition of the physical act required to constitute theft occurred with the enactment of the Theft Act 1968, which replaced the old requirement of a 'taking and carrying away' with the less clear term 'appropriation',[28] itself further defined as 'Any assumption by a person of the rights of an owner'.[29] While it was probably not the intention seriously to loosen the *actus reus* of theft,[30] commentators immediately recognised that 'assuming the rights of an owner' could occur some time before there had been any taking and carrying away, so that cases which would not have been classified as larceny would fall within the definition of theft.[31] One, with considerable foresight, went so far as to suggest that 'assuming the rights of an owner' was such a broad conception that any case which would have constituted attempted larceny would now have to be classified as the full offence of theft.[32] This very broad interpretation was accepted by the House of Lords in the leading case of *Morris*:[33] an 'appropriation' could be constituted by any minimal interference with another's property. Nevertheless the underlying idea of carrying off remains central to the popular conception of theft,[34] and continues to exert a considerable influence over the operation of the law.

The primacy of the mental element

The attenuation of the physical element in *furtum* led inevitably to an increasing sharpness of focus on the mental state of the wrongdoer. It was only by paying attention to the wrongdoer's state of mind that it was

---

[25] (1664) Kel. 31.   [26] S. 1(1).
[27] J. W. C. Turner (ed.), *Kenny's Outlines of Criminal Law* (19th edn, Cambridge, 1966), 257.
[28] S. 1(1): 'A person is guilty of theft if he dishonestly appropriates property belonging to another with the intention of permanently depriving the other of it.'
[29] S. 3(1).
[30] See the eighth report of the Criminal Law Revision Committee, *Theft and Related Offences* ((1966) Cmnd. 2977), para 35: '[T]he offence will extend to ordinary stealing by taking property from another's possession.' It was this report that laid the basis for the new offence of theft.
[31] J. C. Smith, *The Law of Theft* (1st edn, London, 1968), para. 27; E. Griew, *The Theft Act 1968* (1st edn, London, 1968), para. 2.23 (implicitly); R. R. Stuart, 'Reform of the Law of Theft' (1967) 30 Modern Law Review 609, 624–5.
[32] Stuart (1967) 30 Modern Law Review 626.   [33] [1984] A.C. 320.
[34] See, for example, *Shorter Oxford English Dictionary*, s.v. 'steal', 'thief'. The primacy of the popular conception is transparently visible in S. Gardner, 'Is Theft a Rip-Off?' (1990) 10 O.J.L.S. 441. It is central to the speech of Lord Lowry in *Gomez* [1993] A.C. 442.

possible to distinguish between interferences which were theftuous and interferences which were not. It was not sufficient simply to specify that the interference had to be against the will of the owner, for such a test would not enable the Romans to draw any line between *furtum* and those cases of *iniuria* or *damnum iniuria datum* that involved a deliberate invasion of property.

So long as liability was limited to cases of actual taking away, there was little need for precision in the specification of the mental element of the wrongdoer; it was enough that he had acted deliberately. Thus in D.47.2.67.2 Paul reports the view of the *veteres* that *furtum* was committed by the man who *dolo malo* summoned a muleteer to court with the result that his mules disappeared.[35] By the end of the Republic, though, as the physical element had become more attenuated we find increasingly an emphasis that the wrongdoer had acted with a view to gain, *lucri faciendi causa*.[36] This also served to put a stop to the later republican tendency to extend the delict from the straightforward paradigm of taking to include cases of wrongfully causing loss, even where there was no gain. As well as the problematic case of the muleteer,[37] liability in *furtum* may have attached to the man who chased a peacock with the result that it was lost,[38] or by the person who waved a red rag at cattle, causing them to flee.[39] By the middle of the second century this expansive tendency had been checked, and the conception of *furtum* restricted to cases where there

[35] Paul, 7 *ad Plautium*: 'Eum qui mulionem dolo malo in ius vocasset, si interea mulae perissent, furti teneri veteres responderunt'. There is nothing in the text to suggest that the mules have been taken away by a third party; the clear implication is that they have wandered.

[36] For example, Sabinus' definition reported in *Noctes Atticae* 11.18.21. See generally J. A. C. Thomas, 'Animus Furandi' (1968), 19 Iura 1, 2–6.

[37] D.47.2.67.2 (Paul, 7 *ad Plautium*). Watson has argued that this would mean that the wrongdoer was liable without *animus furandi*, which he would regard as an untenable belief ('Contrectatio as an Essential of Furtum' (1961) 77 L.Q.R. 526–7, '"Contrectatio" Again' (1962) 28 S.D.H.I. 337); yet this is what the text seems to say. But it does not seem too far-fetched to see this as indicating a broadening of the mental element and the causal connexion between the acts of the wrongdoer and the loss of the goods, analogous to the extension of the physical element visible in the move from subtraction to *contrectatio*. The only difference is that the latter became established law while the former did not.

[38] D.47.2.37 (Pomponius, 19 *ad Sabinum*: 'Si pavonem meum mansuetum, cum de domo mea effugisset, persecutus sis quoad is perit, agere tecum furti ita potero [si aliquis eum habere coeperit].' 'Si . . . coeperit' has all the marks of an explanatory comment, though whether a comment of Pomponius on Sabinus or of a later hand on Pomponius is less easy to determine; the parallel formation 'cum quis fugitivi fur esse coeperit' in D.47.2.36 *pr.* (Ulpian, 41 *ad Sabinum*, quoting Pomponius) suggests that it might be genuine Pomponius, but for present purposes it does not matter. See Watson (1961) 77 L.Q.R. 526, 527–9.

[39] D.47.2.50.4 (Ulpian, 37 *ad edictum*), G.3.202. Analogous situations were discussed: knocking coins out of the hand or throwing goods overboard with the result that they are lost (D.9.2.27.21 (Ulpian, 18 *ad edictum*); D.19.5.14.2 (Ulpian, 41 *ad Sabinum*); D.19.5.23 (Alfenus, 3 *Digestorum a Paulo Epitomatorum*); D.47.2.52.13 (Ulpian, 37 *ad edictum*)); freeing an animal or a slave (D.4.3.7.7 (Ulpian, 11 *ad edictum*); D.41.1.55 (Proculus, 2

was some intention to make a gain either for the wrongdoer himself or for some person acting in concert with him.[40] The malicious waver of the red rag was now liable to the *actio furti* only if he was assisting another to take the cattle, and not if he merely caused them to charge over a precipice or to be lost;[41] in the latter case he might still be liable, but only to a decretal *actio in factum*.[42]

As the physical element of *furtum* became attenuated, so it became necessary to be more specific in the formulation of the wrongdoer's mental state. No longer was it sensible to require simply that the act have been done *dolo malo*; it had to have been done *furti faciendi causa*,[43] or *animo furandi*.[44] Any handling of a thing may constitute *furtum*, but only if it is part of a removal of the thing; and normally the only way to determine whether it is part of a removal is to examine the state of mind of the wrongdoer.[45] This had the effect of narrowing the potential scope of *furtum*, and also of anchoring the legal scope of *furtum* to its popular conception.

In the same way as the Romans, as the physical requirement of the crime of theft became broader the English lawyers shifted from a loose and undefined 'felonious intent'[46] to a more precisely defined requirement that there must have been an intention to deprive the owner of his property.[47] Nevertheless, English law has not yet gone as far as the Romans did in delimiting the *mens rea* in order to keep the offence of theft within reasonable bounds. There is no requirement in the legislation that

---

Epistularum)). That the texts say so consistently that an *actio furti* is not available suggests that there was once a view that it would lie. See generally J. L. Barton, 'The *Lex Aquilia* and Decretal Actions', in Watson (ed.), *Daube Noster*, 15.

[40] For the development of *furtum ope et consilio* see G. MacCormack, 'Ope Consilio Furtum Factum' (1983) 51 T.v.R. 271.

[41] See the texts referred to supra, n. 39. Similarly the glossed reference to falling into the hands of thieves in the case of the peacock, D.47.2.37 (supra. n. 38).

[42] Tradition treats the *actio in factum* as an offshoot of the *lex Aquilia*, but this is too simplistic. For present purposes it is enough to recognise that in his Institutes (G.3.202) Gaius treats it as a case of not-*furtum*. Whatever analytical nicety might have suggested, from a pedagogical point of view it was this that had to be stressed.

[43] D.47.2.1.1 (Paul, 39 *ad edictum*); D.47.2.22 *pr.*, 1 (Paul, 9 *ad Sabinum*); D.47.2.21.7 (Ulpian, 41 *ad Sabinum*); D.47.2.39 *pr.* (Ulpian, 41 *ad Sabinum*); D.47.2.91.1 (Javolenus, 9 *ex Posterioribus Labeonis*). D.47.2.39 *pr.*, holding that *rapere* a prostitute is not *furtum* if the motive is lust rather than theft, appears to cause difficulties, but they are convincingly dispelled by Thomas (1962) 13 Iura 72–6.

[44] D.47.2.43.5 (Ulpian, 41 *ad Sabinum*); D.47.2.52.20 (Ulpian, 37 *ad edictum*); D.47.2.76 (Pomponius, 21 *ad Quintum Mucium*); P.S.2.31.35 (FIRA 2.356). Thomas (1968), 19 Iura 1.

[45] Handling after removal (supra, n. 20) is an exception to the normal rule.

[46] E. H. East, *A Treatise of the Pleas of the Crown* (London, 1803), 662.

[47] *Cabbage* (1815) R. & R. 292. Cf. *Holloway* (1848) 3 Cox 241 (where the increasing precision is treated by Denman, C.J. as a recent, and not wholly desirable, development).

the wrongdoer should have any view to gain, merely that he should intend permanently to deprive the other of his property.[48] In theory, therefore, the deliberate release of a caged bird[49] or the intentional destruction of another's property could be treated as theft, even though in practice they would invariably be regarded as criminal damage.[50] The popular conception of theft as unauthorised taking may still essentially determine the scope of the offence, but only by directing the way in which prosecutorial discretion operates rather than by dictating formal legal rules.

The physical element

The most obvious difficulty stemming from the adoption of a definition of *furtum* based on *contrectatio*, assuming that we should take this to connote an improper handling, was that there may have been cases which were generally regarded as *furtum* but where there was no physical touching.[51] What of the hypothetical case put by Buckland of the chasing of your hen into my hen-house?[52] What of the refusal to return a pledge or to hand over another's swine which have been rescued from wolves?[53] What of the person who lends a seller false weights with the result that he obtains a lesser price for his goods?[54] In all of these situations the owner is deprived of his property, and it can hardly have made a difference

---

[48] S. 1(1).
[49] Williams, *Textbook of Criminal Law*, 766.
[50] J. C. Smith and B. Hogan, *Criminal Law* (7th edn, London, 1992), 504 n. 14; Williams, *Textbook of Criminal Law*, 765–6. E. Griew, *The Theft Acts 1968 and 1978* (6th edn, London, 1990), para. 2.79. Sometimes, however, a charge of theft is preferred when property has simply been destroyed: J. N. Spencer, 'Mere Baubles' (1978) 42 Journal of Criminal Law 125, 126–7. It has, however, been suggested that it is necessary to consider the mental state of the accused in order to determine whether an act constitutes an appropriation: *Morris* [1984] A.C. 320, 332–3 (already recognised by one far-sighted commentator in 1968: E. Griew, *The Theft Act 1968* (1st edn), para. 3.23): switching price labels as a malicious prank would not be an appropriation. Perhaps in the light of this theft can to some extent be marked off from criminal damage. But see *Gomez* [1993] A.C. 442, 460.
[51] Even Watson, who argues most strongly for the requirement of actual physical contact, seems to concede that there may be cases of *furtum* without it: 'The Definition of Furtum and the Trichotomy' (1960) 28 T.v.R. 197, 198.
[52] (1941) 57 L.Q.R. 468.
[53] In both of which cases Ulpian would allow the *actio furti*: D.47.2.52.7 (Ulpian, 37 *ad edictum*); D.41.1.44 (Ulpian, 19 *ad edictum*). For the more difficult case of the denial of deposit, see J. A. C. Thomas, 'Infitiando Depositum Nemo Facit Furtum', in *Studi in onore di Edoardo Volterra*, vol. II (Milan, 1971), 759.
[54] D.47.2.52.22 (Ulpian, 37 *ad edictum*), D.4.3.18.3. (Paul, 11 *ad edictum*); discussed by P. G. Stein, *Fault in the Formation of Contract in Roman Law and Scots Law* (Aberdeen, 1958), 94–7. The latter text refers to Trebatius' argument for the appropriateness of the *actio de dolo*, and therefore by implication his denial of the *actio furti*; Trebatius may have taken an extreme view; supra, n. 14.

whether or not the wrongdoer or his accomplice had fortuitously touched it.

If the essence of *furtum* had been simply a wrongful interference, it might have been possible to hold that there could be *furtum* of land. This was Sabinus' view[55] and others may have agreed with him, but the popular opinion that there could not be *furtum* of land came to prevail in classical law.[56] It might have been possible to explain this away on the grounds that the wrongful occupier of land[57] could not in the nature of things ever have had an *animus furandi*, assuming that this connoted an intention to take away. What, though, of the analogous case of the person who handles a chest with the intention of carrying it off but finds he is incapable of moving it? This, by definition, cannot be explained away on the grounds of lack of intention, yet Ulpian is clear that it cannot be *furtum*.[58] Nor can it be explained as a crude rule that a man cannot be liable for the *furtum* of a thing too heavy for him to lift.[59] Apparently, and quite logically, he is not guilty of *furtum* of the chest on the straightforward grounds that he was not stealing it.

The case of the heavy chest is just one instance of a more general problem raised by the Roman definition of *contrectatio*, the problem of the measure of damages for the theft of part of a whole. In English law if I handle a purse with the intention of taking away some of its contents it does not really matter whether I am treated as stealing the purse-plus-contents or merely the money which it contained;[60] it is simply a question of how the charge is drafted. In Roman law the problem was acute, though, since the damages recoverable were assessed as twice the value of the thing stolen. It was in this context that the tension between handling and carrying off, *contrectatio* and *asportatio*, received its most substantial consideration.

---

[55] *Noctes Atticae* 11.18.13.
[56] D.47.2.25 *pr.* (Ulpian, 41 *ad Sabinum*): 'Verum est quod plerique probant, fundi furti agi non posse.'
[57] Or, to use Sabinus' example, the person who dishonestly sold land belonging to another: *Noctes Atticae* 11.18.13.
[58] D.47.2.21.8 (41 *ad Sabinum*), considered below, p. 67. The reference to the same problem in 21 *pr.* suggests that it might have been a commonly discussed hypothetical. I am not convinced by Thomas' assumption, not demanded by the wording of the text, that Ulpian must have been considering the situation where the chest was so obviously heavy that the wrongdoer could not have had the intention of carrying it off: 'D.47.2.21', in *Synteleia Arangio-Ruiz*, vol. II (Naples, 1964), 607, 613.
[59] Hence the immediate qualification in D.47.2.21.9 that he might have helpers, all of whom would (in accordance with general principles of cumulative liability in delictual actions) be liable in full.
[60] Cf. *Easom* [1971] 2 Q. B. 315. There might be a problem if the purse was empty and I could show that I had no intention of taking in such circumstances, but the better view is

Contrectatio and appropriation 63

The question is discussed at some length by Ulpian, in D.47.2.21 *pr.*-8,[61] a passage of no little complexity. The text may simply be irredeemably corrupt, but the fact that it is extremely difficult to make sense of the highly condensed argument is not in itself a reason for so concluding; what follows is based on the assumption that the text is substantially genuine, and that it makes substantial sense. If I follow Ulpian's reasoning, his argument takes the form of an extended critique in four sections (*pr.*, 1–4, 5–6, 7–8) of the notion (of Sabinus?) that the simple handling of the thing with the appropriate mental state is sufficient in itself to constitute *furtum*.

The first section – 21 *pr.* – introduces the problem, drawing attention to the tension between the idea of *furtum* as *contrectatio* and *furtum* as *subreptio*.[62] The conflict is stated starkly. The man who takes a measure out of a whole heap of corn or a small quantity of wine from a barrel is held – presumably by Sabinus[63] – to commit *furtum* of the whole, for he has committed a *contrectatio* of the whole; on the reasonable assumption that the heap is a *universitas*, this seems an unavoidable conclusion, indistinguishable from the analogy (cited by Ulpian) that a person who touches a slave's ear must be regarded as touching the slave. On the other hand, says Ulpian, the damages should be assessed solely by reference to the amount that he took.[64] The conclusion that it is the taking away that is relevant is then supported by two analogous situations ('Nam et ... Sed et

---

that I am still guilty of the offence: Smith, *The Law of Theft* (6th edn, London, 1989), para. 136.

[61] Ulpian, 40 *ad Sabinum*. The inscription attributes the passage to Paul, but this seems an obvious mistake, and the emendation to Ulpian is almost universally admitted. 21.9 and 10 constitute a brief coda to what I take to be the main argument. For discussion of the text, see in particular K. Olivecrona, *Three Essays in Roman Law* (Lund, 1949), 43–51 and Thomas, *Synteleia Arangio-Ruiz*, II.609–15.

[62] 'Volgaris est quaestio an is qui ex acervo frumenti modium sustulit totius rei furtum faciat an verum eius tantum quod abstulit. Ofilius totius acervi furem esse putat; nam et qui aurem alicuius tetigit inquit Trebatius totum eum videri tetigisse; proinde et qui dolium aperuit et inde parvum vini abstulit non tantum eius quod abstulit verum totius videtur fur esse. Sed verum est in tantum eos furti actione teneri quantum abstulerunt. Nam et si quis armarium quod tollere non poterat aperuerit, et omnes res quae in eo erant contrectaverit, atque ita discesserit, deinde reversus unam ex his abstulerit, et antequam se reciperet quo destinaverat deprehensus fuerit, eiusdem rei et manifestus et nec manifestus fur erit. Sed et qui segetem luce secat et contrectat eius quod sequente nocte asportans deprehenditur manifestus et nec manifestus fur est.'

I have followed Mommsen's generally accepted emendation of the last sentence; for a different view, see MacCormack [1977] Acta Juridica 129, 135.

[63] Albanese, 23 *Annali Palermo* 140 n. 126.

[64] I cannot accept Olivecrona's view that this sentence ('sed verum ... abstulerunt') is interpolated (*Three Essays in Roman Law*, 44 n. 3). On the contrary, the opposition between it and the preceding part of the text is essential to the logic of the argument.

...'). First, the person who handles all the contents of a chest[65] and goes away, who then returns and is caught in the act of carrying off one individual item; here he is a *fur manifestus* of the item he actually takes. But this might be distinguished from the initial situation of taking part of a heap, for here the separate items are clearly individual *res*. Hence the second, stronger, analogy: the person who cuts corn by day and goes away, who then returns by night and is caught carrying off part of it; again he is a *fur manifestus* of the part he carries off.[66] In both cases it is the carrying off rather than the simple handling that determines the liability of the wrongdoer.

The second section, 21.1–4,[67] explores the same problem from a different angle. A man deposits a bag containing twenty coins and then, by mistake of the depositee, receives back a bag containing thirty; on the assumption that he knows that the bag contains thirty, but believes that twenty of these are the coins originally deposited, he is held liable[68] for *furtum* of only ten.[69] We must take it that this is a straightforward deposit and not *depositum irregulare*, and that the depositor is wrong in believing that his own twenty are contained in the bag.[70] Here, then, is the case of the *subreptio* of the whole, but with the *animus furandi* only as to a part; liability is determined by the animus. Ulpian immediately puts the con-

---

[65] The chest is stated to be too heavy to lift, so as to avoid the argument that he might be liable for *furtum* of the entirety.

[66] In both cases the text as it stands states that he commits *furtum nec manifestum* (by handling) as well as *furtum manifestum*. Thomas' arguments (*Synteleia Arangio-Ruiz*, II.609–10) that the reference to *furtum nec manifestum* are interpolated are compelling.

[67] '1. Si is qui viginti nummorum saccum deposuisset, alium saccum, in quo scit triginta esse, errante eo qui dabat, acceperit, putavit autem illic sua viginti esse, teneri furti decem nomine placet.

2. Si quis aes subripuit, dum aurum se subripere putat, vel contra, ex libro octavo Pomponii ad Sabinum, aut minus esse cum plus esset, eius quod subripuit furtum committit: idem Ulpianus.

3. Sed et si quis subripuit furto duos sacculos, unum decem, alterum viginti, quorum alterum suum putavit, alterum scit alienum, profecto dicemus tantum unius, quem putavit alienum, furtum eum facere, quemadmodum si duo pocula abstulerit, quorum alterum suum putavit, alterum scit alienum; nam et hic unius fit furtum.

4. Sed si ansam in poculo suam putavit [vel vere fuit], totius poculi eum furtum facere Pomponius scripsit.'

There is an obvious problem with 21.2, most easily explained by treating it in part as a text from Pomponius *ad Sabinum* (presumably book 18, which dealt with *furtum*) which has become embedded in the extract from Ulpian. For an elaborate palaeographical explanation of the difficulties of this text see J. Miquel, 'Mechanische Fehler in der Überlieferung der Digesten' (1963) 80 Z.S.S. 233, 256–8.

[68] 'Teneri ... placet' suggests that this is not just Ulpian's opinion.

[69] There are admittedly formal difficulties with the passage, but Albanese's suggestion (23 *Annali Palermo* 145–6) that Ulpian's actual decision was that he was liable for the full thirty involves too radical a change and disregards the inner logic of the argument.

[70] Otherwise it is a straightforward case of knowing receipt of an over-payment, which would not fit with the sense of the passage.

Contrectatio and appropriation 65

trasting case: if I take copper believing it to be gold, for example, I am liable for what I actually take, and not for what I believe I am taking. The problem is to reconcile these two decisions; this is done by considering closely the nature of the *universitas*. If I take two purses, one containing ten and the other twenty coins, believing that one belongs to me, then I am only liable for the one which I knew was not mine.[71] Hence, applying the reasoning back to 21.1, the bag containing thirty has to be treated as two logically distinct parts: the twenty to which I think I am entitled and the ten to which I do not.[72] In 21.4 the contrast is finally underlined between the *universitas* and the single *res*: if I take a cup, believing that the handle which is attached to it belongs to me,[73] I am liable for the *furtum* of the whole cup.

The function of 21.1–4 in the context of Ulpian's argument can thus be seen. When dealing with *furtum* as a *universitas*, logic demands that it be treated not as a single entity, but in terms of its component parts. The implication for the resolution of the initial problem, taking the measure of corn from the heap, is obvious: liability cannot simply be determined by considering the heap as a single thing.

The next section – 21.5–6[74] – returns to the initial problem, applying this reasoning to it. What if a man removes a *sextarius* of corn from a shipload, or a small quantity of wine from a ship's hold? Working from the simple case of the removal of goods from a warehouse (*horreum*), which (he says) could hardly be *furtum* of the whole of the contents of the warehouse, Ulpian concludes that we should similarly not say that the abstracter of the corn or wine was liable for the *furtum* of the whole cargo.[75] We must see here three distinct questions, in increasing order of difficulty:

[71] 'The case is too simple for argument' (C. H. Monro, *Digest XLVII.2. De Furtis* (Cambridge, 1893), 28 n. 3). This is precisely the point of it.
[72] Ulpian's treatment of unitary sums of money may not have been typical. In D.45.1.1.4 (48 *ad Sabinum*) he holds that an obligation to pay ten arises where there is a *stipulatio* to pay ten and a promise to pay twenty or a *stipulatio* to pay twenty and a promise to pay ten; 'licet enim oportet congruere summam, attamen manifestissimum est viginti et decem inesse'. This passage is normally regarded as interpolated (see R. Backhaus, 'In Maiore Minus Inest' (1983) 100 Z.S.S. 152–5), but the reasoning closely parallels the present passage.
[73] 'Vel vere fuit' is clearly a gloss.
[74] '5. Sed si de navi onerata furto quis sextarium frumenti tulerit, utrum totius oneris an vero sextarii tantum furtum fecerit? Facilius hoc quaeritur in horreo pleno; et durum est dicere totius furtum fieri. [Et quid si cisterna vini sit, quid dicet? Aut aquae cisterna?] Quid deinde si nave vinaria (ut sunt multae in quas vinum effunditur), quid dicemus de eo qui vinum hausit? An totius oneris fur sit? Et magis est ut et hic non totius dicamus.

6. Certe si proponas in apotheca amphoras esse vini easque subtractas, singularum furtum fit, non totius apothecae, quemadmodum si ex pluribus rebus moventibus in horreo reclusis unam tulerit.'
[75] 'Et quid si cisterna ... cisterna?' has all the marks of a marginal gloss incorporated into the text; this would also explain the active voice and third person of *dicet*.

66   *David Ibbetson*

(a) the simple case of taking goods from a *horreum*; this is not *furtum* of the whole, for it is easy to see that the individual items are obviously separate *res*.
(b) the removal of corn from the shipload;[76] following Pomponius, Ulpian might allow that the ownership of the corn remained vested in its original owners, if the mixing had been done without their consent,[77] so that the taking of the *sextarius* could be logically indistinguishable from the easy case of the removal of goods from the *horreum*.
(c) the removal of wine from the cistern; here the mixing of different persons' wine would have destroyed the individual ownership, and the resultant mass would have been subject to common ownership even if the mixing had been done without the owners' consent.[78] It could not therefore be treated as individual *res*. Still, though, we would not treat this as *furtum* of the whole.

It is this last case which marks the true equivalent of the original situation of 21 *pr*., and which is the logical parallel with the bag containing thirty coins dealt with in 21.1. Strengthening this parallel, Ulpian now uses exactly similar reasoning as that used to link 21.1 and 21.3 to analogise the wine in the hold of a ship to *amphorae* of wine in a farmer's warehouse (*apotheca*[79]); just as a bag of thirty coins can be treated as two distinct entities of twenty and ten, so a shipful of wine can be treated as if it were distinct *amphorae*. Even if what is taken is part of a *universitas*, the wrongdoer's liability is determined by what he removes.[80]

This leads on to the final section of Ulpian's argument, 21.7–8.[81] He

[76] It seems to be assumed that the ship contains corn belonging to several owners.
[77] D.6.1.5 *pr*. (Ulpian, 16 *ad Edictum*); cf. J.Inst. 2.1.28.
[78] D.41.1.7.8 (Gaius, *rerum cottidianarum*); J.Inst. 2.1.27.
[79] It is possible that *apotheca* is here used in contrast to *horreum*; the former would normally contain only one man's goods, whereas the latter would commonly be a public warehouse containing many men's. More probably, though, Ulpian is treating *apotheca* as the normal word for the storehouse of wine and *horreum* for the storehouse of grain: cf. D.30.47.1 (22 *ad Sabinum*); D.33.7.12.9 (20 *ad Sabinum*). See generally G. Rickman, *The Corn Supply of Ancient Rome* (Oxford, 1980), 138–43.
[80] We may be able to draw additional support for this conclusion from the contrast in form between 21 *pr*. ('in tantum eos furti actione teneri quantum abstulerunt') and 21.5 ('Et magis est ut et hic non totius dicamus'). The latter, perhaps, marks a strengthening of the conclusion. It is not merely that damages are assessed by reference to the amount abstracted; we would not even *say* that this was *furtum* of the whole.
[81] '7. Qui furti faciendi causa conclave intravit, nondum fur est, quamvis furandi causa intravit. Quid ergo? Qua actione tenebitur? Utique iniuriarum: aut de vi accusabitur, si per vim introivit.'

8. 'Item si maioris ponderis quid aperuit aut refregit, quod tollere non possit, non est omnium rerum cum eo furti actio, sed earum tantum quas tulit, quia totum tollere non poterit. Proinde si involucrum quod tollere non potuit solvit ut contrectet, deinde contrectavit quasdam res; quamvis singulas res quae in eo fuerint tollere potuerit, si

Contrectatio and appropriation

begins, summing up what he has said about the *horreum* and the *apotheca*, by making the seductively obvious point that entering a room with the intention of stealing does not in itself constitute *furtum*.[82] Equally, if someone breaks open a chest which is too heavy to lift, he is liable for the *furtum* of such of the contents as he carries off, but not of the whole;[83] breaking into a chest is essentially the same as breaking into a room. Similarly, though slightly less obviously, if he unstraps a bundle which is too heavy to lift, intentionally handles the contents and carries some of them off, this is *furtum* only of those that he takes;[84] his liability is determined by what he removes.

With the final sentence of 21.8 Ulpian ties together his whole argument, although not in a way to make his meaning immediately clear:

Quod si totum vas tollere potuit, dicimus eum totius esse furem, licet solverit ut singulas vel quasdam tolleret: et ita et Sabinus ait.'

But if he could take the whole receptacle, we say that he is thief of all, even though he opened it to take one or some items; and so says Sabinus.[85]

This seems logically indistinguishable from the two cases just dealt with, yet the opposite result is reached; in consequence even such a conservative scholar as Buckland has agreed in the conclusion that the text has suffered badly at the hands of compilers who misunderstood what Ulpian was saying.[86] If we think simply in terms of 21.8 itself, there is no doubt at all that this last sentence looks very odd indeed. But if we consider it in terms of the whole argument beginning at 21 *pr.* then its force becomes clearer.

    tamen totum involucrum tollere non potuerit, singularum rerum quas tulerit fur est, ceterarum non est. Quod si totum vas tollere potuit, dicimus eum totius esse furem, licet solverit ut singulas vel quasdam tolleret: et ita et Sabinus ait.'

[82] See too Ulpian in D.47.2.39 *pr.* (41 *ad Sabinum*). The same point is made by Paul in P.S.2.31.35 (FIRA 2.356) and D.47.2.54 *pr.* (35 *ad edictum*). The text had been treated by several commentators as having been introduced from a wholly different context, but it is vigorously and convincingly defended by F. Raber, *Grundlagen klassischer Injurienansprüche* (Vienna, 1969), 152–9.

[83] 21 *pr.* (supra, p. 63). Thomas (*Synteleia Arangio-Ruiz*, II.613) is clearly right to suggest that what is envisaged is the person who breaks open the box intending to ransack it, but I do not think it is necessary (or possible) to assume from the text that the box is so heavy that he could not have contemplated moving it.

[84] Compare the analysis of D.47.2.22.1 (Paul, 9 *ad Sabinum*): if he handles the other things in the box with the intent to steal them, even if he does not carry them off, he commits *furtum* of them; if he handles them only to move them out of the way of the object of his theft, it is not *furtum*. Ulpian would presumably not disagree even with the first case: the difference is that for Paul there is liability if the things were handled *furti faciendi causa*, while for Ulpian the bundle was unstrapped simply *ut contrectet* the contents. If I understand him rightly, his whole point is that *contrectatio* alone is insufficient.

[85] The translation is from the Pennsylvania edition of the Digest.

[86] 'Digest XLVII.2 and the Methods of the Compilers' (1930) 10 T.v.R. 117, 131–2. To the same effect: Albanese, 23 *Annali Palermo* 156–9; Thomas, *Synteleia Arangio-Ruiz*, II.613.

The starting-point is Sabinus' assertion that the person who takes part of a *universitas* is liable for the *furtum* of the whole. Ulpian has cast doubt on this first (21.1–4) by showing that sometimes we must take into account the *animus* of the wrongdoer as determining not simply *whether* he stole but *what* he stole, and then (21.5–7) by showing that we cannot coherently conclude that a person who breaks into or breaks up a collection of objects which have been gathered together as a unity commits *furtum* of the whole collection. Having thus weakened Sabinus' position by these flanking arguments, in 21.8 he attacks Sabinus head-on. The first two cases lead inexorably to the conclusion that the person who ransacks a container which he could carry off, but which he has no intention of taking, should only be liable for what he does in fact carry off. In starkly stating the contrary conclusion as Sabinus' opinion, he is not politely referring to the view of an earlier jurist but brutally if implicitly pointing out that it is wrong. 'Et ita et Sabinus ait', with its emphatically repeated 'et ... et', should be translated not simply as 'Sabinus says the same'[87] or 'And so says Sabinus',[88] but rather as 'But this is what Sabinus says.' *Modo suo*, he teases out the weak point in the opponents' position, and rips it to pieces.[89]

Even here, Ulpian does not resolve the tension between handling and carrying away. It cannot be resolved, since it is implicit in the opposition between the definition of *furtum* as *contrectatio* and the conception of *furtum* as taking away. Similarly, we can only point to the existence of the same tension in English law.

The English world 'appropriation' does not have the overtones of physical touching which are associated with the Roman *contrectatio*, and in consequence English law has avoided some of the problems which had to be faced by the Romans. It is able, for example, to impose liability for theft in a case where one person holds himself out as owner of another's property and purports to sell it to a third party.[90] In addition, since English law does not have to calculate damages by reference to the value of the thing stolen, it has not had to deal with the difficult problem of the theft or part of a *universitas*. Notwithstanding this, it is generally recognised that the courts' exegesis of the concept of appropriation has been

---

[87] Jolowicz's translation.
[88] As in the Pennsylvania edition.
[89] T. Honoré, *Ulpian* (Oxford, 1982), 81–2. Honoré's comments on Ulpian's treatment of D.24.1.32.14 could be applied equally to the text we have been discussing: 'The structure is that of a dialogue between the author and himself. He asks himself a question, searches for the answer, suddenly finds the decisive reason, and pounces.'
[90] *Pitham and Hehl* (1976) 65 Cr.App.Rep. 45. But see the severe criticisms of Williams, *Textbook of Criminal Law*, 763–5.

Contrectatio and appropriation

regrettably unclear and that the law today is something of an impenetrable forest.[91]

At the root of the difficulties lies the apparent conflict between the decisions of the House of Lords in *Lawrence* v. *Metropolitan Police Commissioner*[92] and *Burnside and Morris*.[93] In the former case D, a taxi-driver, was held to have been rightly convicted of theft when he had taken money in excess of the lawful fare from the wallet of a passenger; it did not matter that the passenger had proffered the wallet and hence consented to the taking. In the latter, D was held to have been rightly convicted of the theft of a joint of meat in a supermarket when he replaced its original label with one showing a lesser price, and then tendered this price at the supermarket check-out. In the course of his elaborate discussion of the concept of appropriation, Lord Roskill stressed that it involved an act which was not expressly or impliedly authorised by the owner, 'an act by way of adverse interference with or usurpation of [the owner's] rights'.[94] If there is a single concept of 'appropriation',[95] then there is clear conflict between these two decisions. In *Lawrence* the conviction was upheld notwithstanding that the owner consented to the taking; in *Morris* an act was said to constitute an appropriation if and only if the owner did not consent to it.

Subsequent cases have striven to reconcile these decisions, but without signal success.[96] No attempt will be made to do so here; the logic-chopping involved should have no part to play in the criminal law. What is more interesting from a comparative perspective is why English law has managed to get itself into such a mess. Behind the conflict, it is argued, there is the same tension as we have seen underlying the Roman law, the tension between the definition of the minimal conditions which need to be satisfied in order to ground a conviction and the basic conception of the offence.

---

[91] See, for example, the remarks of Griew, *The Theft Acts 1968 and 1978*, paras. 2–50.
[92] [1972] A.C. 626.
[93] [1984] A.C. 320 (hereafter referred to simply as *Morris*). The fundamental conflict between these decisions is explored at length, though not satisfactorily resolved, in *Gomez* [1993] A.C. 442.
[94] [1984] A.C. 320 at 332.
[95] It has been argued that the Theft Act in fact contains two concepts of appropriation, one in s. 1 and one in s. 3; A. Halpin, 'The Appropriate Appropriation' [1991] Crim.L.R. 426. While I am sympathetic to Halpin's general standpoint, I do not think his specific argument withstands analysis; s. 1 provides the definition of theft, and ss. 2–6 thereafter clearly function only as an elaboration of the five principal elements of the offence. See C. M. V. Clarkson, 'Authorised Acts and Appropriation' (1992) 55 Modern Law Review 265, 267 n. 14.
[96] *Dobson* v. *General Accident Fire and Life Assurance Corporation plc* [1990] 1 Q.B. 274; *Gomez* [1993] A.C. 442; *Shuck* (1992) Crim.L.R. 209; *Rader* [1992] Crim.L.R. 663 (all in the Court of Appeal).

Morris is clearly a case of minimal conditions. The question was not *what* offence had been committed, but *whether* an offence had (yet) been committed. In this context appropriation has the same function for the English lawyers as *contrectatio* had for the Romans. This question can arise in a range of situations: when D has been interrupted in an apparently theftuous course of conduct;[97] when D has undoubtedly stolen the goods by a series of acts beginning in England but only completed in a foreign jurisdiction;[98] when the question is of the liability of secondary parties who only became involved at a late stage of the theftuous course of conduct;[99] when D is charged with dealing with property which he has already dishonestly come by;[100] or where there is a question whether D has committed one single theft or a number of distinct thefts which are required to be charged separately.[101]

In this context there are a number of good reasons why appropriation should be limited to acts which are not authorised by the owner. If appropriation involves 'an assumption of the rights of an owner'[102] it is difficult to give this any real meaning when D's acts are precisely those which the owner has permitted; such acts do more to confirm the owner's rights then to assume them.[103] If a theftuous course of conduct is held to involve a single act of appropriation, rather than a continuing act or a series of acts,[104] then it makes good sense to ensure that so far as possible the appropriation should be held to occur at a time when it is possible to prove the other elements of the offence; this is best achieved by requiring that D's behaviour on its face raises the inference that he is stealing.[105]

---

[97] *McPherson* [1973] Crim.L.R. 191 (shopper in supermarket placing goods in own shopping basket rather than basket provided by store: guilty); *Monaghan* [1979] Crim.L.R. 673 (supermarket cashier putting money in till but failing to ring up payment, intending subsequently to take money for self: guilty); *Eddy* v. *Niman* (1981) 73 Cr.App.Rep. 237 (shopper in supermarket putting goods in store's basket, intending not to pay for them: not guilty, but questionable in the light of *Gomez*).

[98] *Morgan* [1985] Crim.L.R. 447, 596 (see Smith, *The Law of Theft*, (7th edn), para. 33 n. 33); *Fritschy* [1985] Crim.L.R. 745; cf. *Figures* [1976] Crim.L.R. 744.

[99] *Meech* [1974] Q.B. 549 (*sed qu* the application of the principle on the facts of the case).

[100] *Hircock* (1978) 67 Cr.App.Rep. 278.

[101] *Skipp* [1975] Crim.L.R. 114.

[102] Theft Act s. 3(1); *Morris* [1984] A.C. 320, 321–2.

[103] Similarly it is argued that there must be a distinction between assuming the rights of another and invading the rights of another: L. H. Leigh, 'Some Remarks on Appropriation in the Law of Theft after *Morris*' (1985) 48 Modern Law Review 167. There is an exact parallel with the Roman requirement that the *contrectatio* be *invito domino*.

[104] The law on this point is by no means clear; academic writers prefer to see it as a continuing act (see, for example, Smith and Hogan, *Criminal Law* (7th edn), 512–13), but judicial authority is more equivocal.

[105] This is of particular importance in determining whether a store detective has a power of arrest: H. Levenson and F. Fairweather, *Police Powers* (2nd edn, London, 1990), 87–8; Police and Criminal Evidence Act 1984, s. 24(4), 24(5). Hence also the sense of the rule

Moreover, as a matter of reality we do not normally regard someone as stealing (as opposed to preparing to steal) whose acts are apparently perfectly innocent.

A case like *Lawrence* is very different. Where D has actually taken P.s property (assuming that he has acted dishonestly and with intent permanently to deprive P), there is a clear case of criminality. There may, legitimately, be a question of *what* offence he has committed, but there is no room for any doubt *whether* he has committed an offence. It is necessary therefore to face up to two distinct questions: (a) whether D.s conduct *prima facie* falls within the ambit of the offence of theft; (b) if so, whether the fact that he was clearly guilty of the offence of obtaining property by deception[106] should preclude a conviction of theft. Both the Court of Appeal and the House of Lords were (rightly) of the opinion that the answer to the second question was in the negative.[107] Hence the only question for resolution is the first; and it is hard to disagree with the conclusion that this is a perfectly clear case of appropriation, of taking another person's property, and that there is no warrant for reading into the statute a wholly artificial requirement that the taking be without the consent of the owner. The case is the English analogue of Buckland's hypothetical Roman question of inducing the hen to enter the henhouse;[108] if we are satisfied that D has wrongfully obtained P's property, we do not need to look a great deal further into the definition of the offence. The same point is visible even more strongly in *Dobson* v. *General Accident*.[109] Here the wrongdoer had deceived the owner of a watch and a diamond ring into parting with them in exchange for a worthless cheque; the question was whether this loss fell within the clause in P's insurance policy covering 'loss or damage caused by theft'. The obvious answer, reached by the Court of Appeal, is that it did; as a matter of the construction of an insurance contract, anything else would have been absurd. Similarly in two further recent cases, *Shuck*[110] and *Rader*,[111] the Court of Appeal has upheld convictions of theft where D has obtained –

---

that D's state of mind is one factor which determines whether his external acts constitute an appropriation.

[106] Theft Act 1968, s. 15(1).
[107] [1971] 1 Q.B. 373 at 377–8; [1972] A.C. 626 at 633. Equally the fact that he was no doubt guilty of a number of statutory offences was irrelevant. The Theft Acts are full of apparently overlapping offences; if they were held to be wholly distinct it would be all too easy for a person to escape conviction for one offence by arguing that he was guilty of another, perhaps more serious, one. See P. R. Glazebrook, 'Thief or Swindler: Who Cares?' [1991] C.L.J. 389.
[108] Supra, n. 52.
[109] [1990] 1 Q.B. 274.
[110] [1992] Crim.L.R. 209.
[111] [1992] Crim.L.R. 209.

taken – P's property; it has been held not to matter that D's taking has merely been the opposite side of the coin to P's giving.[112]

The courts have in general attempted to analyse all these cases as if they dealt with the same problem, whether an appropriation can be said to have occurred when the owner of the goods consented to D's acts. When faced with a statutory definition of theft couched in terms of appropriation it is hard to see that they could have done otehwise; yet in truth the two questions – *whether* an offence has been committed and *what* offence has been committed – are distinct, and it is by no means obvious that the answer to the first question should also provide the answer to the second. Roman law provides no easy answer to the English lawyers' problem. Nor should we expect it to do so. What can be learned, though, is that the problem stems not from the nature of the definition of theft but from the fact that it is being used to fulfil two functions. Ulpian's demonstration of the inadequacy of framing the question of liability simply in terms of *contrectatio* should lead us to recognise the parallel inadequacy of asking simply whether and when there has been an appropriation. The apparently conflicting answers of *Lawrence* and *Morris* can be reconciled; but only if we realise that they are answers to different questions.

---

[112] The contrary line was taken in *Gomez* [1991] 3 All E.R. 394, but on appeal the House of Lords resolved in favour of the line in *Lawrence, Shuck* and *Rader*: [1993] A.C. 442.

5 Going to the fair – Jacques de Révigny on possession

William M. Gordon

Having begun my studies in mediaeval Roman law under Peter Stein's supervision it seemed to me appropriate to turn to that subject in offering a tribute to him. Jacques de Révigny taught in the Orléans law school from around 1260 to around 1280, and the importance of that law school in the thirteenth and early fourteenth centuries is now well established, particularly as a result of the work of E. M. Meijers. The work which he began in the University of Leiden has been continued there under the leadership of R. Feenstra[1] and attention has focused on the writings of Jacques de Révigny, which, so far as they had been printed before Meijers brought out their importance, had been printed under the names of others – Pierre de Belleperche in the case of his commentary on the Code and Bartolus in the case of his commentary on the Institutes.[2] The modest addition to what has since been achieved by way of publication of his writings which follows has been made possible by association with the Leiden project. I gratefully acknowledge the help which I have received from Leiden in preparing it.

The text edited is a commentary by Jacques de Révigny on D. 41.2.6.1–7, in the mediaeval form of reference, ff de acquirenda vel amittenda possessione l.Clam possidere § Qui ad nundinas and l. Sed et si.[3]

---

[1] See his collected studies, *Fata Iuris Romani. Etudes d'histoire du droit* (Leiden, 1974) and *Le Droit savant au moyen âge et sa vulgarisation* (London, 1986), the latter of which contains at pp. 13–29 a review of researches on the law school of Orléans conducted since those of Meijers.

[2] For the Code see Meijers, *Etudes d'histoire du droit*, vol. III (Leiden, 1959), 72ff. and H. Kiefner, 'Zur gedruckten Codexlectura des Jacques de Révigny' (1963) 5 *Tijdschrift voor Rechtsgeschiedenis* 5; for the Institutes see Meijers, *Etudes*, 68ff. and L. J. van Soest-Zuurdeeg, *La Lecture sur le titre De actionibus (Inst. 4,6) de Jacques de Révigny* (Leiden, 1989).

[3] Ulpian, 70 *ad edictum*: 'Qui ad nundinas profectus neminem reliquerit et, dum ille a nundinis redit, aliquis occupauerit possessionem, uideri eum clam possidere Labeo scribit: retinet ergo possessionem is, qui ad nundinas abiit: uerum si reuertentem dominum non admiserit, ui magis intelligi possidere, non clam.'
Paul 54 *ad edictum*: 'Sed et si nolit in fundum reuerti, quod uim maiorem uereatur, amisisse possessionem uidebitur: et ita Neratius quoque scribit.'
('Suppose a man to go to market without leaving someone in charge and, while he is

It is taken from a *lectura* on the *Digestum novum* of which the part from which this text comes is preserved in two manuscripts, one formerly held in Chartres and the other held in Paris.[4] In his excellent study of the *repetitiones* of Jacques de Révigny[5] Bezemer cautiously refrains from identifying the commentary on D.41.2.6.1–7 definitely as a *repetitio*, that is, as a ceremonial special lecture treating a text at length outside the regular course of lectures. Nevertheless he expresses a suspicion that it and other lengthy commentaries included in the *lectura* were in fact *repetitiones*, and he is perhaps unduly cautious in refusing to include this particular one. He points out that D.41.2.6.1–7 was the subject of a *repetitio* by another famous teacher at the Orléans law school, Pierre de Belleperche, which is preserved at Paris in the Bibliothèque Nationale, MS lat 4488 fos. 216r–219r.[6] The Digest text is also described as intricate and subtle by Odofredus,[7] is said by Albericus de Rosate to be regarded as subtle and difficult,[8] and is called by Bartolus a *notabilis et magistralis textus*,[9] all of which comments would indicate that it was appropriate for a *repetitio*. However this may be, the commentary is an interesting example of Jacques de Révigny's work.

The structure of the commentary follows roughly the pattern of *repetitiones* of Jacques de Révigny as identified by Bezemer.[10] This, as he notes, does not differ greatly from the structure of commentaries

returning from market, someone seizes possession; Labeo says that this person possesses by stealth, and so the man who went to market remains in possession; but if the trespasser does not admit the owner on his return, he is regarded as possessing by force rather than by stealth.

But if the owner declines to return to his land because he fears superior force, he will be deemed to have lost possession. Neratius writes the same.')

The text and translation are taken from *The Digest of Justinian*, Latin text edited by T. Mommsen with the aid of P. Krueger, English translation edited by W. A. J. Watson, vol. IV (Philadelphia, 1985), 506–7.

[4] The Chartres MS Bibliothèque Municipale 145 in which the text edited appears on fols. 91ra–92vb (= C in the edition) was destroyed during the Second World War. Fortunately some of the photographs of it held by E. M. Meijers have survived – see Meijers, *Etudes*, 77 n. *; the Paris MS Bibliothèque Nationale Latin 14350 (in which the text edited appears on fos. 83vb–84vb (= P in the edition) survives but is a less complete record. Another incomplete MS of the *lectura* is in Douai, Bibliothèque Municipale 648, and there are fragments in Paris MS BN lat. 4488 and Frankfurt-on-Main MS MPI 1 fos. 7–10. The edition in general follows C, which has been written by a more careful scribe.

[5] C. H. Bezemer, *Les Répétitions de Jacques de Révigny* (Leiden, 1987), at 239 n. 12.

[6] This *repetitio* makes a number of references, some critical, to Jacques de Révigny's commentary on the text, identified as *scripta* – see Meijers, *Etudes*, 95.

[7] Odofredus, *In Digestum Nouum Lectura* ... (Lyons, 1552; reprinted in *Opera Iuridica Rariora*, IV), *ad h.l.* (fol. 57va, no. 3).

[8] Albericus de Rosate, *Commentaria ... super Prima Parte ff noui* ... (Venice, 1585; reprinted in *Opera Iuridica Rariora*, XXV) *ad h.l.* (fol. 81vb, no. 1).

[9] Bartolus, *Commentaria in Primam Digesti Novi Partem* ... (Lyons, 1552), *ad h.l.* (fol. 93ra) *in principio*.

[10] *Les Répétitions*, 61–71.

delivered in the normal run of teaching. The main difference lies in the greater emphasis on *quaestiones*, questions arising out of or in relation to the text being commented on. First comes the statement of the cases dealt with in D.41.2.6.1–7 – the *casus positio* (paras. 1–3). Three situations are identified. In the first, A has left his land to go to a fair, leaving no one on the land. In his absence B, 'an untrustworthy neighbour' in Révigny's description, has entered on the land. In the second situation, on A's return he is denied access to the land by B and in the third he is too afraid even to make an attempt to obtain access. According to Révigny the text lays down three propositions (*dicta*): first, that when B enters on the land he possesses secretly; secondly, that when B denies A access he now possesses by force and not secretly; and thirdly, that if A is afraid to return to his land he loses possession. Having set the scene in this way Révigny proceeds to discussion of the three propositions in paragraphs 4–21, 22–8 and 29–32 respectively.

The first element in the discussion of the first proposition (paras. 4 and 5) is the wording of the text – why does it say that no one was left on the land, and why does it say that A 'therefore' retains possession when B takes possession secretly? This is an *expositio literae*, the part of a lecture, whether a normal or a special lecture, in which textual difficulties are disposed of. The explanation of the 'no one', attributed in the gloss to Jo(hannes), that is, Johannes Bassianus, is accepted. If anyone had been there, B would have acquired the whole possession if he had expelled him or nothing if he had failed to expel him. The gloss explains the 'therefore' on the basis that the words 'only naturally' are to be understood; what B acquires secretly is only natural possession. Révigny thinks it unnecessary to read anything into the text. A person possessing secretly is afraid of the person who is, and whom he believes to be, in possession, and so that person remains possessor.

Révigny then raises a series of questions on the first proposition. They are concerned with the nature of the possession held by A and B respectively, civil or natural, and the remedy available to A to recover the land from B. The terminology of possession in the texts is notoriously difficult to disentangle, and it is by no means clear what is meant by civil and by natural possession. Révigny attacks the view of Johannes Bassianus that A has both civil and natural possession while on the land and civil possession only, meaning possession held *animo*, when he leaves, allowing B to take natural possession (paras. 7 and 8). He also attacks the view of Azo that natural possession means the possession of someone who is on the land or in sight of it or near it and is retained when one leaves (paras. 8 and 9). In his view civil possession means the possession of an owner, possession which he holds whether he is on the land or not, and natural possession means the possession held by someone who has the use of land (para. 9), for example a usufructuary (see para. 13);[11] the person who enters secretly is like a usufructuary in that he holds the land although illegally (*iniuste*), but the illegality is irrelevant because possession can be held either legally or illegally (paras. 13 and 14). In each case only one possession is involved and the owner does not have a combination of civil and natural possession but a single civil possession which carries the benefit of natural possession. This gives him a right to claim the natural possession from someone who interferes with it as B has done in this case. The fact that he has this civil possession does not prevent someone from taking natural possession because possession is a matter of fact, but the taking is not to his prejudice (paras. 10 and 12). B has only natural possession, and a statement in the gloss that Ro(gerius) held that he had civil possession is perhaps a mistake (para. 15).

Révigny then turns to the remedy available to A. First he disposes of an argument by *quidam* that the action will have to take place on the land because if B is summoned to a court at some distance he will lose his natural possession, which he holds only so long as he is on the land or near it or in sight of it. He has no doubt that B has to appear before the judge (para. 16) and will not lose the natural possession which he has by doing so. He rejects the conception of natural possession which gives rise to the difficulty, in particular as applied to moveables, where it seems to mean that natural possession of them is lost if they are not held or in sight (paras. 17 and 18). He also rejects the view of the gloss that the remedy available will be an interdict *uti possidetis* for recovery of possession as opposed to retention of it, in turn based on the view that A is suing for recovery of his civil possession, which is disturbed by B's retention of the natural possession (paras. 19 and 20). So far as Révigny is concerned A still has civil possession and does not need to recover it. He sues with the interdict *uti possidetis*, which is an interdict for retention of possession, to give effect to his right to have the land back, and he could sue even a bona fide possessor on this basis.

Turning to the second proposition Révigny begins with questions (paras. 22 and 23), but these seem to be in essence an *expositio literae*. The questions are whether B possesses by force or secretly or by force and secretly, and if he possesses by force and secretly, whether he holds the same possession in these two ways. The gloss states that when the text says that B now holds by force and not secretly when he refuses A admission to

---

[11] He even argues in para. 11 that if there is both an owner and a usufructuary and they each leave the land intending to retain possession, a third party coming in cannot have possession – he stands there like an ass because all the possession, both civil and natural, is already held, by owner and usufructuary respectively.

his land it means that he holds by force and not only secretly and that he holds two possessions, the natural possession secretly, in the way he began, and the civil possession by force. B cannot have one possession held in two contrary ways. Révigny says, rather tartly, that he thinks one should stick to the text rather than the gloss and that B now holds one possession by force, the natural possession strengthened by ejecting the owner.

Then, following the usual order of treatment in lectures, he disposes briefly of an apparently contradictory text (a *contrarium*) in para. 24, and embarks once more on questions. The first question is one raised by the gloss which argues that B would not be liable to the interdict *unde vi* if he turned A away but did not claim A's (civil) possession; Révigny firmly disagrees (para. 25). He disagrees even more firmly (para. 26) with the view of the gloss that A would require to bring two actions. The first would be the interdict *unde vi* to recover his civil possession from which he has been ejected; the second would be the interdict *uti possidetis*, which becomes available after he has recovered his civil possession, to deal with the disturbance of his civil possession by B's retention of natural possession – 'thus he reaches his goal with two actions, very laboriously' (para. 26, ll.42–3). This is rubbish. A can simply sue with the interdict *unde vi* to recover the civil possession which he has always had and which is held by force against him (para. 27). *Uti possidetis* is, however, available for the interim profits before his ejection (para. 28).

Finally, Révigny turns to the third proposition which he deals with fairly summarily. He again begins with what is essentially an *expositio literae* explaining that he assumes possession is lost only where the fearful owner, A, has given up his intention of possessing and not where he chooses to bring an action rather than confronting B on the land (para. 29). Thereafter he discusses two questions, whether B would acquire civil possession if A gave up his intention of possessing even if B did not know of A's change of mind and what action there would be if B had entered on the land in good faith. On the first question he appears to agree with the gloss that B would acquire civil possession because he could be assumed to intend to acquire it if it were open to acquisition, this despite his differing view on what constitutes civil possession (para. 30). On the second question he rejects the use of the interdict *unde vi* if there was no intention to eject the owner (para. 31). He also rejects other suggestions – a remedy based on C.8.4.11; a suggestion that there is no remedy because A should not have given up his intention of possessing; a suggestion that there would be force with retroactive effect if B defended an action to recover the possession and Azo's suggestion of an extended interdict *unde vi*. For him there can be no action based on a supposition of the use of force. He suggests recourse to C.11.48(47).14, giving a summary remedy to the bona fide possessor of *coloni* until title to them can be established.

It is not possible to assess the work of Jacques de Révigny on the basis of this relatively brief extract from his writings, but it is possible to gain some impression of his qualities. The *Ultramontani* had a reputation for constantly criticising the gloss. Chevrier[12] has already shown that this did not mean that Jacques de Révigny had a policy of criticising it. He could accept views expressed in the gloss where he thought them well founded or merely suggest modification or correction, and instances of these attitudes can be found in the extract below, for example in paras. 4, 30 and 15. On the other hand Jacques de Révigny shows no particular respect for the gloss and is an unsparing critic where he thinks it clearly wrong, as in para. 27. It is not difficult to see how the *Ultramontani* gained their reputation when one reads the commentary as a whole. The picture which emerges is that of a man of incisive mind with a vigorous style, concerned to reduce the texts to a clear system and to provide from them practical and straightforward solutions to legal problems. It is much easier to understand why it is thought that his work should be restored to prominence in the history of mediaeval law than to understand how it fell out of sight.

[12] G. Chevrier, 'Jacques de Révigny et la glose d'Accurse', *Atti del Convegno Internazionale di Studi Accursiani. Bologna 21–26 Ottobre 1963*, vol. III (Milan, 1968), 979ff.

Qui ad nundinas etc.

1. Casus: ego possideo fundum meum. Exeo de fundo meo, animo retinende possessionis semper, nemine relicto in fundo meo, et uado ad nundinas. Me absente quidam uicinus meus
5 infidelis ingressus est fundum meum clam, nam si ego fuissem presens, pro oculo capitis non esset ausus intrare fundum. Queritur, quid iuris? Numquid ingressus possidet fundum meum? Dicitur quod sic: clam possidet. Ego autem retineo
10 possessionem animo meo.
2. Set ponamus in casu secondo: ego intellexi quod uicinus meus est in fundo meo. Ego reuertor ad fundum meum. Dico ego sibi: domine, quid facitis hic? Exeatis fundum meum. Dicit ipse: ymo uos eatis, uos non intrabitis fundum.
15 Dicit iurisconsultus: ego expulsus sum, unde ui possidet qui prius possidebat clam.
3. Set ponamus: ego scio quod uicinus meus est in fundo meo. Dico ego: non sum ausus ire ad fundum meum. Ipse crudelis est. Statim me expelleret. Ego, qui suspicatus
20 sum me repellendum, amitto possessionem. Hoc dicit.

4. Dicit ergo hic: profectus ad nundinas neminem reliquit in fundo. Quare dicit, 'neminem reliquit'? Jo. dixit quod si aliquem reliquisset in fundo, dicit glosa,[1] ille ingressus nullam possessionem sibi acquireret uel utramque sibi
5 acquireret; uerbi gratia, si ille clandestinus possessor ingrederetur fundum existente eo quem dominus dimisisset in fundo, nichil acquireret sibi ingressus, nam dominus animo suo habet ciuilem, item animo eius quem dimisit retinet naturalem et sic ingressus inueniret omne genus possessionis
10 occupatum, unde nullam sibi acquireret, ut infra eodem l. Si coloni.[2] Vel si ingressus expelleret eum quem dominus ibi

---

[1] Gl. 'Qui ad nundinas' *ad h.l.*   [2] D.41.2.31.

80 William M. Gordon

dimisisset ingressus haberet omnem possessionem, nam expulso
eo qui est in fundo meo, ego uideor expulsus arg. legis infra
eodem l. Peregre,[3] in fine legis.

15 5. Dicit ergo hic: ingressus clam possidet.
Retinet ergo possessionem qui ad nundinas iuit. Dic michi:
unde procedit illud 'ergo'? Dicit glosa,[4] illud
'ergo' sequitur ex subaudito. Ingressus clam possidet,
subaudi naturaliter tantum; ad illud subauditum
20 refertur li 'ergo'. *ergo possessionem retinet etc.*:
nam ingressus non habet omnem. Ego credo quod hec conclusio
inferatur sine subauditione. Dico quod ille possidet clam
qui metuit possessorem. Unde si ego ingredior fundum
uacantem et timeo aliquem quem credo possessorem et non est,
25 ego non possideo clam. Non enim inspicitur animus meus,
quemadmodum si contrecto rem tuam te uolente in ueritate et
ego te inuitum credam et sic in animo meo ego credo facere
furtum, tamen ex quo tu uolens ego non sum fur, ut infra de
furtis l. Inter omnes § ult.[5] Similiter dico hic: si ego
30 ingredior fundum clam, credens eum possessorem, ego essem
possessor clam, scilicet si ego timerem possessorem, ego
essem possessor clam. Unde Jo. concludit: hic clam
possidet, ergo credit alium possessorem.

6. Explicata litera, ego quero hic duo. Ille qui est
extra possidet. Quero, quam possessionem habet? Item ille
qui est ingressus possidet. Quero quam possessionem habet,
et quomodo habeat? Iste tres questiones sunt literales.
5 7. Primam questionem uos habuistis. Sententia Jo. est
quod ille qui egressus est habeat animo ciuilem. Unde dicit
Jo.: dum modo ipse erat in fundo, ipse habebat ciuilem et
naturalem. Si exit de fundo, ciuilem retinet animo,
naturalem uero amittit et ideo naturalem uacantem potest
10 habere ingressus suo ingressu et ita dixit Jo.
8. Dominus Azo dixit quod egressus fundum possidet sicut
possidebat dum erat in fundo et habet naturalem existens
extra fundum, illam eandem quam habebat dum erat in fundo.
Pro sua sententia inducit C. eodem l. Licet[6] et istam[7] que
15 non distinguit possessionem. Item lex[8] dicit, nulla
possessio amittitur sine corpore et animo. Sequitur ergo
secundum te, Jo., existens in fundo habebat ciuilem et

[3] D.41.2.44.2   [4] Gl. 'Possessionem' *ad h.l.*   [5] D.47.2.46.8   [6] C.7.32.4
[7] D.41.2.6.1.   [8] D.41.2.8.

Jacques de Révigny on possession

naturalem. Secundum te, si ergo exeo de fundo animo
retinende possessionis, nullam possessionem amitto, nam nulla
20 possessio amittitur sine animo et corpore. Ergo naturalis
non amittitur solo corpore, ut infra eodem l. Quemadmodum.[9]
9. Quid ergo dicemus? Ego dico quod egressus habet eandem
possessionem quam habebat intra fundum, unde exeans de fundo
non habebat nisi unam possessionem quam habebat dum erat
25 intra, unde non dico sicut dixit Azo. Ipse dicebat quod
dominus existens in fundo habet naturalem, et extra habet
naturalem, et ego dico, quod ymo ille qui possidet fundum
pleno iure iacens in fundo habet ciuilem, et extra fundum
habet ciuilem eandem. Unde ego non dico, ut ipse dixit,
30 quod naturalis sit illa quam habet ille qui est in fundo, uel
in conspectu fundi uel prope; ciuilis quam habet ille qui est
extra fundum uel fundi conspectum uel fundi presenciam. Ymo
dico ut iam dixi. Ciuilem habet ille qui non possidet, ut
ille qui dominus est, naturalem habet ille qui possidet ad
35 quem spectat rei utilitas. Unde isti modi possidendi non
uariantur per intra et extra. Unde dico dominus, siue
iacens in fundo siue extra fundum, semper habet ciuilem et
iste § me urget ad hoc.
10. Ego ostendo quod existens extra fundum habet illam
40 eandem quam habebat existens in fundo. Et Azo hoc dicit.
Hic constat quod existens extra fundum non habet naturalem
possessionem. Si haberet eam, ergo non esset uacans. Ergo
ingressus eam non haberet. Ergo necesse est michi dicere
quod dum est in fundo non habeat naturalem nec eciam extra.
45 Hec est prima questio. Dico enim quod dum est intra et
extra habet possessionem ciuilem et intelligo de eo qui
possidebat fundum ut suum pleno iure.
11. Si nos intelligeremus casum huius § de fundo in quo
habebat unus proprietatem et alter usumfructum, uerbi gratia,
50 ego habeo in fundo usumfructum, tu proprietatem. Ambo
eximus fundum, quilibet animo retinende possessionis sue.
Tercius ingreditur fundum. Dico quod ipse stat ibi sicut
asinus. Nullam enim habet possessionem, cum omnem inueniat
occupatam.
55 12. Tu dicis michi quod ille qui possidet ut dominus
pleno iure habet possessionem unam, que habet uim et effectum
duarum possessionum, sicut ille qui dominus est pleno iure

[9] D.41.2.8.

habet unum ius quod quidem ius habet utilitatem duorum iurium, scilicet ususfructus et proprietatis. Dic ergo
60 michi: quando iura sunt diuersa, quod unus habet proprietatem alter usumfructum, quilibet retinet suum ius. Quare ergo erit ita quod dominus dum est extra fundum retineat suum ius, quod habet effectum duorum iurium? Ymo uidetur arg. lex supra de hiis quibus ut indignis l.
65 Tutorem.[10] Ego dico possessio plus habet facti quam habeat reale dominium uel ususfructus. Unde ego concedo, quod quando ipse est extra fundum ipse habet possessionem que ualet duas, et est tante efficacie quante est illa possessio quam habet existens in fundo et dormiens. Unde quemadmodum
70 est reperire dominium separatum ab usufructu, et dominium pleno iure quod habet secum utilitatem ususfructus, ille qui est dominus pleno iure suum dominium habet eque plenum dum est in fundo et dum est extra. Ita dico quod suum ius possidendi habet eque plenum, dum est in fundo et dum est
75 extra. Tu non dicis uerum, nam secundum te ingressus nullam haberet. Dico quod ingressus nichil habet in preiudicium absentis domini, unde non est simile quantum ad hoc de dominio et de possessione, quia possessio plus habet facti quam dominium. Unde fructuarius usumfructum non potest
80 habere nisi per me dominum, set possessionem quam habet fructuarius, tu potes habere me existente, non tamen in preiudicium meum. Unde totum ius et utilitatem meam ego retineo extra sicut intra.

13. Tu dicebas alia die quod ille possidet ciuiliter qui
85 possidet rem ut dominus; ille possidet rem naturaliter qui possidet rem ut possidet ille ad quem spectat rei utilitas, et hoc bene dicebas de superficiario et emphiteota et similibus. Set quid dices de isto, nam ad istum qui ingressus est non spectat rei utilitas? Ego respondeo:
90 uerum est, quod non habet rei utilitatem, set uerum est quod ipse possidet eo modo quo possidet fructuarius si esset in fundo. Iniuste tamen possidet. Nichil tamen ad rem, quia in summa possessionis non refert utrum sit iusta uel iniusta, ut supra eodem l. iii § Econtrario.[11]
95 14. Vel aliter, et sic redit in idem. Dic michi quare tu dicis quod iste ingressus possidet sicut fructuarius, et fructuarius sicut ipse? Quid commune habent inter se? Ego

[10] D.34.9.22.   [11] D.41.2.3.5.

possum sic dicere: dic michi quis primo possidet,
proprietarius uel fructuarius? Certe proprietarius, nam
100 fructuarius habet ius suum per constitutionem sibi factam a
proprietario. Unde primo fuit proprietas et secundo
ususfructus, nam ususfructus et seruitus communis habetur per
constitutionem domini. Ergo dominus primo fuit quam esset
fructuarius. Unde sicut in constitutione ususfructus, ego
105 constituo tibi usumfructum et relinquo te in fundo et
possides naturaliter, sic si ego exeo fundum et tu intras
fundum, ego relinquo te in fundo. Unde propter istam
similitudinem potest dici quod tu possides et fructuarius ad
modum fructuarii.
110 15. Modo uidimus quam possesionem habet ille qui exit.
Modo uideamus quam possessionem habet ille qui ingreditur.
Dicit Ro., ut glosa[12] sibi imponit, naturalem et ciuilem
habet. Nos dicemus, quod ymo naturalem tantum. Ego nescio
utrum glosa recitet hic infideliter sententiam Ro., nam supra
115 eodem l. iii Econtrario,[13] glosa[14] recitauit Rogerium
dixisse, quod duo possunt possidere ciuiliter in certis
casibus tantum, de quibus casibus iste non est unus. Sic
ergo iste ingressus habet naturalem tantum.
16. Set queritur: dic michi, si dominus qui est egressus
120 uult agere contra ingressum, numquid potest, et quomodo
potest? Verbi gratia, ponamus, ego fui ad nundinas.
Reuersus intellexi quod quidam ingressus est fundum meum.
Dico ego: non depono animum possidendi, tum illum qui est in
fundo meo ego faciam in iudicium euocari et agam contra eum.
125 Dic michi quomodo agitabitur illud iudicium. Dicunt quidam
agitabitur in ipso fundo, nam ingressus habet solam naturalem,
set si compelleretur uenire coram iudice, amitteret eam, nam
ille habet naturalem possessionem, qui est in fundo, uel
fundi conspectu uel in presencia. Si ergo recederet longe,
130 usque ad locum iudicii, amitteret possessionem, et ipsi ideo
dicunt iudex ueniet in fundo et ibi agitabitur causa, arg.
legis supra finium regundorum 1. Si irruptione § 1.[15] Nos
dicimus, quod ymo ibit coram iudice, arg. C. de episcopis et
clericis l. Iubemus,[16] in fine. Ergo secundum hoc, amittet
135 naturalem possessionem, quia non est in fundo, nec uidet eum
nec in presencia.

[12] Gl. 'Clam' *ad h.l.*   [13] D.41.2.3.5.   [14] Gl. 'Ex contrario' *ad* D.41.2.3.5.
[15] D.10.1.8.1.
[16] C.1.3.37.

17. Resp.: dicit glosa,[17] naturalem amittit qui non est in
fundo nec in conspectu fundi, subaudi qui habebat utramque
possessionem, set ille qui non habet nisi naturalem, quocumque
loco eat retinet, et probatur de fructuario, infra de ui et
ui armata l. iii § Unde ui interdictum.[18] Quidam dicunt:
fructuarius possidet iuste, et ideo si exeat fundum retinet
naturalem, set ingressus possidet iniuste, unde exiens
amittit eam. Dico non est uerum, nam in summa possessionis
non refert sit iuste uel iniuste quesita, ut supra eodem l.
iii § Econtrario.[19]
18. Ego non possum ita respondere, nam ego dico quod nullus
est qui non habeat nisi unam possessionem, unde ego dicam
quod falsum dicunt. Azo dixit, quod naturalem habet ille
qui est in fundo, uel in conspectu fundi uel in presencia,
ciuilem habet ille qui non est in fundo, uel fundi conspectu
uel in presencia. Dico, quod hoc non est uerum, nam ego non
distinguo possessionem per intra et extra. Dixit ergo Azo:
ille habet naturalem qui est in fundo, uel fundi conspectu
uel prope, ueluti si fundus sit retro se. Quod uerum est in
rebus immobilibus. Set in mobilibus dicit ipse, si non
tenet nec uidet librum suum, amittit naturalem. Unde licet
liber suus sit in presencia eius uel in custodia, si non
tenet nec uidet, amittit naturalem et de hoc ego non credo
ei, et de hoc habetis supra l. iii § Nerua.[20]
19. Set quis libellus dabitur sibi? Resp.: dabitur sibi
libellus in interdicto uti possidetis. Unde dicit sic: ego
retineo possessionem fundi mei in animo meo. Tu turbas me
in mea possessione et iniuste. Exi de fundo meo. Ego
ostendo quod iste libellus non consuleret agenti interdicto
uti possidetis, quod est retinende possessionis. Dicet ei
ingressus: tu contendis de retinenda possessione. Quam
possessionem habes tu? Dicet ille: ciuilem. De qua
retinenda tu contendis, bene retineas. Ego non curo de ea.
Habeas eam, quocumque loco ineris. Set scias quod naturalem
quam ego habeo tibi non restituam. Dicit glosa:[21] ingressus
habet naturalem uiciose, scilicet clam, unde eo ipso quod
tenet naturalem, turbat possidentem in sua ciuili, retinendo
naturalem; unde interdictum uti possidetis erit in casu isto
recuperande possessionis; unde compelleretur exire, nam
turbatio cessat si exeat.

[17] Gl. 'Naturaliter' *ad* D.41.1.1 *pr.* (?).   [18] D.43.16.3.13.   [19] D.41.2.3.5.
[20] D.41.2.3.13.   [21] Gl. 'Non clam' *ad h.l.*

20. Querit glosa[22] ultimo: tu dicis quod racio est hic, quod ille ingressus uiciose habet possessionem. Set ponamus, quod ingressus non habuit animum celandi possessionem, set habuit animum celandi quendam qui non possidebat, quem ipse credebat possessorem, et sic non habet uiciose possessionem a possessore. Ergo in causa ista non compelleretur restituere possessionem possessori. Dicit glosa,[23] quod ymo semper cogitur ei restituere possessionem, quia turbat eum in sua ciuili, retinendo naturalem. Pro glosa uidetur lex.[24] Lex dicit: ego edifico quendam locum tuum quem possides, habens animum celandi alium qui nullum ius habet. Numquid ego uideor fecisse clam quoad te? dicitur quod sic, infra quod ui aut clam l. Aut qui § Si quis dum putat.[25] Et sic dicit glosa,[26] retinendo naturalem, turbat ciuilem, unde oportet eum exire.

21. Advertatis: ego non credo aliquo casu quod interdictum uti possidetis sit possessionis recuperande. Unde ego dico quod interdictum uti possidetis non erit interdictum recuperande possessionis. Si tu diceres quod agenti restitueretur possessio aliqua, iam sequeretur quod habeat duas possessiones. Ego autem, secundum me, non possum dicere quod ipse habeat nisi unam. Dico enim, quod eque possidet dum est extra fundum sicut dum est intra, unde non indiget restitutione possessionis. Quid ergo dicemus secundum me? Ego dico quod detentio quam habet ingressus, non facit eum possessorem; unde egressus habet unam possessionem, scilicet ciuilem plenam; unde ius habet, unde potest agere contra ingressum, ut ingressus qui est in fundo patiatur eum esse in fundo de facto, sicut sibi est ius ne turbet eum. Unde dicet sic: ego habeo ius eundi in fundo meo. Volo quod fiat michi facultas de facto detinendi, sicut michi est ius, et tu exeas. Et hoc est agere proprissime uti possidetis. Unde non est interdictum recuperande possessionis, set retinende possessionis. Unde ego non dico quod racio sit hic, quod clam ingressus est. Ymo et si esset ingressus bona fide, cogeretur exire ut fieret michi facultas detinende de facto, sicut michi ius est. Nam ego, quocumque loco sum, siue intra siue extra, habeo ius; unde ingressus compellitur exire, ut sic michi fiat facultas detinendi de facto et esse in fundo meo, sicut michi ius est.

[22] Gl. 'Non clam' *ad h.l.*   [23] Gl. 'Non clam' *ad h.l.*
[24] D.43.24.5.5.   [25] D.43.24.5.5.   [26] Gl. 'Non clam' *ad h.l.*

22. Hoc est uerum, quod in primo casu huius legis ingressus possidet clam. Modo ueniamus ad secundum dictum. Egressus uult uenire ad fundum suum. Dicit ingressus: certe uos non intrabitis, et sic me reuertentem non admisit. Possidet ui, non clam. Ego quero unum quod est contra literam: utrum ingressus possidet ui uel clam? Si tu dicis quod possidet ui, et non clam, tu omittis racionem legis. Lex dicit: origo adipiscende possessionis intuenda est. Ergo cum ab inicio possedit clam, adhuc possidet clam, ut supra hac eadem lege circa principium.[27] Dicit glosa[28] quod hic dicit possidet ui, non clam, subaudi tantum. Unde dicit glosa,[29] quod dicit magis comparatiue, accipe, non electiue. Possidet enim ui et clam.

23. Quero ergo ultra: si possidet ui et clam, numquid eandem possessionem habet ui et clam? Dicunt quidam quod sic, arg. legis infra, quod ui aut clam l. Is qui in puteum § Hoc interdictum.[30] Glosa[31] dicit contrarium. Ymo possidet unam ui, aliam clam, nam ui et clam contraria sunt. Unde non compatiuntur se in eadem possessione, quia posito uno de contrariis, remouetur et reliquum, ut supra de procuratoribus l. Pomponius § Set et hiis[32] et infra de exceptione rei iudicate l. Inter me.[33] Unde dicit glosa,[34] naturalem habet clam, ciuilem ui, nam antequam dominus expelleretur, ingressus haberet naturalem et clam. Unde adhuc habet eam clam. Eo autem ipso quod dominum reuertentem non admisit, expulit eum. Unde ciuilem habet ui. Quid ergo dicemus? Ego non sum ausus dicere quod ingressus habeat duas possessiones. Quid ergo dices? Ego melius credo adherendum litere quam glose. Unde dicam quod possidet ui, et non clam. Quam ergo possessionem habet ui? Dico quod ipse possidet uno modo tantum. Set ponamus: quam habet post deiectionem domini? Illam quam habebat ante deiectionem. Unde prius habebat naturalem possessionem, post deiectionem non habet nisi unam possessionem, pleniori iure coadunatam. Unde dico quod ante deiectionem ingressus habebat unam possessionem, et dominus aliam. Domino deiecto, ista duo iura per coadunationem faciunt unum ius in

---

[27] D.41.2.6 *pr.*   [28] Gl. 'Non clam' *ad h.l.*   [29] Gl. 'Magis' *ad h.l.*
[30] D.43.24.11.5.
[31] Gl. 'Non clam' *ad h.l.*   [32] D.3.3.40.2.   [33] D.44.2.15(?).
[34] Gl. 'Non clam' *ad h.l.*

Jacques de Révigny on possession

persona ingressi, arg. supra si ususfructus petatur l. Uti
frui circa principium[35] et supra quemadmodum seruitutes
40 amittuntur l. Non satis[36] in fine.

24. Ad literam istam opponitur et signatur contrarium.
Dicit hic, quod qui non admittit dominum reuertentem,
possidet ui. Lex dicit contrarium in eisdem terminis infra
de usucapionibus l. Sequitur § Si occupaueris.[37] Dicendum
5 est: ibi loquitur de eo qui ingressus est fundum uacantem
animo et non corpore.

25. Glosa[38] mouet hic unam questionem. Ponamus: ille non
admittit dominum reuertentem et dicit: amice, tu non
introibis et scias quod possessionem quam tu habes, ego uolo
scilicet te habere. Modo querit glosa:[39] ex quo ingressus
5 non curat habere possessionem quam absens habet, numquid in
casu isto agetur interdicto unde ui? Dicit glosa[40] quod
non, et male dicit. Inducit legem contrariam, infra de
usucapionibus l. Non solum § Si dominus.[41] Lex illa dicit:
ego te expello de facto. Possessionem non apprehendo.
10 Fundus tuus non est ui possessus, nam hic, ex quo ingressus
expulit dominum et animo non apprehendit possessionem domini,
non possidet. Ego dico, quod etiam ubi ingressus non
possidet, glosa haberet apparenciam. Set dico quod ubi
possidet, alius non possidet. Eciam glosa non potest
15 deffendi, quin ingressus teneatur interdicto unde ui. Lex
enim dicit: ego deicio te de fundo tuo, non apprehendendo
possessionem. Ego non possideo ui, et tamen teneor
interdicto unde ui, ut infra de usucapionibus l. Sequitur §
Si tu me.[42] Quid ergo dicemus in ista questione? Ego dico
20 quod ex quo non patitur dominum intrare et detinet de facto,
uidetur eum deicere, ex quo non patitur eum uti sua
possessione et oportet dominum recedere et deponere animum
possidendi.

26. Set queritur. Ponamus: ille qui exiuit de fundo suo
25 reuersus est ad fundum suum. Non est admissus, unde
deiectus est. Quomodo aget contra deicientem? Dicit
glosa[43] quod aget duobus iudiciis. Aget enim primo iudicio

---

[35] D.7.6.5 pr.   [36] D.8.6.6.   [37] D.41.3.4.27(28).   [38] Gl. 'Non clam' *ad h.l.*
[39] Gl. 'Non clam' *ad h.l.*   [40] Gl. 'Non clam' *ad h.l.*   [41] D.41.3.33.2.
[42] D.41.3.4.22.
[43] Gl. 'Non clam' *ad h.l.*

recuperande possessionis, secundo agit retinende
possessionis. Verbi gratia: clam ingressus habet ab inicio
30 naturalem, et dominus ciuilem. Quando ingressus non
admittit dominum reuertentem ad fundum suum, ipse deiecit eum
de sua ciuili, et ideo dominus, quia non possidet, non habet
interdictum uti possidetis. Habet ergo interdictum unde ui.
Set ad quid? Ad possessionem de qua fuit deiectus, scilicet
35 ad ciuilem, nam de ciuili fuit deiectus. Unde aget ante
interdicto unde ui, ut restituatur ciuilis de qua fuit
deiectus. Ciuili habita, possessor est, et ex quo habet
ciuilem in sua ciuili turbat eum ingressus, retinendo
naturalem; unde, recuperata ciuili per interdictum unde ui,
40 adhuc non recedet ingressus; unde dominus aget interdicto
uti possidetis contra ingressum, ut recedat de fundo et
restituat ei naturalem; et sic ad intentionem suam perueniet
duobus libellis, multum laboriose.
27. Ego miror quomodo ipsi dicunt, quod restitueretur sibi
45 ciuilis. Dic michi, reponetur-ne sibi in animo primo
ciuilis? Ego bene dicerem pro eis unam trupham. Dico
tamen, quod restituatur sibi possessio ut possideo animo.
Non est res magne apparencie. Unde dico ego, quod non est
dicendum ut ipsi dicunt, nam iste est circuitus et
50 circuitus uitandus est, ut supra de condictione indebiti l.
Dominus.[44] Quid ergo dicemus? Dico: uisa mea prima
positione, patet quid sit dicendum. Dico enim quod aget
recta uia interdicto unde ui ut restituatur sibi possessio
omnis, et istud sequitur ex premissis necessario. Dico quod
55 ingressus qui dominum deiecit, non habet nisi unam
possessionem; unde illam quam prius habebat clam, modo habet
ui. Idem deiectus tempore deiectionis, et in omni tempore,
habuit eandem possessionem. Unde deiectus aget interdicto
unde ui ut restituatur illa possessio qua fuit deiectus, que
60 semper fuit una et intra et extra. Set ingressus post
deiectionem habuit pleniorem possessionem, illam eandem
possessionem quam prius habebat minus plenam. Contra;
origo possessionis inspicitur, ergo non potest esse quod
illam quam habebat clam, habeat ui. Dicendum est illud:
65 uerum est nullo extrinsecus accidente. Set deiciendo enim
dominum enim accedit extrinsecus, et probatur supra eodem l.
iii § Illud[45] ad finem §. Sic ergo uidetis, si non

[44] D.12.6.53. [45] D.41.2.3.19.

admittatur, uidetur deici, et habet interdictum unde ui pro
recuperanda possessione, et sufficit sibi illud interdictum.
70 28. Set queritur, numquid et post deiectionem
habet interdictum uti possidetis? Ego credo quod sic hic, pro
utilitate medii temporis quod cucurrit ante deiectionem, nam
utilitas preterite turbationis non uenit in interdicto unde
ui; unde datur sibi interdictum uti possidetis ut infra uti
75 possidetis l. Si duo[46] ad finem et supra de usufructu l.
Quesitum[47] ad finem, et sic intelligo glosam[48] que obscure
loquitur in suo fine.

29. Modo ueniamus ad ultimum dictum. Dominus meticulosus,
timens se repellendum, non uenit ad fundum. Possessionem
amittit. Quod ego intelligo, ubi deponit animum possidendi.
Unde ponamus quod egressus est quidam bonus homo, qui execratur
5 lites et maluit procedere per iudicem. Semper tamen habet
animum retinendi possessionem. Nam tucius est procedere per
iudicem, ut infra de solutionibus l. Si stipulatus.[49] Ego
non dicerem eum amisisse possessionem, quemadmodum ille qui
nunciat uerbo tenus amittit possessionem; ille qui nunciat
10 per pretorem non amittit possessionem, ut supra de operis
noui nuntiatione l. De pupillo § Meminisse[50] et supra eodem
titulo l. i § De operis.[51]
30. Set queritur: tu dicis quod absens suo animo habet
ciuilem, ingressus naturalem. Ponamus: absens, ignorante
15 ingresso, deponit animum possidendi. Mode quero, numquid
ingresso, et ignoranti, acquiritur possessio ciuilis? Dicit
glosa[52] quod sic, non per ius accrescendi, nam ius
accrescendi accedit saltim inuito in hereditatibus. Dic
michi ergo, quare differtur sibi possessio? Dicit glosa:[53]
20 quia ab inicio dum ingressus est fundum, presumitur habere
animum quod uellet habere ciuilem si esset uacans, quia sine
animo nulla est possessio, infra l. proxima.[54]
31. Set queritur ultra, et illud est hic necessarium.
Absens possidet animo, ingressus corpore. Ponamus: absens,
25 ignorante ingresso, deponit animum possidendi. Ingressus
bona fide ingressus est. Quid remedium dabitur absenti
contra ingressum? Numquid interdictum unde ui? Non

---

[46] D.43.17.3. [47] D.7.1.37. [48] Gl. 'Non clam' *ad h.l.* [49] D.46.3.81.
[50] D.39.1.5.10.
[51] D.39.1.1.6. [52] Gl. 'Amisisse' *ad h.l.* [53] Gl. 'Amisisse' *ad h.l.*
[54] D.41.2.8.

uidetur, quia non est deiectus, nam uoluntas distinguit
maleficia, et certe, ingressus bona fide ingressus est, nec
30 habebat animum deiciendi egressum. Nam si haberet animum
deiciendi dominum si uenerit, ego concederem quod teneretur
interdicto unde ui, arg. infra de furtis l. Si quis ex domo[55]
et l. Qui iniurie.[56]
32. Quid ergo remedium dabitur sibi eo casu?
35 Dicunt quidam: dabitur sibi remedium per legem C. unde
ui l. Querebatur.[57] Dicunt alii: nullam habebit remedium.
Miser est et miser erit. Dampnum quod quis sua culpa
sentit;[58] de se ipso queri debet, quare deposuit animum
possidendi. Dominus Azo admisit in casu isto, quod detur sibi
40 interdictum utile unde ui, nam licet non deiecit eum, tamen
occasione sui egressus amisit possessionem; unde tenetur ei
interdicto unde ui utili de eo quod ad eum peruenit, arg.
infra de ui et ui armata l. i § Familie[59] et Si quis tamen
se,[60] et de hoc habebitis in eodem titulo l. iii § Si quis
45 autem uisis armatis.[61] Dicunt alii: uerum est quod
ingressus non deiecit eum, set si contenderet de possessione
et non admitteret eum, ille actus retro traheretur, et
uideretur eum deiecisse, arg. infra de itinere actuque
priuato l. i § Si quis propter,[62] supra ad Macedonianum l.
50 Set Julianus § Proinde.[63] Ego non uideo per quam uiam iste
habet interdictum unde ui, ubi ingressus non habuit animum
deiciendi eum, set dico ei consulendum per legem que dicit,
celeri reformatione succurrendum possessori ut C. de
agricolis et censitis l. Si coloni.[64]

---

[55] D.47.2.53(52). [56] D.47.2.54(53). [57] C.8.4.11. [58] D.50.17.203.
[59] D.43.16.1.18.
[60] D.43.16.1.19. [61] D.43.16.3.6. [62] D.43.19.1.9. [63] D.14.6.7.12(?).
[64] C.11.48(47).14.

1	ETC *om.* P
2	meo *om.* P
3	quidam] quia C^{ac}
5–6	clam – fundum *om.* P
10	meo *om.* C
11	ponamus] po(ne) P in secundo casu *tr.* P
12	meus *om.* C in fundo meo est *tr.* P Ego reuertor] uenditor uenit C meum *om.* C
13	facitis] facis P exeatis] exeas P
14	dicit – fundum *om.* P (*homoiotel.*)
17	ponamus] pone P quod uicinus *om.* P

1	Dicit] Dico C *om.* P
2	dicit] dixit C reliquit – quod] i.e. l. quid adeo dixit quia P
3	in fundo *om.* P
4	sibi possessionem *tr.* P
6	fundum *bis scr.* P
7	ingressus – dominus *om.* P
7–8	animo suo *tr.* P
8	habet *om.* P
12–13	expulso eo] expellendo eum P
13	arg. legis *om.* P
14	legis *om.* P ergo] hic *praem.* C
20	refertur] infertur C
21	ego] ergo P
22	inferatur] refertur P
23	metuit possessorem] uetuit pos(essionem) P
24	quem *om.* P possessorem] pos(essionem) P
25	non] nemo P
26	rem tuam] rem meam tuam C^{ac}
26–7	uolente in ueritate – credam] nolente inuito te et ego te inuitum P
27	credam] C² *marg.* facere *om.* P
29	§ ult.] penultimo C² *marg.*
31–2	scilicet – clam *om.* P
32	Jo.] non P

1	quero] extra(?) *add.* P
5	questionem] questiones P^{ac}
6	egressus] ingressus C^{ac}
11	dixit] dicit P
12–13	et habet – in fundo *om.* P (*homoiotel.*)

14	istam (?) que] ista questio P que] scilicet sic intelligit *praem.* C² *marg.*
18	exeo] exit P
19	amitto] amittit P
21	ut *om.* P
22	egressus] ingressus C^{ac} P
23	intra] utrum(?) P exeans de] existens in P C^{ac} exeans C² *marg.* de C² *inter.*
25	intra] in fundo uel *praem.* P non *om.* P dixit] dicit P
26	dominus *om.* P
28	et extra] ymo ille qui possidet fundum *praem.* P^{ac}
30	sit *bis scr.* C
31	prope] proprie P quam] est *praem.* P
31–2	est extra] e P
32	conspectum] conspectu P
33	iam *om.* P ciuilem] nam *praem.* P
34	qui possidet *om.* P
36	uariantur] uariatur P
39	quod] §(?) P
39–41	habet – extra fundum *om.* P (*homoiotel.*)
43	michi *om.* P
44	habeat] habet P
45–6	hec est – intra et extra *om.* P (*homoiotel.*)
48	casum] conversum P
50	in fundo *tr.* P *post* usumfructum
56	uim et *om.* P
57	sicut] non *praem.* P
58	ius] inde C
59	ususfructus et proprietatis] usumfructum et proprietatem P
60	iura] iussa C
61	alter] alius P ius suum *tr.* P
65	dico ego *tr.* P
66	reale] realem C
67	quando] quandoque(?) C est ipse *tr.* P
67–8	que ualet – possessio *om.* C (*homoiotel.*)
69	in fundo *om.* P
71	quod habet] habet *praem.* P^{ac}
71–2	secum – pleno iure *om.* P (*homoiotel.*)
72	habet *om.* C eque plenum] eam plenam P
73	ius *scr., om.* C.
73–5	ita dico – est extra *om.* P (*homoiotel.*)
75	Tu non *scr.*: tuum C *om.* P

Jacques de Révigny on possession

79	fructuarius] usufructuarius P usumfructum *om.* P
80	dominum] dominium P possessionem] posseossionem C
85	rem naturaliter] rem *om.* P
86	ut possidet] possidet *om.* P
87	hoc] hic C emphiteota] emph(yteuta)rio P
88	Set *om.* P nam] non P
90	non habet – quod *om.* C (*homoiotel.*)
92	tamen possidet] eam possidet P
95–6	dicis tu *tr.* C
97	Quid commune habent] qui habet commune P
99–100	Certe – fructuarius *om.* C (*homoiotel.*)
102–3	nam ususfructus – constitutionem] et seruitus communis habetur constitutione P
105	usumfructum *om.* C fundo] fundum P
108	et] ut(?)
110–11	exit – qui *om.* P (*homoiotel.*)
114	nam] ut C
115	recitauit] recitat P Rogerium] C² Ro. C P
117	casibus *om.* P
118	tantum] habet P
119	egressus] ingressus P
121	ponamus] po(ne) P
123	illum] ille P
125	michi *om.* P agitabitur] agebatur P illud iudicium *om.* C
125–6	Dicunt quidam agitabitur] P Uidetur quod in ipso fundo quidam(?) C² *marg.*
126	in fundo ipso *tr.* P
127	set] qui C *marg.* compelleretur uenire] compelletur ire P amitteret] et *praem.* P
130–1	ideo dicunt ipse *tr.* P
131	ueniet] ueniret P agitabitur] agitabatur P
133	ibit] ibi P
137	qui] quia P
140	eat] exeat P
143	unde] et ideo P
144	in] s *praem.* P^ac
147	possum – respondere] non ita respondeo P
148	non *om.* C unam *om.* P
149	Azo] Az. P alias est Jo. C² *marg.*
150	uel in presencia *om.* C
151–2	ciuilem – in presencia *om.* P (*homoiotel.*)
153	Azo] alias Jo. C² *interl.*

154	fundi conspectu] in conspectu fundi P
157	naturalem] naturaliter P licet] liber *praem.* C[ac]
160	ei *om.* P
161	sibi? Resp. *om.* P
161–2	libellus dabitur sibi *tr.* P
162	dicit sic] dic si P
163	in animo meo] immobilis P Tu] set *praem.* P
164	possessione *om.* C Exi] et *praem.* P
165	ostendo] ostendi P agenti] agentem C
165–6	interdicto – quod] interdictum uti possidetis P
167	retinenda] restituenda C
168	habes tu?] habetis P
169	bene retineas] unde ne timeas P
170	ineris] meus C scias *scr.*: sciam C *om.* P
172	naturalem] ciuilem *praem.* P
173	tenet naturalem] retinet corporalem P ciuili *om.* P
174	interdictum *om.* P erit *om.* P
176	exeat] extat P
183–4	possessori – possessionem *om.* P (*homoiotel.*)
185	eum] eam P[ac]
186	lex] quod P
189	l. Aut qui] l. Aut qui aliter P
191	unde oportet] *post* ciuilem C *lacuna* eum] Azo *praem.* C
194	erit interdictum] interdictum *om.* P
196	aliqua] aliquam P sequeretur] iam *om.* C
197	me non] eum P
199	sicut] et P intra] in fundo P unde *om.* P
201	detentio] detentatio P
206	dicet] dicit P eundi] exeundi P C[ac]
207	quod] quidem C
208	exeas] exiens P Et *om.* P
209	recuperande] retinende C
211	sit] sic C
212	est michi ius *tr.* P
214	sum] eam P siue intra] siue *om.* C
215	compellitur] compelleretur P sic michi fiat] sit michi P
216	esse] etiam C
6	possidet] possideat P
6–7	Si tu – clam *om.* P (*homoiotel.*)
7	omittis racionem legis] committis in legem P racionem] C² *marg.* in C[ac]

9		possedit] possiderit (?) C eadem *om.* P
11		subaudi *om.* P
13		et] non P
16		Is qui] C² *marg.*, *om.* P
17		Glosa dicit] Clam dic C dicit C^ac
19		non] C² *interl.* quia] nam P
20		et] in C^ac
21–2		de exceptione – Inter me] de re iudi(cata) si mea P Inter me *scr.*: Si mei C
23		ui nam *om.* P
26		eum] eam C^ac unde] C² *interl.* ut C
27		quod] quidem C
29–30		quod – dico *om.* P (*homoiotel.*)
31		ipse *om.* P
31–2		quam – deiectionem] quod habet prius adfectionem P
32		illam] quam *praem.* C^ac
33		possessionem *om.* P
34		nisi *om.* P, *add.* C² *interl.* pleniori] pleniorem C
35		coadunatam *scr.*: coadunatio c ordinatam P quod *om.* C
36		et *om.* P
1		opponitur *bis scr.* P contrarium *add.* C² *marg.*
4		usucapionibus] usur(pationibus) P Sequitur] C² *marg.* P, Seius C^ac
5		est *om.* C loquitur *om.* C
6		non *om.* C
1		mouet] monet C Quaestio *add.* C² *marg.* ponamus] pone P ille *om.* P
2		admittit] amittit C et dicit] et *om.* P
3		introibis] intrabis P
4		scilicet te habere] C² *marg.*, *om.* P
7		contrariam *om.* P infra *om.* C
9		de facto] C² *marg.*, *om.* P
10		nam] ita P
11		animo *om.* P non] C² *interl.* domini] dominum P
12		non *om.* P etiam quod *tr.* P
14		alius] alium C non *om.* C glosa eciam *tr.* P
16		apprehendendo] apprehendo C^ac P
17		teneor] tenetur P
18		de usucapionibus] unde ui P
22		oportet *om.* P

24	Ponamus] po(ne) P Quaestio *add.* C² *marg.*
28	agit *om.* P
31	admittit] C² admit C admisit P
32	dominus *om.* C
36	interdicto] interdictum C ut] aut C^ac
37	possessor] pos(sessione) *praem.* P et *om.* P
38	retinendo] C² *interl.* ueniendo C
40	adhuc] aut restituatur ciuilis de qua fuit deiectus *praem.* C^ac
42	perueniet] uenient P
44	restitueretur] restituetur P
45	primo] prima P
46	bene *om.* P
47	disce *add.* C *post* tamen
48	ego *om.* C
50	uitandus] uitantus P
51	prima *om.* P
53	unde ui interdicto *tr.* C
54	istud] illud P
59	qua] e *praem.* P
60	semper fuit] superfluit P
61–2	illam eandem possessionem *om.* P (*homoiotel.*)
64	est illud *om.* C
54	accidente] adueniente te P enim *om.* P
66	accedit] accedat P extrinsecus] extrinsecum C et] ut P
67	ad finem §] § fi. P
68	admittatur] amittatur P
70	et] etiam P
71	credo] concedo P quod] quidem C hic *om.* P
72	cucurrit] incurrit P
73	interdicto] interdictum C
77	suo] sui C
1	ueniamus ad] uideamus P
2	timens] timet P
3	quod *om.* P
4	quod *om.* P
5	maluit] mauult P
7	solutionibus *scr.*: usu(capionibus) C P Si] sti(?) *praem.* P^ac stipulatus] stipulatur P
8	amisisse] amittere P quemadmodum] quandam C
9	nunciat] uenit C nunciat] ueniat C
10	non *om.* P

10–11	noui operis *tr.* C
11	supra *scr.*: infra C P
12	titulo *om.* C
13	queritur *om.* P
14	Ponamus] po(ne) P
16	ignoranti] ignorante C[ac]
18	in] et *praem.* P
19	quare] queritur P differtur] differatur P
20	fundum] in *praem.* P
21	quod] quia P uellet] C[2] *interl.* nellet C
22	est *om.* P
23	ultra] utrum P
24	Ponamus] po(ne) P absens *om.* P
29–30	egressum – deiciendi *om.* P (*homoiotel.*)
32	domo] domi P
34	eo casu *om.* C
35	sibi *om.* P
37	quod *bis scr.* C
37–8	sentit sua culpa *tr.* P
38	queri] conqueri P quare] queritur P
39	Azo] Az. P
40	deiecit] deiecerit P
41	egressus *scr.*: ingressus C *om.* P amisit] admisit P[ac]
43–4	et Si quis tamen se] C[2] *marg.*, *om.* P
45	autem uisis] C[2] *marg.* iure C, *del.* C[2] uiris P
46	contenderet de possessione] concederet eum de pos(sessione) C de *del.(?)* C[2] *post* pos. *add.* s(ess)orem C[2] *interl.*
47	admitteret *scr.*: amitteret C P eum *om.* P retro] secus P
49	i §] C[2] *interl.*, *om.* P
50	Proinde *scr.*: p. C p(enultimo) P
51	habuit] habet P
53	celeri *scr.*: sceleri C P succurrendum] ei consulendum siue *praem.* P ut *om.* C C. *scr.*: infra C P

6 Bembo giureconsulto?

Michael H. Crawford

When Antonio Agustín arrived in Rome in the autumn of 1544, followed in the spring by his friend and collaborator Jean Matal, he had already formulated the amazing project of a corpus of the sources of civil and canon law; he was already the author of the *Emendationum et Opinionum Libri IV* and the *Ad Modestinum*, the fruit of his work on the Florentine manuscript of the Digest; and he had begun work on the *De Legibus et Senatus Consultis*.[1] Central to the activity of the two in Rome was a continued search for manuscript copies of imperial constitutions and novels; but they also devoted a great deal of time and energy to an attempt to collect and arrange in order reliable copies of the inscriptions of the Roman world, which could furnish evidence for the Roman institutions which had produced the legal texts on which they worked.

Much of the material which they collected survives to reveal their methods of work, which attached high importance to the verification of copies against stone or bronze and to the assembly of parallels from juristic and literary texts:[2] an annotated copy of *Epigrammata Antiquae Urbis* (Rome, 1521), now in the Biblioteca Apostolica Vaticana, MS Vat.Lat. 8495; and a series of notes and drafts for an epigraphic sylloge, which form part of five later miscellanies, MSS. Vat.Lat. 6034 and 6037–40. One of these, MS Vat.Lat. 6039, contains a curious text, in the form of a decree of the senate of Renaissance Rome.

Petri Bembi Cardinalis
Quod Curtius Fregepanius, Tiberius Marganius, Jo. Petrus Draco, Consules[3] de Q. Fabio et Theophrasto Rullis Lupi filiis posterisque eorum civitate donandis verba fecerunt, D(e) E(a) R(e) V(niversi) I(ta) C(ensuerunt). Cum Rullorum gens urbe Roma oriunda, ob Agrariae legis invidiam olim premeretur quam P. Servilius Rullus trib(unus) pleb(is) promulgasset, cumque propterea nonnullorum

---

[1] See J.-L. Ferrary, *Correspondance de Lelio Torelli avec Antonio Agustín et Jean Matal 1542–1553* (Como, 1992), introduction; J.-L. Ferrary, 'La Genèse du *De Legibus et Senatus Consultis*', in M. H. Crawford (ed.), *Antonio Agustín between Renaissance and Counter-Reform* (London, 1993).

[2] R. C. Cooper, 'Epigraphical Research in Rome in the Mid-Sixteenth Century: The Papers of Antonio Agustín and Jean Matal', in Crawford (ed.), *Antonio Agustín*.

[3] Here and at the end Matal has wrongly expanded *cons* as *consules* instead of *conservatores*.

potentiae cedendum sibi esse potius decreverit quam propter civium dissensionem Rempub(licam) in discrimen adducere, ac Lupiam antiquissimam et nobilissimum (sic) magnae Graeciae oppidum se contulerit, ibique splendide semper ac honorificentissime vixerit, cum postremo Q. Fabius et Theophrastus, optimae indolis magnaeque spei adolescentes, ut civitati longo intervallo restituerentur magnopere petierint: His de rebus senatum existimare Rullae genti civitatis ius quod illius nobilitati splendori egregiaeque in Rempub(licam) voluntati debeatur quasi postliminio reddendum restituendumque esse, atque etiam si res ita postulet de integro condonandum; senatuique placere uti Q. Fabius et Theophrastus fratres posterique eorum Romanae civitatis immunitatibus, privilegiis, beneficiis, honoribus frui ac fungi omnibus possint utique cives patritiique Romani eodem iure sint perpetuoque futuri sint, quo sunt qui cives patritiique iure optimo esse censentur. Qui impedierit, senatum existimaturum eum contra Rempub(licam) fecisse. Hanc autem s(enatus) c(onsulti) auctoritatem iidem consules V. Id. Januar. perscribendam curarunt Anno a Christo nato MDXLII. (Vat.Lat. 6039, fol. 335^r (Matal's numbering) = 111^r (modern numbering)

The fact that the grant of citizenship is not to be found in the list of grants drawn up by F. Gregorovius on the basis of the archives is not in itself significant.[4] The same is true of numerous other grants attested by other sources: Montaigne, mentioned by Gregorovius; but also Mariano de Blanchellis de Leonardi of Palestrina, about 1510;[5] Giovanbattista Paladino, by 1538;[6] Jacopo Strada; Camillo Capranica, by 1547;[7] Carlo Gualteruzzi, in 1564 (see below). The list could no doubt be much lengthened.

There is nothing mysterious about the proposers, Curzio Frangipane, Tiberio Margani and Giovanni Pietro del Drago. The first came from one of the oldest families of the Roman nobility, even if we decline to follow Onofrio Panvinio in tracing it back to the Anicii of the Late Empire; the family was closely tied to the Farnese; Curzio and his twin brother Mario were together responsible for the funerary monument of their father Antonio in 1546;[8] he himself held the office of *Urbis cancellarius* in 1545 and died in 1554;[9] and his brother Mario was his *coadiutor* and was then the holder of that office himself, when Panvinio dedicated *De Gente*

---

[4] 'Alcuni cenni storici sulla cittadinanza romana', *Memorie dell'Accademia dei Lincei*, Serie Terza, Cl.Sc.Mor. 1 (1876–7), 314–46 = 'Römische Bürgerbriefe seit dem Mittelalter', *Kleine Schriften zur Geschichte und Cultur*, vol. I (Leipzig, 1887), 265–323.

[5] P. A. Petrini, *Memorie prenestine disposte in forma di annali* (Rome, 1795), s.a.

[6] J. Wardrop, 'Civis Romanus sum. Giovanbattista Paladino and his Circle', *Signature*, n.s. 14 (1952), 3–39.

[7] Bodleian Library, MS Auct.S.10.25, fol. XVI^r; see M. H. Crawford, 'Benedetto Egio and the Development of Greek Epigraphy', in Crawford (ed.), *Antonio Agustín*.

[8] V. Forcella, *Inscrizioni delle chiese e d' altri edificii di Roma dal secolo XI fino ai giorni nostri* (2 vols., Rome, 1869, 1873), vol. II, p. 306, no. 945; O. Moroni, *Corrispondenza Giovanni della Casa Carlo Gualteruzi (1525–1549)* (Vatican City, 1986), no. 196, p. 322, for the news of the death of Antonio; cf. p. 76 n. 5.

[9] Moroni, no. 50, p. 110; Forcella, vol. II, p. 535, no. 1610.

Fregepania Libri Quatuor to him on 1 May 1556.[10] The second came from a less distinguished, but none the less notable, family.[11] The last is himself attested in 1558 and 1559, and his son (presumably) is attested as *conservator* in 1584.[12] I know of no independent attestation of the three as *conservatori* in 1542;[13] but it is surely easier to suppose that the three were *conservatori* and that the decree was passed in their names in 1542 than that they were all parties to an elaborate joke. For their names would surely not have been invoked without their knowledge and consent.

Comparison of our decree with those for Giovanni Vitelleschi of 1436, Cardinal Otto Truchsess of 1560 and Carlo Gualteruzzi of 1564 makes a number of things clear.

In nomine etc. ... Ad laudem, gloriam et honorem omnipotentis Dei ... ac aeternam memoriam Joannis de Vitelleschi ... congregatis, et coadunatis insimul et ad invicem, in Domibus solitae residentiae magnificorum D. D. Conservatorum Camerae Almae Urbis apud Capitolium et Aracaeli situatis, Magnificis Viris [*the names of three* conservatores *and 69 others follow*] propositoque per supradictum Laurentium alias lo Mancino primum Conservatorem quid agendum foret circa mirabilia gesta invictissimi Patriarchae ... praedictus magnificus Laurentius alias lo Mancino Conservator praedictus pro ipsius Collegis et toto Conservatoratus officio laudibilia et fortia gesta praedicta D. Patriarchae mirabilesque operationes pro Urbis liberatione enarrando singulariter commendavit ... (P. A. Petrini (n.5), 175–6, 448–52)

Privilegium Ro(manae) Civitatis obtentum per R(everendissimum) card(inalem) Augustanum. Quod Pyrrhus Tharus, Pamphilus Pamphilius, Jo. Bapt. Cicchinus Conservatores de Ill(ustrissi)mo et R(everendissi)mo Cardinali Othone Truchses Civitate donando ad senatum retulerunt, SPQR de ea re ita fieri censuit. Cum veteri more et instituto in Civitate Ro(mana) cupide illi semper studioseque suscepti sint, qui ... Quam quid(em) S. C. auctoritatem iidem Conservatores per

---

[10] Biblioteca Apostolica Vaticana, MS Barb.Lat. XXXI, 1 = 2481, esp. fols. 121^v–127^r; Padua, Biblioteca Universitaria, MS 263; Biblioteca Angelica, MS A.7.16 = 77; see Fr. Ehrle, 'Die Frangipani', in *Mélanges Emile Chatelain* (Paris, 1910), 448–85, at 453 n. 1. Panvinio does not mention the office of *conservator*, concentrating rather on that of *cancellarius urbis*.

[11] See C. Cecchelli, *I Margani, i Capocci, i Sanguigni, i Mellini* (Rome, 1946), 7–20. Cecchelli follows *La storia delle famiglie romane di Teodoro Amayden con note ed aggiunte del Comm. Carlo Augusto Bertini*, vol. II (Rome, [1910]), 55 n. 1, without source, in claiming that Tiberio Margani was *conservator* in 1552; I suspect that this is a mistake for 1542.

[12] See G. Presutti, 'I Colonna di Riofreddo', *Archivio della Società Romana di Storia Patria* 61 (1938), 241–90, at 267 n. 2, for our man; Forcella, vol. I, p. 42, no. 80; vol. II, p. 14, no. 44, for the son.

[13] There is nothing in L. Pompilj Olivieri, *Il senato romano* (Rome, 1886), who, however, lists Giovanni Pietro del Drago as *conservator* in 1583, by mistake for 1584; and there are no further volumes to F. Bartoloni, *Codice diplomatico del senato romano dal MCXLIV al MCCCXLVII* (Rome, 1948).

SPQR scribam perscribendam curarunt. Ann(o) ... Julius Horologius scriba
SPQR. (F. Gregorovius (n.4))

Referentibus ad Senatum, Pamphylo Pamphylio, Gabriele Vallato, Octavio Graccho Cons, De donando Civitate Romana Deq(ue) in Senatum legendo Carlo Gualterutio cive Fanensi, Qui per annos quattuor et viginti urbem incoluerit, complures in ea liberos susceperit, bonam existimationem quesierit, rem pararit, Senatui placuit, hominem excellentis in civilib(us) reb(us) industriae, spectatae integritatis atq(ue) virtutis, in civitatem atque in hunc ordinem asciscere. Itaq(ue) censuit, uti is eo iure civis Romanus sit, quo qui optimo sunt, Bona habeat immunia, Magistratus gerat, Omnia alia Civium Romanor(um) commoda ac iura potiatur ipse liberiq(ue) eius ac posteri, Utiq(ue) ei in Senatum veniundi, sententiae dicundae ius sit, Eosq(ue) honores, eaq(ue) emolumenta capiundi, quae caeteri Senatores, Utiq(ue) liberi eius ac posteri, patritii sint, gentemq(ue) habeant. Quae ut nota testataq(ue) in posterum essent, in publicas litteras referri consignariq(ue) iusser(unt). (Archivio Segreto Vaticano, Misc. Arm. XLIV, v. III, c. 91[r] = O. Moroni, *Carlo Gualteruzzi (1500–1577) e i corrispondenti* (Città del Vaticano, 1984), 129 (inaccurate) = MS Vat.Lat.6038, fol. 113[r])

Our decree is peculiar in its systematic use of the formulae of ancient decrees of the senate, *uerba fecerunt, de ea re ita censuerunt, senatui placere uti*, which do not appear in mediaeval and Renaissance decrees earlier than ours and appear only randomly later; in the use of legal terminology, *promulgare, restituere, postliminium*, indeed the whole of the end of the decree; in the high style adopted; and in the elaborate nature of the reasons given for the grant and for their historical and literary character, though there are elements of this in the decree of Carlo Gualteruzzi, notably the reference to *gentem habere*. This reasoning leads on to the observation of another oddity: Roman citizenship was granted in this period to those who had established residence in Rome, witness, the example of Carlo Gualteruzzi; to those who had conferred signal benefits on the city; and, increasingly, on major figures of the world of the arts. But this was an innovation as the sixteenth century advanced, as is shown by the uproar caused by the attempt to grant it to Christopher de Longueil in 1519.[14]

It is very surprising that citizenship should be granted to two nonentities with a spurious Roman ancestry, even if they could invoke a learned account of that ancestry evidently composed by Pietro Bembo: for the genitive of 'Petri Bembi Cardinalis' presumably indicates authorship rather than ownership, since Matal elsewhere uses 'apud so-and-so' to identify texts which belonged to others and which he copied. The connex-

---

[14] D. Gnoli, *Un giudizio di lesa romanità sotto Leone X* (Rome, 1891).

ion between Pietro Bembo and Donato Rullo, financial adviser to Ascanio and, above all, Vittoria Colonna, is straightforward enough. But who on earth were Quinto Fabio and Teofrasto Rullo, sons of Lupo?

The high style is in any case intelligible enough in the greatest Ciceronian of the age. But a different problem lurks beneath the surface. The reasoning in the decree, with its sympathy for the author of the *lex agraria* of 63 BC which Cicero succeeded in blocking, is actually hostile to Cicero. And what is more, one only has to read the speeches of Cicero after his return from exile to see that his virtuous claim that he had preferred exile to provoking civil strife, is here transferred to P. Servilius Rullus.

It is, however, the interest in Roman legal formulae that reveals an unsuspected side to Pietro Bembo, though one may suspect that his sources in general were Frontinus and the famous letter of Caelius to Cicero of 51 BC, rather than any epigraphic or juristic source.[15] Bembo was no doubt drawing on his earlier reading, directed at the acquisition of a mastery of Latin style, in the course of which he systematically noted and recorded formulae and turns of phrase suitable for the composition of Latin letters.[16] In one case, indeed, both the source of a phrase in our decree and the edition used can be identified: the 1513 edition of Frontinus of Fra Giocondo, which has in ch. 106 the reading D.E.R.V.I.C., unsupported by the manuscript tradition and abandoned in modern editions, but also adopted by Agustín. On the other hand, the phrase 'Hanc autem s(enatus) c(onsulti) auctoritatem iidem consules V Id. Januar, perscribendam curarunt ...' is clearly drawn from the letter of Caelius. But such a literary pedigree would not have diminished the interest of the text to Agustín and Matal. They wished to learn about Roman institutions from one of the great figures of the distant days of Leo X, even if these institutions were mediated through a decree of the contemporary senate. For they were lawyers and it was as lawyers that they were in the process of transforming the antiquarian culture of mid-sixteenth-century Rome. And they not only remarked, of course, on the great treasures of Bembo, the manuscripts of Virgil and Terence, when they called on him.[17] Agustín and Matal, 'che annotarono ogni minima minutia', together made a copy of the Terence, which was later

---

[15] Frontinus, *De Aquis* 100–1, 104, 106, 108, 125, 127; (Cicero), *Ad Fam.* VIII. 8 = 84 Shackleton Bailey, 5–8.

[16] Evidence of this reading survives in Biblioteca Apostolica Vaticana, MSS Chigi L. VIII.304; and Barb. Lat. XXXI, 17; Vat.Gr. 1347 contains a classified list of place names. See V. Cian, 'Contributi alla storia dell'enciclopedismo nell' età della Rinascità. Il Methodus Studiorum del Cardinale Pietro Bembo', in *Miscellanea Giovanni Sforza* (Lucca, 1915), 289–330.

[17] C. Flores Sellés, *Epistolario de Antonio Agustín* (Salamanca, 1980), no. 149, pp. 213–15, L. Torelli to Agustín, 20 August 1546; J.-L. Ferrary, *Correspondance* (n. 1), nos. 52–3, 58–9.

available to Gabriele Faerno;[18] and on 31 May 1545 Matal wrote to their jurist friend of their Bologna and Florence days, Lelio Torelli, 'ego a paucis diebus utor Terentio et Virgilio Petri Bembi Cardinalis, in quibus expressa uideo non contemnenda uestigia nostrarum *Pandectarum*'. It would be hard to exemplify better the humanist jurisprudence of the sixteenth century.

[18] British Library, Add. MS 10266, fol. 119, G. Faerno to P. Vettori, 29 April 1558.

7 Gentilis and the *interpretatio duplex*

J. L. Barton

One of the reasons for which, in Maitland's opinion, the history of English law was not written was that much mediaeval English legislation remained in force:

That process by which old principles and old phrases are charged with a new content, is from the lawyer's point of view an evolution of the true intent and meaning of the old law; from the historian's point of view it is almost of necessity a process of perversion and misunderstanding[1] ... I make no doubt that it is easier for a Frenchman or a German to study medieval law than it is for an Englishman; he has not before his mind the fear that he is saying what is not 'practically sound', that he may seem to be unsettling the law or usurping the functions of a judge.[2]

The sixteenth-century student of Justinian's compilations was in much the same difficulty as the nineteenth-century student of the mediaeval sources of English law. His predecessors had been content to treat the compilations as a code. No doubt the provisions of any code have a history, but what that history may have been is a curious rather than an important question for the expositor who is considering their present application, and the glossators had either ignored historical questions altogether, or treated them very casually. D.29.2.60 is an extract from Javolenus' epitome of Labeo's *Posteriora*. It concludes with a note of Paul's which, in the Vulgate, had become part of the passage of Javolenus:

Paulus et Labeonis sententiam improbant, et in Iavoleni sententia sunt.

The gloss suggests that Javolenus is referring to himself in the third person, or that Neratius, from whom L.59 of the same title was taken, is citing Javolenus with approval. This was held a particularly shocking proof of Accursius' barbarous ignorance of antiquity, for not only was this suggestion chronologically impossible; that it was chronologically impossible clearly appeared from Pomponius' account of the succession

---

[1] F. W. Maitland, 'Why the History of English Law is not Written', in *Collected Papers*, vol. I (Cambridge, 1911), 480 at 491.
[2] *Ibid.*, at 492–3.

of the jurists in D.1.2.2.[3] For the glossator, the sense of the passage was clear, and the reason for its rather odd form was not of sufficient importance to require him to go to the trouble of checking references. The gloss may note an interpolation upon occasion. According to D.33.5.19, if the legatee of an option dies before he has made his choice, his heir may choose. The gl. 'Placuit' notes that this passage has probably been altered, for in Inst. 2.20.23 Justinian states that it is his constitution which has permitted the legatee's heir to make the choice which his testator failed to make. On the other hand, the gloss may pass over an equally obvious interpolation without comment. According to D.4.4.27.4, 'Adversus eos quoque restitutio praestanda est, quorum de dolo agere non permittitur, nisi si quaedam personae speciali lege exceptae sint.' The gl. 'Lege' refers the reader to Justinian's constitution in C.2.42.2 for the persons who are 'speciali lege exceptae'. If the reference be correct, this latter text is as clearly interpolated as the former, but this the reader may be left to infer for himself. Since an interpolated text is no less authoritative than a text which has not been interpolated, there is no reason to attempt to list interpolations systematically, and it is of no consequence whether an apparent inconsistency should be ascribed to interpolation or to oversight. In D.2.41.5 Justinian provides that prescription shall no longer run against a minor in those cases in which he was formerly granted restitution after time had run. A constitution of Gordian in C.5.72.1 and another of Diocletian and Maximian in C.7.53.3 assume that *longi temporis praescriptio* does not run against a minor. Placentinus suggested that Justinian had been drinking, and had forgotten these constitutions.[4]

This was not an attitude which an expositor trained in the new learning could easily maintain consistently, whatever his theoretical opinions. Montaigne's early education was influenced by the suggestion of a friend of his father, that the true reason that we cannot attain the greatness of mind and of knowledge of the Greeks and Romans is that we are obliged to devote many years to mastering the languages which they learned in the cradle. Montaigne was inclined to doubt whether this were the only reason, but though he cannot be accused of an uncritical deference for received opinion, it did not occur to him to question the superiority of the ancients.[5] Tribonian, who had been principally responsible for the compilation of the Corpus Iuris, was hardly one of the ancients. In the sixth century, the long decline into barbarism was already well begun.

For the honour of his own faculty, Alciatus was willing to defend him against the attacks of others – more particularly of the grammarians, who

---

[3] Gribaldus Mopha, *De Methodo ac Ratione Studendi* (ed. Lugduni, 1564), book I, ch. 15, 131ff.
[4] Gl. 'Quaerere', C.2.41.5.   [5] *Essais*, book I, ch. 25.

were the worst possible judges of the merits of any jurist[6] – but he did not always speak very well of him himself. Bartolus deserved the gratitude of posterity for opening eyes which would otherwise have been obscured by the *graeculae tenebrae* in which Justinian's compilers had involved the Roman texts. Had the works of the ancient jurists still existed, the labours of Accursius and of those who wrote after him would not have been necessary.[7] Tribonian was capable of error, and if he could be shown to have erred, it might be questioned whether posterity were obliged to err with him.

Balduinus was firmly of opinion that posterity was under no such obligation. His views upon the compilation are expounded in most detail in his *Iustinianus, sive de Iure Novo*.[8] Tribonian and his colleagues had been guilty of two faults not easily pardoned in the draftsmen of a code: haste and negligence. The passages which they had extracted from the classical jurists had too often been left unrevised, or had been revised insufficiently, and to attempt to make good law of them by construction was to labour in vain. In proof of his thesis, he reviewed Justinian's reforms in chronological order, and showed how imperfectly the new law was reflected in the Digest. Justinian, for example, had provided that all legacies, and indeed *fideicommissa* also, should be enforceable in the same manner and by the same remedies. Not only did many texts distinguish still between *fideicommissa* and legacies; the texts on legacies could not be understood without a knowledge of the different legal effects of the different classical forms of legacy, for the compilers had too often struck out the jurist's reference to the form of legacy which he was considering, but left his decision upon its effect unaltered, and the effect varied with the form.[9] The Digest must be interpreted historically, not because this method of interpretation was appropriate, but because without a knowledge of legal antiquities the expositor could not disentangle the law in force from that mass of wholly or partially obsolete matter which the compilers, in defiance of their instructions, had incorporated into the Digest.

Antony Faber was of opinion that the surest means of detecting the interventions of the compilers was to bear in mind that in their unin-

[6] *Dispunctionum*, in *Opera* (ed. Basileae, 1571), book IV, ch. 7.
[7] *Comment ad Tit. Dig. De Verborum Significatione*, at D.50.16.246. I have used the edition of his works which was published at Basle in 1571.
[8] See H. Troje, 'Peccatum Triboniani, zur Dialektik der Interpretatio Duplex bei François Baudouin' (1970) 36 S.D.H.I. 341.
[9] 'Ac in Pandectis quidem, ubi hac de re quaeritur, vidimus vindicationis et damnationis mentionem expunctam saepius, deletamque esse. Sed tanto magis interea queror, non solum lituram esse relictam, sed et rem ipsam tam varie, adeoque contrarie nihilominus proponi, ut necesse videatur ad conciliationem, repetere vetus illud discrimen, et nos ad illud iterum confugere.' *Justinianus, sive de Iure Novo* (ed. Basileae, 1560), book II, at 110.

telligent haste they commonly mistook the true reason of the law.[10] In the *rei vindicatio*, restitution *manu militari* had replaced the *iusiurandum in litem*. The *iusiurandum in litem* appeared in the Digest only because Tribonian did not understand the mechanism of the *actio arbitraria*. It served no purpose, if the thing itself might be restored *in specie*.[11] This is reasoning of which Balduinus might not have disapproved, but if Tribonian did not understand the law which he had undertaken to digest, it might be questioned whether it were invariably necessary to attribute legislative force to his blunders. In his *De Erroribus Pragmaticorum et Interpretum*, which he wrote for the instruction of practitioners, Faber observes at one point that the reader may object that he is discussing the errors not of the interpreters, but of Tribonian. He, however, holds Tribonian to be an interpreter, and an unskilful one, not a *iuris auctor*,[12] and he seems willing upon occasion to act upon his opinion. It is Tribonian and not Paul who holds in D.26.7.43.1 that a curator who has promised a dowry which exceeds his ward's fortune is not answerable to her husband for the overplus, save in so far as she is able to indemnify him, though she must give her husband security to pay the balance, which he cannot claim from her curator should she come to better fortune. Faber makes no apology for treating this passage at length, for it is of great importance, and proper to be explained according to Paul's opinion and the right reason of the law, rejecting the notes of Tribonian and the errors of the interpreters.[13] It is not obvious why it should be of great importance, or indeed of any importance at all, unless we are to hold that a judge as well as an expositor is at liberty to follow the right reason of the law, rejecting the notes of Tribonian and the errors of the interpreters.

For Heineccius, Balduinus and Faber were two of the three principal members (Hotman was the third) of the 'secta Tribonianomastigum'.[14] He found their opinions so unreasonable that he was driven to conclude that they had been inspired by academic jealousy. They were led to attack Justinian's compilations because they had very justifiably despaired of ever rivalling the great Cujas as interpreters of them.

[10] *Coniecturae Iuris Civilis* (ed. Aureliae Allobrogum, 1609), book XII, ch. 1.
[11] *Coniecturae Iuris Civilis*, book XVI, ch. 17: 'An ergo, inquies, legem hanc e libris nostris delebimus, cum non sit Ulpiani? Immo vero pro imperatoria constitutione habebimus, sed ad eam interpretandam in perquirenda iuris ratione quam aperte labefactat operam, si mihi credis, non impendemus, potiusque fatebimur arbitrarias actiones hodie nullas esse, posteaquam placuit Triboniano, manu militari faciendum esse ut omnimodo arbitrio pareatur.' See also *De Erroribus Pragmaticorum* (ed. Lugduni, 1598), Decas XVIII, Error 5.
[12] *De Erroribus Pragmaticorum*, Decas XVIII, Error 6.
[13] *Coniecturae Iuris Civilis*, book VI, ch. 18.
[14] Heineccius, 'De Secta Tribonianomastigum', in *Opera* (Genevae, 1767), vol. III, 171 at 174ff.

108   J. L. Barton

Cujas was certainly no Tribonianomastix. Tribonian, he held, was another Papinian.[15] Those who criticised the arrangement of the Digest, or who wished to change it, were *ineptissimi* and *imperitissimi*, who knew neither what was an art, nor the art of the Digest, and could never have understood the clear principles of the civil law, though this arrangement was not Tribonian's own, but that of the earlier jurists whom he had followed.[16] He was prepared none the less to hold Tribonian capable of error, and indeed of negligence – in some instances, of rather grave negligence. In D.50.4.7 Marcian states that imperial constitutions have provided that one accused of crime may not stand for public office though sentence be not yet given, but if a year have elapsed since proceedings were commenced he is not prohibited, 'nisi per ipsum steterit, quominus causa intra annum expediretur'. Criminal proceedings, as we may see from the Theodosian Code, formerly lapsed if judgment were not given within a year. Justinian extended the term to two years, but the compilers have failed to correct this passage,

quod a me adnotatum est, non tam ut ille locus explicaretur, quam etiam ut Triboniani non curantia proderetur.[17]

The compilers, in his opinion, did not always understand the texts which they excerpted. According to D.2.15.6 (Gaius, 17 *ad edictum provinciale*):

De his controversiis, quae ex testamento proficiscuntur, neque transigi neque exquiri veritas aliter potest, quam inspectis cognitisque verbis testamenti.

This is taken from the same passage of Gaius as D.29.3.1, where the verb *transigere* is applied 'per translationem ... ad iudicata, non ad conventa sive composita'. It therefore does not properly belong in the title *De Transactionibus*, for the jurist was speaking of a settlement by judicial decision, not by the agreement of the parties.[18] Elsewhere, Cujas takes occasion to explain that he did not say, as he is alleged to have said, that in C.4.23.4, 'Praetextu debiti restitutio commodati non probabiliter recusatur', we should read *commendati* for *commodati*. This could be an impossible emendation, for the constitution is in the title *De Commodato*. What he did say, and he is of this opinion still, was that *commendati* was the original reading of the constitution. The emperors were speaking not of *commodatum* but of deposit, in which there was no set-off. In the copy which the compilers used, *commodati* had been substituted for the rarer

---

[15] *Comment. ad Lib. VI Cod. tit. 43*, upon the rubric. I have used the edition of the works of Cujas (omitting the posthumous works) which was published at Frankfurt in 1623.
[16] *Paratitla ad L Libros Digestorum*, at D.17.1.
[17] *Observationes et Emendationes*, book I, ch. 8.
[18] *Comment. ad tit. D. De Transactionibus*, at 1.1, *in fine*.

Gentilis and the *interpretatio duplex*

commendati by the error of a scribe, and the compilers therefore assumed that the constitution was intended to apply to *commodatum*.[19]

Cujas had the good fortune to be writing in a country in which the compilations of Justinian did not have the force of imperial legislation. He was not, therefore, obliged to consider whether, if Gaius were not speaking in D.2.15.6 of a settlement of a disputed claim by agreement between the parties, a judge might hold that there was no difference in law between a settlement of a claim under a testament and a settlement of any other claim, or whether, if C.4.23.4 were written of deposit, a judge before whom a defendant who was sued for the return of a thing which had been lent to him for his use attempted to rely upon a set-off might ignore it. Gribaldus Mopha was less discreet. One of his illustrations of the importance for the student of a knowledge of the methods of the compilers and of the principles of textual criticism is D.41.2.8 (Paul, 54 *ad edictum*):

Quemadmodum nulla possessio adquiri nisi animo et corpore potest, ita nulla amittitur, nisi in qua utrumque in contrarium actum est.

Paul says precisely the opposite elsewhere.[20] The contradiction is easily resolved if for *Quemadmodum* we read *Non quemadmodum* – a locution which is frequent in the jurists – but the *lex geminata* (D.50.17.153 (Paul, 65 *ad edictum*)) is not so easily amended:

Fere quibuscumque modis obligamur, iisdem in contrarium actis liberamur, cum quibus modis adquirimus, isdem in contrarium actis amittimus. Ut igitur nulla possessio adquiri nisi animo et corpore potest, ita nulla amittitur, nisi in qua utrumque in contrarium actum est.

If it be an illustration of the principle of *contrarius actus* that possession is lost, as it is acquired, *animo et corpore*, and neither *animo solo* nor *corpore solo*, it is hardly possible to argue that a negligent scribe has omitted a negative which would have made the doctrine of *contrarius actus* inapplicable to the loss of possession. Gribaldus was equal to the challenge. The extracts which compose the title *De Regulis Iuris* have been put together from fragments of different jurists by the compilers or by others

unde quidquid ibi primo versiculo (qui ex Pomponio desumptus est) adiectum reperitur, ex nullius iurisconsulti auctoritate, vel sententia prolatum est. Quare expungendum omnino putarem.[21]

---

[19] *Observationes et Emendationes*, book IX, ch. 27.
[20] D.41.2.3.6 (Paul, 54 *ad edictum*).
[21] *De Methodo ac Ratione Studendi*, book I, ch. 16 (ed. Lugduni, 1564), 145–6.

If we may take it that Tribonian, or another, has borrowed Pomponius' observation upon *contrarius actus* from D.46.3.80 (Pomponius, 4 *ad Q. Mucinum*), and added it to an extract from Paul which did not mention the point, and that this passage of Paul originally (whether or not when it came into the hands of the compilers) contained a negative which has dropped out, or been struck out, of the text which we now have, we may quite properly strike out the reference to *contrarius actus* and restore the negative. That the compilers clearly thought that the negative had been properly omitted is neither here nor there, for an opinion supported only by the authority of Tribonian is 'ex nullius iurisconsulti auctoritate vel sententia prolatum'.

From Faber or from Hotman, this would not have been a very remarkable observation. Gribaldus, however, was an Italian, and like most of his compatriots at this period, more conservatively than radically inclined. The authors whom he particularly recommended to the student (who would, he held, profit more from the diligent study of a few good writers than from indiscriminate reading) were Bartolus, Baldus, Paulus Castrensis, Alexander Tartagnus, Jason Maynus and Imola.[22] That a writer who was certainly no opponent of the *mos italicus* should still be capable of holding it self-evident that the authority of the compilers was of no weight if they could be shown to have differed from the jurists of the classical age is a very striking testimony to the prestige of antiquity.

It was not an opinion universally professed by the exponents of the *mos italicus*. Pacius, who thought the method of the French school of his own day more proper for grammarians than for legists,[23] held it unnecessary to labour to detect interpolations in Digest and Code, for it was no longer of any consequence how the law stood before Justinian.[24] However, he was not perfectly consistent:

post editas ex Pandectis Florentinis inscriptiones legum Pandectarum per quas inscriptiones licet capita coniungere a Triboniano seiuncta, iam multa facile et feliciter enarrantur, quorum veram sententiam veteres interpretes ea conferendi leges commoditate destituti assequi non potuerunt.[25]

To put together the fragments which Tribonian has separated is no doubt a help to discovering the meaning of the jurist from whom the extracts were taken, but if this be the only way in which it may be discovered, it might seem fairly arguable that we should infer that the meaning of the jurist was not the meaning of the compilers. This was the opinion of Albericus Gentilis, who, almost alone among his contemporaries, distinguished clearly and consistently between historical and dog-

---

[22] *De Methodo ac Ratione Studendi*, book I, ch. 12 (ed. Lugduni, 1564), 123–4.
[23] *De Iuris Methodo Libri II* (Spirae, 1597), book II, at 72.
[24] *Ibid.*, at 66. [25] *Ibid.*, at 51.

matic interpretation. The latter, in his view, was the province of the legist, who was not concerned to discover what law the Romans had followed, whether at Rome or at Constantinople, but to determine how the law now stood.[26] It was absurd to criticise Accursius for inferring that if, as Modestinus states in D.23.2.1, marriage involves *divini et humani iuris communicatio*, spouses must be of the same religion.[27] Modestinus was indeed a pagan, and it might be that when he spoke of *divini iuris communicatio* he was referring to the family worship of pagan Rome,[28] but whether this were in fact the case was of no more importance than whether by the phrase *damnati ad ferrum* in D.28.1.8.4 Gaius meant those condemned to the arena,[29] or by the *Judaica superstitio* which, Ulpian tells us in D.50.2.3.3, Severus and Antoninus had declared not to be a disqualification for municipal office, Ulpian meant the Christian religion, or whether the *ignaviae sectatores* whom Valentinianus and Valens mention in C.10.32.26 were monks. The names of the jurists from whom the passages which are excerpted in the Digest were taken are preserved only for the honour of antiquity. Since all the texts of the compilation, from whatever source they have been taken, are to be taken as legislation of Justinian, it is no concern of the legist in what sense a pagan jurist, or one or other of Justinian's predecessors, may be more or less probably held to have used this or that expression. He is to consider what sense these expressions should be held to bear in the legislation of a Christian emperor, under whom gladiatorian contests were prohibited. What was the original meaning of a text is in any case a speculative question, for the compilers have altered many passages, so that we cannot be certain whether any particular expression should be attributed to the jurist whose name appears at the head of the extract or to the compilers.[30]

[26] *De Iuris Interpretibus Dialogi Sex*, ed. G. Astuti (Torino, 1937), 86.
[27] Connanus, *Commentariorum Iuris Civilis*, book VIII, ch. 4 (ed. Lutetiae, 1553).
[28] Alciatus, *Parergon*, book V, ch. 25.
[29] Alciatus, *Parergon*, book I, ch. 23. See also Gentilis, *Lectiones et Epistulae quae ad Ius Civile Pertinent* (Londini apud Wolfium, 1583), book I, ch. 7. Cujas (*Observationes et Emendationes*, book XIII, ch. 10) holds that in the original of the rescript cited in D.47.14.1 *pr.* Hadrian, after observing that *abigei* who are to be severely punished are ordinarily *damnati ad gladium*, went on to add that in case of a very grave or of a second offence *damnatio ad metallum* might be appropriate. We must therefore take *damnatio ad gladium* to be condemnation to the arena, and Tribonian should not have omitted these words, since *damnatio ad metallum* is mentioned subsequently in the same passage. Gentilis' comment is, 'At is non debuit eo modo tractare Hadriani rescriptum. Itane loqui possunt? Et nos manus damus.' Cujas, however, was of opinion that the abolition of *gladiatorum spectacula* had not entailed the abolition of the *ludus gladiatorius*, and that *damnatio ad ferrum* was therefore to be taken to bear its classical meaning in the law of Justinian.
[30] *De Iuris Interpretibus Dialogi Sex*, 167ff. See also at 208, 'Credo potius controversias, labyrinthos inexplicabiles ex illis monumentis [antiquitatis]; quoniam innumera aliter relata sunt a compilatoribus, innumera translata in alium sensum.'

Since it is not the meaning of the jurist which is in question, it naturally follows that the inscription of the passage is useless as an aid to its interpretation, and indeed that it is improper to make use of it. Justinian has not only stated that the inscriptions are preserved merely for the honour of antiquity; he has expressly forbidden resort to the original text. If the original text would be of no authority had it survived, a conjectural reconstruction of the original text is of even less authority. Whether or not Ulpian was speaking of the *lex Falcidia*, or of the interdict *Quod legatorum*, when he said that 'Per omnia exaequata sunt legata fideicommissis',[31] the compilers were not. That a fideicommissary manumission differs in effect from a direct testamentary manumission is no objection to this generalisation, for since *libertates* are to be deemed repeated if legacies be repeated,[32] a gift of liberty is not a legacy.[33] Whether it were of the Edict *Quod quisque iuris* that Ulpian said 'Cogitationis poenam nemo patitur'[34] is of no consequence whatever. To object that this is hardly correct if we take it as a general proposition, since 'in aliis plerisque causis non tantum effectus punitur, sed etiam voluntas',[35] is to ignore the elementary distinction between simple cogitation and the purpose with which an act is done.[36] It is an even graver error to argue that a jurist is not necessarily to be held to have adopted an opinion which he cites. For Cujas, the opinion of Callistratus in D.5.1.37 and of Marcian in D.48.6.5.1 that if violence and possession come in question together the question of violence should be determined before the question of property was no authority that the judge should decide the question of possession before the question of property if *possessorium* and *petitorium* be brought together. Had the jurists been speaking of the interdict *Unde vi*, they could hardly have treated violence and possession as two distinct questions, for a plaintiff who had not been in possession could not be violently ejected. We must take them to have meant that if the party injured chose to proceed criminally for the violence, and civilly for the possession or for the property, the criminal proceedings were to be first determined. Since, however, C.4.62.1 and C.9.12.7 can hardly be explained in this manner, it would seem that the imperial constitution which both jurists cite did refer to proceedings to recover possession rather than to punish the intruder.

---

[31] D.30.1 (Ulpian, 67 *ad edictum*). Cujas, *Paratitla ad L Libros Digestorum*, book 30. The gl. 'per omnia' makes a rather similar suggestion: 'Vel dic quod aliquid est hic detractum ex verbis Ulpiani a compilatoribus novi iuris, et illud detractum inducit novitatem.'

[32] D.50.16.80.

[33] Gentilis, *Lectiones et Epistulae quae ad Ius Civile Pertinent*, book I, ch. 17.

[34] D.48.19.18 (Ulpian 3 *ad edictum*).

[35] Cujas, *Observationes et Emendationes*, book VIII, ch. 22.

[36] Gentilis, *Lectiones et Epistulae quae ad Ius Civile Pertinent*, book I, ch. 13, book II, ch. 12. See also book I, ch. 17, where he observes that in D.30.1 the draftsman 'in alium sensum omnino deduxerit Ulpiani verba, quam fuerunt ab ipso prolata'.

That they cited it, however, is not proof that they accepted it as sound.[37] For Gentilis, the question of possession and the question of violence were no more distinct in criminal than in civil proceedings, for violence might be committed only against a possessor. There was therefore no inconsistency between C.9.12.7 and C.4.62.1: 'Prius de possessione pronuntiare, et ita crimen violentiae excutere praeses provinciae debuit', for to say that the judge must first determine the question of violence and to say that he should have first determined the question of possession and thus determined the offence of violence is to state the same proposition in different words. Both these texts are perfectly consistent with the constitution cited in the two Digest passages, for Marcian states in D.48.6.5.1 that Antoninus Pius decided 'ut prius de vi quaeratur, quam de iure dominii sive possessionis'. He was speaking not of actual possession, but of the right of possession, and though it cannot be known whether I have suffered violence until it appear whether I were in possession, whether I have suffered violence and whether I have a right to possess are undoubtedly two distinct questions.[38]

If the texts of the compilation are to be taken as different parts of a single law, it is no less improper to argue that one passage states the old law, and another the new. In D.50.16.88 Celsus says that a man is commonly said to leave as much money as his goods are worth, but the case is different if he leave a legacy of another's land, though he leave money enough to buy it, for one who has money is not said to have what he may buy with it. In D.35.2.61 Javolenus assumes that a legacy of an estate which is not the property of the testator is valid. If these two passages require to be reconciled, to hold that Celsus was speaking of a *legatum per vindicationem* and Javolenus of a *legatum per damnationem* is no way to reconcile them.[39] Similarly whether the jurists differed in opinion, or a particular jurist hesitated, is not a question for the legist, who is concerned to discover the intention of Justinian, not the opinions of the jurists upon whom his compilers drew.[40] In D.18.7.6.1 (Papinian, 27 *Quaestionum*) Papinian confesses that he formerly held that if a term which had been inserted into a contract for the sale of a slave at the seller's instance were intended as a penalty upon the slave, no action would lie against a buyer who ignored it unless the seller had a pecuniary interest in its performance, as if the breach would render him liable to a penalty which he had promised to another. However, the argument of Sabinus,

---

[37] *Observationes et Emendationes*, book V, ch. 15.
[38] *Lectiones et Epistulae quae ad Ius Civile Pertinent*, book II, ch. 12. See also book I, ch. 13.
[39] *Lectiones et Epistulae quae ad Ius Civile Pertinent*, book I, ch. 13; Cujas, *Observationes et Emendationes*, book XIV, ch. 36.
[40] *Lectiones et Epistulae quae ad Ius Civile Pertinent*, book I, ch. 13.

that the action should lie because a slave sold subject to a restriction of this kind may be assumed to have been sold at a lower price for that reason, now inclines him to hold the contrary. In D.18.7.7 (Papinian, 10 *Quaestionum*) Papinian states that if a slave be sold 'ne in Italia esset', and the buyer agree, but do not promise by stipulation, that he will pay a penal sum if the slave be brought to Italy, an action will hardly lie for the penalty unless the buyer's breach make the seller liable to pay a penalty which he has promised to another. For Cujas, Papinian evidently changed his opinion after he had composed the tenth, and before he had composed the twenty-seventh, book of his *Quaestiones*.[41] For Gentilis: 'Variaverit igitur auctor eorum Papinianus: an ideo dicendum est, compilatores etiamnum pugnantia loqui?' We are to take D.18.7.6.1 with its reason. A term of this kind will be enforceable if it appear that because of this restriction the slave was in fact sold at a lower price.[42]

It is an even more fundamental error to suggest that one provision of the compilation has abrogated another.[43] According to a passage from the *Sententiae* in D.23.2.38, a provincial governor may be betrothed to a woman of his province, though he may not marry her until he has laid down his office, and she may then refuse to marry him, upon returning the *arra sponsalicia*. C.5.2.1 provides that if the governor's betrothed, or her relatives, change their minds the *arra sponsalicia* need not be returned. Cujas held that this constitution abrogated D.23.2.38.[44] Gentilis adopted the first solution of Accursius. The *arra sponsalicia* need not be returned if the betrothal were repudiated while the *sponsus* was still governor of the province, but must be repaid if he had already laid down his office.[45]

Gentilis does not altogether neglect the 'secta Tribonianomastigum'. In his final dialogue he has something to say of Hotman, who was the most violent of the three, though the dreadful truth that he thought very little better of the classical jurists than of Tribonian did not become publicly known until his *Anti-Tribonianus* was published, after his death. Gentilis concentrated his attack, however, principally upon Cujas. This was a judicious choice, for the vices of the historical method might be better illustrated from the work of a writer who applied it to the interpretation of Justinian's compilations than from the writings of a Tribonianomastix who was more concerned to determine how much of the compilations

---

[41] *Observationes et Emendationes*, book II, ch. 36.
[42] *Lectiones et Epistulae quae ad Ius Civile Pertinent*, book II, ch. 12.
[43] *Lectiones et Epistulae quae ad Ius Civile Pertinent*, book I, ch. 13.
[44] *Observationes et Emendationes*, book IV, ch. 21.
[45] *Lectiones et Epistulae quae ad Ius Civile Pertinent*, book II, ch. 12. This was a point upon which Gentilis grew somewhat less rigid in his later years. In his *De Libris Iuris Civilis* he is prepared to admit that one part of the compilation may correct another. See, for example, ed. Hanoviae 1605, at 10–11.

must be given up as unsavable. For an author barely thirty years of age to attack the modern school with this vigour was perhaps bold, but is hardly sufficient in itself to explain Gentilis' bad reputation with posterity. In a remarkable passage of his *Respublica Iurisconsultorum* De Januario observes:

illud tamen miror quamquimaxime, eo furoris devenisse Albericum Gentilem, ut pro hisce ineptiis arma viriliter sumat, putetqe arroganter nimis, Accursium recte coniectare, sacra, quae in Pandectis memorantur, ab religione nostra nequaquam abhorrere, cum opus illud ad Iustiniani mentem, Christianique cultus formam sit concinnatum, utut, in veterum iurisconsultorum obsequium, horum nomina in fronte legum prae se ferat.[46]

The charge of arrogance is hardly very well supported by the particulars. Gentilis' offence is merely to take Justinian's intimation that

constitutionum vicem et has leges optinere censuimus quasi ex nobis promulgatas[47]

at face value. The charge of insanity is a little extreme, coming from anyone but a convinced Tribonianomastix, who would no doubt have argued that in what sense the references to *sacra* in the juristic texts were intended to be taken in the legislation of a Christian emperor was an idiotic question, since only an idiot would imagine that the compilers had considered the point at all.

Gentilis, however, had been guilty of a worse offence than supporting Accursius against the moderns. He had spoken of the new learning in a manner which could hardly fail to shock contemporaries, though not altogether without provocation from those ambitious souls who recommended the legist to make himself master of the whole circle of the sciences. The task of mastering the law was occupation enough. Since the province of the legist was dogmatic, not historical interpretation, he need not acquire that knowledge of antiquity which would have been necessary to qualify him to interpret the texts historically. It was not merely a knowledge of ancient history that might be dispensed with. He need not aspire to write a Latin of classical purity, and would do better not to attempt it, for the time which he would be obliged to spend polishing his language might be more profitably devoted to the study of the texts.[48] Greek might be neglected altogether. The old translation was admirably literal, and a perfectly satisfactory substitute for the original, save where the meaning of the original was disputable, and in that case the legist would be obliged to rely on the opinions of others unless he were a profound Grecian. If he aspired to become a profound legist he could

---

[46] Ed. Neapoli 1731, at 24–5.   [47] Const. *Tanta*, 20a.
[48] *De Iuris Interpretibus Dialogi Sex*, II (Paulus), at 45–83.

hardly spare the time to become a profound Grecian. If he possessed an elementary knowledge of Greek, he would be no better for it than if he had known no Greek at all. To be able to read the Greek commentators was not an advantage of much value.[49] Gentilis did not stop there. Since the study of languages exercised the memory rather than the reason, it had ordinarily no very good effect upon the higher intellectual faculties of those who spent much time upon it. Few scholars profoundly skilled in languages attained much distinction in any other branch of learning, and it might be doubted whether the modern practice of requiring schoolboys to learn Greek as well as Latin were good for their future development.[50] The older commentators were the superiors of the moderns certainly in method, and, Gentilis was prepared to argue, even in style. That they encumbered their commentaries with superfluous references was a criticism which came singularly ill from those who were given to appropriating the solutions of their predecessors and superiors without acknowledgment.[51] The superfluous and sophistical questions with which they were alleged to complicate the exposition of the texts were not superfluous, and not necessarily the worse for being sophistical. The study of the laws was not a preparation for practice in Plato's republic, or in Utopia, and the legist must come to court prepared to meet the specious as well as the substantial arguments which might be relied upon against his client. This, Gentilis asserted, had been the practice of the ancients, and in their manner of argument, and in the form of their exposition, the jurists of the *mos italicus* resembled the jurists of classical Rome very much more closely than did their detractors.[52]

When Pantagruel studied the law at Bourges, he was accustomed to say that the books of the law seemed to him a beautiful robe of gold, marvellously triumphant and precious, bordered with filth – for, said he, there are not in the world books so fine, so well adorned, so elegant, as are the texts of the Pandects, but their border, that is to say the gloss of Accurius, is so dirty, so infamous and stinking, that it is merely ordure and villainy.[53] This is not an opinion which he would have imbibed from Cujas, who held Accursius the superior of any other interpreter of the law, whether Latin or Greek.[54] Pantagruel's creator was a physician, not a

[49] *De Iuris Interpretibus Dialogi Sex*, III (Cato), at 86ff.   [50] *Ibid.*, at 104.
[51] See, for example, *De Iuris Interpretibus Dialogi Sex*, VI (Antipater) at 225: 'An legatum in extranei voluntatem transferri possit; magna est quaestio. Tu vide meos interpretes ad l. *capitatorias, de her. inst.* et ad l. *captatoriae, de leg.* 1, et si Cuiacius quidquam ex se dicit, mentiar ego in aeternum.' Cujas considers this question in *Observationes et Emendationes*, book II, ch. 2.
[52] *De Iuris Interpretibus Dialogi Sex*, IV (Trebatius) at 115.
[53] Rabelais, *Pantagruel*, ch. 5.
[54] *Observationes et Emendationes*, book III, ch. 11. He was even prepared to defend the style, if not of Accursius, at least of Bulgarus and Johannes: *Observationes et Emendationes*, book VII, ch. 36.

legist. It was one thing, however, to argue that the faults of the older commentators were those of the less happy times in which it had been their misfortune to live, and that they might be pardoned the barbarity of their style and their ignorance of good letters in consideration of their other merits. It was a very different matter to suggest that elegance of style and a knowledge of good letters were not accomplishments which any legist need trouble to cultivate, and that the commentaries upon the texts of Justinian which had been written in an age of Gothic barbarism were more truly classical than the works of contemporaries. This was to argue that ignorance was to be preferred to enlightenment, and it was perhaps inevitable that this apparent perversity should distract attention from the substantial point that Gentilis was making; a point upon which he was exceptionally clear-sighted.

Nearly two centuries after his time Bynkershoek, who was both a historian of Roman law (and a very learned one) and a judge, found it impossible to hold that whether a text were interpolated was a merely historical, not a legal question:

Quemadmodum vero ... ipsius iurisprudentiae interresset, nullum omnino dari emblema, ita et interest, dari quam paucissima. Quapropter non oportet nos esse liberales in his vel temere iactandis, vel anxie investigandis; quin nec ullum largiendum, si res aliter salva esse possit, et an possit, tentanda prius omnia, omnis movendus lapis.[55]

The legist should approach the question whether a passage of the Digest be interpolated in the same manner as he should approach the question whether it be impossible to reconcile it with another passage in the same compilation. If two provisions in the same legislative code might appear to the superficial eye to be inconsistent, the office of the expositor is to reconcile them, and if they may be so construed that they can stand together, this is to be deemed their true construction. Whether, as a matter of historical fact the difficulty may not be due to the oversight of the draftsman is a question upon which it is not necessary, or indeed proper, to speculate. Since both provisions are equally authoritative, effect must be given to both. Interpolation, we are to take it, is as much a defect as bad draftsmanship. It would be better for the science of jurisprudence if Justinian's compilations contained no interpolations. Since it cannot be denied that some passages are interpolated, it is better to hold that the compilations contain as few interpolations as may be, and the office of the expositor of a text is to discover reasons to hold it genuine.

The English reader may be reminded of the controversy between

---

[55] *Observationum Iuris Romani libri Quattuor, Quattuor prioribus additi* (ed. Lugdini Batavorum, 1732), Praefatio ad Lectorem.

Challis and Maitland upon the question whether a remainder might be limited after a conditional fee in the reign of Henry III. Maitland had been at pains to stress that he was not suggesting for a moment that a remainder limited after a conditional fee might be good in the reign of Victoria. Challis, while admitting that such remainders appeared in thirteenth-century settlements, was reluctant to hold this evidence of anything save the ignorance of the draftsmen, or, to put it at its highest, of the uncertainty of the law, which encouraged conveyancers to experiment with speculative limitations.[56] We should not admit that a limitation which would be clearly invalid at this day would have been supported six centuries ago if the evidence can be made to bear any other interpretation, for to do so would be to throw doubt upon the claim of the modern rule to be deemed a rule of the common law. Similarly for Bynkershoek, to admit that a doctrine to be found in the Digest was not classical would be to give more countenance than was desirable to conclusions which were not 'practically sound'. That the law is one study and the history of the law another is not a position which it is easy to maintain consistently, if the law is founded upon ancient texts. That Gentilis was capable of doing so might be held a singular merit, though it was one which gained him little esteem in his own day.

[56] *Challis's Law of Real Property* (3rd edn by Charles Sweet, London, 1911), appendix II.

8   *Ius gentium* in the practice of the Court of Admiralty around 1600

Alain Wijffels

Traditionally, the reputation of the early modern English Civil lawyers has to a large extent been based on their supposed expertise in international law. At an academic level, writings by Gentili, Zouch and others are presented as pre- and post-Grotian 'classics'. Much in the same way as on the European continent, jurists trained in *ius civile* at law faculties were usually called upon for diplomatic missions. Their role, however, was mostly a subordinate one. In the new literary genre on ambassadors and embassies which flourished from the last two decades of the sixteenth century onwards, the 'perfect ambassador' was deemed to be well-versed in history, but much less in law. Apart from diplomatic service, the practice of the High Court of Admiralty, a preserve for members of Doctors' Commons, provided the Civil lawyers with the aura of a specialism in international law. Litigation at the Court of Admiralty, fostered by privateering or more peaceful foreign trade, reflected the world-wide commercial interests of late Elizabethan England and, consequently, the need to settle international disputes according to universally accepted legal standards among European nations. This need was acknowledged at the paramount level of government, as evidenced in a notorious (and often-quoted) speech by James I in 1610:

It is true, that I doe greatly esteeme the Civill Law, the profession thereof serving more for generall learning, and being most necessary for matters of Treatie with all forreine Nations. And I thinke that if it should be taken away, it would make an entrie to Barbarisme in this Kingdome, and would blemish the honour of England: For it is in a manner Lex Gentium, and maintaineth Intercourse with all forreine Nations: but I only allow it to have course here according to those limits of Jurisdiction, which the Common law it selfe doth allow it.[1]

---

[1] Quoted after *The Kings Maiesties Speach To the Lords and Commons of this present Parliament at Whitehall, on Wednesday the xxj. of March. Anno Dom. 1609.* Imprinted at London by Robert Barker, Printer to the Kings most Excellent Maiestie (copy: Cambridge UL Syn. 7.60.63); also in: *The Workes of the Most High and Mightie prince, Iames By the Grace of God, King of Great Britaine, France and Ireland, Defender of the Faith, &c.* Published by IAMES, Bishop of Winton, and Deane of his Maiesties Chappel Royall. London, Printed by Robert Barker and Iohn Bill, 1616, 532.

The assimilation of Civil law and *ius gentium* is of course not unequivocal. It raises the question of the foundation of the Civil law's authority in England, and hereby the controversial problem whether the Civil law was to be considered as part of the *lex terrae* or not. The King's speech also illustrates another ambiguity regarding the concept of *ius gentium*. The reference to the law of treaties suggests something similar to the modern notion of the law of nations as inter-state law, whereas the latter part of the quotation is characteristic of a far less positivistic era, when the national municipal laws of the sovereign states had not yet acquired a monopoly of the authoritative legal sources regulating the relations between private persons.

The theoretical and political aspects of these controversies have often been discussed.[2] In what follows, which implicitly relies much on Peter Stein's fundamental publications on the 'character and influence of the Civil law' both in England and in the rest of the world, I shall try to express the English Civil lawyers' concept of *ius gentium* from a more pedestrian, and at the same time very different, perspective. Drawing on Julius Caesar's notes as Admiralty judge (c. 1582–1606),[3] the following paragraphs will show how the Civil law practitioners at the High Court of Admiralty referred to *ius gentium* in their pleadings and memoranda.[4]

In general, technical references to the learned law (*allegationes*) reflect the method followed by civilian practitioners throughout European courts at the time. Both Roman Civil law and Roman Canon law are extensively quoted.[5] Besides the fundamental texts (the *corpora iuris*), a wide range of doctrinal authorities are constantly being referred to. The

[2] On various uses of the terms *ius gentium* and *ius naturale* in the English context, see D. R. Coquillette, *The Civilian Writers of Doctors' Commons, London. Three Centuries of Juristic Innovation in Comparative, Commercial and International Law*, Comparative Studies in Continental and Anglo-American Legal History 3 (Berlin, 1988), 32–7.

[3] On Julius Caesar as Admiralty judge: L. M. Hill, *Bench and Bureaucracy. The Public Career of Sir Julius Caesar, 1580–1636* (Cambridge, 1988), chapter 2.

[4] The notes are mainly concentrated in BL MSS Lansdowne 129, 130, 131 and 135. In many cases, the notes are not very elaborate, and sometimes they simply consist of a few references to authorities. In 1992–7, a research project sponsored by the Netherlands Scientific Organisation (NWO) will try to establish a data-base combining the Caesar Papers at the British Library (both the notes which are referred to in the present contribution and various other documents collected or transcribed by Caesar) and the records of the court (PRO, HCA).

[5] Throughout the sixteenth century, and well after the Counter-Reformation, English Civil lawyers kept abreast of current developments in the Roman Canon law. This attitude was not inspired by religious motives, but by the need to keep pace with changes in legal methods affecting the whole of the *ius commune* tradition. For the English ecclesiastical courts a convincing reassessment of the Civil lawyers' approach is offered by R. H. Helmholz, *Roman Canon Law in Reformation England* (Cambridge, 1990). Since Canon law also influenced to a considerable degree the general principles and the law of procedure, it is not surprising that a similar observation can be made in the practice of the Admiralty Court, even for the early Stuart period.

bulk of the latter belong to the *mos italicus* tradition and some monographical works (in particular, treatises) heralded the early *usus modernus*, while legal humanistic scholarship is virtually ignored. On the whole, these tendencies confirm the findings of recent research into the academic legal library holdings in England during the last quarter of the sixteenth century. The predominance of *mos italicus* authorities is also a clear indication that the characteristic method of that school still governed the forensic argumentations of the late Elizabethan and early Stuart Civil lawyers. Their arguments, therefore, very much resemble those of their contemporary continental counterparts. Predictably, a large proportion of the references are concerned with procedural questions, and more in particular with the law of evidence. General principles, or specific rules drawn from any area of the law, on which a general applicability is then conferred, play a greater role than any form of strict systematisation of the law in which only the rules belonging specifically to a particular field are applicable. In the same vein, references to rules by analogy are common practice. On the other hand, there are also clear signs that the more systematic approach of the (early) *usus modernus* was under way. A major impediment, however, was the absence of a specialised legal literature on international maritime law. Privateering and prize-law, probably the most important issues the Admiralty Court had to deal with, were a subject which no legal work treated systematically. Nevertheless, the pleadings show that the English practitioners endeavoured to incorporate in their arguments the more specialised legal publications offered on the bookmarket. These included works in the *ius commune* tradition, for example the popular collection on maritime law edited by B. Straccha, but also foreign municipal law, for instance, de La Popelinière's compilation *L'Admiral de France*. In a more traditional way, yet expressing the tendency to restrict the authorities *ratione materiae*, many arguments concentrate their quotations around specific titles of the Corpus Iuris Civilis, notably (for example on questions of liability of factors or their principals) C.4.25, D.14.1 and D.14.3, and the corresponding commentaries. For (mostly, incidental) questions on the law of war, Civil lawyers were keen to quote the late sixteenth-century treatises by Ayala, Bellus and a few others.[6] In short, the authorities referred to in the pleadings reflect the transition from *mos italicus* literature and method to *usus modernus*.

This transitory character implies that, although many arguments ignore

---

[6] See, for example, BL MS Lansdowne 135, fol. 98^r (Dr Hammond): 'and other that have written particuler treatises de bello, or de re militari, as Martinus Laudensis, Joan. de Lignano, Claudius Cotereus, Petrinus Bellus, Balthasar ab Ayala, Ferdinandus Vasquius lib. quest. illustrium, the places whereof wanting my bookes I can not more particularly recite'.

any systematisation *ratione materiae*, questions of international law were often treated with a certain degree of concern for its specific nature. However, international law as such was not yet fully perceived as a particular discipline, and its method was therefore still very much integrated in the general, developing, *ius commune* approach. In that sense, one could say (paraphrasing James I) that international law was 'in a manner (part of) *ius commune*'. In this context, it is not surprising that references to international law did not require any specific justification. The paucity of explicit mentions of *ius gentium* in the Admiralty pleadings somehow reflects the lawyers' view that it was simply a component of the European *ius commune* tradition. On the other hand, it may have been more irksome to warrant the application of Civil law by referring to *ius commune* as such, rather than to the *lex gentium*. In practice, however, references to *ius commune* authorities only exceptionally presented a difficulty and did not need any particular legitimation.[7] A negative example of such a controversy appears briefly in a case where, shortly after the Anglo-Spanish peace treaty of 1604, Portuguese merchants claimed that their ship, which had been captured off Lisbon by a man-of-war commanded by a Dutchman to whom Dutch commissions had been granted, could not be held to be a lawful prize when it was brought into neutral English territorial waters and seized by the English authorities. The controversial argument was that under those circumstances the fiction of *ius postliminii* might be applicable in favour of the Portuguese.[8] One of the counsel for the Dutch captain, Dr Trevor, argued

quod l. postliminii et l. postliminium non extenditur ad nos, sed ad Romanos et eos qui erant sub iure eiusdem magistratus.[9]

From a Civil lawyer, the argument may seem surprising, all the more so since the principle in question (the fiction of *ius postliminii*) was said to have been 'naturali aequitate introductum' (D.49.15.19 *pr.*). Perhaps Julius Caesar's note is too brief to allow a proper reconstruction of

[7] References to 'ius commune', 'imperial law', 'pontifical law' appear occasionally in the pleadings. One draft contains different quotations which might be used for solving the question: 'Touching an Englishmans ship taken by a man of Newhaven being enimy and afterwards recovered by a Frenchman a friend, and brought into England; howe to bee disposed, 1591'. The quotations appear under the headings: 'Out of the ordonnances of France'; 'Out of the civill lawe'; 'Out of history' (Lansdowne 131, fol. 4ᵛ). The historical examples are taken from Livy, and the reference to civil law is a fine specimen of an argument by analogy: D.49.15.6.
[8] On this case, a more elaborate reconstruction of the different arguments is discussed in: *Alberico Gentili and Thomas Crompton. An Encounter between an Academic Jurist and a Legal Practitioner*, Studia Forensia Historica 1 (Leiden, 1992). Eventually, the argument was dropped when Alberico Gentili appeared in the proceedings as counsel for the Portuguese.
[9] BL MS Lansdowne 131, fol. 276ᵛ. The references are to D.49.15.5 and D.49.15.19.

Trevor's reasoning. Did the latter imply that in his time positive rules from Justinian's compilations applied only to those nations which had been fully incorporated in the Roman empire and subjected to Roman law, but that this had not been the case with England? This was, indeed, a serious matter of dispute among scholars,[10] but it is hard to understand why a Civil lawyer who himself constantly referred in his pleadings to the various sources of *ius commune* would have made such an assertion. Alternatively, for reasons which do not appear in Caesar's notes, Trevor may have restricted the argument to some specific rules, in this case those governing the *ius postliminii*.

When a more elaborate approach was required, as in the 'note' of which a transcript is printed hereafter in the appendix, the theoretical foundation of the applicability of Roman law is better documented.[11] Although the note's main concern is the extension of writs of prohibition, i.e. a jurisdictional conflict, the authors included a full paragraph on substantive law, perhaps because the application of a different legal system was, in their view, a strong argument in support of a specialised jurisdiction. The arguments expressed in favour of the application of Civil law in maritime causes are threefold. First, it is founded on the very authority of the Kings of England. Further, and to some degree justifying that royal policy, it is made necessary by the 'reception' of Roman law 'throughout all nations about us', which constitutes in that sense a form of *ius gentium*. Finally, the authors proclaim the intrinsic value of the Roman law for dealing with maritime cases, both international and domestic. In addition, the note contains an historical argument in its references to provincial jurisdictions in the Roman Empire and to the incorporation of Rhodian maritime laws. The whole argumentation remains, perhaps for purely opportunistic reasons, very specific regarding the applicability of Roman law in England, for its proper field is strictly confined to maritime law. Ironically, the note itself betrays that Civil lawyers were all too prone to extend the authority of *ius commune* sources well beyond the area of maritime disputes, for the Civil law provides in the same text ammunition for highly controversial considerations of the King's prerogative powers.

When counsel refer to *ius gentium* in their pleadings, the expression is in most cases borrowed from their *ius commune* source. The references fall into two broad categories which correspond to the equivocal meaning of

---

[10] A. Duck, *De Usu et Authoritate Juris Civilis Romanorum, in Dominiis Principum Christianorum, Libri Duo* (London, 1653), book II, chapter 8, first part, no. 11.

[11] The note is discussed by Hill, *Bench and Bureaucracy*, 47–52. Hill's attribution of the authorship of the note to Julius Caesar is, considering the heading of the memorandum (the whole text is written in Caesar's hand), questionable.

the term. In the first place, it is used in the sense of Gaius' definition, i.e. a set of legal rules which, in principle, is observed by all men and applied in all nations. More particularly, this is apparently the meaning of *ius gentium* when, in prize-cases, the acquisition of spoils is justified. The principal authorities are the parallel texts D.41.2.1 *pr.* (s.v. 'item bello capta') and J.Inst. 2.1.17, the first of which was discussed at great length in *mos italicus* commentaries.[12] The mere reference to *ius gentium* in the Corpus Iuris left, however, many practical questions unanswered. Prize-law litigation was precisely fostered by the uncertainty of rules applicable to privateering. When no compromise could be found between the conflicting economic interests, Civil lawyers had a field day quoting *ius commune* authorities. Customary law is admittedly not altogether ignored, but it appears to play only a modest part in the Admiralty lawyers' arguments. Moreover, the precise purport of a maritime customary rule could be challenged and was often difficult to establish.[13] When it became necessary to formulate a substantive rule of *ius gentium*, the Civil lawyers effectively fell back on *ius commune*. For the frequently occurring questions of acquisition, principles based on *ius civile* (in the strict sense) could provide the thread of their argumentation. For example, when it was stated that captors acquired their spoils by virtue of *ius gentium*, the question was often raised whether the goods had been captured as *res derelictae*, *res nullius*, or as the enemy's property (in which case it could be relevant to examine the validity of the enemy's title to the goods).[14] The

---

[12] In Caesar's notes, the best example of references to *ius gentium* as the legal foundation for the acquisition of goods taken at war appears not in an English civilian's pleading, but in a transcript of a legal opinion delivered in 1593 by the Faculty of Tübingen (Lansdowne 129, fols. 112ᵛ–131ʳ). An edition of this *consilium*, which will not be discussed here, is forthcoming.

[13] For example, in *Bromley* c. *Oliver and Gold* (Lansdowne, 130, fols. 92ᵛ ff.), the plaintiff produced several witnesses to testify 'that the common use among marchants is, that if a factor shall first consigne goods to any cert. person, hee may not afterwards alter his consignation to an other'. The counsel for the defendants objected 'that the deponents touch. the custome prove nothing for that they mention not of any such cause ever in question of theire knowledge' and produced a new witness, who '[deposed] of a contrary custome: unles there were a speciall commission for the buyeng of the goods consigned in particular; for then the factor cannot alter his first consignation' (fol. 93ᵛ).

[14] A *ius commune* argumentation could also be buttressed by other authorities, as in a more complex opinion delivered by Dr Hammond in *Dominus Admirallus* c. *Thomas Gorge militem* (Lansdowne 135, fols. 95ʳ–103ʳ). The facts leading to the case are only alluded to in Caesar's notes. Possibly, Sir Thomas Gorge, who held Hurst Castle (commanding the entrance of the Solent), claimed goods from a Spanish ship. The goods may have been cast away during a storm, for the corresponding texts of the Corpus Iuris are quoted. The claim gave rise to a dispute regarding the jurisdiction of, respectively, the Lord Admiral and Sir Thomas. In his opinion, structured as an extensive refutation of the latter's claims, Dr Hammond addressed various questions which would now qualify as problems of public and international law. He first considers the extension of the powers of someone to whom the King has granted a *castrum*, a complex topic which was familiar to civilian

Ius gentium in the Court of Admiralty 125

way to acquire possession was also often discussed by the standards of *ius commune*,[15] but occasionally a lawyer could take advantage of the distinction between *ius civile* and *ius gentium*, as in the following example:[16]

lawyers: see G. Vallone, *Iurisdictio domini, Introduzione a Matteo d'Afflitto ed alla cultura giuridica meridionale tra Quattro e Cinquecento*, Collana di Studi storici e Giuridici 1 (Lecce, 1985). The conclusion is that 'for so much as that castle is appointed for the safety of the countrie, it may bee that the capten hath in that respect marshall authoritie. But it followeth neither hereof nor of the wordes aforesaide [*namely of the letters patent*], that hee may lay handes uppon straungers' goods uppon the streame, or exercise any part of an Admirals authority' (fol. 96ᵛ–97ʳ). In a second paragraph, he discusses whether, at the time, there was a state of war between England and Spain. Subsequently, he deals with the acquisition of the property, disproving (*inter alia*) the thesis 'that hee [i.e. Sir Thomas Gorge] tooke [the goods] iuregentium, as goods held pro derelictis' (fol. 95ᵛ; for the arguments of Hammond's opponent, Dr Goldingham, see fol. 95ʳᵛ). The argumentation follows mainly *ius commune* authorities (including the opinions of the Roman jurists reported in the Digest), but also refers to *ius proprium* sources: 'they are taken to bee of other nature then those which as left *pro derelicto*; and are by the wisdome of our lawe assigned to certaine persons to keape to th'use of th'owner, if hee come within his time. Which it is like wee received from the costume of Normandie. For the booke of those customes hath one proper title, *De varech et choses gaynes*, where th'author of the commentary written thereuppon, expounding the word *choses gaynes* writeth thus, *ne sont pas proprement res habitae pro derelicto, mais delaissées à possider par celuy à qui elles appartiennent, veluti animalia aberrantia*. Which is th'example which Paulus useth before recited [cf. D.41.2.3.13]. And Bracton our countreman in his title *de rerum divisione*, cap. 12, maketh a difference betwene *res habitae pro derelicto*, and those *quae pro waynio habentur*, using th'example of cattle strayed whereto no owner maketh claime, adding this, *et que olim fuerunt inventoris de iure naturali, iam efficiuntur principis de iure gentium*' (fols. 101ᵛ–102ʳ). Bracton's authority allows Hammond to conclude that since 'by our lawe ... wayved goods ... are given to the L. Admirall by her Majestie ..., it must of necessity followe, that my L. Admirall hath a cleere and a direct right to them, to keape them for th'owner if they bee demanded in time, or otherwise to enjoy to his owne use' (fol. 102ᵛ).

[15] For example, in *Eyrning* c. *Nokes* (Lansdowne 131, fols. 35ff.), it was disputed which of two ships had taken the decisive action to capture a prize. Large interests were at stake, and several lawyers appeared for both parties. They all argued about which rules governing the acquisition of goods were applicable. Dr Styward, for instance, held that 'que acquiruntur iure gentium, acquiruntur non aliter quam adprehensione vel occupatione possessoris, Jason in rubr. D. de acquir. possessio. num. 7 et 8 et 2 et 3. Alberic. in l. naturalem, D. de acquir. possessio., § illud quesitum, etiamsi fera sit ità vulnerata, quod certum sit ex vulnere non posse evadere, tamen nostrum non fit, antequam capiatur. Et Alberic. in l. in laqueum, D. de acquir. rer. domin. num. 2, potest quis acquirere dominium agri illaqueati per conspectum oculorum. Petr. Bel. par. 4, cap. 8, num. 15 et 16, rem que neque oculis conspicitur, neque corpore comprehenditur, possumus animo acquirere, num. 17 et 18' (fol. 38ʳᵛ, several articles omitted).

[16] From *Pots* c. *Newton* (Lansdowne 130, fols. 53ᵛ, 78ᵛ–81ʳ, 91ᵛ–92ʳ), involving again the captains of two ships who contested each other's part in the capture of a prize. Dr Styward appeared for Newton and quoted several authorities on which he also relied in the case cited in the previous note. The quotation in the text, Dr Crompton's argumentation for Pots, is preceded by a summary of an argument developed by Dr Dun, also appearing for the plaintiff. It begins: 'l. 1 de acquir. possessio. D. in princip. Instit. de rer. divisio., § item illa que ex hostibus, que ex hostibus capiuntur, ex iure gentium nostra fiunt. In acquisitione dominii ex iure gentium, is primo acquirit dominium, qui prius nanciscitur possessionem, id est apprehensionem naturalem, d. l. 1, D. de acquir. possessio., § Item bello capta' (several paragraphs omitted).

In acquisitione ex iure gentium, consideratio est solummodo naturalis apprehensio, Jason in rubricam de acquir. possessio D., num. 7, 8 et 9. Dominium ex iure gentium nunquam causatur sine apprehensione sive occupatione possessoris, et ubi aliter sine traditione acquiritur, id fit ex iure civile, non ex iure gentium. Et iure gentium statim ex possessione acquiritur dominium, ita ut nihil sit temporis medium inter possessionem et dominium. Jo. Francisc. Ripa in d. l. 1, D. de acquir. possessio. num. 63 et 64, ad hoc ut transferatur possessio per aspectum, opus est ut possessor tradat vacuam possessionem: sed adversario possidente non acquirit possessionem, nisi primo adversarius eiectus sit. Mynsing. in § possideri, Instit. de interdictis, ver. animo solo, opus est corporali apprehensione ad acquirendam possessionem.[17]

Although the link with an act of war may suggest some association with the law of nations in its modern sense, the different arguments clearly indicate that the questions regarding the law of war and the acquisition of private property were considered separately, even when they appear in the same context.[18] Besides, references to *ius gentium* as a common law of mankind governing private acts were also borrowed from the *ius commune* by the English Civil lawyers outside the jurisdiction of the Court of Admiralty.[19]

In the second type of reference to *ius gentium*, the expression approaches more closely the modern concept of public international law. Again, the civilian practitioners did not work out the concept on their own, but borrowed it from traditional *ius commune* literature. In Caesar's Admiralty notes, the English Civil lawyers seem mostly to rely on the authority of *ius gentium* when they discuss the freedom of international

[17] *D. Crumpton ex parte Pots*, Lansdowne 130, fol. 80^{rv}. It was alleged that the crew of the prize had meant to surrender to the captain of the other ship, but not to Pots: 'That Pots with 3 Flemings entered not into the prize till long after that shee had yealded to the Julian' [i.e. the other man-of-war], and 'that Pots should not have come on bourd them, but that they took him to bee capt. of the Julian' (fol. 79^{rv}).

[18] For example in a short memorandum, 'Bona amicorum onerata in navi hostium capta in bello una cum navi fiunt capientium' (Lansdowne 131, fols. 188^{r}–189^{r}): 'Ex iure gentium introducta bella et commercium, eque igitur sunt consideranda iura belli et iura commercii, cum ex eodem iure procedant, l. ex hoc iure, D. de iustit. et iure, glos. et DD. ibi in ver. bella et commercium. Ea, que ex hostibus capimus, iure gentium statim nostra fiunt, § item ea que ex hostibus, Instit. de rer. divis. et acquir. earum dominio, et l. naturalem, in fine, D. de acquir. rerum dominio, glos. et DD. ibi' (fol. 188^{r}).

[19] For example, in *Henry Newton* c. *Georges Brooke*, a testamentary cause (Lansdowne 130, fols. 136^{v}ff.): 'Probatio iuris gentium non restringitur ad duos testes in testamento, Vasquius lib. 2, de testament, § 13, num. 23, requisito, 6, idem § 11, num. 68, Zuntius in responso pro uxore, num. 477. Quando probatio est iurisgentium, potest quomodocumque suppleri, Corneus in l. hac consultissima, C. de testament., § ex imperfecto, num. 1, et sequent., Natta ibid., num. 151, Wesembec. consil. 98, num, 65, Zuntius in responso pro uxore, num. 66, Linwood in cap. statutum, ver. probatis, de testibus' (Dr Dun and Dr Hove for the defendant); countered by Dr Styward: 'Probatio iurisgentium est que fit per duos testes, glos. in ver. probationibus, l. Lucius, D. de milit. testam., l. 15, C. de milit. testam., ver. sub ipso tempore, Angelus in § plane, Instit. de milit. testam., Alexand. in l. militis, C. de testam. milit. num. 1, 2, 3' (fols. 137^{r}–138^{v}, several articles omitted).

trade. Both the principle of free trade and the right of the prince to restrict foreign trade under certain circumstances, viz. when the security of the realm is under threat, are founded on *ius gentium*. The two sides are highlighted in an opinion written in support of the principle: 'Tempore belli nullæ merces ad hostes deferri debent.'[20] Because of the general purport of the opinion, the emphasis is not on the foundation of free trade, but rather on its restrictions:

Commercia non sunt simpliciter libera, quia ex causa prohiberi possint. Quanquam homines liberi nascantur, commerciaque libera esse debeant, attamen secus, si a Principe prohibeantur, M. Mantua in l. comparandi, C. que res vendi non possunt.
Commercia sunt de iure gentium libera, nec princeps ipse nisi ex magna causa potest derogare, Laur. Silva. consil. 35, num. 14.
Principes possunt prohibere transeuntes per viam publicam, item navigantes per publicum flumen; in fluminibus publicis etiam inhibere possunt piscationes; item et vectigalia navigantibus per flumina publica, ac transeuntibus per vias publicas necnon pro piscationibus et venationibus imponere possunt, atque huiusmodi prohibitiones iure et usu gentium universali probantur, M. Anto. Peregrinus de iure fisci lib. 1, cap. num. 21.[21]

The ultimate justification for the priority of the King's prohibition of foreign trade is the national interest.[22] However, the defence of the realm is seen to be an application of a general and more fundamental principle of natural law and *ius gentium*, which in this context tends to lose again its connotation of inter-state law:

Vim et iniuriam propulsare iuris naturalis et gentium est. Est hec non scripta sed nata lex, quam non didicimus, accepimus, legimus, verum ex natura ipsa arripuimus, hansimus, expressimus, ad quam non docti sed facti, [non] instituti, sed imbuti sumus, et si vita nostra in aliquas insidias, si in vim, in tela aut latronum aut inimicorum incidisset, omnis honesta ratio esset expediende salutis, Cicero pro Milone. Bellum pro tuitione rerum suarum est licitum iure naturali, gentium et divino, Jason in l. ex hoc iure, D. de instit. et iure, num. 39. Propulsare vim atque iniuriam de iure nature atque gentium est, Decius in l. ut vim, D. de iustit. et iure.[23]

---

[20] Lansdowne, 130, fols. 161^r–165^r. The purpose of the opinion is not clear. Caesar's notes begin with various allegations of law on the question, followed by a more elaborate opinion attributed to Dr Crompton (fols. 161^v–164^v); the text ends with a brief concurring opinion from Dr Dun. Similar arguments can be found later in the same volume, under the heading: 'An ulla bona tempore belli ad hostes deferri possunt?' (fols. 180^{r}f–181^r). There are no references to facts or to any particular proceedings.

[21] Lansdowne 130, fol. 162^r.

[22] 'Salus reip. suprema lex esto, L. 12 tabularum. Neque ulla potest esse sanctior aut reip. magis salutaris quam ipsa salus populi, cuius tanta vis est, ut que natura erant illicita, commutentur eo respectu fiantque contraria' (fol. 164^v).

[23] Fol. 161^v.

As a result, and in spite of the conventional references to *ius gentium*, the decisive source for restricting foreign trade became the will of the sovereign.[24] Not surprisingly, even the principle of free trade was sometimes founded primarily on the national interest, and thus on royal legislation.[25] Similarly, the task of fighting piracy is presented as a rule imposed by *ius gentium*, but in practice entrusted to the prince.[26]

Neither these various principles of *ius gentium* nor their applications by Civil lawyers at the Court of Admiralty in London were innovative. The counsel still relied mainly on the late mediaeval *mos italicus* and the early modern legal literature which showed a large degree of continuity with that tradition. These authorities, partly of ancient, partly of mediaeval origin, did not reflect the new European international order which emerged during the early modern period. Yet, the emphasis on the constitutive role of the territorial sovereign in regulating international relations does to some extent express the changing approach in legal scholarship.

In the absence of a uniform, clearly defined, concept of the law of nations, one should not expect that practitioners would have used the term *ius gentium* differently from its various meanings in the extensive library of *ius commune*. In the same way as the burgeoning literature on specific topics of international law (in particular, the law of war, the law of embassies, the law of the sea) incorporated much traditional *ius commune* learning, the late Elizabethan civilian practitioners contributed to adapting late mediaeval doctrines to early modern developments. In addition to the few explicit references to *ius gentium* that were discussed in the

---

[24] A further example will be found in *J. Requeti, N. Dornel (= du Renel), Ch. Dornel etc.* c. *Capt. Duffield, the Crown intervening* (Lansdowne 130, fols. 239^{v}ff.). In this case, the question was whether trade with a city in Normandy which had rebelled against the King of France during the religious wars was prohibited or not. Dr Crompton argued for the plaintiffs that 'commerce is lawefull by the generall lawe of nations, and unlesse the K. doe especially prohibite the same by edict, the same is still lawefull, and the rather betwene them, by reason of a convention betwene them to the same purpose' (fol. 245^v). See also Lansdowne 132, fol. 82^r (author unknown).

[25] In *Le Porte* c. *Grenfield, Hals*, Dr Steward quoted first a statute of Edward III: '9 E. 3, cap. 1, a libertie of traffick graunted to all nations and to all places, saving th'enimy. Declarat. an 1589 after the taking of certeine Easterlings goods. Saluti regni non convenire, ut hostes frumento armari sinamus, nulla neutralitatis facienda excusatione; quod de iure gentium obtinet, ut constat an. 1545, Galli et Angli hostes, Carolus 5. confederatus ... (Lansdowne, 131, fol. 70^r).

[26] Lansdowne 131, fols. 253^{r}ff. ('Whether piracies were pardoned by the King's generall pardon at the time of his most happy coronation?'; possibly a note by Caesar himself, cf. fol. 253^r): 'Iure gentium omnes principes obligantur ad debellandos piratas tanquam hostes publicos et totius Christianitatis, authent. navigia, C. de furtis, nam sunt eiusmodi latrones et pirate diffidati omni iure, et impune occidi ex iure gentium, ubicumque reperiuntur, ut ibi et alibi DD.' (fol. 253^v).

previous pages, their main arguments effectively dealt with a host of questions which would later be recognised as proper topics of international law: the law of reprisals (often including, in connexion herewith, the determination of denizenship), prize-law, the law of war. The cases always produced particular questions and in order to provide answers and arguments the practitioners necessarily relied on *ius commune*, combining both rules which were more or less specifically applicable and general principles of 'topical' principles borrowed from other areas.[27] It was precisely the versatility of the *mos italicus* and early *usus modernus* methods which made it possible to address these questions of international law *avant la lettre*, i.e. before the modern concept of the law of nations had been established.

[27] The term 'topical' here refers to the literary genre of *loci* or (in Greek) *topoi*.

Appendix: BL Lansdowne 129, fols. 80ʳ–82ᵛ[1]

[80ʳ]
A briefe note of certaine reasons giving occasion to judge that the King's Bench prohibitions and other proceadings against the Admiralty should bee voyde; delivered mee by Duck Lambe etc. 26. febr. 1591.

First it appeareth not that there hath bene at any time till of late yeres any prohibitions or other such like proces against th'Admiralty, but onely against Curiam Christianitatis, beecause as it seemeth the Court of Admiralty being alwaies the King's Court as well as anie other Court of the Land, was not to bee restrained or enlarged but as it pleased the Princes to order it in th'Admiral's commissions. Whereas the Court Christian (that is to say the spirituall Court) was till H. 8. alwaies a forreine Court, and therefor to bee withstood by the King's prohibitions: least the crowne's inheritance by forreine commissions might otherwise in time bee wholy taken away.

And whereas the statutes of 13. and 15. R. 2. and 2. H. 4.[2] doe forbid th'Admirall to meddle with any thing done within the bodies of counties, or within the realme, and suffereth him to meddle with things done uppon the sea (saving for meames[3] and deaths of men happening uppon greate rivers beneath the first bridges to the sea) the power of the prince is not therein denied or restrained, as that shee shall graunt no further commission, but onely that th'Admirall is forbidden to meddle, as meerely Admirall, further then with things done uppon the sea; and therefor the power and right of the Prince must bee considered. For the Prince being alwaies seized without impeachement of any lawe, in the right of her imperiall crowne of this realme, of all jurisdiction as well by sea as by land, and devinding the same, as by nature they are separated, into 2. severall goverments, hath ordeined the magistracy of the bodie of the land

---
[1] Written in Julius Caesar's hand. Additions in the manuscript are indicated by the angle brackets.
[2] 13 Rich. II c. 5, 15 Rich. II c. 3, 2 Hen. IV c. 11.
[3] Read: 'mayhem' (compare 15 Rich. II c. 3, in: *The Statutes of the Realm*, vol. II (London 1816, reprint 1963), 78–9; and in: Sir Travers Twiss (ed.), *The Black Book of the Admiralty, with an Appendix* (4 vols., London, 1871–6), vol. 1, 412–3).

to be exercised by severall officers, as the King's Bench for Plees touching the crowne, the Common Place for ordinary actions betwixt private persons, the Chauncery for causes of equitie, th'Exchequeur [80ᵛ] for rent, issues, fines and forfeitures accrewing to the prince, with other peculiar Courts of like nature to theise. And the magistracy of the sea, to bee exercised by the L. Admirall onely, called the great Admirall of England, in respect there is included in his onely office all th'offices abovesaid with charge also of military affaires, as doth appear in the severall clauses of his letters patents.

As it is written in the civill lawes of the Romane Emperors, that unto the president of any place did continually belong all offices whatsoever, which were executed in the citie of Rome by severall magistrats, as[4] at this day the same seemes to bee resembled in the provinces of Ireland and Wales, and the counties Palentine, and so in like manner in the province of the sea. The wordes in the civill lawe bee theise, Cum plenissimam iurisdictionem proconsul habet, omnium partes, qui Rome sunt, vel quasi magistratus, vel extra ordinem ius dicunt, ad ipsum pertinent, et ideo maius imperium in ea provincia omnibus post principem habet. And againe, omnia enim provincialia desideria, que Rome varios iudices habent ad officium praesidum pertinet, l. 7. et 8. < D. > de offic. Proconsulis[5] et l. 10. et 11. D. de offic. praesidis.[6]

And < according to > this division of[7] magistraces, the Princes of this realme have likewise devided the maner of goverment with 2. soundry lawes, th'one the common lawe of this land,[8] appropriate to our nation onely, as best fitting those causes that happen within bodies of counties, where the eyes of iurors may give them intelligence to enquire and give veredict of truth, in fact of all controversies; th'other is the civill lawes imperiall for the sea, which for that by long continuance in the most florishing commonwealth of Rome, they have bene many ages since, the most perfect and the most equal [81ʳ] lawes of the world, are generally received throughout all nations about us. And therefor are not onely most fittest for our traffick and other dealings with straungers, but also (for such causes as concerne the sea) are most necessary to bee practised amongst ourselves. And in this division of lawes they seeme to followe th'example of the Romane Emperors, who in deciding seacauses referred suters to the Rhodian lawes in all things, wherein theire owne lawes imperiall did not specially abrogate the same, l. deprecatio, D. ad l. Rhodiam de iactu.[9] The Honorable seagouverment of which Rhodian

---

[4] Crossed out: 'by'.   [5] D.1.16.7–8.
[6] D.1.18.10–11 (text quoted from the latter *lex*).
[7] Crossed out: 'magistrats'.   [8] Crossed out: 'the other'.   [9] D.14.2.9.

lawes (as Tullie saith) was in his time famous, Cicero pro lege Manilia.[10] And that bycause the resort of all marchants to the citie and Isle of Rhodes was now exceading there, then in all the places of the worlde, and by that meanes the lawes of traffick were there most triedly qualified with all points of equity, Peck. in rubricam, ad l. Rhodiam de iactu.[11] And also[12] bycause the commodiousnes of the place, and skill in navigation, and use of greate shipping obtained to that citie and island the space of manie yeres all gouverment by sea. And theise lawes of Rhodes nowe encorporated to the civill lawes Imperiall. And so to the whole bodie of both with th'aunceint customes of th'Admiralty of England and actes of parliament concerning the same have alwaies governed seacauses by expresse commission from the Prince. Hereby it is manifest, that the magistrates both of sea and land, are equally authorised in theire severall offices to governe by severall lawes in like immediate degree from the Prince: and therefor if it falles out, that a question doth arise concerning the limits of either their iurisdictions, it seemeth that [81ᵛ] this question is not fit to bee decided by either of themselves, but rather by the Prince her selfe, in her owne person, or by such speciall commissioners or delegates as her Matie shall appoint superiour and indifferent to them both.

[13]Adversus sententiam eius, qui vice Principis iudicavit, solus princeps restituet, auxilium apud Pretorem flagitare non potes, l. 3, C. si adversus rem iudicatam.[14]

Magistratus qui sunt pares imperio, nullo modo possunt alter ab altero cogi, l. nam magistratus, D. de arbitris.[15]

Praetor in praetorem, et consul in consulem nullum habet imperium, sed (ut inter eos ius dicatur) auxilium principis est impetrandum, l. ille a quo, § penult. D. ad Senatuscons. Trebellia.[16]

And therefor, whereas her Matie hath graunted by her letters patents to the L. Admirall, magistrate of the sea, the cognizance of all causes, arising within th'ebbing and flowing of the sea and fresh water to the full, and beneath the first bridges to the sea, and of all other causes concerning the sea, wheresoever they happen to bee done under which termes the commission of all his iurisdiction is limited. It cannot seeme to bee lawefull for magistrats of the land, to prohibite the course of the said commission

---

[10] M. Tullius Cicero, *De Imperio Cn. Pompei ad Quirites Oratio* 18.54, in A. C. Clark (ed.), *M. Tulli Ciceronis Orationes* (Oxford, 1938) ('Rhodiorum quorum usque ad nostram memoriam disciplina navalis et gloria permansit').
[11] Petrus Peckius, *Commentaria ... in omnes titulos ad rem Nauticam pertinentes*. Hagae-Comitis, Ex Officina Hildebrandi Iacobi, 1603, *Ad Legem Rhodiam de Iactu, ad rubricam D.14.2*, 141.
[12] Crossed out: 'And also'.   [13] Crossed out: 'Adv'.   [14] C.2.26.3.
[15] D.4.8.4.
[16] D.36.1.13.4.

within those limits, without greate impeachment of her highnes prerogative and power, and uniust iniury to their equall. For whereas the statutes of R. 2. and H. 4.[17] are supposed to warrant the judges of the land to restraine the Queen's power in graunting such a commission, as though the lawe of parliament were not by her Ma[tie] to bee qualified in the rights belonging to her selfe: the truth is, that as the same statutes themselfes have not anie wordes to restraine or denie the power of the prince in making such a commission: so if they have it may well bee saide, that the prince may make a graunt [82[r]] merely contrary to statute, and anie lawe positive to preiudice herselfe by such graunt, by a clause non obstante,[18] l. finali, C. si contra ius vel utilitatem publicam,[19] Baldus in authent. hoc inter liberos, C. de testament.,[20] Francisc. de Aret. consil. 25, col. 4.[21] And the same statute is hereby sufficiently dispensed withall, especially where theise wordes *ex certa scientia et mero motu nostris*, are therewith also inserted, Alexander in glossa l. 3, § si is, D. quod quisque iuris,[22] Baldus in l. final., C. sententiam rescindi non posse.[23] And this power of the prince is grounded uppon that most certaine observation, that every prince imperially raigning is at free libertie from all lawes positive to annihilate the same, Zazius in l. 2, D. de origine iuris, § eodem tempore,[24] vide de hoc pulchre distinct. Minsinger. centur. 5, observat. 97,[25] so they impeach not the rules of the lawes of nations and nature. And therefor the penalty of the same statute of 13. R. 2. and 2. H. 4.,[26] videlicet, that the statute and the common lawe shall bee holden against th'Admirall, and that the pursuant in th'Admirall Court shall forfaite to the partie grieved double dammages, and 10. lib. to the Queene, being in this dispensation[27] avoyded, and no prohibition being therein mentioned, (as it is in all the statutes prohibiting the spirituall Courtes), it followeth, that the said

---

[17] Supra, n. 2.   [18] Crossed out: 'fi'.   [19] C.1.22.6.
[20] Baldus de Ubaldis, *Commentaria in Sextum Cod. Lib.*, Lugduni 1585, ad auth. Hoc inter liberos (C.6.23.21.3), no. 3, fol. 69[rab].
[21] Franciscus de Accoltis de Aretio, *Consilia* (Lugduni per magistrum Johannem, Moylin alias de chambray), 1529, Consilium 15 (Reverendissime. Pater et domine mi. singularis et amantissime), nos. 6–9, fol. 14[vab].
[22] Alexander Tartagnus (Imolensis), *In Primam et Secundam Digesti Veteris Partem*, Lugduni (per Georgium Regnault) 1547, ad D.2.2.3.3., esp. no. 7, fols. 55[vb]–56[ra].
[23] Baldus de Ubaldis, *Commentaria in vij. viij. ix, x. et xi. Cod. lib.*, Lugduni 1585, ad C.7.50.3, esp. nos. 5–9, fol. 76[rab].
[24] Udalrichus Zasius, *Singularia Responsa, sive Intellectus Iuris Singulares ...*, Basileae, Apud Mich. Isingrinum, 1541, *In Iuris Civilis Originem Scholia, quibus L. II, FF. De Orig. Iur. Elucidatus*, ad D.1.2.2.10–2, ad verba 'ratum esset', 228–30.
[25] Ioachimus Mynsingerus a Frundeck, *Singularium Observationum Iudiciis Imp. Camerae Centuriae VI.*, Helmstadii, Ex officina Iacobis Lucii, 1584, Centuria V, Observatio XCVII (*Quae sit potestas principis in tollendo iure tertii, et an contra ius divinum, naturale, gentium, vel civile statuere possit?*), esp. no. 10, p. 521 (sum.: 'Princeps contra ius civile, seu positivum statuere et rescribere potest, cum ipse sit supra ius').
[26] Supra, n. 2.   [27] Crossed out: 'avoydded'.

magistrates have no warrant at all to countermaund the iurisdiction of their equall, by anie such courses, in th'exercise of the marine authority graunted them by commission.

And least this resolution shoulde bee a meanes for th'Admirall to deale further with causes of the land, then the commission authoriseth, when anie such proceading is offered, the partie greived may except against the judge's competency for such a cause. And if th'Admirall notwithstanding, will uniustly persist in proceading, [82ᵛ] the same partie may appeale to her Matie in the Chauncery, and then the iudgement and sentence of such delegates,[28] as by commission, from thence shall bee appointed, shall determine that controversie 8. Eliz. cap. 5.[29]

Which authority of delegates is so confirmed by that statute of 8. Elizab. that theire iudgement must bee taken as finall in all civill and marine causes, and no further appeale or complaint to anie other Court is allowed.

To the maintenance therefor of this Admirall seagoverment according to every clause of her highnes commission, her Matie enioyneth and commaundeth her L. Admirall to enioyne all subiects, of this realme to obey the tenour of the same her commission uppon paine of contempt and perill ensueng. And the contempt thereuppon growing to punnish by fine and imprisonment. Th'example of which iniunctions all other her highnes Courts doe put in ure, to defend the limites of their severall[30] iurisdictions. And by this meanes onley the L. Admirall hath from time to time, and < so >[31] hereafter shall avoyde all such impeachments of the landcourts, offered nowe commonly at every common man's sute, uppon bare untrue suggestions, to the dammage of her highnes imperiall crowne of this realme, and to the overthrowe of that settled goverment, which hath alwaies remained in the same, to[32] the greate encrease of traffick and navigation.

Ordinatum fuit tempore E. 1. anº reg. 2, that all marine causes should be tried before the L. Admirall.

---

[28] Crossed out: 'as by commission'.   [29] 8 Eliz. I c. 5.   [30] Crossed out: 'iudi'.
[31] Crossed out: 'shall'.   [32] Crossed out: 'theire'.

9   Stair's title 'Of Liberty and Servitude'

John D. Ford

I

The problem with the title 'Of Liberty and Servitude' in James Dalrymple, first Viscount Stair's *The Institutions of the Law of Scotland*, is to explain what it is doing there.[1] On the one hand, Stair expressed himself satisfied that the institution of slavery had little relevance in seventeenth-century Europe, and none at all in the Scotland of his day. Adopting the definition in Justinian's Institutes, in turn derived from Florentinus' *Institutes*,[2] Stair described slavery as a creation of the law of nations, at first arising when prisoners of war 'did loss their Liberty in lieu of their Life', later resulting from sale or birth (2.10/1.2.10). Though contrary to nature, slavery was none the less lawful, 'yet Christian Lenity and Mercy, hath almost taken away Bondage, except amongst the *Spaniards*, *Portugals*, and other Christian Nations, bordering upon the *Turks*' (2.11/1.2.11). Some southern nations, he explained, still found it necessary to maintain a supply of slaves to exchange for those taken from them.

Otherwise the nearest Christian Europe came to practising slavery was in recognising the status of *adscripticii glebae*. 'Such are the *English* villains', Stair remarked, 'but in *Scotland* there is no such thing.' Although he did concede that until recently there had been 'a kind of Bondage, called Man-rent', he added that those subject to manrent 'were rather *in clientela*, than in Bondage', and pointed out that the institution had since

---

[1] Quotations are from the first edition of the *Institutions* (Edinburgh, 1681) unless otherwise indicated, but since copies of the second edition of 1693 or of later editions derived from it are more readily available, references take the form first edition/second edition. In the first edition the second title is actually headed 'Of Liberty', though a fuller heading appears in some of the manuscripts.

[2] J.Inst. 1.3.2; D.1.5.4.1. W. M. Gordon, 'Stair, Grotius and the Sources of Stair's *Institutions*', in J.A. Ankum, J.E. Spruit and F.B.J. Wubbe (eds.), *Satura Roberto Feenstra* (Fribourg, 1985), 571, at 582, points out that Stair's account of slavery 'was very closely modelled on and sometimes even simply translated from' Petrus Gudelinus, *Commentariorum de Iure Novissimo Libri Sex* (Arnhem, 1639), 1.3–6.

been abolished by both statute and custom (2.12/1.2.12).[3] In Scotland there was no 'middle condition' between *ingenui* and *servi* (2.13–14/1.2.13–14). 'The Servants which now retain that name', he concluded, 'are judged free persons, and have at most but hired their labour and work to their Masters for a time, which is a Contract betwixt them; of which afterward' (2.15/1.2.15).[4] The only relevant form of service would be dealt with in a later title of contract law eventually under the heading 'Location and Conduction' (10.70–7/1.15).[5]

On the other hand, if slavery was obsolete in Scotland, that might at least have been taken to imply that liberty was the common condition of the Scottish people. Again following Justinian and Florentinus,[6] Stair defined liberty as 'a Natural Faculty, to do that which every man pleaseth, unless he be hindered by Law or Force' (2.1/1.2.1). As a former Cambridge Regius used to observe, that definition appears to make everyone free, and as such fails to provide an adequate basis for contrasting liberty with servitude.[7] Its value, as Stair understood it, lay more in contrasting liberty with coercion, whether by restraint or constraint (2.4/1.2.4), and it was with this conception of liberty that he was primarily concerned in his title.

Once more, however, he was forced to concede rather lamely that 'The Customs of this Nation have little peculiar, in relation to Liberty directly, but the injuries done against the same, especially constraint, fall under the consideration of Delinquencies, and are so punished' (2.16/1.2.16). Whereas special actions for wrongful imprisonment were available under the laws of ancient Rome or Israel and of modern England, the Scottish

---

[3] J. Wormald, *Lords and Men in Scotland* (Edinburgh, 1985) indicates that Stair's observations were substantially accurate, though, as Stair noted in the dedication of the first edition, a not dissimilar institution survived in the Highlands.

[4] In a much later passage in the second edition he admitted that 'some vestiges' of slavery remained in the condition of salters and colliers (4.45.17), yet no amendment was made to the title 'Of Liberty and Servitude'. It is clear from T. B. Smith, 'Master and Servant', in G. C. H. Paton (ed.), *An Introduction to Scottish Legal History* (Edinburgh, 1958), 130, and 'Master and Servant: Further Historical Outlines' [1958] Juridical Review 215, that something might easily have been made here of the quasi-servile condition of many Scottish workers.

[5] The heading does not appear in the first edition, where contract law was covered in one title. That Stair did not take the opportunity to deal with the relations of master and servant in his title on liberty and servitude is revealing. J. W. Cairns, 'Blackstone, Kahn-Freund and the Contract of Employment' (1989) 105 Law Quarterly Review 300, points out that it was still common for institutional writers to include the topic in their discussions of the law of persons in the eighteenth century. That Stair did not do so suggests that he had some other purpose in mind.

[6] J.Inst. 1.3.1; D.1.5.4 *pr.*

[7] W. W. Buckland, *The Roman Law of Slavery* (Cambridge, 1908), 1, *The Main Institutions of Roman Private Law* (Cambridge, 1931), 39, and *A Text-Book of Roman Law* (3rd edn, revd P. G. Stein (Cambridge, 1963), 61.

courts punished incarceration as a crime, and awarded civil damages, 'according to the Circumstances and Attrocity, and according to Equity'. It was in a later title on 'Reparation, whereof Delinquence, and Damages thence Arising' that Stair discussed liberty as one of several 'interests' protected by the general law of delict, also dealing there with the more specific delict of extortion by force or fear (9.4 and 8/1.9.4 and 8).[8]

So why devote a separate title to liberty and servitude? One answer might be that Stair was himself constrained by the conventions of the institutional tradition in which he was working: after writing about justice and law and about *ius naturale, ius gentium* and *ius civile* in his opening title, it was only to be expected that he would start his account of the law of persons with the distinction between freemen and slaves. Yet Alan Watson, who has done more than anyone to stress the force of traditional thinking in legal history, has noted that Stair was more liberated than many other institutional writers when it came to making adjustments to Justinian's arrangement.[9] Stair's treatment of persons is a case in point: after his title on liberty and servitude he went on to discuss 'Obligations in General', before dealing with familial, quasi-contractual, delictual and contractual obligations as species of personal rights, all prior to rights in things.

Reflecting on that shift from persons to personal rights, A. H. Campbell demonstrated over thirty years ago how examination of the structure of the *Institutions* can afford important insights into the structure of Stair's thought.[10] According to Professor Campbell, the title 'Of Liberty and Servitude', far from being a lifeless witness to the force of the institutional tradition, formed the cornerstone of Stair's treatment of personal rights and connected his work with the most recent advances in legal and political theory. The key to understanding what the title was doing in the *Institutions* lay in realising that in the succeeding titles Stair was 'presenting obligations less in their aspect of rights than as limitations upon the right of liberty'.[11] In keeping with the burgeoning natural rights theories of the seventeenth century, Stair was arguing that men were at

---

[8] Stair's explanation for the absence of a special action was that 'these crimes are very rare'. Yet something might perhaps have been added about public imprisonment, even in a treatise on private law. The Claim of Right of 1689 listed the imprisonment of persons 'without expressing the reason' as one of the grounds for depriving James VII of the crown, and Sir George Mackenzie indicated in his *Vindication of the Government in Scotland, during the Reign of King Charles II* (London, 1691), 11–12 and 24, that the issue had been sensitive for some time, with periodic suggestions that habeas corpus legislation should be introduced.

[9] W. A. J. Watson, *Legal Transplants* (Edinburgh, 1974), 37, and 'Some Notes on Mackenzie's *Institutions* and the European Legal Tradition' (1989) 17 Ius Commune 303, 310–13.

[10] *The Structure of Stair's Institutions* (Glasgow, 1954).   [11] *Ibid.*, 16.

138   John D. Ford

liberty to do as they pleased except where constrained by their obedience to God or by their voluntary undertakings to each other.

Now Peter Stein has not only had occasion to examine the structure of Stair's *Institutions* in his work on the transmission of the institutional system,[12] but has also commented several times on Stair's part in the development of legal thought in Scotland.[13] In doing so he has warned of the tension that must have existed between the new thinking on *ius naturale* and Stair's Calvinist principles.[14] What follows is an attempt to pay heed to that warning, first by looking more closely at the suggestion that Stair viewed liberty as a natural right in the modern sense, then by looking in an appropriate Presbyterian source for an alternative explanation for the inclusion of his title. The essay derives from an inquiry conducted with Peter's advice and encouragement. He may find some of what is said familiar and recognise his own influence; he may find other parts unconvincing and regret that more was not made of his advice; it is hoped that he will at least find something of interest.

II

Professor Campbell's contention was that Stair had learned to conceive of liberty as a natural right and of law as a body of obligations restricting the scope of liberty from Samuel Pufendorf's *De Iure Naturae et Gentium*, another treatise in which consideration of man's natural liberty preceded consideration of the general duties of humanity and of the duties added by human agreement.[15] Although there was no direct evidence of Stair's acquaintance with Pufendorf, the similarities in structure between the *Institutions* and the *De Iure Naturae* made it seem more likely that Stair had read Pufendorf's book than that the two writers had drawn from a common source. What we now know, however, is that manuscript copies of the *Institutions* were made a full decade before the appearance of the *De Iure Naturae* in 1672. To sustain the thesis that Stair was thinking

---

[12] 'The Fate of the Institutional System', in J. van der Westhuizen, P. J. Thomas, S. Scott and D. van der Merwe (eds.), *Huldigingsbundel Paul van Warmelo* (Pretoria, 1984), 218, 224–5, repr. in *The Character and Influence of the Roman Civil Law* (London, 1988), 73, 79–80.
[13] 'Legal Thought in Eighteenth Century Scotland' [1957] Juridical Review 1, 3–7, repr. in *Character and Influence*, 361, 363–7, 'The General Notions of Contract and Property in Eighteenth Century Scottish Thought' [1963] Juridical Review 1, 2–4, 'Law and Society in Eighteenth-Century Scottish Thought', in N. T. Phillipson and R. Mitchison (eds.), *Scotland in the Age of Improvement* (Edinburgh, 1970), 148, 148–51, and 'The Theory of Law', in D. M. Walker (ed.), *Stair Tercentenary Studies* (Edinburgh, 1981), 181.
[14] In part following Campbell, *Structure of Stair's Institutions*, 26–30.
[15] *Ibid.*, 23. The most accessible edition of Pufendorf's book is in the Carnegie Endowment series, tr. C. H. and W. A. Oldfather (Oxford, 1934).

along the same lines as Pufendorf we have to look for a common source after all.[16]

In fact, Professor Campbell was able to cite one other writer who contrasted liberty with obligation in the manner ascribed to Stair, a writer with whom Pufendorf at least was undoubtedly familiar. In the chapter of his *Leviathan* 'Of the First and Second Naturall Lawes, and of Contracts' Thomas Hobbes had made the often-quoted remark that:

> though they that speak of this subject, use to confound *Jus*, and *Lex*, *Right* and *Law*; yet they ought to be distinguished; because RIGHT, consisteth in liberty to do, or to forbeare; Whereas LAW, determineth, and bindeth to one of them: so that Law, and Right, differ as much, as Obligation, and Liberty; which in one and the same matter are inconsistent.[17]

Immediately before this Hobbes had defined liberty as 'the absence of externall Impediments', explaining in a later chapter 'Of the Liberty of Subjects' that the term could be used with reference to inanimate objects as well as to rational beings.[18] In the case of men, however, 'Artificiall Chains, called *Civill Lawes*', could be added by agreement,[19] and Hobbes argued in the earlier chapter that the first and second laws of nature required men to create these artificial bonds by contract. A distinction then had to be drawn between *ius civile* and *lex civilis*, 'For *Right* is *Liberty*, namely that Liberty which the Civil Law leaves us: But *Civil Law* is an *Obligation*; and takes from us the Liberty which the Law of Nature gave us'.[20] The liberty in question was *ius naturale*, the right of every man to do as he thought best for his own preservation, as opposed to *lex naturalis*, the duty to do so.

Following A. P. d'Entrèves, Profesor Campbell regarded Hobbes' distinction between right and law as a radical reworking of the traditional distinction between *ius* as *facultas agendi* – subjective right – and *ius* as *norma agendi* – objective right.[21] Where previously it had been said that a person had a right to do something when it was right for him to do it, and thus when others had a duty to allow him to do it, now it was being said that he had a right to do the thing unless he himself was bound by a duty. More recently Richard Tuck has stressed that the new rights theories were concerned with the individual's sovereignty over his own domain.[22] The

---

[16] Professor Campbell could find no parallel in structure between the *Institutions* and Pufendorf's earlier *Elementorum Iurisprudentiae Universalis Libri Duo*, again in the Carnegie Endowment series, trans. W. A. Oldfather (Oxford, 1931).
[17] Quotations are from the Cambridge Texts edition, ed. R. Tuck (Cambridge, 1991). References (here p. 64) are to the pagination of the 1651 edition, included in most modern printings.
[18] *Ibid.*, 107.   [19] *Ibid.*, 108.   [20] *Ibid.*, 150.
[21] *Natural Law* (2nd edn, London, 1970), 61–2.
[22] *Natural Rights Theories* (Cambridge, 1979), *passim*.

crucial point for Hobbes was that although men were bound by the law of nature to preserve themselves, they had some freedom in deciding how best that might be done.[23] The individual's freedom of choice was his natural right of liberty, a moral residue untouched by natural and civil laws; what was chosen consistently with those laws was necessarily within the individual's right.

The new theorists represented by Hobbes also effected a radical reworking of the traditional definition of liberty. If *libertas* was still man's *naturalis facultas* of doing what he pleased except where prevented by *vis*, it was no longer limited by *ius*; rather, liberty itself was *ius*, restricted by *vis* and *lex*.[24] In so far as men who naturally defended themselves against attack had the choice of the best means of defence, they could be said to possess a liberty or right. Their right was limited to the extent that they were in fact compelled in particular circumstances to adopt one means of defence, to the extent that reason dictated a specific course of action. Even where men did in principle have the freedom of choice, their liberty could be further curtailed by a voluntary transfer of their *ius* to an artificial sovereign, when *ius naturale* became *ius civile*, the liberty restricted not only by actual force but also by the laws backed up by threat of force. By this way of thinking, man's natural power was a matter of right while the law that limited his power was a matter of force.

Now Stair clearly could have read the *Leviathan* before he wrote the *Institutions*, but he never mentioned Hobbes by name, and Professor Campbell was certainly correct in supposing that he would not have had much sympathy with many of Hobbes' ideas. In a later treatise on physics he dismissed the 'Horrendus Hobbesius' as an atheist 'who subverted all moral and political principles, and substituted in their place natural force and human agreement as the first principles of morality, society and political government'.[25] These words might well be read as a resounding rejection of the new thinking, yet Stair was clearly indebted to another leading rights theorist, for he made no secret of his admiration for Hugo Grotius' *De Iure Belli ac Pacis*.[26] Although Professor Campbell could see no parallel between the structure of the *Institutions* and the arrangement of the *De Iure Belli*, Grotius is now acknowledged as the key figure in the emergence of the new thinking, making the vital move from saying that men naturally did what they could to defend themselves to saying that men had a natural right to do what they could to defend themselves.[27]

---

[23] R. Tuck, *Hobbes* (Oxford, 1989), 62–3.   [24] See Tuck, *Natural Rights Theories*, 26.
[25] *Physiologia Nova Experimentalis* (Leiden, 1686), 17.
[26] Quotations are from the Carnegie Endowment edition, tr. F. W. Kelsey (Oxford, 1925).
[27] Tuck, *Natural Rights Theories*, 58–81, 'The "Modern" Theory of Natural Law', in A. Pagden (ed.), *The Languages of Political Theory in Early-Modern Europe* (Cambridge,

Grotius began by defining the terms *bellum* and *ius*.[28] The latter meant 'nothing else than what is just, and that, too, rather in a negative than in an affirmative sense, that being lawful which is not unjust'. *Ius* was therefore a residual category of right, and it could be defined more subjectively as 'a moral quality of a person, making it possible to have or to do something lawfully'. *Ius* was something that people had whenever the law did not prohibit them from doing what they wanted to do. Used properly the term was synonymous with *facultas*, whether understood as man's power over himself (*libertas*), his children (*patria potestas*) or his slaves (*dominica potestas*), or as his power over things (*dominium*), or as his power over debts (*creditum*, correlative to *debitum*).

For present purposes two features of this classification are especially important. First, the traditional discussion of status categories in terms of the distinctions between freemen and slaves and persons *sui iuris* and *alieni iuris* was replaced by discussion of rights over persons akin to rights over things and debts; when Grotius eventually returned to the law of persons it was in the course of an account of the acquisition of rights of all kinds.[29] Secondly, in accomplishing this transition Grotius did not simply replace discussion of the first distinction with treatment of the acquisition of *patria potestas* and of the second with treatment of the acquisition of *dominica potestas*, but also recognised *libertas* as a right capable of acquisition; like Hobbes, he believed that civil government was established when men transferred their natural rights over themselves to a ruler.[30]

Stair's debt to Grotius' analysis is manifest in the opening titles of the *Institutions*. He accepted that a treatise on law should focus on the rights of men, that there were basically three kinds of right – 'Liberty, Dominion, and Obligation' – and that 'all Rights consist in a Power or Faculty' (1.21/1.1.22). Liberty in particular he described as 'the power to dispose of our Persons, and to live where, and as we please, except in so far, as by Obedience, or Ingagement we are bound', adding in the second title that it was a right 'maintained by that Common received Principle in the Law of Nature, of self defence and preservation' (2.3/1.2.3). After dealing with liberty Stair went on to present a series of titles on 'Conjugal Obligations', 'Obligations between Parents and Children' and 'Obligations between

---

1987), 99, and 'Grotius and Selden', in J. H. Burns and M. Goldie (eds.), *The Cambridge History of Political Thought, 1450–1700* (Cambridge, 1991), 499.

[28] *De Iure Belli* 1.1.2–5.

[29] *Ibid.*, 2.5. R. Dagger, 'Rights', in T. Ball, J. Farr and R. L. Hanson (eds.), *Political Innovation and Conceptual Change* (Cambridge, 1989), 292, shows how the language of rights came into its own only when more traditional notions of status began to prove inadequate.

[30] *De Iure Belli* 1.3.8.

Tutors and Curators, and their Pupils and Minors' (4–6/1.4–6), in preference to the usual titles *de statu hominum*. That he had decided to focus on rights, and that he had learned the language of rights from Grotius, can hardly be doubted. What should be doubted, however, is his full endorsement of the new thinking on *ius naturale*.

The first cause for concern is his statement that liberty was maintained by a common received principle in the law of nature. Although Stair remarked in the extract just quoted from the first title that liberty was limited by obedience or engagement, he stated his position with greater precision in the second title: 'This Right ariseth from that Principle of Freedom, that man hath of himself, and of other things beside man, to do in relation thereto, as he pleaseth, except where he is tyed thereunto by his Obedience or Ingagement' (2.3/1.2.3). The right of liberty, but the principle of freedom: Stair had already presented freedom, obedience and engagement as the 'first Principles of Equity', three common principles of natural law providing the foundations of the rights of men (1.17–20/1.1.18–21), yet distinct from the rights of men (1.21/1.1.22). It was not liberty but freedom – of which self-defence was a facet – that was limited by the obligations of obedience and engagement. Stair understood that liberty was limited by restraint and constraint (2.4/1.2.4).

He went on in the second title to list several possible bases for legitimate restraint or constraint, such as the failure of those under the control of spouses, parents or guardians to fulfil their obediential duties (2.5/1.2.5), the commission of a delict (2.6/1.2.6) or the breach of an engagement (2.7/1.2.7). In each case careful reading confirms that the point was not that the person's liberty was limited by the obligation but that his liberty was limited by the coercion which would result from failure to fulfil the obligation. Though the list ran parallel to the order of the ensuing titles, those titles were concerned with examining the obligations that set limits to freedom; the restrictions on liberty were discussed in these earlier paragraphs on restraint and constraint.

Strictly speaking, then, Stair did not contrast liberty with obligation, but contrasted liberty with coercion in a general framework of law and obligation. If *libertas* was *ius*, *ius libertatis* was 'the Law of Liberty' as well as the subjective right – there was nothing here to suggest that *facultas agendi* had been divorced from *norma agendi*. Nor would it have been easy for an orthodox Calvinist to have made that division, since far from accepting that *ius* was the absence of force and law, Calvinists were inclined to believe that fallen men could only hope to obtain *ius* in conditions of force and law. To maintain, moreover, that men in the state of nature had sufficient *ius* to construct an appropriate system of government was to come dangerously close to saying that men could work towards their own salvation without the gracious intervention of God. Although Stair could have followed Grotius (unlike Hobbes) without being accused of concurring with an atheist, Peter Stein has warned that he would still have been adopting the views of an author who was known to have supported the Arminians in the controversy culminating at Dort.[31]

Stair did in fact continue his list of the bases of legitimate coercion by adding after breach of engagement that 'Liberty is diminished by subjection unto Authority' (2.8/1.2.8), and finally that 'Liberty is wholly taken off by Bondage, Slavery, or Servitude' (2.9/1.2.9), with the clear implication that both civil government and slavery resulted from engagement. But at no point did he suggest that men created authority by transferring their natural rights to a ruler. His riposte to Hobbes remains significant, and I have argued elsewhere that his views on the origins of government owed less to the new rights theories than to the Presbyterian theory expounded in Samuel Rutherford's *Lex, Rex: The Law and the Prince*.[32]

One other reason for doubting Stair's full endorsement of the new thinking is the separation of his treatment of liberty from his titles on the rights of husbands and wives, parents and children, and guardians and wards. Whereas Grotius had included the relations of masters and servants in his title *De Acquisitione Originaria Iuris in Personas*, Stair dealt first with liberty and servitude and only then, after a fresh introductory title on 'Obligations in General' (3/1.3), with personal rights. One explanation might be that his thinking was even more advanced than Grotius', that he was drawing an analytical distinction between the liberty correlative (in W. N. Hohfeld's terms) to 'no-right' and the personal rights correlative to obligations in others. But to the danger of attributing an anti-Calvinist opinion to Stair this adds the danger of anachronism.[33] An alternative would be to conclude that the title 'Of Liberty and Servitude' was still essentially *de statu hominum*. That possibility will be considered in the fourth section of this essay. We turn now to Rutherford's *Lex, Rex* in search of an ideological context in which it might have made sense to

---

[31] 'The Theory of Law', 181.
[32] (London, 1644). My argument was presented to the annual conference of the Scottish Legal History Group in 1989 in a paper abstracted in (1990) 11 Journal of Legal History 134.
[33] This is not to dispute the point made by D. N. MacCormick, 'Stair as Analytical Jurist', in Walker (ed.), *Stair Tercentenary Studies*, 187, that modern positivists have continued the analytical tradition of the natural lawyers. It might be added that, as Peter Stein commented in 'Continental Influences on English Legal Thought, 1600–1900', in *La formazione storica del diritto moderno in Europa*, Atti del terzo congresso internazionale della società Italiana di storia del diritto, vol. 3, 1105, 1119–25, repr. in *Character and Influence*, 209, 223–9, modern analytical jurisprudence had its roots in the Roman law tradition.

talk of government, like servitude, as an encroachment on man's natural right of liberty, yet without it being implied that liberty was, as Grotius put it, a moral quality of the person.

III

When Samuel Rutherford first started working on his *Lex, Rex* he was persuaded by another Presbyterian divine to abandon the project as one 'proper for jurisconsults, lawyers and politicians', only to resume the task at the instigation of Archibald Johnston of Wariston, an Edinburgh advocate who was later to sit on the Bench with Stair around the time he began writing the *Institutions*.[34] Johnston, however, does not appear to have been the sort of jurisconsult, lawyer or politician referred to.[35] By 'the law' Rutherford understood the learned law, by 'jurisconsults' and 'lawyers' civilians and canonists like Bartolus, Baldus, Petrus Rebuffus, Covarruvias, and Vázquez, and by 'politicians' jurists like Bodin and Althusius. Though conscious of the distance between the disciplines of divinity and law,[36] Rutherford read these authors as reliable guides to the universal jurisprudence with which scholastic Natural lawyers were equally concerned. In other words, he envisaged himself working in the same general area as the new rights theorists.

Johnston's encouragement apart, the other reason why Rutherford decided to complete the *Lex, Rex* was the appearance of John Maxwell's *Sacro-sancta Regum Maiestas*.[37] It was Maxwell's avowed aim to undermine the 'Puritanicall, Jesuiticall, Antimonarchicall' thesis that civil government was a human institution established by positive law, and to defend the rival thesis that 'the King is onely and immediately dependent from Almighty God, the King of Kings, and Lord of Lords, and independent in his Soveraigntie and Power, from the Communitie'.[38] The king ruled *iure divino*, and his rule could be shown to be necessary *de iure naturae*. Maxwell was prepared to concede that the people had the task of designating a particular person to be king, but he insisted that 'the *reall constitution, the collation of soveraignty and Royalty* is immediately from

---

[34] *The Life of Mr Robert Blair*, ed. T. McCrie (Edinburgh, 1848), William Row's 'Supplement', 365–6.

[35] Like Stair, but unlike many other Scots lawyers, Johnston had not studied law at any of the continental universities. It is perhaps worth noting that when one royalist opponent of the Presbyterians, John Corbet, complained in *The Ungirding of the Scottish Armour* (Dublin, 1639), 43, of the Presbyterians' failure to cite 'judicious Lawyers' in support of their argument, accusing them of relying instead on Jesuit divines, he added: 'I know your Advocate Master *Iohnstone* is for you, but the question is too *Deepe* for his *shallow* brain.'

[36] See, for example, 114 and 204; and cf. 156.   [37] (Oxford, 1644).

[38] *Ibid.*, long title and 6.

God'.[39] In no sense could it be claimed that the king derived his authority from the people.[40] Not only did the people lack the power of governing themselves, but they did not even have the power of submitting actively to government. It could hardly be denied by orthodox Calvinists that 'every singular and individuall person, by corruption and selfe love hath *naturalem repugnantiam*, a natural aversenesse and repugnancy to submit to any'.[41] The most that could be said was that the people had a '*potestas passiva regiminis*, a capacity or susceptibility to be governed'.

It must have seemed a bitter irony to the Presbyterians to be accused of taking the Jesuit line by a reputedly Arminian bishop.[42] Rutherford, who had established his academic reputation with a treatise on divine grace written 'against Jacobus Arminius and his followers, and the Jesuits',[43] was as open as Maxwell in setting his aim: where Maxwell had given his book the English title *The Sacred and Royall Prerogative of Christian Kings*, Rutherford gave his the subtitle *A Dispute for the Just Prerogative of King and People*. It was Rutherford's purpose to show that both the king and the people participated in the political process *iure divino* or *naturali*. To begin with he pointed out that no one contested the fundamental principle that 'All civill power is immediately from God in its root.'[44] But where Rutherford had to admit that the Presbyterians came close to the Jesuits was in recognising that the people played an active part in the appointment of the king. Though all forms of government were 'instituted' by God, he argued, particular governments were 'constituted' by the popular choice of one form in preference to others. Maxwell had said that the people were only really capable of '*consensus passivus, a necessary necessitated consent*', a scarcely voluntary

[39] *Ibid.*, 20–3. [40] *Ibid.*, 90–1.
[41] Calvin himself had observed in his sermons on Job, quoted in C. Hill, *Religion and Politics in Seventeenth Century England* (Brighton, 1986), 123, that 'The nature of man is such that every man would be lord and master over his neighbours, and no man by good will will be subject.'
[42] N. Tyacke, *Anti-Calvinists* (Oxford, 1987), 234–5. Dr Tyacke mentions Grotius' role in the introduction of Arminianism into Britain at pp. 20, 68, 70 and 119 of his book. Further discussion can be found in A. W. Harrison, *The Beginnings of Arminianism* (London, 1926), 200–3, W. S. H. Knight, *The Life and Works of Hugo Grotius* (London, 1925), 55–60 and 127–57, P. White, *Predestination, Policy and Polemic* (Cambridge, 1992), 172–8 and 205–7, and H. R. Trevor-Roper, 'Hugo Grotius and England', in *From Counter-Reformation to Glorious Revolution* (London, 1992), 47.
[43] *Exercitationes Apologeticae pro Divina Gratia* (Amsterdam, 1636), long title.
[44] *Lex Rex*, 1–2. For a fuller account of Rutherford's argument see J. D. Ford, '*Lex, Rex, Justo Posita*: Samuel Rutherford on the Origins of Government', in R. A. Mason (ed.), *Scots and Britons* (Cambridge, forthcoming); and for differing perspectives W. M. Campbell, 'Lex Rex and its Author' (1941) 7 Records of the Scottish Church History Society 204; and I. M. Smart, 'The Political Ideas of the Scottish Covenanters, 1638–88' (1980) 1 History of Political Thought 167, at 175–80.

submission elicited by force or constraint.[45] In contrast, Rutherford maintained that they exercised a 'free, voluntary, and active power'.[46]

The theological argument could be turned round against Maxwell.[47] Although Rutherford had to agree that the people 'through corruption of nature are averse to submit to Governours, *for conscience sake, and as to the Lord*, because the naturall man remaining in the state of nature can doe nothing that is truely good', he still felt able to speak of a 'naturall moral active power' of submission, 'though it be not Evangelically, or legally in *Gods* Court, good'. What, after all, was Maxwell saying? That fallen men could only submit to government with the assistance of divine grace? The fact was that all over the world and throughout most of history men had submitted to government voluntarily, so that Maxwell could only be claiming that the grace essential to faith and to the works that were the fruits of faith was available to all those who would receive it. As expected, it was Maxwell who was taking the Jesuit and Arminian line that the submission of the people was 'not naturall, but done by the helpe of universall grace'.

Here we come to the polemical crux of Rutherford's theory. On the one hand, he wished to argue against Maxwell and like-minded royalists that the people had an active part to play in the establishment and maintenance of godly government, that they too had a just prerogative. On the other hand, in response to the same critics he wished to advance his argument without attributing to men in the state of nature capabilities for just living which they could only be said to have had in the state of grace. To a considerable degree the *Lex, Rex* represents a sustained struggle to find a language in which it could be claimed that men had by nature powers which were properly supernatural. Whether Rutherford succeeded in his task need not detain us, nor need we attempt to identify all the different languages he used. What matters for the moment is that we find here one context in which it might well have made sense to talk of natural rights while still denying that men were endowed with a natural faculty enabling them to act lawfully. It might have made sense, that is, to try out the language of rights even if what was said in that language could not have made perfect sense.

In the opening pages of his book Rutherford borrowed from Fernando Vázquez (also one of Grotius' sources) the proposition that civil government 'hath its *rise from a positive and secundary law of Nations, and not from the law of pure Nature*'.[48] There were two sides to this claim. In the

---

[45] *Sacro-sancta Regum Maiestas*, 92.   [46] *Lex, Rex*, 50.   [47] *Ibid.*, 51.

[48] *Ibid.*, 2–5. To begin with, Rutherford simply provided a selective paraphrase of Vázquez's *Controversiarum Illustrium Aliarumque Usu Frequentium Libri Tres* (Venice, 1564), 1.41.28–9, incorporating citations from D.1.1.1.3 and J.Inst. 1.2 *pr.* which made sense in

first place, Rutherford was arguing that since all men were born 'equally free', civil government was in a way 'Artificiall and Positive', that government in effect involved 'some servitude, whereof Nature from the womb hath freed us'. In the second place, however, he was trying to show that it was also grounded on a law of nature, 'which *Lawyers* call, *secundario jus naturale*, or *jus gentium secundarium*', namely the precept that it was lawful *vim vi repellere*. He explained that men were inclined by an 'instinct of nature' to defend themselves, which meant both that they were not inclined to submit individually to coercive power, and that they were inclined to agree collectively to the constitution of coercive power as the best means of defending themselves.

In this passage Rutherford talked of men resigning their liberty to the king and of the people devolving their power. He made use of similar vocabulary in a later chapter headed 'Whether or no Royall Dignitie have its Spring from Nature, and how that is True (Every Man is Born Free) and how Servitude is Contrary to Nature'.[49] He acknowledged there that some forms of subjection were indeed purely natural, above all the subordination of children to their parents. Civil government, on the other hand, was to some extent contrary to nature, and once again Rutherford used the imagery of liberty and servitude to press his message home. 'The originall of servitude', he observed (citing the Institutes), was that 'when men were taken in warre, to eschew a greater evill, even *death*, the captives were willing to undergoe a lesse evill, *slaverie*.' This, of course, was a standard misreading of the text from Florentinus in which the captor was said to preserve the lives of his prisoners, designed to emphasise that while the people naturally did what was necessary to save themselves, their consent to an intrinsically unnatural condition was also required.

Not surprisingly, Dr Tuck has concluded that Rutherford came as close as any Presbyterian writer to espousing a natural rights theory.[50] Close, but not close enough, for Rutherford made it plain that he did not equate man's natural liberty with the power of government.[51] What he was dealing with here was the people's power of submitting to government, not a power of self-government that could be transferred to the ruler. Put shortly, Rutherford's contention was that the people ruled themselves by submitting to the rule of God's vicegerents. It was natural for the people to submit to the rule of those placed in authority over them, just as children naturally submitted to the rule of their parents, wives to the rule of their husbands.[52] But not all forms of subjection were purely natural.

---

the original – where *ius naturale* was said to be common to all animals – but not in the paraphrase, where that point was omitted.
[49] *Lex, Rex*, 89–96.   [50] *Natural Rights Theories*, 145.   [51] *Lex, Rex*, 87 and 151.
[52] *Ibid.*, Preface, 6, 111, 319.

That it was lawful *vim vi repellere* proved that men were not always required to submit passively to coercion. The people had to determine for themselves where their right of self-defence ended and their duty of obedience started.

The value of the language of rights therefore lay in the facility it provided for stressing the free, voluntary and active character of the people's part in politics. None the less, Rutherford was conscious that this sort of language could be seriously misleading:

> Individuall persons in creating a Magistrate, doth not properly surrender their right which can be called a right; for they do but surrender their power of doing violence to these of their fellows in that same Communitie; so as they shall not now have Morall power to do injuries without punishment; and this is not right or libertie properly, but servitude; for a power to do violence and injuries, is not liberty, but servitude and bondage.[53]

A moral power to do injuries? Rutherford was alluding here to a distinction commonly drawn by Calvinist writers between the morality of the state of nature – the condition of unregenerate men, or 'naturall *Moralists*', as Rutherford sometimes called them – and the virtue of the state of grace – the condition of the elect, those destined to renewal and fulfilment as *viri*.[54] In the state of nature men were sometimes moved by instinct to perform deeds in external conformity with the law, such as defending themselves by violence or by submitting to government, but this fell far short of the willing obedience offered by those in the state of grace. The conduct of 'morall and naturall' men, in Rutherford's terms, was *factum* as opposed to *ius*. Indeed, where the instinct of self-defence was concerned it was more *iniuria* than *ius*.

What made it plausible to talk of rights was simply the absence of any threat of punishment, an absence that seemed to entail a measure of individual liberty. From Rutherford's perspective, however, a negative conception of liberty like this was in danger of obscuring the genuine character of liberty as the freedom to participate in the godly life. As participation in the godly life was only possible in the setting of a Christian polity, it followed that man's so-called liberty was really servitude. Although it was Rutherford's opinion that the truly Christian polity could not be built without the free and active participation of the people, he never questioned the more fundamental assumption that the godly life could not be achieved without the aid of executive authority. The coercive apparatus of church and state served both to compel external obedience

---

[53] *Ibid.*, 44.
[54] Rutherford explained the distinction with particular clarity in his *Divine Right of Church-Government and Excommunication* (London, 1646), 79–80.

Stair's title 'Of Liberty and Servitude' 149

from the reprobate and to provide the discipline necessary to habituate the elect to virtue.

Like many Calvinist writers, Rutherford was striving to put into words an elusive vision of a Christian polity in which believers would have the opportunity to offer up to God the willing obedience that was more acceptable to him than sacrifice. Willing obedience was by definition the opposite of coerced obedience, yet it had to be acknowledged that obedience was impossible without a measure of coercion. Thus although the language of rights could be used to mark the limits of coercion and to describe the active and voluntary participation of the people in government, it had to be admitted that *ius* was only to be looked for under government. Moreover, the term *ius* was always bound to have objective overtones, less free choice than free obedience – at one place Rutherford actually wrote of 'the right of servants to obey' their masters[55] – and properly speaking it was quite inaccurate to apply the term *ius* to the moral conduct of the reprobate.

Now here we surely do find a context in which Stair's use of the language of rights begins to make sense. Here we find a line of thought in which government, like servitude, was regarded as an encroachment on liberty, yet with liberty opposed to coercion, not obligation; a manner of speaking in which man was said to have a natural right of liberty without it being implied that whatever he did in the exercise of his liberty was necessarily lawful. The right of liberty was still grounded on the principle of self-defence, it is true, and W. M. Gordon has pointed out that Stair's citations from Cicero and Gaius in support of the principle may well have been borrowed from Grotius.[56] If so, however, what seems interesting for our purposes is Stair's omission of Grotius' next reference, to the text in which Florentinus remarked that whatever a person did to protect himself could be said to be done *iure*.[57] Stair added instead that the principle of self-defence was 'only to be extended to private and unlawful violence' (1.3/1.2.3). Like Rutherford, he simply took the principle to mark the limits of legitimate coercion.

After defining restraint and constraint (2.4/1.2.4), Stair went on as we have seen to list the bases of legitimate coercion (2.5–9/1.2.5–9). On the one hand, he indicated that it was no encroachment on liberty to restrain a person from breach of an obediential duty or engagement, or to constrain him to performance. On the other hand, while he understood infringement of the law to be a necessary condition of legitimate coercion,

[55] *A Dispute Touching Scandall and Christian Libertie* (London, 1646), 86.
[56] 'Stair, Grotius and the Sources of Stair's *Institutions*', 575. The citations were from Cicero's *Pro Milone* 11.30 and D.9.2.6.1, quoted in *De Iure Belli* 1.2.3.1.
[57] D.1.1.3.

he did not consider it sufficient of itself. No more than Rutherford did Stair subscribe to the opinion that all men had authority to enforce the law of nature. As he later explained, the authority of fathers over their families, initially of husbands over their wives, was 'the only Natural Authority and Government, which had in it self all Authority, Public, Private, Civil and Criminal, till by Humane Constitution, and Divine Approbation, most of that power is now devolved into Magistracy' (5.6/1.5.6).[58] It was therefore convenient to deal with the enforcement of the law in relation to the family before commenting on the coercive power of civil government.

All this was perfectly consistent with Rutherford's thinking, with the exception of Stair's use of the expression 'Divine Approbation' to describe God's institution of government. Rutherford disliked the expression because it seemed to diminish God's role in creating government and to impute undue freedom to men.[59] It was against 'learned and pious' authors like Rutherford that Stair sought to defend the equitable principle of freedom in his opening title, insisting that where God had neither expressly enjoined nor prohibited an activity men were free to decide for themselves what was most conducive to the glory of God and the edification of each other (1.19/1.1.20). We cannot explore this argument further here,[60] crucial as it was to Stair's enterprise, but it needs to be mentioned because it connects with something he said in relation to liberty:

> in matters of utility and profite, where the Natural Liberty is not hemmed in with an Obligation, there, unless by his own delinquence or consent, man cannot justly be restrained, much less constrained upon pretence of his utility or profite: for Liberty is far preferable to profite, and in the matter of utility, every man is left to his own choice, and cannot without injury to God and Man, be hindered to do what he pleaseth, or be compelled to do what he pleaseth not, in things wherein he is free. (2.5/1.2.5)

Note first that Stair was again talking loosely of liberty being hemmed in by obligation: he clearly meant that liberty was hemmed in by the lawful coercion used to enforce man's obligations. Note too that although Stair

[58] See too 4 *pr.*/1.4 *pr.*; 1.9.2 may seem to contradict this in editions later than the second, but not in the editions for which Stair himself was responsible.
[59] *Lex, Rex*, 5–9, 17–20 and 416.
[60] The argument was examined in a paper I presented to a seminar at the Centre for Criminology and the Social and Philosophical Study of Law at Edinburgh University in 1991. The background to Stair's three principles of equity will be examined in J. D. Ford, 'Conformity in Conscience: The Structure of the Perth Articles Debate in Scotland, 1618–38', forthcoming in the Journal of Ecclesiastical History, and 'The Lawful Bonds of Scottish Society: The Five Articles of Perth, the Negative Confession and the National Covenant', forthcoming in the Historical Journal. Details of Stair's reaction should be published in the not too distant future.

regarded freedom as the absence of obedience and engagement, he did not regard it as the absence of duty: he had already explained that in the area of freedom men were bound by duties of expediency (1.19/1.1.20). His argument here was that liberty was preferable to profit, that the expediency of enforcing particular actions in this doubtful area would be outweighed by the expediency of leaving men to make up their own minds. What they chose to do might sometimes involve injury to God and man, yet it was most conducive to divine glory and human edification to let them have their choice.

The right of liberty was thus correlative to the duty of expediency: the point was not so much that men had a natural right to do what they pleased as that others had a natural obligation to allow them to do what they pleased.[61] Nor was Stair anxious to show that governments would have to derive their authority from the consent of the governed. Although he suggested in the passage just quoted that no one could be coerced in the area of expediency 'unless by his own delinquence or consent', he maintained elsewhere that the heads of families, from whom power was devolved on civil governors, did have authority to compel those under their control to do what they believed to be most conducive to the common good (4.3/1.4.9). If Stair agreed with Rutherford that it was necessary for the people to consent to the transfer of authority from family heads to civil rulers, he also agreed that the authority exercised by rulers was not itself derived from the people's consent.

IV

Stair's use of the language of rights has now become more intelligible, but it is still not entirely clear why he included his title 'Of Liberty and Servitude' in the *Institutions*. Attention has focused in the last two sections on his interpretation of Florentinus' definition of liberty as the opposite of coercion, yet the fact is that Stair only needed seven of the sixteen paragraphs in his title to make the contrast (2.3–9/1.2.3–9), and it is not without significance that we have had little cause so far to examine the opening two paragraphs, in which he set out the definition and distinguished liberty from dominion and obligation. The reason is that apart from quoting the Roman definition Stair was more concerned there

---

[61] This is intended to mean what it says, not that liberty was a right surrounded by a protective perimeter of rights correlative to obligations imposed on others. None the less, Stair clearly did give marginally more substance to the right of liberty than Rutherford had done, and it is not surprising to find him quoting an inoffensive passage from the *De Iure Belli*, 2.22.12, in support of his position.

with Florentinus' other contrast between liberty and servitude. It was to the elucidation of this other contrast that he devoted the second half of his title (2.9–15/1.2.9–15), and we have still to see why he did so. After all, to make the point that government like servitude was an encroachment on man's natural liberty it would surely have been enough to have added servitude to the list of bases of coercion, without going on to elaborate on its characteristics and variants. Besides, it is by no means obvious why it should have been thought necessary to make an essentially political point in a treatise on private law.

Though it is more obvious why Rutherford should have made the point, even in his case it had the serious drawback that assimilating submission to government with submission to slavery tended to imply that once the people had submitted, their ruler would exercise absolute authority over them. That, of course, was precisely what Rutherford wished to deny. As a means of doing so the conventions of political theory suggested a further comparison between the powers of masters over their slaves and of fathers over their children,[62] a potentially felicitous manoeuvre, since likening kings to fathers had long been envisaged as a way of stressing the care and affection kings owed to their subjects.[63] Calvin himself, moreover, had used this sort of comparison to distinguish between the servitude of those left under the yoke of the law and the willing obedience of the regenerate: the former came before God as a master to receive a penalty for their failure to perform his assigned tasks, while the latter approached him as an indulgent parent to receive a blessing for their earnest though imperfect endeavours.[64]

For Rutherford, however, there was the additional problem that many of his royalist opponents, John Maxwell amongst them,[65] were advancing the patriarchalist argument that the power of the king could be shown to come immediately from God because it was identical with the natural power of fathers over their families. To say that kings were more like fathers than masters might therefore have involved Rutherford in making a dangerous concession, especially since he already accepted that the constitution of civil government did in practice amount to a shift from

---

[62] Hobbes, for instance, after explaining the nature of sovereign power in his *Leviathan*, went on to discuss 'Dominion Paternall, and Despoticall' immediately before the chapter mentioned above on the liberty of subjects. His move, however, was to deny that there was any real difference between the various forms of rule.

[63] D. K. Shuger, *Habits of Thought in the English Renaissance* (Berkeley, CA, 1990), 218–49.

[64] *Institutes of the Christian Religion*, trans. H. Beveridge (Edinburgh, 1845), 3.19.5. He did not say so, but Calvin was presumably thinking of Romans 8.14–15.

[65] *Sacro-sancta Regum Maiestas*, 85–6. G. J. Schochet, *The Authoritarian Family and Political Attitudes in Seventeenth Century England* (New Brunswick, NJ, 1988), explores the setting.

paternal to royal rule.[66] His solution was presented in a series of chapters in which he asked, first, 'Whether or no the King be Univocally, or only Analogically, and by proportion a father?', secondly, 'Whether or no a despoticall and masterly dominion of men and things, agree to the King, because he is King?', and thirdly, less conventionally, 'Whether or not the Prince have properly a fiduciarie, and ministeriall power of a Tutor, Husband, Patron, Minister, head, father of a family, not of a Lord or dominator?'.[67]

In the first chapter Rutherford argued that although Aristotle and Justinian had referred to the prince as a father, he was 'only a father *Metaphorically*, and by a *borrowed speech*'.[68] Having made that apparent, Rutherford was able to go on in the next chapter to argue that 'The *King* hath no proper, masterly, or herile dominion over the subjects', and that his power was 'rather fiduciary and ministeriall, than masterly', since he was to feed, rule, defend and govern his subjects 'as the father doth his children'. The master was entitled to make use of his slaves for his own benefit, so that slaves could be bought and sold as goods, but the king was to act in his people's interest. The king did not own his subjects, nor, as Petrus Rebuffus taught,[69] did he own all their goods. 'If the subjects had no proprietie in their own goods', Rutherford observed, 'but all were the Princes due, then the subject should not be able to make any contract of buying and selling without the *King*, and every subject were in the case of a slave.' He had gleaned from his reading that in Roman law a slave could only incur a natural, not a civil, obligation, 'because the condition of a servant, he not being *sui juris*, is compared to the state of a beast'.

That comparison expressed the essence of servitude for Rutherford. If royal power were *dominica potestas*, as the royalists seemed to be claiming, if subjects were like slaves, 'no better than bruit beasts', that would mean the people obeyed the law 'not because good and honest, but because their prince commandeth them so to do'.[70] By contrast, Rutherford's vision was of a polity in which the people would obey the law (in St Paul's words) not only for wrath but also for conscience' sake, which he took to mean obeying the law voluntarily because it was conceived to be the will of God. In the truly godly polity the people would obey as rational beings, consenting freemen rather than coerced slaves, and that could only happen where the king's decrees were in keeping with God's

---

[66] See again Ford, '*Lex, Rex Iusto Posita*'.   [67] *Lex, Rex*, 111–30.
[68] The reference here to '1. 3. *c*. 11' of the *Politics* makes no sense. Rutherford may have had in mind book 1, chapter 2, often cited by patriarchalists. For Justinian he cited Novel 12.2.
[69] *Tractatus Congruae Portionis* (Lyons, 1564), n. 125.
[70] This had been the Presbyterians' complaint for decades: see again Ford, 'Conformity in Conscience'.

commandments. It followed, as Rutherford concluded in his third chapter, that 'the Law is not the Kings own, but given to him in trust', to be enforced for the good of the people. Though various metaphors could be used, ultimately it was best to say that '*The King* is more properly a Tutor then a Father', a guardian appointed in the father's place to take care of the people and their inheritance. The inheritance – political power – was not the king's to do with as he pleased, and like any tutor he could be called to account.

Master and slave, father and child, guardian and ward: there cannot be much doubt about the origin of Rutherford's categories, especially given the number of citations from the Corpus Iuris in these chapters.[71] The categories were closed, yet we may find it instructive to ask why Rutherford did not go on to explain that in Roman law a freeman was usually also a citizen.[72] He was, after all, employing the concept of freedom to stress the equality of men at the political level, and to defend the active participation of the people in their own government. He made use of republican vocabulary elsewhere in his book,[73] and Quentin Skinner has indicated that at least some of the things he wanted to say could have been said coherently in the language of civic humanism.[74] Furthermore, a related language had been in use in Scotland at least since the time of the Declaration of Arbroath in 1320,[75] a language that continued to dominate political discourse at the end of the sixteenth century.[76]

A few moments' reflexion, however, suggest that Rutherford would have had good reason to frame his argument in terms of natural jurisprudence. For one thing, the liberty of the citizen was by definition a civic right, not a natural right,[77] and Rutherford was committed to meeting the

[71] Not that Rutherford need necessarily have consulted the texts himself, still less understood what they said (cf. n. 48 above). Peter Stein cautioned against too readily imputing knowledge of Roman law to authors in this area in 'Calvin and the Duty of Guardians to Resist: A Comment' (1981) 32 Journal of Ecclesiastical History 69. The Roman law influence is less manifest in Rutherford's guardianship chapter than in the other two.

[72] After dealing with paternal and despotical dominion it was Hobbes' chief aim in his chapter on the liberty of subjects to deride the republican account of liberty.

[73] See, for example, pp. 48, 168, 211–12, 238, 259, 350, 376 and 387.

[74] 'The Idea of Negative Liberty: Philosophical and Historical Perspectives', in R. Rorty, J. B. Schneewind and Q. Skinner (eds.), *Philosophy in History* (Cambridge, 1984), 193, and 'The Republican Ideal of Political Liberty', in G. Bock, Q. Skinner and M. Viroli (eds.), *Machiavelli and Republicanism* (Cambridge, 1990), 293.

[75] G. W. S. Barrow, 'The Idea of Freedom in Late Medieval Scotland' (1979) 30 Innes Review 28.

[76] R. A. Mason, 'Covenant and Commonweal: The Language of Politics in Reformation Scotland', in N. Macdougall (ed.), *Church, Politics and Society* (Edinburgh, 1983), 97, and 'Kingship and Commonweal: Political Thought and Ideology in Reformation Scotland', unpublished Ph.D. dissertation, Edinburgh University, 1983.

[77] C. Wirszubski, *Libertas as a Political Idea at Rome during the Late Republic and Early Principate* (Cambridge, 1950), 1–4.

episcopalians and royalists in their own terms: if the king's prerogative were grounded on *ius naturale*, the same would have to be said of the people's prerogative. Similarly, a central aim of the *Lex, Rex* was to maintain the principle that the king received his power from the people without denying that government had to be imposed on men from above: however free and equal the people may have been to begin with, Rutherford had to accept that they became subjects rather than citizens. Above all, while Rutherford defended the active participation of the people in their own government, he was not so much concerned with their involvement in the institutional machinery of the state as with their exercise of conscience in response to the decrees of their superiors: in so far as he took 'the people' to mean ordinary men and women, as opposed to the *pars valentior*, he was less concerned with the public practice of politics than with the private application of the law. He had in mind a polity in which governed yet autonomous individuals would take responsibility for their actions, and to that end it helped to say that freemen were *sui iuris*, though not citizens.

If we turn once more to the title on liberty and servitude in the *Institutions* we can see that Stair was moved by a similar concern. Servitude, he remarked, was

Diametrically opposite to Liberty; for as Liberty is that power, by which men are *sui juris*, so by Servitude, they became *alieni juris*, in the power of another, unto whom they became as the rest of their Goods in their Patrimony, and are possessed by them, and may be gifted, legated, sold, and otherways disposed of at their pleasure. (2.9/1.2.9)

At least in earlier law, Stair went on, masters had enjoyed *ius vitae necisque* over their slaves. Since slaves were 'wholly their Masters' they could have owned nothing – any *peculium* was 'in their Masters power, and might be taken away at his pleasure' – nor could they have incurred obligations, been party to civil actions, or been witnesses, procurators or arbiters. No wonder 'they were accounted as no body, or as dead men'.

Could it have been a deliberate ploy to describe liberty as the power by which men were *sui iuris*, apparently collapsing the two distinctions between freemen and slaves and between persons *sui iuris* and *alieni iuris* into one? It is hard to be sure. Rutherford had implied that anyone *alieni iuris* was in the state of a beast, technically a slave. Stair seemed to indicate more clearly still that those subject to paternal or analogous power were in subjection yet *sui iuris*,[78] which certainly ties in neatly with

---

[78] In contrast, Gudelinus, *De Iure Novissimo* 1.17, expressed the following view: 'Surely guardianship and supervision is also a certain force and power *in personam*. But it is provided entirely for the favour and advantage of those who are subject to the power, nor does it detract from but rather adds to and assists their *ius*, whence they are yet said to be

Rutherford's theory. The move may not have been conscious, though Stair did observe in a later title that the Romans had at first erred in making the power of parents 'almost Dominical, and the Children as Servants' (5.11/1.5.11). Scots law, he believed, was closer to the law of nature, in which children were distinguished from slaves yet placed under the authority eventually devolved upon magistrates (5.6/1.5.6).

Since children were not like slaves it followed that their relationship with their parents was interpersonal. That meant in juridical terms that parents and children were best considered as parties to personal *iura* or *obligationes*, objective 'bonds' between two persons, one of whom could be said subjectively to have the right, the other to have the obligation (2.1/1.3.1). It meant in addition that the relations of husbands and wives, parents and children and guardians and wards could be dealt with alongside quasi-contractual, delictual and contractual obligations. Liberty, on the other hand, though also subjectively taken as a right correlative to obligation (and as such identified as a topic requiring discussion in the title on delict), was a right of unique significance. As Stair said at the outset, since 'Bondage exeemeth man from the account of persons, and brings him rather in among things, *quae sunt in Patrimonio nostro*', liberty was not only a right distinct from dominion and obligation but was 'the most native and delightful Right of man, without which, he is capable of no other Right' (2.2/1.2.2). To be free was, quite simply, to be a person, a rational being capable of living in accordance with law.

The reason why the title on liberty and servitude had to be separated from the other titles on persons was thus that the relationship between master and slave was not interpersonal, and consequently was not susceptible of treatment in terms of personal rights and obligations – the focus was still by and large on status. The reason why the title had to be included at all was that no other relationship could be interpersonal unless the distinction between liberty and servitude was maintained. The reason why Stair insisted that there was no servitude in Scotland was not so much that he wished to state the facts as that he wished to affirm that the Presbyterian vision of the legal order was capable of achievement in Scotland.[79] While his vision differed significantly from Rutherford's, it was still very much a modern version of the Presbyterian ideal.

It has not been possible to spend much time here on the points of disagreement between Stair and Rutherford, which may have given a

sui iuris, not to be *in potestate* (J.Inst. 1.13 *pr.*), just as citizens bound by the authority of the magistrate still are (D.50.16.215). Far different is the rationale of *dominica potestas* and *patria potestas*, which are brought about very much in favour of masters and fathers, not in favour of slaves and sons. For that reason we say that those are *in potestate* and *alieni iuris* (J.Inst. 1.8).'

[79] See again n. 4 above.

rather misleading impression of uniformity among the Presbyterians. Nevertheless, at the risk of reinforcing that impression, it may be worth closing with a brief comparison between the treatment of persons in Stair's *Institutions* and the treatment in the rival *Institutions* of the Episcopalian royalist Sir George Mackenzie.[80] For if the reading of Stair's title that I have presented is sound, it ought to follow that an author of contrasting ideological commitments would take a markedly different approach.

What we find is that Mackenzie began like Stair with a title on law and justice, then started his second title by explaining that 'Having resolved to follow *Justinians* method' he would work through persons, things and actions.[81] His second title, however, was headed 'Of Jurisdiction and Judges in General', and two further titles were devoted to the jurisdiction of civil magistrates before the fifth dealt with ecclesiastical dignitaries. Only then did he move on to conclude his treatment of persons with titles on marriage and guardianship, '*Having spoken fully of Persons, as they are considered in a Legal sense*'. If the problem with Stair is to explain why he included a title on liberty and servitude, the problem with Mackenzie is to explain why he omitted both master and slave and parent and child, and why he dealt primarily with the jurisdiction of judges.

The omissions were accounted for in the closing sentence of Mackenzie's section on persons:

We have little use in *Scotland*, of what the *Institutions of the Roman Law* teach, concerning *slaverie*, or *Patria potestas*, for we as *Christians* allow no Men to be made *Slaves*, that being contrare to the *Christian liberty*; and the *Fatherly power* or *Patria potestas*, has little effect with us; for a *Child* in *Familie* with his *Father*, acquires to himself and not to his *Father* as in the *Civil Law*.

Although Stair would clearly have agreed that the Roman notions of slavery and *patria potestas* were out of date, we may surmise that he would not have found Mackenzie's reasons for ignoring the topics satisfactory. In the first place, the fact that *patria potestas* was no longer similar to *dominica potestas* was no reason for saying nothing about it; quite the contrary, it was precisely because children were no longer treated like slaves that their relations with their parents could be discussed in terms of right and obligation. Mackenzie apparently had trouble with a conception of paternal power which was not dominical and absolute, presumably because of its implications for his understanding of royal power. Conversely, Stair would no doubt have objected, in the second

---

[80] *Institutions of the Law of Scotland* (Edinburgh, 1684).
[81] Watson, 'Mackenzie's *Institutions*', 312–13, argues persuasively that Mackenzie meant to criticise Stair for departing from Justinian's arrangement.

place, that although the Roman texts on slavery had limited practical significance in modern conditions they still had ideological relevance.

Yet Mackenzie also wore his politics on his sleeve. He defended his approach in the opening titles by stating that the law concerned itself with civil or ecclesiastical persons, of whom the most important 'in a Legal sense' were the judges vested with powers of jurisdiction.[82] 'The *King*', he noted at the beginning of his third title, 'is the *Author*, and *Fountain*, of all power, as any King, or Potentate, whatsoever, deryving his power from GOD Almighty alone, and so not from the people', a thesis he defended at length against the Presbyterians in his *Ius Regium*.[83] In contrast to Stair, who based his account of private law on a political theory that sought to reconcile ascending and descending principles of government, and so began by dealing with the legal status of ordinary people, Mackenzie adhered uncompromisingly to a descending principle, and so began with the legal deputies of the king deputed by God. To some extent at least we may conclude that the Scottish development of the institutional tradition was divided along party lines, as other commentators have in the past suggested,[84] but we may do so without implying that Stair had abandoned his Calvinist convictions. Peter Stein was surely wise to be wary of that implication.

[82] Watson, *ibid.*, 309–10, shows that Mackenzie's approach was not without precedent in the institutional tradition. At p. 313, however, he adds that it 'may seem rather forced', and it is highly significant that a scholar with Professor Watson's extensive knowledge of the institutional literature should have been unable to find 'a precise model for Mackenzie's arrangement'.

[83] (London, 1684). It may have been more than a coincidence that Mackenzie's *Institutions* appeared in the same year as his *Ius Regium*. The latter was designed to remind ordinary people stirred up by Presbyterian assertions of their active role in politics of their proper place.

[84] H. Ouston, 'York in Edinburgh: James VII and the Patronage of Learning in Scotland, 1679–88', in J. Dwyer, R. A. Mason and A. Murdoch (eds.), *New Perspectives on the Politics and Culture of Early Modern Scotland* (Edinburgh, 1982), 133, 147, and 'Cultural Life from the Restoration to the Union', in A. Hook (ed.), *The History of Scottish Literature, 1660–1800* (Aberdeen, 1987), 11, 23, and H. L. MacQueen, 'Mackenzie's *Institutions* in Scottish Legal History', 1984 Journal of the Law Society of Scotland 498, 500.

10 The *actio communi dividundo* in Roman and Scots law

Geoffrey MacCormack

In a characteristically lucid and elegant essay written some thirty years ago Peter Stein observed that 'The vague proposition that Scots law is "based on Roman law" is still widely canvassed today.'[1] At that time there were few detailed treatments of the precise extent of the debt owed by Scots law to Roman law; nor have many appeared since.[2] Professor Stein's own writings have constituted an important step towards remedying this deficiency.[3] This paper is intended as a modest contribution in the same direction.[4]

Decisions of the Scots courts arising from disputes between persons holding ownership of land in common have on occasion referred to two actions known to Roman law. These are the *actio familiae erciscundae* and the *actio communi dividundo*, the former lying for the division of property falling within an inheritance, and the latter being available to co-owners other than heirs. Scots law did not in fact, from the point of view of the remedies, distinguish between the case in which heirs sought a partition of land inherited in common and that in which other co-owners sought a partition. Although references to both the Roman actions are found in the works of the institutional writers and the judgments of the courts, the *actio communi dividundo* has tended to assume the larger role. Hence I have omitted specific consideration of the *actio familiae erciscundae*.[5]

---

[1] 'The Influence of the Roman Law in Scotland' [1963] Juridical Review 205.
[2] A forthcoming volume of the Stair Society to be edited by R. Evans-Jones under the title *Roman Law in Scotland: Essays in Scots Law* will contain a number of essays on aspects of the 'debt'.
[3] Apart from the essay cited at n. 1, see especially his *Roman Law in Scotland* (Milan, 1968) *Ius Romanum Medii Aevi*, part V 13b.
[4] The fullest account of the *actio communi dividundo* in relation to Scots law in the post-institutional literature can be found in J. Rankine, *The Law of Land-Ownership in Scotland* (4th edn, Edinburgh, 1909, repr. 1986), chapter XXX.
[5] Cf. below at n. 52.

The Roman background

In Roman law the *actio communi dividundo* lay at the suit of any co-owner, whether or not he was in partnership with the other owners, to compel a division of the property held in common. A fundamental principle, expressed in a constitution of AD 294, was that *in communionem vel societatem nemo compellitur invitus deteneri*: no one is to be compelled to remain as co-owner or partner against his will.[6] The late classical jurist Paul also states that agreements between co-owners prohibiting partition have no force, although they may be valid if limited to a particular period of time.[7] The action was directed primarily at the physical division of the property in question, land being by far the most common example. It was recognised that it might prove impossible to divide the land in such a way that each former co-owner received a portion of identical value. Hence provision was made by the action for the payment of compensation by an owner who had received more than his proper share to an owner who had received less.[8] What does not seem to have been normally contemplated was that the land might be sold to a third party and the price divided between the co-owners in proportion to their interests. However, one passage in the Codex states that, as a last resort, the land might be sold to third parties in order to achieve a proper price, and that the former owners might then receive a portion of the proceeds.[9]

Although the *actio communi dividundo* was primarily a remedy to compel division of the property held in common, it also lay to rectify the consequences of mismanagement or other improper acts committed by any co-owner with respect to the property. Nor does it seem that actual division was necessary before such matters could be adjusted. Digest texts speak generally of the *actio communi dividundo* lying to remedy loss incurred by one co-owner through another's misdealing with the property. The late classical jurist Ulpian states generally that 'in an action *communi dividundo* nothing is admitted save the division of the actual things which are owned in common and that of any damage caused or done to any of these things or of any loss or expenditure being incurred by one of the co-owners or of anything coming to his hands out of common property'.[10] He also says that a co-owner by means of the action can recover a portion of any money he has legitimately spent on the property or of produce to which he is entitled[11] or of rent kept solely by another

[6] C.3.37.5.   [7] D.10.3.14.2.
[8] The procedural technicalities need not concern us here.
[9] C.3.37.3.1.
[10] D.10.3.3 *pr.* (C. H. Monro (trans.), *The Digest of Justinian*, vol. II (Cambridge, 1909), 197).
[11] H.t. 4.3.

co-owner[12] or to compel some necessary repair.[13] Paul states that the action lies for damages where one co-owner has spoilt or damaged the property under circumstances that would normally give rise to an Aquilian action.[14]

The treatment of the *actio communi dividundo* in the Institutes of Justinian deserves to be mentioned because the relevant passages have sometimes been directly relied upon by the Scottish courts. The Institutes discuss the *actio communi dividundo* not in the context of property but in that of obligations and actions. It mentions the action first under the head of quasi-contract. Where persons own property in common without being in partnership[15] and one is held to be liable to the other on the ground, for example, that he took all the fruits for himself, the obligation in question arises not from contract but from quasi-contract.[16] In the book on actions the role of the judge in the *actio communi dividundo* is examined. His primary duty is to allocate the property between the co-owners and, in so doing, to require anyone who has received property of greater value than the others to make to them an appropriate compensatory payment. Where the property is not readily divisible, the judge should award it all to one of the parties, condemning him to pay appropriate compensation to the others.[17]

The institutional writers

We may first consider how much of this Roman learning is reflected in the treatment of the institutional writers, and then consider the attitude of the Scots courts themselves. Craig discusses the question of common ownership in two paragraphs of *Ius Feudale*.[18] The first[19] adverts to a peculiarity of Scots law described as 'common pasturage and commonty', that is, an immemorial right enjoyed by a number of people to the use of the same land for the pasturing of animals or some other common purpose. After noting that 'by the civil law no person can be compelled to remain in the position of co-owner along with others' and that agreements between co-owners not to divide were treated as void on the ground of public policy, Craig observes that by Scots law persons who have a right to common pasturage and commonties may not divide the land unless all those entitled concur. This rule is, however, said not to apply to the case

---

[12] H.t. 6.2.   [13] H.t. 12.   [14] H.t. 10 *pr*.
[15] In fact the action might also lie at the suit of a *socius* (D.17.2.38.1).
[16] J.Inst.3.27.3.   [17] J.Inst.4.6.20; 4.17.4, 5.
[18] J. A. Clyde (trans.), *The Jus Feudale*, vol. I (Edinburgh, 1934). I have used the edition published at Edinburgh in 1655.
[19] 2.8.35.

in which co-heirs succeed *pro indiviso* to some item of property, since it can be divided at the suit of any one of them.

The second paragraph[20] deals explicitly with the division of common property. The only case treated is that of co-heirs, for which it appears there had been some dispute as to the circumstances under which the inheritance might be divided. Craig cites the view of 'some authorities' that all co-heirs had to agree to the division. The reason adduced by these authorities (omitted in Clyde's translation) is the civilian principle under which the person who prohibits is in the stronger legal position (*melior est condicio prohibentis*). Craig himself states the law to be that any one heir might insist on a division against the opposition of the others, and cites the Digest text already noted[21] for the proposition that any agreement between the co-heirs not to divide was void unless limited to a particular period of time. It is clear, therefore, that for the case of co-heirs Craig is stating the law of Scotland to be the same as that of Roman law in that each heir has a right to compel division. The appropriate model, although he does not mention it, is the *actio familiae erciscundae* rather than the *actio communi dividundo*. It is also clear that the opposing view, rebutted by Craig, was itself supported by a maxim derived from Roman law. Hence the discussion in the *Ius Feudale* of the right of co-heirs to divide the property held in common proceeds entirely in the context of the Civil law. It is accepted that the Roman rules or principles are to be taken as showing what the position in Scots law is, though the correct interpretation of the Roman authorities may be subject to doubt.

Stair[22] cites the Roman actions *familiae erciscundae* and *communi dividundo*[23] in the course of his discussion of the obligation of restitution. Within this obligation, he says, 'is comprehended the obligation of division, whereby what we possess in common with others, or indistinct from that which they possess, we are naturally obliged to divide it with them, whensoever they desire to quit that communion, and we are not obliged thereto by any contract or delinquence'.[24] After noting that the Roman actions were derived from this ground, he adds that, since they chiefly concern immoveables, he will deal with them in that context. In fact the only other explicit references to the actions *familiae erciscundae* or *communi dividundo* are made in the context of partnership (society), where the elliptic nature of the reference does not really permit any useful conclusion to be drawn as to the scope of these remedies in Scots law.[25]

---

[20] 2.8.41. [21] D.10.3.14.2.
[22] D. M. Walker (ed.), *The Institutions of the Law of Scotland* (2nd edn, Edinburgh, 1981).
[23] He also adds the *actio finium regundorum*, being virtually the same as the old Scots possessory action of molestation (4.27.2).
[24] 1.7.15. [25] 1.16.4.

In book 4 Stair discusses the procedure for effecting a division of property held in common, but does not in fact mention the *actio communi dividundo*. He instances the brieve of division which is said to be available to 'portioners ... such as bruik *pro indiviso*, whether they be heirs portioners, or portioners by apprising or adjudication, or if there be divers tercers who have not been kenned to a particular division'.[26] This passage identifies only a very limited class of *pro indiviso* proprietors who might have resort to a judicial remedy for division of the property, namely daughters inheriting in common (heirs-portioners), creditors who have jointly been put in possession of their debtor's land, and widows entitled to a third of a deceased husband's land under the rules of succession. Probably these were the principal classes of case for which at Stair's time the brieve of division was commonly invoked; they should not be taken as exhaustively defining its scope.

Bankton,[27] following Stair, introduces a reference to the *actiones familiae erciscundae* and *communi dividundo* in the context of restitution.[28] Nothing is said as to the scope of these actions in Scots law. The brieve of division is stated to apply to 'co-heirs, co-adjudgers or other conjoint proprietors'. A note of the special rules applicable to heirs-portioners is added.[29] The phrase 'other conjoint proprietors' suggests a wider sphere of application for the brieve than the range of examples given by Stair.

Erskine[30] speaks of the 'communion of goods' as a quasi-contract, 'for where two or more persons become common proprietors of the same subject by legacy, purchase or gift without the view of any copartnership an obligation is thereby created among the proprietors, without any covenant, by which they are mutually obliged to communicate the profit and loss arising from the subject while it remains common'. He then notes that 'common subjects' in Roman law were subject to division by the action *communi dividundo*, adding that 'such division when limited to moveable subjects has been always competent by the law of Scotland'.[31] There is an implication here that immoveables by Scots law are not subject to division in the same way. This implication is confirmed by the following discussion, which cites a number of special cases in which Scots law provides a remedy by way of division or the like, namely the action by which a ship might be sold at a public roup and the proceeds divided between the co-owners, the brieve of terce by which land held in common between heir and tercer was divided, and the brieve of division by which

---

[26] 4.3.12.
[27] *An Institute of the Law of Scotland*. I have used the edition published in 1751.
[28] 1.8.36.   [29] 1.8.38.
[30] *An Institute of the Law of Scotland*. I have used the edition by J. Badenach Nicholson, published in 1871.
[31] Inst.3.3.56.

heirs-portioners might secure a division of the land they inherited. The only other example given by Erskine of land which Scots law permitted to be divided is that of 'commons or commonties', division of which was authorised by a statute of 1695. One might, therefore, extract from Erskine the conclusion that the Roman action *communi dividundo* was accepted into Scots law only with respect to the division of moveables, and that land held in common was not divisible unless the common (feudal) law of Scotland or the legislature had developed a special remedy.

An important point emerges from Erskine's analysis, namely that the relevance for Scots law of the old Roman *actio communi dividundo* is confined to the case of co-ownership of moveables. There is at least an implication that for land it was Scots law itself which had independently evolved its own remedy, i.e. the brieve of division, for the case where any co-owner sought a separation of interests. This brieve was not modelled on, or inspired by, the *actio communi dividundo*. One can see that this view could be supported from the treatment in Stair and Bankton (though not Craig), which discusses the brieve of division without explicit reference to the Roman action, even though Stair had originally implied that the latter was primarily relevant to the case of immoveables.

Not until Bell[32] is there a systematic discussion of the nature of rights in common. He points out that the previous Institutional writers have not adequately distinguished between three kinds of rights in common:

1. Common Property, in which the several parties have, *pro indiviso*, the same equal but undivided right, each being entitled to the joint use and enjoyment of the subject, and mutual consent being necessary in all acts of management or disposal; 2. Common Interest, in which there is a mixture of property in one, restrained or qualified by an interest in another for the maintenance and preservation of the subject; and 3. Commonty, in which a right, not of common property, but only of common use, is conferred on several persons by the proprietor of the subject.[33]

Of particular importance is the distinction between common property and commonty, only the former arguably falling within the ambit of the *actio communi dividundo*. Bell himself makes no reference to this action or directly to the Roman law, although certain of the rules which he cites show a clear Roman origin. Among the rules for the management of common property he lists *in re communi melior est conditio prohibentis* (for the case of property held in common the person who prohibits is in the better legal position), which is derived from D.10.3.28.[34] When speaking

---

[32] *Principles of the Law of Scotland.* I have used the tenth edition, by W. Guthrie, published in 1899.
[33] *Ibid.*, para. 1071.   [34] *Ibid.*, para. 1075.

of the division of common property,[35] he states 'it is a rule that no one is bound to remain in community, but may insist for a division'. For this topic he states the following rules: (1) if the parties cannot agree, the subject, where possible, must be divided, co-adjudgers formerly being entitled to have the property adjudged by them divided by brieve of division, replaced later by judicial sale;[36] (2) joint proprietors may still have the subject divided by brieve of division or by an action of declarator and division;[37] (3) if the subject cannot be divided, it should be sold at the instance of any of the co-owners and the price divided between them;[38] and (4) heirs-portioners, females succeeding jointly *ab intestato*, are entitled to equal shares, subject to some special benefits accorded the eldest.[39]

Although the institutional writers undoubtedly show some influence from the Roman law in their treatment of common property, notably in the adoption of the principle that no one might be forced to remain in communion against his own will, the attention paid to the *actio communi dividundo* is small. Probably the classification of the action in the Institutes of Justinian under the head of quasi-contract was responsible for its inclusion by the Scottish writers under the head of restitution, although nowhere is the Justinianic source directly acknowledged. But it does not seem that there is any firm institutional authority for the proposition that the *actio communi dividundo* was the model from which the brieve of division, applicable where co-owners of land sought a separation of interests, was derived. This remedy appears to have been treated as a part of the indigenous customary law. Erskine is the writer who most clearly demonstrates such an approach, but it may have been implicit in the thought of Stair, Bankton and Bell. It is the judges who firmly established the *actio communi dividundo* as the basis of the general law of co-ownership in Scotland.

The cases

Not all the cases considered below make an explicit reference to the *actio communi dividundo* or even to Roman law. Indeed broadly they may be divided into two groups: those which appeal to the Roman law as a source for the rules to be adopted in Scotland, and those which make no such appeal but simply discuss and develop the rules governing ownership in common as part of Scots law itself. The latter group has been included to

---

[35] *Ibid.*, para. 1079. [36] *Ibid.*, para. 1080.
[37] *Ibid.*, para. 1081. [38] *Ibid.*, para. 1081, 2.
[39] *Ibid.*, para. 1083. See also the brief remarks in J. M'Laren (ed.), *Commentaries on the Laws of Scotland* (7th edn, Edinburgh, 1870), vol. I, 62.

show the main outlines of the way in which the remedy for division or sale of property held in common has been deployed in Scots law, but no attempt has been made to offer an exhaustive account of the law relating to common ownership. As will be seen, the cases of this group evidence a state of the law broadly consistent with that which obtained in Roman law as to the circumstances governing the availability of the *actio communi dividundo*.

A point related to the above concerns individual judicial preference (or indeed the preference of counsel) for an appeal to Roman law. Some judges and counsel make much of this; others prefer to discuss the position purely in terms of contemporary Scots law itself. However, it should be noted that, even where a decision makes no express mention of Roman law, it is often founded either on earlier decisions which do, or on broader principles of the law which are unanimously accepted as derived from the Roman law, such as the principle that no one should be bound in communion where he is unwilling. Something further on these issues will be said in the concluding remarks.

Prior to the opinion of Lord Rutherfurd in *Brock* v. *Hamilton* (1852) the courts showed some uncertainty in the determination of the principles upon which any co-owner might be entitled to seek a division of the land. The earliest case to be discussed is that of *Cowie* v. *Cowies*, which came before the courts at various times during the years 1707 and 1708.[40] It concerned the claims which arose between five sisters who had inherited an estate as heirs-portioners. The first issue raised concerned the entitlement of the eldest sister to the mansion house without the necessity of paying compensation to the others. The latter had argued on the basis of a number of civilian authorities that under the *iudicium familiae erciscundae* there should be equal division of the property falling within the inheritance, or, if that was not possible, that compensation should be paid by those who had received more to those who had received less. However, the court rejected this appeal to civilian authority on the ground that by the feudal law obtaining in Scotland the custom was that the eldest daughter should receive the mansion house without the obligation to pay compensation to her sisters, Stair 3.5.11 being cited as decisive in this respect. The second issue concerned the eldest daughter's claim that, in addition to the mansion house, she was also entitled to the orchard appending to it, the court by a 'scrimp majority' holding in her favour.

The third and final issue concerned the claim of the eldest sister that the remaining lands should be divided between her and her sisters on the basis

---

[40] M.2453, 5362.

that she would receive that portion of the land adjacent to the orchard with compensation being paid to her sisters should it be more valuable than the portions left for them. In support of her claim she cited two texts from the Corpus Iuris Civilis, Inst.4.17.4,5 and D.10.3.2.1.[41] On this matter the court could not agree. Some judges thought that the old brieve of division was available, others that there was no power in the court to order a division, since no specific Act of Parliament or other law could be found in Scots law authorising such a division. The report of the case concludes with the observation that the court demurred as to its power.

Why should there have been doubt as to the availability of the brieve of division? Although the *Ius Feudale* is not cited specifically by the court, the judges may have had in mind the difference of opinion to which Craig refers. Some authorities had in effect treated land held in common by heirs-portioners in the same way as a commonty: division was not to be permitted without the consent of all those entitled. The court in *Cowie* may therefore have considered the principle with respect to co-heirs to be insufficiently settled. The extent to which the judges, or some of them, regarded the availability of the brieve of division as controlled by the feudal law or by the principles of Roman law cannot be determined.

Stewart v. *Feuars of Tillicoultry* in 1739[42] concerned the interpretation of the Act of 1695 which regulated commonties. One may merely note an argument made by the pursuers to the effect that 'common properties might have been divided upon the footing of the common law, *actione communi dividundo*'.[43] This shows that lawyers were prepared to argue that Scots law had received the principles governing the *actio communi dividundo*, at least to the extent of permitting division of land held in common ownership.

Milligan v. *Barnhill* in 1782[44] illustrates a different legal approach being taken to the competence of Scots law to order division of land held in common. The case arose from a partnership between the pursuer and defender in a brewery business, each being entitled *pro indiviso* to one half of the premises. Upon the dissolution of the partnership one of the former partners brought an action to compel the other either to buy his share at a certain price or to sell him his own share at the same price, or to agree to a public sale followed by division of the price. The defender argued that the enactment of the 1695 Act relating to commonties permitted the inference that at Common law proprietors holding *pro indiviso* shares in property could not be compelled to divide except in the case of a ship. This argument is directly opposed to that raised by the pursuer in *Stewart's Case*.

---

[41] See above, p. 161.   [42] M.2469.   [43] M.2469, 2470.   [44] M.2486.

The pursuer in *Milligan* replied to the effect that the right of a co-owner in a ship to insist upon a division was only an example of a general rule recognised by the Common law, according to which the differing interests of joint proprietors could be effectively realised in one of the ways now proposed. In support of this proposition the pursuer cited Stair[45] and Bankton,[46] and instanced the same rule as obtaining in Roman law. Apart from certain passages from the Codex,[47] he cited D.10.2.55, which stated that, where under the *actiones familiae erciscundae* or *communi dividundo* a division proved in practice to be impossible, the judge might award the whole of the property to one of the claimants. He also argued that, had the remedy been sought in the context of the *actio pro socio* while the partnership still subsisted, the defender would have had no plea.

The Bench, finding for the pursuer, succinctly observed:

No person in such a case as the present is to be compelled to remain longer *in communione* then he chooses. Long before the act of 1695 the brief of division was known respecting property in lands. That statute, with a view to the improvement of agriculture, refers to the particular nature of commonties and does not relate to common property in general. With regard to this, as in the case of heirs portioners, such remedies as those here proposed, must always have been competent.[48]

Although the court in this passage does not directly refer to Roman law or mention the *actio communi dividundo*, it clearly accepted as received into Scots law the basic Roman and civilian principle according to which any co-proprietor could insist upon a division of the property. This applied irrespective of whether the ground of the common ownership had been a partnership or some other legal state of affairs such as an inheritance. Further, the court may have accepted the pursuer's argument, derived from texts of the Codex and the Digest, that, where the property was difficult to divide physically, the appropriate course was a sale of the whole and division of the price, unless any one owner was prepared to purchase at a fair price the shares of the others.[49]

Scots law had to wait until 1852 for an authoritative judicial exposition of the main principles governing division of land held in common. In that year Lord Rutherfurd in the case of *Brock* v. *Hamilton*[50] delivered a judgment which has since been accepted as the *locus classicus*. An action of declarator for division and sale was raised at the instance of the trustee

---

[45] Walker (ed.), *Institutions* 1.7.15.   [46] *Institute* 1.8.40.   [47] C.3.37.1, 3.
[48] M.2486, 2487.
[49] Some decades later it was held in the case of *Stewart* v. *Simpson* (1835, 14 S.72), where the essential facts were similar to those of *Milligan*, that the pursuer's right was that of sale of the premises held in common and division of the price. It was not necessary first for either of the former partners to attempt to buy the share of the other.
[50] Reported in a note to *Anderson* v. *Anderson* (1857, 19 D.701).

in bankruptcy of one of two *pro indiviso* proprietors of certain lands in Glasgow. Both parties had agreed that in practice the lands were incapable of division. The defender, founding on Erskine 3.3.56, had apparently first argued that the right to division in Scots law was in principle limited to moveables and that, with respect to immoveables, the brieve of division lay only as between heir and tercer or as between co-heirs. However, the court found, in the light of Stair's exposition of the law, that this contention was unfounded. Lord Rutherfurd stated, 'There can be no question it is thought, after the authority of Lord Stair, referring to the Roman law, that an action for division of heritable property held *pro indiviso*, though by singular titles, was imported into the law of Scotland in the form of a brief of division in very ancient times.'[51] Erskine's remarks on this point were to be discounted. His Lordship thus interpreted Stair as stating that the brieve of division itself was modelled on the *actio communi dividundo*. As has been seen, there is some doubt on this point. A possible interpretation of Stair's language, notably his assertion that, since the *actio communi dividundo* is concerned mainly with immoveables, he will deal with it in that context, would support Lord Rutherfurd's conclusion. Nevertheless, it is perhaps odd that Stair says nothing explicitly about the Roman action when discussing the Scots brieve of division.

In reviewing the authorities Lord Rutherfurd made two important points. First, he asserted that 'we have borrowed from the Roman law, and introduced into our common law actions of the same nature and import with those of the Roman law *familiae erciscundae*[52] and *communi dividundo*'.[53] Secondly, he cited the cases of *Milligan* and *Stewart*[54] as showing that upon the principles of Roman law, incorporated into Scots law, an action for division lay with respect not only to property actually held in co-partenary but also to that held under circumstances creating *quasi ex societate* the relation of co-partenary.

The defender then accepted this view of the law, but founded his argument upon the fact that, although an action for division might be competent should the lands in fact be divisible, where they were not physically divisible no action for sale and division of the price was competent. His point was that Scots law had borrowed from Roman law

---

[51] 19 D.701, 702.
[52] It is interesting in the light of this remark to record the opinion of Lord Justice-Clerk Hope given a few years earlier in *M'Neight* v. *Lockhart* (1843, 6 D.128, 136): 'The brieve of division has been likened to the action *familiae erciscundae*. That point was fully discussed in the Court in the case of the daughters of Lord Roseberry Nov. 8, 1744 (Elch. II p. 3) when, as Elchies mentions, Arniston argued, long and well, that there is no such action in the law of Scotland, and so the Court found.'
[53] 19 D.701, 702.   [54] See n. 49 above.

merely the right of a co-proprietor to insist on a division of the property as against the others. The question whether the property should be sold and the price divided related merely to the form of the remedy, and an affirmative answer could not be derived from the principles underlying the *actio communi dividundo*.

This argument was decisively rejected by Lord Rutherfurd. He found that the basic principle of Roman law applicable to the case, namely that 'no one should be bound to remain indefinitely *in communione* with another or others as proprietors of a common property',[55] entailed not only the right at the instance of any one of the co-proprietors to a physical division but also, should such a division prove to be impracticable, the right to have the whole property sold and the price divided. The Civil law itself, like the European systems influenced by it, had permitted the public sale of the property as a last resort. This was permitted not only in the case of obligations arising from contract (*societas*) but in those arising from quasi-contract, as through succession, where the Roman law treated the co-proprietors as though they were partners and accorded similar remedies.

In Scots law, following Roman law, the primary object of the action for division or sale was physical division of the property between the co-proprietors; but should this not be practicable either because the property was incapable of physical division or because the parties could not agree on the amount of compensation that should be paid where one of them wished to acquire the whole, 'public sale, under the authority of the Court, becomes plainly the only course'.[56] His Lordship added that, whereas the pursuer was not bound to advance equitable considerations entitling him to the remedy of physical division of the property or, should that be inappropriate, to sale and division of the price, it was open to the defender to show that division or sale might in the circumstances of the case be inequitable. Both the observations as to 'public sale' and 'equity' caused some difficulty in later cases.[57]

The decision in *Brock* v. *Hamilton* settled three points with respect to the law of Scotland, points which had been raised and discussed before, but which had not been fully elaborated or authoritatively settled. First, the principles underlying the *actiones familiae erciscundae* and *communi dividundo*, in particular that which stated that no one should be bound to remain *in communione* when unwilling, were stated to be part of Scots law. Secondly, these principles applied equally to heritage as to moveables, and equally to persons holding in common as partners and to those

[55] 19 D.701, 703.   [56] *Ibid.*
[57] See the cases of *Crathes Fishings Ltd* v. *Bailey's Executors* and *Campbell* v. *Murray* discussed below.

holding in common on some other ground. Thirdly, under these principles there was a right not only to the physical division of the property but also to its sale with subsequent division of the price. The latter right was presented as subordinate to the former in the sense that in Roman as in Scots law the right to sell and divide the price was available only should the physical division of the land between the co-proprietors prove to be impracticable. One point of uncertainty did perhaps remain. Some of Lord Rutherfurd's language could be construed in the sense that all the rules governing the applicability of the *actiones familiae erciscundae* or *communi dividundo* had been received into Scots law. Whether he actually meant this should be regarded as doubtful.

After the decision in *Brock* v. *Hamilton* problems continued to surface both with respect to the relationship between the right to divide physically and the right to sell and divide the price, and with respect to the former right itself. In *Anderson* v. *Anderson* Lord Deas stated that at Common law the right of the *pro indiviso* proprietor was 'to have the subject divided, and, if not divisible, to have it sold. The ordinary rule is that no man is bound to remain longer in communion than he pleases.'[58] The implication of this remark, admittedly *obiter*, is that the right to have the property divided physically is primary and that the right to have it sold and the price divided is subsidiary, being available only should the property not be divisible.

In *Thom* v. *MacBeth*[59] the question as to what is meant by 'divisible' was raised. The defender, who was one of the proprietors with a *pro indiviso* interest in a landed estate, argued that the estate should not be divided at all, or, if the interests of the proprietors were to be split, then the estate should be divided physically. It was held by the Inner House that this contention could not be sustained, and that the pursuer was entitled to insist upon sale of the whole property and division of the price between the co-proprietors. The Lord Justice-Clerk (Lord Moncreiff) deduced from the judgment of Lord Rutherfurd in *Brock* that, where a division was not 'reasonably practicable without sacrificing to an appreciable extent the interests of some or all of the parties the only resort is a sale and division of the price'.[60] Lord Ormidale took a similar approach, observing that, where physical division of the property would adversely affect its value, the proper course was to authorise sale and division of the price.[61] Lord Gifford emphasised that, while almost any property could be physically divided, regard should be had to questions of 'expense of division and of deterioration or possible destruction of the value of the subject';[62] it was a consideration of these factors which would determine

[58] 1857, 19 D.700, 704.   [59] 1875, 3 R.161.   [60] 3 R.161, 164.   [61] *Ibid.*
[62] 3 R.161, 165.

whether a property should be physically divided or sold and the price divided. The case as a whole is authority for the proposition that a co-proprietor can insist upon sale of the property and division of the price where a physical division would reduce its market value.

In *Provost Magistrates and Councillors of Banff* v. *Ruthin Castle Ltd*,[63] the essential question before the court was whether certain lands gifted to the provost, magistrates and councillors of the burghs of Banff and MacDuff in the form 'jointly and to their assignees' became part of the 'common good' of each of the burghs. If it did, a lease granted by the pursuers was void by statute. Hence the pursuers were concerned to argue that the effect of the words 'jointly and to their assignees' was to constitute them 'joint' and not 'common' proprietors. This contention was rejected by the Inner House. Lord MacKay refused to allow that there was a general class of 'joint ownership' characterised by the fact that 'the common proprietors were tied to one another indissolubly until they mutually agreed on some specific mode of untying the knot', thus excluding the remedy of division or sale. He admitted the existence only of some exceptional cases where this was true, most arising under the law of trust.[64] Lord Wark held that

A destination to A and B jointly and their heirs and assignees imports a right of proprietorship in each of the disponees to the extent of one-half *pro indiviso*, with full power of disposal thereof independently of each other ... Any attempt to restrain that right of disposal is inept as being contrary to public policy. The right of division has been imported into Scots law from Roman law.[65]

The Lord Justice-Clerk (Lord Cooper) noted that the institutional treatment of 'common property' as well as that of Pothier[66] could all be traced back to a paragraph in the Institutes of Justinian[67] which treated the obligation between persons who owned a thing in common without being in partnership as arising from quasi-contract and as enforceable by the *actio communi dividundo*. The absolute right of each co-owner to terminate the communion at will is derived both in Roman and Scots law from public policy. Joint property, on the other hand, where no such right to leave the communion is present, arises only in a limited number of cases in which the parties stand in some special relationship to each other, as in the case of a partnership or an unincorporated association.[68]

The question of the appropriate remedy (division or sale) also arose in

[63] 1944 S.L.T. 373. [64] 1944 S.L.T. 373, 382. [65] 1944 S.L.T. 373, 385.
[66] This is a reference to Pothier's essay *Du quasi-contrat de communauté*, printed as an appendix to his *Traité du contrat de société*, in *Œuvres de Pothier* (1819), vol. 6, 619.
[67] J.Inst.3.27.3.
[68] 1944 S.L.T. 373, 388. It is not proposed here to go into the complex question of the relationship between common property and partnership. See J. Bennett Miller, *The Law of Partnership in Scotland* (Edinburgh, 1973), 65f., 376f., 387f.

Crathes Fishings Ltd v. *Bailey's Executors*.[69] Here the dispute concerned salmon fishings. The executors of one of two *pro indiviso* proprietors had sold his share to a company, and the share of the other had passed to his executors. The company sought a declarator of its right to insist on a sale of the salmon fishings and a division of the price. It averred that the property was incapable of division, but in any event insisted that it had an absolute right to a sale. The defenders argued that, since the salmon fishings were capable of division, this was the appropriate remedy. They further argued that, since the company had acquired its share in order to sell fishing rights on a commercial basis and had not acted in good faith, it was not entitled to a sale.

The Lord Ordinary (Lord Clyde) analysed Lord Rutherfurd's opinion in *Brock* and concluded that the references to equity in that case did not support the defender's view that equitable objections might be raised to the whole action of division or sale. All that could be extracted from the judgment was that equitable considerations might determine whether the appropriate remedy was division or sale. His Lordship dismissed as irrelevant the defender's allegation of mala fides on the part of the pursuers. On this point he had been referred to certain Digest texts and two textbooks of Roman law. What he found most in point was the statement in Buckland's *Textbook of Roman Law* to the effect that each co-owner had an absolute right to division of the property and that agreements not to divide were void.[70] He then added an important qualification with respect to the utility of the Roman texts for the development of Scots law: 'There was apparently some difference between the Roman *actio* [that is, *communi dividundo*] and the Scottish action as it has now developed and it may be that the Roman texts require to be treated with some reservation.'[71]

When the case went to appeal,[72] the Inner House upheld the Lord Ordinary's judgment and also contributed some observations on the help to be derived from Roman law for the settlement of the rules to be applied in Scotland. The Lord President (Lord Hope) stated the general rule in Scotland to be that a co-owner had an absolute right to insist upon division or sale subject only to the possibility that he might have deprived himself of that right by contract or personal bar. His Lordship noted: 'There are traces in Roman law of an acceptance that an agreement not to demand the subjects for a certain period was valid, although an agreement not ever to do so was not (D.10.3.14.2 and 3).'[73] Lord Allanbridge, with reference to the defenders' reliance upon the bona fide nature of the

---

[69] 1990 S.L.T. 46.   [70] (3rd edn, revised P. Stein, Cambridge, 1963), 540.
[71] 1990 S.L.T. 46, 49.
[72] 1991 S.L.T. 747.   [73] 1991 S.L.T. 747, 749.

Roman *actio communi dividundo*, agreed with the Lord Ordinary's comment that the Roman texts should be treated with caution. While under Roman law there was no doubt that a co-owner had a right to division, there was no clear Roman authority for the view that bad faith (mala fides) deprived him of that right. His Lordship pointed out the possible difference between classical and Justinianic law, the latter but probably not the former treating the action as based on good faith.[74] Lord Mayfield accepted that the *actio communi dividundo* was a *bonae fidei iudicium*, but held that this did not mean that in Scots law equitable considerations might bar a co-owner from recourse to his basic remedy of division or sale.[75]

It is significant that both the Outer and the Inner House gave serious consideration to the question whether rules stated in the Corpus Iuris Civilis should be treated as also being rules of Scots law. The approach of the court may be put in this way. Even though there is general agreement that a branch of the law of Scotland has been derived from Roman law, that branch in this case being the rules governing common ownership of land, it is not the case that each Roman rule relating to that topic will necessarily be deemed to be part of the law of Scotland. Yet, at the same time, the court will consider on its merits whether a particular Roman rule should be adopted. There are suggestions in *Crathes* that a rule may not be accepted into Scots law where its status in Roman law is uncertain or where it does not accord with the way Scots law has already developed.

Subsidiary issues which have arisen before the Scots courts have concerned the possibility of limitations upon the 'absolute' right to sell or divide, the type of sale which the court should permit, and the availability of remedies other than the action for division and sale between co-owners. One of the issues before the court in *Grant* v. *Heriots Trust*[76] was the validity of a clause contained in a series of feu charters granted around the year 1760 to a number of persons constituting them owners in common with respect to certain land. The clause provided that 'it shall not be in the power of the said . . . (disponee) or his foresaids, to pursue for a division of or build up the said common property, it being agreed to by all the parties concerned that the same shall remain an open area in all time coming'. Although this clause in so far as it purported to prevent a co-owner from seeking a division of the property was held by all the members of the Inner House to be unenforceable at the time the case came before the court, they did not analyse its effect in precisely the same way. The Lord President (Lord Dunedin), after observing it to be 'familiar law' that no co-owner might alter the legal or physical state of the property without the consent

[74] 1991 S.L.T. 747, 751–2.   [75] 1991 S.L.T. 747, 754.   [76] 1906, 8 F.647.

of all the other co-owners, held that the clause purporting to prevent a co-owner from seeking a division of the property was a nullity. 'I have no hesitation in saying that to give a thing in common property and at the same time to say that you are not to pursue a division is an impossibility according to the law of Scotland.'[77] Lord M'Laren did not go as far as this. He considered that the obligation not to sue for a division 'might possibly be binding on the original grantee and his heirs, but certainly would not be enforced against a singular successor, because it is an obligation of the same class as the condition *non alienandi sine consensu superiorum* (may not be alienated without the consent of the superior), which by Act of Parliament is declared to be of no effect'.[78] It is of interest that his Lordship referred to an Act of Parliament in this context rather than to the Roman law which contained explicit rules on the effect of an agreement between co-owners not to divide the property. Lord Kinnear simply said 'there was attached to the right of property a condition against division which would probably have been ineffectual'.[79]

In *Morrison* v. *Kirk*[80] the question also arose whether co-proprietors might be barred from resort to an action for division or sale of the property. Here all the co-proprietors had granted a bond over the property, and the bondholders had refused to allocate the bond in the event of a division of the property. Although it was found possible to divide the property into three more or less equal parts, where one co-owner brought an action for division, the others objected on two grounds: (1) that the implied understanding, when the co-owners first obtained the bond, was that no division should be sought until at least the time when the bond fell due in 1912, and (2) that the division would be prejudicial to the interests of the bondholders. Both these arguments were rejected by the Inner House. Lord Salvesen (with whom the other two judges concurred) observed 'Unless a *pro indiviso* proprietor has barred himself by contract from resorting to an action of division or sale, he has an absolute right at common law to insist in such an action. If it should turn out that division is impracticable, or would operate unfairly, then his remedy is to have the properties sold and the price divided.'[81] He also found both that there was 'no relevant averment of any agreement by the pursuer that she should not resort to her common law rights as a *pro indiviso* proprietor',[82] and that the interests of the bondholders were in no way threatened by the proposed division.

Where the remedy sought was the sale rather than the physical division of the property, a further question which the courts have had to consider

[77] 8 F.647, 658. [78] 8 F.647, 665. [79] 8 F.647, 667. [80] 1912 S.C. 44.
[81] 1912 S.C. 44, 47.
[82] 1912 S.C. 44, 48.

has been the kind of sale to be authorised, in particular, whether it was always to be a 'public roup'. In *Campbell* v. *Murray*[83] the pursuers, being the *pro indiviso* proprietors as to two-thirds of a motel, sought the authorisation of the court for its sale by private treaty under circumstances which showed both that the motel could not be physically divided without great loss of value and that sale by public roup would be less advantageous than sale by private treaty. The Lord Ordinary refused authorisation on the ground that the invariable custom in such cases had been sale by 'public roup'. His judgment was overturned by the Inner House. The Lord President (Lord Emslie) referred to the expression 'public sale' found in the judgment of Lord Rutherfurd in *Brock*, upon which the Lord Ordinary had relied, and noted that this was not the same as 'sale by roup'. Lord Rutherfurd had not been 'addressing his mind to the forms of sale which might satisfy the description of public sale under the authority of the Court'.[84] The Lord President found that in 1972 sale by public roup was not necessarily the best way of testing the market and obtaining a fair price. Hence in this case a sale by private treaty should be allowed.

The matter of the kind of sale to be authorised was more fully considered by the Outer House in *Scrimgeour* v. *Scrimgeour*.[85] A divorced husband and wife were jointly *pro indiviso* proprietors of the matrimonial home solely occupied by the wife. The latter brought an action for division and sale seeking to purchase her husband's share at a price to be fixed by a third party appointed by the court. The Lord Ordinary (Lord McCluskey) in granting this request traced the development of the law of the matter in Scotland. He noted that prior to *Campbell* v. *Murray* the practice had been to offer the property for sale at a public roup; since that decision it had been possible to sell by private negotiation. Such procedure did not, however, exhaust the possibilities open to the court. His Lordship accepted the pursuer's contention that the court might order a sale only as between the *pro indiviso* proprietors such that one acquired the whole property with a fair compensation going to the other. In this connexion he relied upon passages from the Institutes of Justinian[86] and the Codex Justinianus[87] which had been cited to the court by counsel. These passages authorised the judge in the *actio communi dividundo* to assign the whole of the property to one of the co-owners with compensating payments to the other(s), either where the property could not readily be divided or where one of several co-owners bid the highest price for the shares of the others. The institutional writers themselves are interpreted

[83] 1972 S.C. 310. [84] 1972 S.C. 310, 312–13. [85] 1988 S.L.T. 590.
[86] J.Inst.4.6.20; 4.17.5.
[87] C.3.37 (wrongly cited in the judgment as title 32).

as recognising the survival of a closed form of sale antedating resort to a public roup under which the co-owners were the only participants. Finally the Lord Ordinary adverted to, and apparently approved, a submission on behalf of the pursuer

that the Scots law on the matter is in fact not just derived from the Roman law but is taken in its entirety from the Roman law. The question of the remedy ... is part of the substantive law or right itself. The practice of the court in Scotland has simply been an application of the principles of Roman law, although the adjectival form has been necessarily Scottish.[88]

Although it is doubtful whether this proposition would be acceptable to all judges, Lord McCluskey's judgment does demonstrate the extent to which texts from the Corpus Iuris Civilis can still be cited and accepted as direct authority for the position in Scots law.

Some of the texts in the Digest suggest that where a disagreement arose between co-owners with respect to the property or damage to it, the appropriate legal recourse was the *actio communi dividundo*. Decisions of the Scottish courts without directly referring to Roman law also take the same approach. In *Price* v. *Watson*,[89] one of two *pro indiviso* proprietors had taken exclusive possession while the other was absent abroad. The latter on his return brought an action of ejectment to secure the removal of the defender from that part of the property of which he himself claimed occupation. The Inner House found for the defender on the ground that the pursuer's proper remedy was the action for division and sale. Lord President Cooper observed that neither *pro indiviso* proprietor without the consent of the other had a right to the exclusive possession of any part of the property, and that at first sight the only remedy afforded by Scots law in a situation such as that before the court was the action of division and sale. Hence he did not wish to exclude the possibility that in certain circumstances an action of ejectment might lie at the suit of one *pro indiviso* proprietor against another.[90] Lord Keith held that the dispute concerned the management of the property. Where co-owners could not agree, Scots law provided only two remedies: either the appointment by the court of a judicial factor to manage the property on behalf of all the co-owners, or an action for division and sale.[91]

A similar, though not identical, issue arose in *Denholm's Trustees* v. *Denholm*.[92] A brother held a two-thirds *pro indiviso* interest in certain farms, and his two sisters each held a *pro indiviso* interest as to one-sixth. The brother, without the agreement of his sisters or the trustees of the estate, was in sole occupation of the farms. The sisters and the trustees

[88] 1988 S.L.T. 590, 593.   [89] 1951 S.L.T. 266.   [90] 1951 S.L.T. 266, 268.
[91] 1951 S.L.T. 266, 269.
[92] 1984 S.L.T. 319.

raised an action for recompense, claiming rent in respect of their share in the farms. The Lord Ordinary (Lord Allanbridge) in rejecting the action took the same approach as that adopted by the court in *Price* v. *Watson*. Referring particularly to the judgment of Lord Keith in that case, he held that the dispute concerned the management of the property, for which the appropriate remedy was either the appointment of a judicial factor or an action for division and sale.

Concluding remarks

In assessing the influence which the *actio communi dividundo* has had on the development of the law relating to common ownership in Scotland, one has to distinguish two questions: what in point of fact has been its influence, and what have writers or judges believed its influence to have been? The distinction is important with respect to the alleged influence of the Roman action on the law of common ownership of land in Scotland. It is generally considered that the remedy of division or sale by which the separation of common proprietors is effected is of primary importance in relation to land. Yet it is precisely in this context that some doubt exists as to whether in fact the old brieve of division from which the action for sale or division is derived was itself modelled on the *actio communi dividundo* or was an independent product of Scots common or feudal law. It is by no means clear that there is solid institutional authority for the former proposition, though it is clear both that there is solid judicial authority for it and that the judges have believed that institutional authority as a whole supports it. Thus one important conclusion which may be drawn from the material studied in this essay is that it is the courts and not the institutional writers who have established the Roman law and specifically the *actio communi dividundo* as the basis of the law of common ownership in Scotland.

However, as has already been noted, not all cases concerned with common ownership in land and not all judges have invoked the Roman law. Indeed, generally speaking, judicial affirmation of the *actio communi dividundo* as the root of the Scots law was very slow in coming. At the beginning of the eighteenth century the courts were certainly not prepared to make such an affirmation.[93] In two other eighteenth-century cases, arguments were submitted to the court on the relevance of Roman law for the Scots law on division or sale of property held in common. Although they were not rejected by the court, they were not explicitly made the foundation of its judgment, at least according to the available

---

[93] *Cowie* v. *Cowies* (1707; above, n. 40).

reports.[94] One has to wait until 1852 for an authoritative judicial statement which locates Roman law and specifically the *actio communi dividundo* as the source of the Scots rules.[95] Was this a piece of 'historical engineering' (even if accomplished in good faith), or was it belated recognition of the true course of evolution taken by Scots law in its treatment of common ownership? Further studies on the early history of the brieve of division will be needed before one can be sure of the answer. It is worth remembering that already Craig in the first part of the seventeenth century had cited authorities to the effect that in Scots law co-heirs had to agree to any division of the inheritance.

Perhaps, however, it is a mistake even to postulate a true course of evolution waiting to be discovered and charted. One might have to accept that, whatever the pre-nineteenth-century history of the rules of common ownership, the effect of Lord Rutherfurd's judgment was to create a new source and fount of inspiration for those rules. From this point of view one simply has to accept that Lord Rutherfurd inaugurated a new start for the development of the law and provided the authority which permitted later judges to go back to the texts of Roman law in their search for a relevant rule to be applied in Scots law.

With respect to the post-*Brock* development of the law of common ownership, it is difficult to avoid the conclusion that specific recourse to rules of Roman law depends very much on the individual predilections of counsel or judges. Of the nine cases decided after *Brock*, considered in this paper, only three[96] make in their judgments an explicit reference to Roman law. In both the most recent of these decisions the judges on the facts found it expedient to go back to Roman law in order to support their rulings. Paradoxically it looks as though appeal to Roman law may again be becoming judicially fashionable in this area of the law, even though judges on occasion may be careful to point out that not all the rules established by the Roman jurists with reference to the *actio communi dividundo* can be assumed to be part of Scots law (*Crathes*). Perhaps the second important conclusion to be drawn is that, although by no means all cases concerned with common property refer to Roman law, this source remains available to help judges in the decision of difficult cases. Not until a court has actually identified which of the specific Roman rules is to be taken as part of the law of Scotland can that rule be so regarded. In other words one has again to distinguish two questions. The first can be

---

[94] *Stewart* v. *Feuars of Tillicoultry* (1739; above, n. 42); *Milligan* v. *Barnhill* (1782; above, n. 44).
[95] Lord Rutherfurd in *Brock* v. *Hamilton* (1852; above, n. 50).
[96] *Provost etc of Banff* v. *Ruthin Castle Ltd* (1944; above, n. 63); *Scrimgeour* v. *Scrimgeour* (1988; above, n. 85); *Crathes Fishing Ltd* v. *Bailey's Executors* (1990 and 1991; above, nn. 69 and 72).

put in this way: is the Scots law of common ownership derived from the Roman law, specifically that concerned with the *actio communi dividundo*? At this broad level the answer, at least since Lord Rutherfurd's judgment in *Brock*, is 'yes'. The second question concerns the extent to which each of the individual Roman rules associated with the *actio communi dividundo* can be deemed to be part of Scots law. The answer can here be affirmative only where one has an express judicial ruling on the point.

Finally, one may ask in what sense can Roman law be said to be 'authoritative' for the Scots law of common ownership? This question itself may be phrased more specifically in the form: what 'authority' have the courts in developing the rules of common ownership ascribed to texts from the Corpus Iuris Civilis? Such questions admit at least of a double answer. In the first place that portion of Roman law subsumed under the head of the *actio communi dividundo* has been judicially held to have been received into the law of Scotland. What remains in some doubt is the extent of the reception. Yet it is clear that the main principles governing the operation of the action have been incorporated into Scots law. These may be summarised as follows. No person with a *pro indiviso* interest in property held in common can be barred from seeking a separation of his interest unless he is personally bound by contract not so to proceed.[97] In giving effect to an application by a co-owner for a separation of interests a court may consider the following options: physical division of the property, requiring it to be sold by public auction or private treaty and the price divided between the co-owners, or permitting one of the co-owners to acquire the share of the other(s) subject to the payment of appropriate compensation. One possible difference between the Roman and the Scots law relates not to the content but to the operation of the rule. It seems that Scots law might be more willing than Roman law to permit the sale of the property to a third person, with consequent division of the price between the co-owners.

The above answer can perhaps be described as 'historical' or 'static' in that it looks at the position in Scots law at a fixed point in time and determines which particular Roman rules have in fact been received into Scots law. Another kind of answer, however, looks at the matter from a more 'dynamic' perspective. It considers the process by which consideration is given to the adoption of a rule of Roman law rather than the result of the process of reception as determined at one particular point in time.

From the 'dynamic' perspective the position can be described as

---

[97] The judgments of the Inner House in *Crathes* (1991, above, n. 72) suggest that the full formulation of the rule in Scots law requires the addition of a reference to the co-owner being personally barred in some other way.

follows. A complex of rules dealing with a certain area of law, here that on common ownership, may either not have been received *in toto* at one particular time or, if they have theoretically been received *in toto*, difficulties may arise at a later time in determining the exact content of what has been received. In either case one will have a continuing process of validation of particular rules for which there is a possible argument that they have been, or should be, received into Scots law.

What is of interest is the nature of the criteria by which a rule is 'validated' as a rule of Scots law. These criteria are not normally defined by judges. The material on the *actio communi dividundo* suggests that, where a question arises as to whether a rule of Roman law is also to be treated as a rule of Scots law, judges look in the first place at earlier decisions of the Scottish courts. If among these decisions there are to be found judgments or *dicta* adopting rules similar in content to that whose 'validation' is immediately in question, it is likely that the latter will also be deemed to have been accepted into Scots law. The judgment of Lord Rutherfurd in *Brock* v. *Hamilton* provides an example of a judicial opinion to which frequent recourse is made for the purpose of the validation of rules. Ultimately, of course, whether or not a judge is prepared to accept a rule of Roman law to be a part of Scots law depends upon his conviction as to its individual equity and appropriateness to the particular case he is called upon to decide.

Hence, when raising the question of the authority of Roman law for Scots law from the 'dynamic' perspective, one has to answer that the former possesses 'authority' in the sense that it is a source to which judges may still today look for help in the decision of difficult cases. Where they are prepared to utilise the source constituted by the Corpus Iuris Civilis, their conclusion probably has to be understood in the sense that the existence of the Roman rule provides a good reason for holding that Scots law possesses a rule of the same content.[98]

---

[98] I would like to thank Dr R. Evans-Jones, Professor W. M. Gordon and Professor M. C. Meston, all of whom have generously allowed me to profit from their knowledge of Scots law.

11 Sale and transfer of title in Roman and Scots law

David Johnston

People who sell goods are by and large interested in obtaining payment of the price for them. The law provides various methods. Most legal systems find little difficulty with the case where the buyer is in possession of the goods but refuses to pay for them. Other questions are harder. How much protection (if any) should be given to a third party who is in possession of those goods in good faith? Should an unpaid seller have a better claim to his goods than any other creditor of the buyer?

In an essay to celebrate Professor Stein's first forty years or so of contributions to the study of Roman law and the Roman law tradition, it seems not inappropriate to discuss some problems arising in the contract of sale; to deal with Roman and Scots law side by side; and to consider a question where the application of a *regula iuris* may help to explain why things were done in one way in Rome but in quite another in Edinburgh.[1]

This essay has little to say about the all sums retention of title clauses which are so prominent in commerce (and litigation) today. Since it deals with the law before the Sale of Goods Act 1893, it is in a sense concerned with the prehistory of those clauses. It is concerned with the various ways in which a seller could attempt to ensure that he was paid the price for his goods in Roman law; and the differences between those ways and the ways adopted by Scottish practice. It attempts to do no more than show how some routes were followed, while others, which might have been thought promising, were closed off.

The Roman law background

The Roman law rules on sale and transfer of title can best be divided into implied and express terms in the contract of sale.

---

[1] P. G. Stein, *Fault in the Formation of Contract in Roman Law and Scots Law* (Aberdeen, 1958); *Regulae Iuris* (Edinburgh, 1966).

Implied terms

By Justinian's day Roman law had adopted the rule that, when an object was sold, title did not pass to the buyer on delivery unless the price had been paid, the sale was on credit, or the seller had in some way 'followed the faith' of the buyer.[2] There is considerable doubt whether this rule existed in classical times and, if so, in what shape.[3] All that need be said here is that it probably did not exist in this shape; that it was watered down by the exception regarding the buyer's faith (in fact, the exception appears to absorb the rule); and that by Justinian's day it was sufficiently well established to feature in his Institutes.

So long as a rule of this sort applied, the seller was adequately protected until payment. He remained able to vindicate the property from the buyer or from a third party[4] until satisfied by payment of the price. The right which he retained in the object sold was *dominium* rather than a right *in rem* of any lesser sort. This rule was a rule of law. It did not depend on the terms of the individual contract, although it could, of course, be departed from, notably by words or deeds amounting to 'following the buyer's faith'.

Express terms

It was open to the seller to introduce into the contract, for his own benefit, an express term to the effect that if the price was not paid within a certain period then the object should be 'unsold' (*inempta*). This was known as a *lex commissoria*. It plainly raised the question whether the term suspended the proprietary effects of the sale until payment was made; or whether the sale was perfected but, in the event of non-payment by the buyer, resolved. It also raised the question whether, if the proper interpretation of the term was that it was resolutive, and the term did in fact come into operation, it operated *in rem* so as to retransfer *dominium ipso facto* to the seller; or whether it merely gave him a claim *in personam* against the buyer.

Roman law did not arrive at an immediate or unanimous answer to these questions. Sabinus apparently treated the condition 'unless the price is paid by a certain day the object is to be unsold' (*nisi pecunia intra diem*

---

[2] J.Inst.2.1.41: 'fidem emptoris secutus fuerit'. It should be noted that throughout this essay the concern is with *traditio* of *res nec mancipi*; clearly, in the days before Justinian, *mancipatio* would raise different considerations.

[3] See, for instance, G.2.20; D.18.1.19 (Pomponius, 31 *ad Quintum Mucium*); D.18.1.53 (Gaius, 28 *ad edictum provinciale*). M. Kaser, *Das römische Privatrecht* (Munich, 1971), vol. I, 418, with literature.

[4] Subject, of course, to *usucapio*.

certum soluta esset inempta res fieret) as suspensive. This emerges from the fact that he took the view that a buyer could not usucapt before he had paid the price.[5] Paul, however, appears to disagree, and Ulpian introduces the title on the *lex commissoria* in the Digest with the statement that the better view is that it is a resolutive term.[6] The prevailing classical position sems to have been that the term was resolutive (a *conventio* rather than a *condicio*). Accordingly, title in the object sold would pass to the buyer in accordance with the normal rules of sale.

What, then, if the condition was realised? That led to a further question, whether the condition should be treated as taking effect *in personam* or *in rem*. The texts give some support for each possibility: so there are texts granting the seller a *vindicatio* of the object sold, thus indicating that property has reverted to him;[7] and there are also texts which indicate that the seller's remedy was *in personam*.[8] There is considerable dispute about which view was taken in classical law.[9]

So long as a solvent buyer retains the object, it does not make a great practical difference how the *lex commissoria* is interpreted, and what kind of action follows from it.[10] But once the object is in the hands of a third party, it plainly makes a crucial difference whether the seller is able to recover the object itself or has merely a claim on the price. For present purposes it does not matter very much which was the received view of the classical jurists. Nor perhaps even what was Justinian's view. The main point is that a variety of approaches were illustrated in the texts. Lawyers of later periods could choose which line of authority to follow.

The following sections trace the fate of these various possibilities in Scots law, beginning with the institutional writers. It should be noted at the outset that (at least) three different rules are involved. While these overlap, they do need to be kept conceptually distinct. Each has a purpose of its own, even if at first sight there appears to be duplication.

---

[5] D.41.4.2.3 (Paul, 54 *ad edictum*); cf. D.35.2.38.2 (Hermogenianus, 1 *iuris epitomarum*), which indicates that views do not clearly divide between early and late jurists respectively.

[6] D.41.4.2.3 (Paul, 54 *ad edictum*); D.18.3.1 (Ulpian, 28 *ad Sabinum*).

[7] D.18.3.8 (Scaevola, 7 *digestorum*); C.4.54.4 (Alexander).

[8] For example, C.4.54.3 (Alexander). Here there is a further division between those who believe that the seller can properly sue *ex vendito*, on the contract of sale, and those who require him to proceed *in factum*.

[9] In favour of the effect *in rem*: L. Mitteis, *Römisches Privatrecht* (Leipzig, 1908), 185ff.; F. Peters, *Die Rücktrittsvorbehalte des römischen Kaufrechts* (Cologne, 1973). *Contra*: W. W. Buckland, *Textbook of Roman Law* (3rd edn., revised P. Stein, Cambridge, 1963), 495, 497; W. Flume, 'Die Aufhebungsabreden beim Kauf – lex Commissoria, in diem addictio und sogennantes pactum displicentiae – und die Bedingung nach der Lehre der römischen Klassiker', in *Festschrift für Max Kaser* (Munich, 1976), 309. For further literature see Kaser, *Privatrecht*, vol. I, 561–2.

[10] It does, of course, matter for the purpose of such questions as when the risk passed in the contract of sale.

(1) The mutuality rule. In a bilateral contract, one party cannot be compelled to perform his side of the contract unless the other offers to perform his. A seller is therefore not bound to make delivery of the object unless the buyer offers him the price.

(2) The implied term that property will not pass on delivery until payment is made. Because of the mutuality rule, this term is of significance only if the seller delivers the object before he is paid. It then withholds title from the buyer until he has made payment. Security or credit suffices as an alternative to payment.

(3) The *lex commissoria*. On account of the implied term that property will not pass on delivery to the buyer until payment is made, this term is of significance only if delivery is made but the implied term is inapplicable: in other words, where the seller either accepts security or follows the buyer's faith, so that property does pass to the buyer.[11] This term provides for its reversion to the seller.

The rule on payment of the price in Scots law

In his *Institutions* (the first edition of which was published in 1681) Stair recognises that the Civil law implies a term of payment of the price, but states firmly that no such rule applies in Scots law.

Sale being perfected, and the thing delivered, the property thereof becomes the buyer's, if it was the seller's, and there is no dependence of it, till the price be paid or secured, as was in the civil law, neither hypothecation of it for the price, Hope, *de empto*, Parker *contra* Law.[12]

It seems that two points are being made in this passage. The first is that payment of the price is not regarded as a condition suspensive of the transfer of ownership. The second is that there is no hypothec over the goods being sold until payment. The first is expressly said to be a rule of Roman law which is not followed in Scotland. The authority cited for these propositions is rather exiguous. Reference is made to the title of Hope's *Major Practicks* on sale; that itself at the relevant point[13] refers to only one case, which it reports as follows:

The Lords fand in venditions that venditor, postquam convenit de pretio, might not claym his goods albeit the pryce was not payed to him; and sic lyke that there

---

[11] This applies on the assumption that the term is resolutive. If it is suspensive, it adds little other than to prevent the buyer becoming owner of the object if he offers the price after the deadline has passed.
[12] Viscount Stair, *Institutions of the Law of Scotland* (2nd edn, 1693), 1.14.2.
[13] Sir Thomas Hope, *Major Practicks* (Edinburgh, 1937), II.4.3.

wes no necessity of delivery where the goods wer els in the buyer's possessione: 26 Jun. 1621, Park *contra* Findlay.[14]

Few facts are given, but it appears that the seller has made delivery of the goods to the buyer and that the buyer has failed to pay the price; the reference to agreement on the price is no doubt to indicate that the contract has been perfected.[15] Presumably the question raised in the case was whether the seller was entitled to *vindicatio* of the goods (property remaining in the seller) or to an *actio ex vendito* (property having passed to the buyer, and the seller therefore relying on his contractual right). It was apparently decided that the seller would have to rely on the contractual action. It may be, given the second part of the 'report', that the seller argued that property had not passed because there had been no delivery of the goods. That argument, if it was made, was unsuccessful. The court found that property had passed to the buyer; there had (in Romanistic terminology) been *traditio brevi manu*. If it is correct to assume that the goods were in fact already in the buyer's possession, this seems to be rather a special instance from which to extract a general rule that ownership passes on delivery without the need for payment of the price. But it is at any rate the earliest authority referred to for the proposition that, in Scotland, title will pass on delivery irrespective of whether the price has been paid to the seller.

It is worth examining Stair's second proposition more closely. There is, says Stair, no hypothecation of the thing sold for the price. Stair's first proposition simply stated that property does in fact pass on delivery independently of any requirement that the price be paid. The second proposition, however, seems to presuppose that property has passed to the buyer. It then appears to go on to say that the seller also retains no real right of the nature of a hypothec against the object of sale until the price has been paid. At first sight, this is odd. The natural way to analyse this situation, one might think, is to ask whether property has passed or not. It is a secondary question, which arises only if it is found that it has, whether the seller retains any real right in the goods less than ownership. The difference, then, between Stair's two propositions – although it is not brought out by Stair himself – is this: under the first (non-Scots) proposition, property cannot pass to the buyer until the condition (payment) is satisfied; whereas under the second, for a hypothec to operate, property must have passed to the buyer in order that the goods can be hypo-

---

[14] It will be noted that the name of the case is different from that mentioned by Stair; but it appears that reference is intended to the same case.
[15] This is suggested also by the previous paragraph, II.4.2.

thecated to the seller.[16] What is intriguing about Stair's account is that these propositions are dealt with as if they are merely variations on the same principle.

There are indications in the cases that this view had a certain currency in the late seventeenth century; and that it was also believed that, while Roman law did indeed recognise a seller's hypothec over the goods against payment of the price, Scots law did not. So in *Prince* v. *Pallat*[17] wine was delivered at Bordeaux by the seller, Mr Pallat, to a factor in order to be sent to the buyer, a Mr Arthur Udny. Before delivery was made to the buyer, the seller instructed the factor not to deliver, as he had heard that the buyer was about to become bankrupt. In the mean time the wines were arrested on board ship by a creditor of Udny, Mr Prince. A question arose between the seller and Mr Prince whether property had passed to the buyer or remained with the seller. The creditor argued that there had been a sale, perfected by delivery of the wines to the skipper of the ship on behalf of Udny; that the seller, having delivered, had only a personal action and no real right to the wine; 'And as to the custom of neighbouring nations, and the citations of several lawyers for that effect; it imports nothing, all these opinions being founded upon the Roman law, by which the seller had a hypothec in the ware for the price.'[18] The court found in favour of the creditor.

Similarly, in *Cushney* v. *Chrystie*[19] there was competition for the ownership of certain goods in the hands of the factor of a deceased merchant, George Angus. The first claimant, Chrystie, had been the deceased's business partner; with him he had bought goods in Danzig. The goods had been sent back to Aberdeen in separate consignments, under separate names and marks. After Angus died, however, Chrystie had been served with a summons in Danzig by the sellers, and had been compelled to pay the whole price (rather than his share of it). The basis of his claim was that he had a hypothec over the goods until payment. The second claimant was the deceased's executor-creditor, who had arrested the goods in the hands of the factor. The basis of his claim was that the arrestment had attached a real right in the goods. The court held that there had been *traditio* of the goods to the deceased's agent, inasmuch as they had been separately consigned; that with *traditio* ownership passed; and that there was no hypothecation of goods for the price. Accordingly, Chrystie's claim could be only a claim for the price against the deceased's estate.[20]

[16] It is, of course, possible for a hypothec to be created over goods which have yet to come into the debtor's possession; but the hypothec has no effect over them until they have done so: cf. D.20.6.14 (Labeo, 5 *posteriorum a Iavoleno epitomatorum*).
[17] 24 February 1680, M.4932. [18] M.4932, 4934. [19] 14 June 1676, M.6237.
[20] The grounds for the decision in this case are as set out above. It is to be noted, however, that this does not appear to be an ordinary contract of sale: the claim by Chrystie is a

This case is reported both by Stair and by Gosford. There is some reason to think that both may have sat as judges in it.[21] In his report, Lord Gosford notes that the decision 'seems hard, and to which I did not agree'. He gives various reasons, but in particular makes the interesting observation that this 'could not be very destructive to all foreign trade, which must be ruled by the laws of the place where the traffic is to be used'. Such policy reasons against recognition of hypothecs crop up frequently in Scots authority. But the reason why he expressed himself in such a way may not be far to seek, if indeed Stair was on the other side, in the majority. Only a few years later Stair was to publish these words in his *Institutions*:[22]

Impignoration is either express by the explicit consent of parties, or implicit, which is introduced by law, without consent of parties; of which tacit hypothecations, there have been many in the civil law; as in the ware, for the price ... But our custom hath taken away express hypothecations, of all or a part of the debtor's goods, without delivery, and of the tacit legal hypothecations hath only allowed a few, allowing ordinarily parties to be preferred according to the priority of their legal diligence, that commerce may be the more sure, and every one may more easily know his condition with whom he contracts: and therefore goods sold were not found under any hypothecation for the price, June 14, 1676, Cushney *contra* Christy.

It may well be, then, that the references to hypothecs over goods against payment of the price are to be traced back to a single source, namely Stair, whether acting as judge or institutional writer. And it may be that they are all motivated by the same concern for commerce and for foreign trade. Yet Stair and the cases purport to find such a rule in Roman law. Whether, in speaking of it, Stair had anything more in mind than the implied term that title did not pass without payment of the price is unclear. But, before arriving at that conclusion, it is proper to see if such a rule is to be found in the Corpus Iuris Civilis. It is very difficult to know on what passages Stair and the other sources rely when asserting that there is such a hypothec in Roman law; no references are given. The passages in the Digest, however, which come closest to suggesting that the seller retains a right of security over the goods are the following, although

claim not by the seller of the goods but by a person who has paid the price and who was a partner of the deceased; it ought in principle therefore to be a claim on the contract of partnership rather than that of sale.

[21] Unfortunately none of the reports states who the judges in this case or in *Prince* v. *Pallat* were, and the Advocates Library does not have Session Papers for the years before 1711. But both Stair and Gosford were on the Bench in 1676 and in 1680, and the terms particularly of Gosford's report suggest that he is summarising his own dissenting opinion.

[22] Stair, *Institutions*, 1.13.14.

Sale and transfer of title in Roman and Scots law 189

(as will appear) they are in fact concerned with a very different situation.[23]

The first is a passage of Ulpian. The context is his discussion of the *actio ex empto*, and in particular the heads of damage recoverable in that action.

> The price must be offered by the buyer when he sues on sale, and even if he offers part of the price he still has no action on sale: for the seller can retain the thing sold as if a pledge.[24]

This appears to be no more than a statement of a rule of mutuality of contract.[25] Although Ulpian does not actually say that the object is held as a pledge, there is some oddity here. The goods are in the seller's possession, so (presumably)[26] *traditio* has not been made. It follows that the seller remains owner. If that is so, it is odd to say even that he retains the object as a sort of pledge, since the fact that he is the owner removes one of the characteristics essential to any kind of pledge. The same, however, is found in another passage of Ulpian, dealing with the question whether one of two joint purchasers can compel delivery of half the goods on payment of half the price (the answer is 'no'): 'for the seller retains what he has sold, by way of pledge, until such time as the buyer gives security' ('nam venditor pignoris loco quod vendidit retinet, quoad emptor satisfaciat').[27] This remark too is made in the context of a discussion about when the buyer can bring the *actio ex empto*. From that context, it seems reasonably clear that little more is intended than to assert that the seller is entitled to retain the goods until the buyer tenders the price; the pseudo-pledge mentioned is merely a right to refuse delivery until payment is offered; it is what in later law became the *exceptio non adimpleti contractus*.[28]

In any event, it is quite clear that these passages have nothing to do with

---

[23] I leave aside D.47.2.14.1 (Ulpian, 29 *ad Sabinum*), which appears to take the matter no further, and where the critical last sentence may well be interpolated; and D.18.4.22 (Scaevola, 2 *responsorum*), where it is unclear in whose possession the objects of sale may be.

[24] D.19.1.13.8 (Ulpian, 32 *ad edictum*): 'Offerri pretium ab emptore debet, cum ex empto agitur, et ideo etsi pretii partem offerat, nondum est ex empto actio: venditor enim quasi pignus retinere potest eam rem quam vendidit.'

[25] D.18.1.78.2 (Labeo, 4 *posteriorum a Iavoleno epitomatorum*); D.19.1.25 (Julian, 54 *digestorum*); D.21.1.57 *pr*. (Paul, 5 *quaestionum*).

[26] The alternative is to suppose that the goods have been delivered to the buyer, but have somehow found their way back to the seller. In that case the buyer would be owner. But the objection to this is that we would surely be told that this had happened; and that it would remain to consider whether the mere fact that the goods had returned to the seller's possession gave him a *pignus* over them.

[27] D.21.1.31.8 (Ulpian, 1 *ad edictum aedilium curulium*). The reference to the buyer's giving security is noteworthy.

[28] Cf. among the Scottish cases *Murdoch & Co. Ltd.* v. *Greig* (1889) 16 R.396; *Armour* v. *Thyssen Edelstahlwerke A.G.* 1989 S.L.T. 182, 187 C-D.

a hypothec over the goods for payment of the price, for the very simple reason that the goods are in the possession of the seller. That is quite a different position from what is found in the Scottish cases, where the issue was whether the unpaid seller could assert his hypothec over goods in the possession of a third party.

So far we have established that Stair denied the existence in Scots law both of an implied term on payment of the price and of a tacit hypothec over the price; that he ascribed the doctrine of hypothec to Roman law; that in fact it is hard to find any trace of it there; and that accordingly one must wonder whether he was not simply referring in another way to the rule on payment of the price. But first it may be appropriate to consider the other authorities.

The Roman rule on payment of price was adopted in both France and the Netherlands, two countries whose authorities, in particular Pothier and Voet, were often followed by the (later) institutional writers.[29] In Scotland itself, the later institutional writers did not follow Stair as a matter of course, but any resistance to his exposition made little impact on the law. Bankton, in his *Institute*, followed the Roman rule: 'if the price is paid, or trust given for it, delivery of the goods will transfer the property that was in the seller; but otherwise the property is pendent, even after delivery, which is taken to be conditional'. He goes on to note that 'by our law no hypothec is granted upon the goods for the price'.[30] Erskine too seems to have been much less clear that Scots and Roman law did in fact differ on this point: 'By the Roman law the property was not transferred till the price was also paid, or the seller satisfied with the security he had got for it. But whether this would be held for the law of Scotland remains a doubt.'[31]

Such doubts, however, seem soon to have been overcome. Erskine's editor was unable to understand why he should have had them;[32] and Bell discussed the rules in much the same way as had Stair:

The Scottish law rejects hypothecs of moveables as destructive to commerce, except in a few special and well-ascertained cases, to be afterwards discussed. It gives no sanction to the idea that a seller continues proprietor of a subject which he has delivered over to the buyer on the title of sale.

---

[29] J. Pothier, *Traité du contrat de vente* (Paris, 1768), paras. 322, 324; J. Voet, *Commentarius ad Pandectas* (Lugduni Batavorum, 1698), 6.1.20. Cf. the reference to the 'custom of neighbouring nations' in *Prince* v. *Pallat* (above, n. 18).
[30] Lord Bankton, *An Institute of the Law of Scotland* (Edinburgh, 1751), 1.19.21. It may be noted that Bankton does distinguish between the rule regarding payment and a hypothec against payment of the price.
[31] J. Erskine, *An Institute of the Law of Scotland* (Edinburgh, 1773), 3.3.8.
[32] N. 106, on this passage.

Bell then quotes Stair.[33] In spite of dissenting voices, the orthodoxy appears therefore to have been established by Stair; and to have been consolidated by Bell, who did little more than follow Stair.

To revert to Stair. What seems to have happened is that he associated the Roman implied term, that property will not pass until payment is made, with a rule about an implied hypothec over the goods until payment of the price.[34] It may be noted that, against the background of a legal system such as Roman law which recognised an implied term that property will not pass until payment is made, an implied hypothec over the goods until payment seems relatively improbable. At least in Justinian's day, a hypothec was unnecessary. Unnecessary, if the buyer did pay the price, since he was no longer indebted to the seller; unnecessary, if he did not pay the price, since he did not become owner; unnecessary, if he arranged security or was given credit, since he became owner, but only on the basis that he gave the seller security (whether personal or real)[35] for payment of the price. The security he gave for payment of the price of the goods was, of course, not a hypothec over those very goods. For the purpose, surely, in allowing the buyer to give security was to allow him to take an unencumbered title to the goods sold.

It has already been noted that, from the standpoint of where title to the goods resides, the rules of payment and of hypothec are conceptually quite different. The similarity between them appears to be only this: that an object is in the hands of one person (the buyer) and yet subject to a right *in rem* vested in another person, whether that right is ownership or a security right. But it makes little sense to subject these to the same analysis: the second may be a security without possession; but the first is not a security at all (as appears when one asks what it is a security over).

While the payment of price rule and the hypothec rule are conceptually different, the idea that a condition that title does not pass until payment is a type of security continues to exercise some attraction.[36] In the recent case of *Armour* v. *Thyssen Edelstahlwerke A.G.*, the following was said:

Despite the generality of that rule of common law [that security over moveables *retenta possessione* is of no effect], the law does recognise the right of a seller to

---

[33] G. J. Bell, *Commentaries on the Law of Scotland* (7th edn, Edinburgh, 1870), vol. I, 257 (237 in older editions). The passage quoted from Stair is *Institutions*, 1.14.2.
[34] This is suggested by the wording of the passage cited above, *Institutions*, 1.14.2.
[35] D.18.1.53 (Gaius, 28 *ad edictum provinciale*).
[36] See, for example, J. Mackintosh, *The Roman Law of Sale* (2nd edn, Edinburgh, 1907), 42, 44; W. M. Gloag and J. M. Irvine, *Law of Rights in Security* (Edinburgh, 1897), 241; T. B. Smith, *Property Problems in Sale* (London, 1977), 107.

stipulate that title will be retained until the price has been paid. In a sense, the seller is thus obtaining security without possession.[37]

Reasoning of this sort is possible only if the question who has title to the goods is postponed to the question what the purpose of a contractual term is. It is possible to suppose that, viewed in isolation, a rule which stipulates that property in goods shall not pass until payment is a sort of security, since it gives the seller a right to the goods which he would otherwise not have. Yet this kind of approach makes sense only if one subscribes to the (now largely ignored)[38] doctrine of reputed ownership; only then can it seem at all troubling that there should be property in the hands of one person which in fact belongs to another.

Treatment of the payment of price rule as equivalent to, or even alongside, hypothec for the price was sufficient to taint the Roman rule with guilt by association. The very word 'hypothec', as appears from Bell's writings, was enough to strike terror into the heart of the Scots commercial lawyer, and to conjure up images of the sterilisation of trade and the destruction of commerce.[39] It was a basic rule of Scots law that, apart from an accepted list of hypothecs such as that of the landlord, there could not be security over moveables without possession. That rule is found in early times; it can be observed in Balfour's *Practicks*, as well as in early cases.[40] It may be regarded as settled law even in Stair's day. It was therefore plain that a seller could not have security over the object sold once he had delivered it to the buyer. And if the implied term on payment of the price was regarded as such a security, neither could that term be part of Scots law.

This is not the place to investigate the origins of the rule in Scots law requiring possession of moveables to constitute security over them. None the less, there may be some reason to associate it with the maxim *traditionibus et usucapionibus dominia rerum non nudis pactis transferuntur*.[41] It is plain enough that this maxim, read literally, is a rule about the transfer of *dominium* and says nothing about the transfer of rights *in rem* less than ownership. Equally, it is a rule about delivery, rather than about

---

[37] 1989 S.L.T. 182, 185L–186A *per* L. J.-C. Ross (overruled by the House of Lords: 1990 S.L.T. 891). Cf. *Emerald Stainless Steel Ltd.* v. *South Side Distribution Ltd.* 1982 S.C. 61, 64, with comments by K. Reid and G. Gretton in 1983 S.L.T. (News) 77, 79.
[38] *Robertsons* v. *McIntyre* (1882) 9 R.772, 778; D. L. Carey Miller, *Corporeal Moveables in Scots Law* (Edinburgh, 1991), para. 1.12.
[39] Bell, *Commentaries*, I.257 (236); II.24–5 (25–6); cf. Erskine, *Institute*, 3.1.34.
[40] Balfour, *Practicks*, 194; *Thomsone* v. *Chirnside* (1558) M.827; cf. Bell, *Commentaries*, II.25. Bell also refers to *Regiam Maiestatem*, 3.3, but the rule is not express there; in general see Gloag and Irvine, *Law of Rights in Security*, 219ff. The rule remains in modern practice with the added exception of floating charges.
[41] C.2.3.20 (Diocletian, 293).

possession. But various Scottish authorities appear to construe it more broadly. Thus Stair says:

But, for utility's sake, not only the Romans, but almost all nations require some kind of possession, to accomplish real rights, that thereby the will of the owner may sensibly touch the thing disponed, and thereby be more manifest and sure; so the law saith, *Traditionibus et usucapionibus, non nudis pactis, dominia rerum transferuntur*, with which our custom accordeth.[42]

And the modern Scottish textbook on rights in security says:

The brocard *traditionibus non nudis pactis dominia rerum transferuntur* implies that a mere contract to transfer corporeal moveable property, though made for valuable consideration, and though that consideration be duly given, will not vest a real right in the subject transferred, nor entitle the transferee to vindicate it in the hands of a third party or on the bankruptcy of the transferor, unless it has been delivered into his possession.[43]

It is perhaps little more than a speculation to suggest that this maxim lay behind the requirement of Scots law that moveables be delivered to the security creditor; and that a maxim which once applied only to the transfer of *dominium* came to be treated as applying to the transfer of any right *in rem*. But what is clear is this: once the payment of price rule had become associated with the notion of an implied hypothec over the goods, it was only a short step to the rejection of the rule as part of the law of Scotland.

The *lex commissoria* in Scots law

Scots law therefore rejected the implied term on payment of the price. It remains to consider express terms. Bell noted, 'But although the law rejects, both in England and Scotland, any implied condition or hypothec for the price, it admits express conditions; and an important question arises of the effect of such conditions as against third parties.'[44] As we have already noted, for such a term as the *lex commissoria* to be effective against third parties, it was necessary that it should be treated either as a suspensive condition or, if treated as a resolutive condition, as one having effect *in rem*.

Now the Digest itself pronounced in a prominent place that the *lex commissoria* was best regarded as resolutive.[45] If that view was to be followed, then the effectiveness of the *lex* depended on Scots law adopting the view exhibited in those texts of the Digest which treat it as having effect *in rem*. Unfortunately for sellers, the opposite transpired. Stair took

---

[42] Stair, *Institutions*, 3.2.5. Note the reference to custom.
[43] Gloag and Irvine, *Law of Rights in Security*, 188.
[44] Bell, *Commentaries*, I.258 (237).   [45] D.18.3.1 (Ulpian, 28 *ad Sabinum*).

the view that such a clause could operate only *in personam*. His reasoning is interesting:

if such conditions or resolutive clauses do stop the transmission of property, and be so meant and expressed, then, as is said before, the bargain is pendent, and the property not transmitted, and the seller remains the proprietor; but if by the contract and clause, the buyer becomes once the proprietor, and the condition is adjected, that he shall cease to be proprietor, in such a case, this is but personal; for property or dominion passes not by conditions or provisions, but by tradition, and other ways prescribed in law.[46]

So Stair appeals – and here he does so expressly – to the maxim *traditionibus non nudis pactis rerum dominia transferuntur*. He argues that the seller cannot expect title in the object sold to revert to him on the strength of a mere pact. Consequently the title remains with the buyer, and the seller has a remedy *in personam*. The *lex commissoria* has no effect on the title.

We have already seen that the Roman jurists were apparently not at one on the effects of a *lex commissoria*. To that extent there is nothing particularly remarkable in the fact that Stair chose to follow the school which construed it as resolutive and as having effect only *in personam*. There was, however, a certain amount of civilian authority for treating the *lex* as operating *in rem*. So, for example, the gloss on the passage of Justinian's Institutes dealing with what it describes as acquisition of ownership *sine traditione* (it deals, in fact, with *traditio brevi manu*) expressly mentions reversion under the *lex commissoria* as an instance of the transfer of ownership without *traditio*.[47]

What is interesting, however, is Stair's application of the maxim. It seems likely that this was a new departure. What survives in the Code title *de pactis* is a single sentence of Diocletian and Maximianus' original constitution of AD 293: 'traditionibus et usucapionibus dominia rerum non nudis pactis transferuntur'.[48] Displaced and truncated, its original context is far from clear and hard to trace. This constitution and another preserved elsewhere may be parts of the same original;[49] they are at any rate addressed to a recipient with the same name, Martialis, on or about the same day. Even so, that other constitution also gives little indication what the subject-matter of the whole inquiry may have been. The only hint is provided by its mention of *bona materna*, which at least suggests that the context is ownership of inherited property and not sale.

In any event as a matter of Scots law the maxim was not wholly true,

---

[46] Stair, *Institutions*, 1.14.5.
[47] Gloss on J.Inst.2.1.44; see W. M. Gordon, *Studies in the Transfer of Property by Traditio* (Aberdeen, 1970), 98, 105.
[48] C.2.3.20.   [49] C.1.18.5 (the title is *de iuris et facti ignorantia*).

since the law – and Stair himself[50] – recognised the possibility of *traditio ficta* (*traditio brevi manu* and *constitutum possessorium*) and with it the principle that property might indeed be transferred by mere agreement.[51] In these circumstances it cannot be said that Stair's argument against the effect *in rem* of a *lex commissoria* on the basis of this maxim is of great force, since there are other exceptions to what is only a general rule.

Erskine appears to have taken a different view:

Among the conditions which are only accidental to a sale, and are not admitted except they be expressed, is the *pactum legis commissoriae*, by which the sale becomes void, *res fit inempta*, if the price be not paid within a determinate day. The condition, where it is stipulated by an express clause, does not suspend the sale; the property is transferred to the buyer upon the delivery; but if he fail to pay the price within the time limited, the sale resolves, and the property returns from him to the seller; L. 1, *de leg. comm.* [Ulp. D.18.3.1].[52]

Unfortunately it is not possible to extract from this passage any conclusion much beyond Erskine's reliance on Ulpian; and his presumed adherence to some of the Digest passages asserting an effect *in rem*.[53] Erskine's editor approaches his statement with disbelief, and suggests that it can be meant to hold only in a question with the buyer and not with third parties.[54] No followers seem to have been attracted to Erskine's position. Both Bankton and Bell follow Stair. Bankton notes:

in sales they [*pacta legis commissoriae*] are good, and strictly to be observed, and expiration of the day is the loss of the right, as I observed formerly; it is founded in the civil law. This is no real quality of the sale, but only personal upon the buyer, who will be liable in damages if he frustrate the paction, by disposing of the subject.[55]

---

[50] Stair, *Institutions*, 3.2.5.
[51] See Gordon, *Transfer of Property by Traditio*, 214–22; Carey Miller, *Corporeal Moveables in Scots Law*, paras. 8.20ff.
[52] Erskine, *Institute*, 3.3.11.
[53] Pothier, however, states (1) that the contract does resolve, although the seller requires to bring an action to demand its resolution; (2) that the action (which he describes as *personelle réelle*) can be brought against third parties in possession (*Traité du contrat de vente*, paras. 459, 463). In other words, effect *in rem* is given to the resolutive condition, but only under the supervision of the court (a requirement which is departed from in *Code civil* 1656).
[54] N. 108, on this passage. N. 2 on Bell, *Commentaries*, I.260 (239), contrasting Stair and Erskine, is not without interest: it takes their differing approaches to the effect of the *lex commissoria* to demonstrate that Erskine wrote 'following out the several divisions and train of his course with admirable perspicuity, but without having his attention turned to the shock of principles which in actual practice ... brings out the true principle'; whereas Stair wrote 'with his mind continually turned to practice and the application of legal rules and principles in the business of life'.
[55] Bankton, *Institute*, 1.19.29.

Bell states:

> It is settled as law in Scotland, that an express paction, made by the seller when delivering the property, that the property shall be reinstated in him if the price be not paid against an appointed day, is quite ineffectual against the buyer's creditors. This is the Pactum Legis Commissoriae of the Roman law, which had not the effect of making the sale conditional, but of making it conditionally dissoluble.[56]

Stair's influence therefore prevailed. It was settled that the only effect of a *lex commissoria* was in a question with the buyer. It was quite open to Scots law to conclude, as some of the Roman jurists had in their day done, that the effect of a *lex commissoria* could be *in personam* only. What was not so obvious was that the means of arriving at this conclusion would be the maxim *traditionibus et usucapionibus dominia rerum non nudis pactis transferuntur*. From this application of the maxim it followed inexorably that the *lex commissoria* was unable to protect an unpaid seller against third parties. Since clauses such as the *lex commissoria* were treated as resolutive, and since resolutive clauses were treated as having effect only *in personam*, it followed that they offered no protection to the seller in the event of the object ending in the hands of third parties.

Some consequences

The preceding two sections illustrated the rejection by Scots law of two rules of Roman law: an implied term on payment of the price, and a *lex commissoria* with effect *in rem* (maintained at least by some of the Roman jurists). The rejection of the implied term followed – illogically – from a hostility towards securities over moveables without possession. The rejection of the *lex commissoria* – and possibly also of the implied term – was associated, rightly or wrongly, with a fondness for the maxim *traditionibus et usucapionibus dominia rerum non nudis pactis transferuntur*.

From the rejection of those two rules, it followed that the only way still open to a seller under Scots law was to incorporate into the contract an express term suspending the transfer of title until payment was received. There is no shortage of cases discussing how certain conditions are to be construed.[57] But the fact that Scots law had rejected the other Roman rules meant that the questions it asked were different from those of the Roman jurists.

First, for Scots law the crucial question was whether a sale had been made on credit or under a suspensive condition. If it was the first, property would have passed to the buyer; under the second it would not:

[56] Bell, *Commentaries*, I.260 (239).
[57] For example *Macartney* v. *Macredie's Creditors* (1799) M.App. s.v. Sale No. 1; *Brandt & Co.* v. *Dickson* (1876) 3 R.375; *Clarke & Co.* v. *Miller & Son's Tr.* (1885) 12 R.1035.

that was an end of the matter.[58] It is true that those conclusions would also follow in Roman law. But, on the one hand, Roman law was of no particular assistance in devising types of suspensive clause, since the implied term on payment of the price had made it unnecessary ever to do so. On the other hand, in Roman law there was an additional question. Property would only have passed if credit had been given. Attention therefore had to be directed to the question whether in fact credit had been given. There is evidence of this in systems which followed more closely upon Roman law than Scots law had done.[59]

Secondly, since Roman law had no rule against security over moveables without possession, the jurists show little interest in intention so far as transfer of title and the validity of a contract of sale are concerned. Both Roman and Scots law required that there be intention, as well as delivery, for the transfer of *dominium* in moveables.[60] But broadly speaking, the only interest Roman law had in intention was to see that there was actually a *causa* for the *traditio*, so that property could pass. In particular, the fact that property in the goods was not to pass on delivery did not suggest to a Roman jurist that the transaction was not a sale. Scots law, because of the rule against security over moveables without possession, had to be more vigilant about the actual nature of transactions which purported to be sales. Early on, there was some concern about the nature of the contract, if title was reserved under it; thus Bell could speak of the buyer, where title had been reserved, as a 'mere depositary'; while Lord Young could not 'conceive a contract of sale in Scotland, followed by *bona fide* delivery, yet leaving the property unpassed'.[61] Statements such as that of Lord Young are no longer of any authority; there is now no difficulty about treating such a contract as a sale even if parties do not intend title to pass on delivery.[62] But with the advent of the Sale of Goods Act in Scotland the question of intention has assumed a new importance, since it is critical not just to the question when title in the goods is to pass, but to the question whether, if the contract provides for title to be

[58] See *Wright* v. *Mitchell* (1871) 9 M.516, where the point is made expressly. It is also worth noting that at 518 L.P. Inglis makes reference to the mutuality rule, and then goes on to deal with express terms suspending the transfer of title: 'in one sense every sale is conditional on payment of the price, for the seller is not bound to deliver the article sold except for payment of the price ... If it is intended that payment of the price in a particular way shall be made a condition of the contract, so that the contract shall be in suspense until the condition is purified, it is easy to say so.'
[59] Pothier, *Traité du contrat de vente*, para. 324.
[60] Stair, *Institutions*, 3.2.4 and 5; Carey Miller, *Corporeal Moveables in Scots Law*, para. 8.03.
[61] Bell, *Commentaries*, I.258 (238). Bell would not, however, have meant that the contract was deposit; *Clarke & Co.* v. *Miller & Son's Tr.* (1885) 12 R.1035, 1042.
[62] *Murdoch & Co. Ltd.* v. *Greig* (1889) 16 R.396; *Cowan* v. *Spence* (1824) 3 S.42; other cases are cited by the court in *Armour* v. *Thyssen Edelstahlwerke A.G.* 1989 S.L.T. 182.

retained until the occurrence of a certain event, the contract falls under the Act at all.[63] This type of focus on intention is foreign to Roman law.

In conclusion, two general observations. First, Scots law rejected the implied term on payment of the price because it regarded it as tantamount to a hypothec over the goods delivered to the buyer. The objection to the term, however, appears to have been not that it was an implied or tacit security, but purely that it was a security without possession, and so destructive of commerce. If that is right, then precisely the same objection applies to an express term reserving title until payment: it constitutes in the seller the same right to his property after delivery to the buyer. In order to salvage some logic, therefore, the law ought either (and preferably) to have accepted that retention of title in goods delivered to a buyer did not amount to a hypothec; or else that, if it did, it was one which was recognised by the law of Scotland. Even if the life of the law has been experience, it should not be too much to expect a little logic.

Secondly, Stair's reasoning on the effect of the *lex commissoria* depended on a maxim. The maxim was broadly true, but his reasoning was defective. There is a proper place for maxims. To arguments they may add the appearance of elegance and learning; but a resounding maxim is all too liable to seduce the writer himself into error. As Cinus and, more recently, Peter Stein have warned, *haec via est brocardica et ideo semper dubia.*[64]

[63] Sale of Goods Act 1979, sections 17 and 62(4).
[64] *Commentarius ad* C.2.4.4, n. 5, cited by Stein, *Regulae Iuris*, 154.

12 'What Marcellus says is against you': Roman law and Common law

Andrew Lewis

I Introduction

The influence of Roman law upon the law in England, whether directly or through the medium of Canon law, has been the subject of much recent attention. Helmholz has shown in a series of studies how the ecclesiastical jurisdictions, often applying Roman notions, anticipated and supported a number of legal developments in the Common law, for example in the fields of guardianship and defamation.[1] Seipp has demonstrated that Common law courts occasionally admitted Civil lawyers to plead – in one 1428 case one Andrew Huls 'argued much in Latin' – or consulted Civil lawyers outside the court in cases involving marriages and wills.[2]

The early brush with Roman legal ideas in the Latin treatises of Glanvill and Bracton are thus shown not to have been the isolated events they were once considered to be.[3] An awareness of Roman solutions – though one might also say a wariness of Roman solutions – is to be found throughout the history of the Common law down to modern times.[4]

---

[1] R. H. Helmholz, 'The Roman Law of Guardianship in England, 1300–1600' (1978) 52 Tulane Law Rev. 223 (= Helmholz, *Canon Law and the Law of England* (London and Ronceverte, 1987), 211); Helmholz (ed.), *Select Cases on Defamation to 1600*, Selden Society vol. 101 (London, 1985), introduction.

[2] D. J. Seipp, 'Roman Legal Categories in the Early Common Law', in T. G. Watkin (ed.), *Legal Records and Historical Reality* (London and Ronceverte, 1989), 9; see also Seipp, 'Bracton, the Year Books and the "Transformation of Elementary Legal Ideas" in the Early Common Law' (1989) 7 Law and History Review 175. The 1428 case is Mich. 7 Hen. 6 pl. 16, fols. 10, 11; I am grateful to Professor Seipp for drawing this case to my attention: it is discussed in his 'Reception of Canon and Civil Law in the Common Law Courts before 1600', (1993) 13 O.J.L.S. 388.

[3] For Bracton see J. L. Barton, 'Bracton as a Civilian' (1968) 52 Tulane Law Rev. 555 and the survey by S. E. Thorne in his introduction to *Bracton: De Legibus et Consuetudinibus Angliae*, vol. III (Cambridge, MA, 1977), xiii–lii. For Glanvill see *Tractatus de Legibus et Consuetudinibus Angliae*, ed. G. D. G. Hall (London 1965), xxxvi–xxxviii. See also T. E. Scrutton, *The Influence of Roman Law on the Law of England* (Cambridge, 1885), chapters 2 and 3.

[4] In addition to n. 1 see R. H. Helmholz, 'Continental Law and Common Law: Historical Strangers or Companions?' [1990] Duke Law J. 1207. In detecting a certain wariness in the Common lawyers' attitudes to laws other than 'our law' I differ from Seipp.

199

These influences upon the substantive solutions advanced in the Common law courts continued into the seventeenth and eighteenth centuries. In his famous and influential judgment *Coggs* v. *Bernard*[5] Chief Justice Holt enumerated a list of contracts utilising Roman categories. In the later eighteenth century a number of leading English judges, amongst them Lord Mansfield and Mr Justice Wilmot, displayed and made use of Roman texts and arguments.[6] Such occasional forays into the Roman world continued into the nineteenth century.

II

The quotation in the title of this essay comes from an exchange between counsel and Bench in the mid-nineteenth-century case *Acton* v. *Blundell*.[7] The occasion was one of the last in which original texts of Roman law were cited and discussed as bearing upon the decision to be made in an English court.[8] The dispute in *Acton* v. *Blundell* arose over water rights. The defendant had sunk mines on his land. The plaintiff water-mill owner claimed that the mines dug by the defendant had so disturbed and diverted the underground streams supplying his mill that the water no

---

[5] (1703) Lord Raym. 909. Holt, C. J. discusses *depositum, commodatum, locatio et conductio* and *vadium* ('a pawn or a pledge').

[6] For example, in *Windham* v. *Chetwynd* (1757) 1 Burr. 414, Mansfield discussed the Roman law relating to the capacity of witnesses to a testament in order to dispose of an earlier decision in Equity – *Anstey* v. *Dowsing* (1746) 2 Stra. 1253 – where the Chancellor had grounded his decision on a Digest text; Wilmot, J. explored the 'very curious' Roman law notion of *nudum pactum* in *Pillans* v. *van Mièrop* (1765) 3 Burr. 1663 and commented on a text of Modestinus – D.32.3.16 – in his advice in *Att.-Gen.* v. *Lady Downing* (1767) Wilmot 1.

[7] (1843) 12 M. & W. 324.

[8] In *Taylor* v. *Caldwell* (1863) 3 B. & S. 826 Blackburn, J. cited two texts from D.45.1 (h.t. 33 Pomponius 25 *ad Sabinum* and h.t. 23 Pomponius 9 *ad Sabinum*), adding 'Although the civil law is not, of itself, authority in an English court, it affords great assistance in investigating the principles on which the law is grounded.' The context makes clear that the source of the citation is the discussion in Pothier's *Traité des obligations* (Paris, 1761; English translation as *Pothier and the Law of Obligations* by W. D. Evans (London, 1806)); Pothier's work exercised a particular fascination for English judges in the nineteenth century. The source of this development appears to have been the notice of Pothier in Sir William Jones' *Essay on the Law of Bailment* (London, 1781), 29: P. Stein, 'Continental Influences on English Legal Thought 1600–1900', in *La formazione storica del diritto moderno in Europa*, vol. III (Florence, 1977), 1105 (= Stein, *The Character and Influence of the Roman Civil Law* (London and Ronceverte, 1988), 209). More recent examples of Roman learning concerned with *res nullius* at Heathrow (*Parker* v. *British Airways Board* [1982] Q.B. 1004) and an alluvial lake in Australia (*Southern Centre for Theosophy Inc.* v. *South Australia* [1982] 1 All E.R. 283) were tied to texts in Bracton rather than original Roman sources. In the most recent example – *Indian Oil Corporation Ltd.* v. *Greenstone Shipping S.A. (Panama)* [1987] 3 W.L.R. 869 – Staughton, J. merely cites W. W. Buckland, *A Textbook of Roman Law* (3rd edn by Peter Stein, Cambridge, 1963), 209 on *confusio* and *commixtio*.

longer reached him. Earlier cases had decided that in respect of surface water, a stream or a river, an owner further downstream was entitled to be protected against any exploitation upstream which diminished the flow of water.[9] The plaintiff sought to argue, unsuccessfully, that a similar rule applied in respect of underground water. In the course of his argument the plaintiff, borrowing from the judgment in *Mason* v. *Hill*,[10] a case on surface water, cited a number of Roman texts to establish the communal nature of water rights, including Justinian's Institutes 2.1.1.: 'Et quidem naturali jure communia sunt omnium haec: aer, aqua profluens et mare', and from amongst a number of texts in D.39.3. this from Ulpian:

Denique Marcellus scribit: Cum eo qui in suo fodiens vicini fontem avertit, nihil posse agi, nec de dolo actionem: et sane non debet habere, si non animo vicino nocendi, sed suum agrum meliorem faciendi id fecit.[11]

The whole catena of texts, according to counsel, amounted to this: 'that, as to flowing water, each party is entitled to use it as it passes through his own land, and if another takes away the water, or draws it off, an action is maintainable against him'.

At this point in the oral argument one of the judges, Maule, J., intervened:

It seems to me that what Marcellus says is against you. The English of it I take to be this: if a man digs a well in his own field, and thereby drains his neighbour's, he may do so, unless he does it maliciously.[12]

Counsel for the plaintiff tried to escape from this trap of his own making by some unconvincing arguments about the limitations of Roman hydraulics: 'that the Romans knew little about cutting off or using underground currents of water appears from their use of aqueducts'. But the damage was done, and he was later in reply driven to abandon the Roman texts which he had himself introduced: 'The extracts from the civil law are, at the most, conflicting.'[13]

In its judgment the Court of Exchequer Chamber was careful to distance itself from Roman solutions:

The Roman law forms no rule, binding in itself, upon the subjects of these realms; but in deciding a case upon principle, where no direct authority can be cited from our books, it affords no small evidence of the soundness of the conclusion at which we have arrived, if it proves to be supported by that law, the fruit of the researches of the most learned men, the collective wisdom of

---

[9] *Shury* v. *Piggot* (1625) 3 Bulstr. 339; *Browne* v. *Best* (1747) 1 Wils. 174; *Mason* v. *Hill* (1833) 5 B. & Ald. 1.
[10] 5 B. & Ald. 1 (per Lord Denman, C.J.).
[11] D.39.3.1.12 (Ulpian, 53 *ad edictum*). For a translation see the text to n. 12 immediately below.
[12] 12 M. & W. at 336.   [13] 12 M. & W. at 347.

ages and the groundwork of the municipal law of most of the countries in Europe.

The court then cited the opinion from Marcellus as being 'decisive ... in favour of the defendants.[14]

In two respects this case casts a useful light upon the relationship between English and Roman Law. In its judgment the court is careful to place the generous tribute of the importance of Roman law in the context of a definite distancing of Roman from English solutions: 'The Roman law forms no rule binding ... upon the subjects of this realm.' Of course, as much might be said of those countries of Europe of which Roman law formed only the 'groundwork'. But it would not be wrong to see in these words an echo of a long tradition which, despite all the observable examples of influence, sought to distance 'our law', the Common law, from what the Year Book lawyers called 'other laws'.[15]

Secondly, however, the formulation of the quotation is of some significance, combining as it does a translation of a recurrent and familiar Latin formula *quod Marcellus ait* with a typical Common law expression 'this is against you' – meaning, in fuller form, 'this matter or argument tells against the position which you are seeking to establish'.[16]

The epigrammatic character of the quotation is not haphazard: its author, Maule, J., was famed for his mordant wit in court. It was he who, on another occasion, uttered the comprehensive dismissal of counsel's argument: 'The last point is perfectly new, and it is so startling that I do not apprehend it will ever become old.'[17]

The juxtaposition of the Common law and the Roman expressions in a context where their respective roles are neatly distinguished illustrates my theme, namely the extent to which the Roman law furnished a model for the comprehension of the Common law in the early modern period.

III

There are two sub-themes: first, what actually happened – how, that is, the Common law acquired a method of analysis drawn from the Roman law, with its divisions into Persons, Property and Actions and subordinate classifications, Property and Obligations further classified into Contract, Delict (Tort) and *ex variis causarum figuris*. Within *this* theme there

---

[14] 12 M. & W. at 353. [15] Cf. n. 4.

[16] It has been pointed out to me (by Reuven Yaron) that this argumentative formulation is not restricted to the Common law but is to be found within other legal traditions. For my present purposes, however, nothing turns on this. It may even be, though I doubt it, that some such phrase formed part of the stock in trade of Roman advocates. What is relevant is that it left no trace in the written Roman texts.

[17] *Whitaker* v. *Wisbey* (1852) 12 C.B. 44 at 48.

is much room for discussion about the extent of penetration of Roman ideas. They are to be found much more in the field of Obligations than outside it – the common use of the notion 'Obligations' in the Common law rather than the combination 'Contract and Tort' is a relatively recent departure which may illustrate the continuing intellectual interaction between the two traditions.[18] However, some would seek to minimise the extent of influence from Roman law, arguing that the divisions to be found in both systems are in some sense natural and intrinsic to the subject-matter. This is a difficult problem to resolve, but it must be at the very least suggestive that around 1600, when the Common law was moving from a remedy-based system in which procedure was dominant in lawyers' minds towards a system in which substantive rules of law were consciously decided in court by judges, we can observe the emergence of a class of institutional writings designed to help organise this new learning.

The second sub-theme, therefore, is the intellectual history of this species of institutional writing in the Common law which stretches from Cowell around 1600 to Blackstone in the 1750s. The borrowing of Roman solutions in particular cases is one thing, the adoption of the Roman institutional scheme another. In terms of unification and general influence the latter is far more important. When we move from practice to theory, from doing law to thinking about it, it is apparent that there is little apparent influence of Roman ideas on the Common law between the thirteenth and the sixteenth centuries. From the thirteenth century, of course, we have the very important treatise *On the Laws and Customs of England* commonly called Bracton, after its supposed author, a royal judge. That the author knew Roman law is now not to be seriously doubted, and that his judicial successors had less opportunity than he to display what knowledge they too possessed is to be ascribed as much to the procedurally orientated nature of the Common law as to their supposed ignorance of Roman ideas. Nevertheless it cannot be denied that in the absence of a framework for discussion and understanding the Common law more sophisticated than the alphabetically arranged abridgments and common-place books there was little place for interaction between the Roman and Common law worlds. There were more sophisticated analyses of the Common law – most notably the Readings or lectures given by senior lawyers in the Inns of Court[19] – but as these took the form of comments on specific pieces of legislation, they offered

[18] See, for example, A. Tettenborn, *An Introduction to the Law of Obligations* (London, 1984).
[19] See S. E. Thorne, *Readings and Moots in the Inns of Court in the 15th century*, vol. I, Selden Society vol. 71 (London, 1954) and P. Brand, 'Courtroom and Schoolroom: The Education of Lawyers in England Prior to 1400' (1987) 60 Bulletin of the Institute of Historical Research 147.

less scope for general reflexion or the borrowing of Roman ideas. Where opportunities occurred, Roman solutions were not ignored.[20]

From around 1600 the situation changed. In what can be recognised as the advent of legal humanism in England there began to appear works designed to introduce and explain the Common law to beginners. These required a structure more rigorous than the alphabetical arrangement of the practitioner's *vademecum*. As we shall note, those which ignored this need were markedly less successful. The first such works were authored by those who were at least part-time academics rather than Common law practitioners and were probably aimed at a scholarly rather than an intending practitioners' market. It has to be remembered that well into the nineteenth century the main avenue for study of the Common law was by attendance as an apprentice in chambers and in court, not at the university or any school of law. The late eighteenth-century law reports still allude to remarks being made by judges 'for the sake of the students' attending the court for instruction in their discipline. When in 1774 a rare type of process by writ of right for land came on for trial in the King's Bench the court ordered that 'the galleries of the Court be open for the admission of students of the inns of Court' and took special care that the door-keeper of the court did not take advantage of the demand for seats to extract improper fees.[21]

The first English institutional writer of the early modern period, Cowell, was in fact a civilian and teacher of Roman law in Cambridge; his work was really an attempt to place Common law decisions in juxtaposition to passages drawn from Justinian's Institutes.[22] Written in Latin and by an author whose political views were at marked variance with those of the majority of Common lawyers, the work, although clearly popular with students at the universities for whom it was in all likelihood intended, was not of great importance for the practice of the Common law. Cowell took little account of the actual structure of the Common law system. It is instructive to compare the near contemporary applications of the Roman institutional model to Canon law by Lancelotti and to French law by Coquille, both of whom make serious efforts to mould their model to the needs of the subject-matter, even to the extent of escaping from the Roman framework altogether.[23]

---

[20] See the examples collected in P. Stein, *Regulae Iuris* (Edinburgh, 1966), 154–5 and in Seipp, 'Roman Legal Categories', 30–3.
[21] *Tyssen* v. *Clarke* (1774) Lofft 496.
[22] J. Cowell, *Institutiones Iuris Anglicani* ... (Cambridge, 1605; English translation, London, 1651).
[23] G. P. Lancelotti, *Institutiones Juris Canonici* (Louvain, 1589); G. Coquille, *Institution au droict des françois* (Paris, 1607); cf. W. A. J. Watson, *Roman Law and Comparative law* (Athens, GA, 1991), chapters 17 and 18.

Cowell had a contemporary, Fulbecke, who has been somewhat overlooked, largely because he wrote for a rather humbler market.[24] He had been a pupil of Gentili at Oxford, and his little introduction to the study of law, published in English in 1599, made one or two attempts at classification which show familiarity with both the method and the substance of the Institutes. His sevenfold analysis of things, made a little more confusing by some poor proof reading, proceeds as follows: '1. Absolute or qualified title; 2. Joint or several ownership; 3. servitudes; 4. wild animals; 5. *occupatio pro derelicto*; 6. treasure trove; 7. *res sacra*'.[25]

Contemporary sceptics of Romanist influence on the Common law have a champion in Coke. A leading lawyer and judge, and contemporary of Cowell and Fulbecke, Coke was of the opinion that 'For bringing the Com. Laws into a better Method, I doubt much of the Fruit of that Labour.'[26] His own attempt at a comprehensive treatise in four books, surely jestingly entitled respectively the *First, Second, Third and Fourth Part of the Institutes of the Laws of England*, illustrates the serendipity of the Common law at its most extravagant.[27] The work, or really works, for it is not a whole, owes nothing to Justinian beyond the title. Coke may well have been right to doubt the possibility of reducing the Common law of his day to method. Bentham was to criticise Blackstone, almost two centuries later, for having ignored the fact that the actualities of the legal system were at odds with Blackstone's description of it, and there are still to be found in law schools in England those who vehemently deny the relevance of theoretical studies of the law.[28]

It should be noted that there was a quite independent tradition of institutional writing on English law starting with the work of Henry Finch in 1613. Finch's work, called *Nomotechnia* but written in the obsolescent French dialect of the Common lawyers, is in four books in the published version, but there exists an early draft (c. 1586) in only two books.[29]

[24] W. Fulbecke, *A Direction, or Preparative to the Study of the Lawe* (London, 1600). I have used the reprint of the London, 1829 edn with introduction by Peter Birks (Godstone, 1987).
[25] *Ibid.*, chapter vii.
[26] E. Coke, *The Fourth Part of the Reports* (London, 1738; the first edn in French was published London, 1644), x; the Latin text has (at xi): 'Quod vero ad reductionem Juris Communis in commodiorem Methodum attinet, de illius laboris fructu plurimum dubito.'
[27] E. Coke, *The First Part of the Institutes of the Lawes of England* ... (London, 1628); *The Second Part* ... (London, 1642); *The Third Part* ... (London, 1644); *The Fourth Part* ... (London, 1644).
[28] J. Bentham, *A Fragment on Government* (London, 1776), preface; reprinted in *A Comment on the Commentaries and A Fragment on Government*, ed. J. H. Burns and H. L. A. Hart (*The Collected Works of Jeremy Bentham* (London, 1977)), 393ff.
[29] H. Finch, *Nomotechnia* (London 1613; English translation, London, 1759); *Law, or a Discourse thereof* ... (London 1627); for a full discussion see W. Prest, 'The Dialectical Origins of Finch's Law' [1977] C.L.J. 326.

Moreover the content of the books does not follow an overtly Justinianic pattern, for though book I starts with the Law of Nature, it does not proceed to Persons. Books II and III deal with what Finch identified as the two parts of the Common law, Property and Crime (the latter subsuming private wrongs) and book IV with Courts and procedure. All in all, though a case could be made for some indirect Roman influence on the published four-book format, it seems best to conclude with Prest that Finch's largest debt was to the Ramist methodological tradition.

These first attempts to institutionalise the Common law in the seventeenth century did not achieve overmuch. This may have been because the need for method was as yet not pressing. Until the Civil Wars of the mid seventeenth century there remained an effective legal educational system at the Inns of Court.[30] Only in the early years of the eighteenth century did it become apparent that in the absence of a programme of lectures or readings in the Inns, mere attendance in court and in chambers, however important in matters of detail, was inadequate to generate an overall and theoretical model of the Common law sufficient to support change and development. The first attempt to meet this need was that of Thomas Wood, whose *An Institute of the Laws of England*[31] was well known until eclipsed by Blackstone in mid-century.

When Blackstone started to lecture at Oxford in 1753 he chose to teach the Common law only because he had been disappointed of election to the chair of Roman law.[32] He claimed to have adopted as his model Hale's *Analysis of the Law*,[33] which was in turn based upon the Justinianic model. Book I of Blackstone's *Commentaries*[34] deals with the law of Persons, Book II Things (i.e. land law) and books III and IV Private and Public Wrongs (essentially procedure and crime). The structure in four books is institutional, as is, broadly, the order of treatment, making allowances for the relatively undeveloped law relating to obligations and the overwhelming importance of the land law. As Lobban has recently observed, 'the *Commentaries* were not a treatise on legal reasoning but a summary of the law',[35] and he might have added 'written *cupidae legum iuventuti*'.[36]

---

[30] J. H. Baker, 'Readings in Gray's Inn, their Decline and Disappearance' in *The Legal Profession and the Common Law* (London and Ronceverte, 1986), 31.
[31] (London, 1720).
[32] Hanbury, *The Vinerian Chair and Legal Education* (Oxford, 1958).
[33] Published anonymously together with his *History of the Common Law* (London, 1713).
[34] W. Blackstone, *Commentaries on the Laws of England* (4 vols., Oxford, 1765–9).
[35] M. Lobban, *The Common Law and English Jurisprudence 1760–1850* (Oxford, 1991), 18.
[36] Const. *Imperatoriam maiestatem* prefixed to J.Inst.

IV

By the beginning of the nineteenth century it could be said that Roman law had played two roles in the life of the Common law. Substantively it had been utilised to help resolve particular problems where there was no Common law authority and, more subtly, it had influenced those areas of law which the Common law shared with or took over from the ecclesiastical jurisdictions. As far as theory was concerned, the Roman institutional scheme had been influential since at least the 1600s, though not until the time of Wood and Blackstone was this of much relevance for the general ordering of understandings of the Common law.

Why was there a turn away from Roman law in the mid nineteenth century? Beginning in the late eighteenth century there was a slow emergence of practical treatises on areas of the Common law hitherto unsystematised except in institutional works.[37] These owed nothing to the Roman tradition. It is notorious that the modern Common law lacks an institutional tradition. No one writes books on the Law of England in fewer than fifty volumes. As far as practical influence is concerned it may not be entirely irrelevant that by legislation in 1857 the old non-Common law jurisdictions were effectively abolished, their control over such matters as marriage, testamentary succession and maritime or Admiralty matters passing to the Common lawyers.[38] Although they continued to operate broadly within the framework of the old law, it was inevitable that in time Common lawyers would approximate solutions in these areas to those found in the Common law generally. More significantly the demise of the old Civil law tradition in which the practitioners of the old jurisdictions had been expert removed from the acquaintance of the Common lawyers those with a detailed and practical knowledge of law based upon Roman texts. Before 1843 the Civil lawyers are frequently and directly involved by name in Common law litigation.

After the mid nineteenth century, although there was, paradoxically, a

---

[37] W. Eden, *Principles of Penal Law* (London, 1771), C. Fearne, *An Essay on the Learning of Contingent Remainders* (London, 1772) and W. Jones, *Essay on the Law of Bailments* (London, 1781) were amongst the first of these dedicated treatises, though the various practical works of Sir Geoffrey Gilbert (ob. 1726) first printed in the middle of the eighteenth century should not be overlooked: see A. W. B. Simpson, 'The Rise and Fall of the Legal Treatise' (1982) 48 Univ. Chicago Law Rev. 632 (= *Legal Theory and Legal History* (London and Ronceverte, 1987), 273).

[38] 20 & 21 Vict. c. 85 (Matrimonial Causes Act 1857) and c. 77 (Court of Probate Act 1857); 22 & 23 Vict. c. 6 (High Court of Admiralty Act 1859). The loss of exclusive audience in these formerly civilian courts prompted the remaining advocates to sell off their professional quarters at Doctors' Commons: G. D. Squibb, *Doctors' Commons* (Oxford, 1977), 104–9. The last judge to have been trained as a civilian was Sir Robert Phillimore, who continued to serve as Admiralty judge until 1883.

growth in the number of Common lawyers exposed to Roman law in the course of their legal education,[39] there was no longer any opportunity to experience Roman law in action. The study of Roman law, although it was to flourish at times in England as an academic legal discipline, was no longer to have direct effects upon the practice of the Common law or its understanding.

V Conclusion

But Roman law had done its work. The incorporation into the Blackstonian model of the Roman – indeed Gaian – institutional categories, however imperfect, supported by the willingness of judges to accommodate Roman solutions, was a permanent contribution to the reworking of our understanding of the structure of the Common law. The influence of Roman law must not be exaggerated, however, either in extent or importance. The Greek for 'Unification' is 'Homogenisation'. Whilst Unification seems to offer practical advantages, Homogenisation threatens to limit rather than increase understanding. Peter Birks has drawn attention to the unfortunate consequences of too ready an acceptance of Roman learning in the eighteenth-century case *Moses* v. *Macferlan*,[40] and he has also noted the willingness of English theorists like John Austin to criticise the Roman scheme of classification where it seemed not to suit local conditions.[41] The caution of earlier generations of Common lawyers towards Roman law was therefore justified inasmuch as it indicated an unwillingness to adopt unsuitable solutions or schemes of understanding. Despite this attitude the influence of Roman law upon the Common law was significant, most notably in providing a framework for understanding the substantive law as it emerged after 1600.

---

[39] Roman law was incorporated in the scheme of legal education resulting from the Report of the 1846 Select Committee on Legal Education (no. 686, 1846); P. Stein, *Legal Evolution: The Story of an Idea* (Cambridge, 1980), 78–82.
[40] (1760) 2 Burr. 1005.
[41] P. Birks, 'English and Roman Learning in *Moses* v. *Macferlan*' [1984] C.L.P. 1; Birks and G. McLeod, 'The Implied Contract Theory of Quasi-Contract' (1986) 6 O.J.L.S. at 83.

13 *Audi et alteram partem*: a limit to judicial activity

Daan Asser

In 1966 Peter Stein, at that time Professor of Jurisprudence at the University of Aberdeen, published his excellent book *Regulae Iuris*, subtitled *From Juristic Rules to Legal Maxims*. While reading it again recently it occurred to me that a famous legal maxim was absent: the rule *audi et alteram partem*, sometimes also formulated in better Latin as *audiatur et altera pars*. Since the rule is of paramount importance to all who are, like myself, professionally concerned with a fair administration of justice, I think it right and proper to devote this contribution to it, as a rather late tribute to Peter Stein's work on the *regulae iuris*.

The principle *audi et alteram partem*, which, in the Common law, is regarded as one of the rules of natural justice,[1] is not only self-evident but also – and perhaps for that very reason – valid for all time, as John Kelly showed some years ago.[2]

Therefore, the fact that we can hardly find any text in the Corpus Iuris Civilis which explicitly refers to it[3] should not lead us to the conclusion that the Romans did not recognise this principle.[4] There is much evidence in sources outside the Corpus Iuris confirming that such a principle was held by philosophers and jurists, as Kelly has convincingly shown. In

---

[1] The other rule is *nemo iudex in causa sua*. See H. H. Marshall, *Natural Justice* (London, 1959), 5, 17–20 (a historical survey), and 53ff.; J. A. Jolowicz, 'Fundamental Guarantees in Civil Litigation: England', in M. Cappelletti and D. Tallon (eds.), *Fundamental Guarantees of the Parties in Civil Litigation* (Milan, 1973), 150; see for the continental notion H. Motulsky, *Le Droit naturel dans la pratique jurisprudentielle: le respect des droits de la défense en procédure civile; Mélanges Roubier*, vol. II (Paris, 1961), 175ff. (also in Motulsky, *Ecrits, études et notes de procédure civile* (Paris, 1973), with a preface by Gérard Cornu and Jean Foyer, 60ff.).

[2] J. M. Kelly, 'Audi alteram partem' (1964) 9 Natural Law Forum 103. See also M. Uhlhorn in *Handwörterbuch zum deutschen Rechtsgeschichte*, vol. IV (London, 1990), s.v. *Rechtliches Gehör*.

[3] Kelly, 'Audi alteram partem', 105–6. See, however, D.48.17.1 *pr*. regarding criminal law.

[4] See M. Kaser, *Das römische Zivilprozessrecht* (Munich, 1966), 9 and 275, where he says that in formulary proceedings one adhered strictly to certain principles of procedure 'die die Römer vielleicht nur deshalb nicht formuliert haben, weil sie sie als Voraussetzungen einer sachgemässen Rechtspflege für selbstverständlich hielten. Hierzu zählt etwa der Grundsatz des "beiderseitigen Gehörs", demzufolge beiden Teilen angemessene Gelegenheit zur Äusserung geboten werden muss.'

addition I would submit that in the classical civil procedure the importance of *litis contestatio*, which could only be achieved by both parties, and the severe consequences of the defendant's remaining *indefensus*,[5] may have meant that normally a judgment would not have been given without the defendant having been given the opportunity to put forward his defence. And as to the more informal procedure of post-classical times, in which *litis contestatio* did not play any substantial role, it should be noted that the rules with regard to judgments by default, *in absentia*,[6] are based on the same principle, as they are in modern times. For that principle is, of course, also to be regarded as an expression of the concern that the defendant be summoned in a proper way, the cornerstone of a fair trial.

Furthermore, the Roman procedure, both classical and post-classical or Justinianic, was basically oral in nature, which meant that the judge would actually hear both parties. This would have guaranteed that both parties could fully give their views of the case. The nature of the Roman civil procedure may therefore have given little cause for concern in respect of the idea of *audi et alteram partem*.

There cannot be any doubt that the principle was also recognised throughout later ages, both in England[7] and on the continent.[8] So an ancient German saying goes: *eines Mannes Rede ist keines Mannes Rede, man soll sie billig hören Bede* ('the word of only one man [i.e. a party] is no word at all; one should rightly hear them both').[9] And in an old manual on procedural law written by the Flemish author Philips Wieland,[10] completed in 1519 and dealing with the procedural law of the courts of Flanders and the Supreme Court of the Low Countries at Malines, one may find several references to the right of the parties to be heard.

The same can be said of the later continental codes of civil procedure; the French *Nouveau code de procédure civile* is very explicit on this point,[11] as we shall see below, certainly as a result of the influence of Henri Motulsky, who was a real champion of the *droit de la défense*.[12]

---

[5] See Kaser, *Zivilprozessrecht*, 204ff.   [6] *Ibid.*, 500–1.

[7] See Kelly, 'Audi alteram partem', 107; Marshall, *Natural Justice*, 17ff.

[8] See Uhlhorn in *Handwörterbuch zum deutschen Rechtsgeschichte*, s.v. *Rechtliches Gehör*.

[9] Cf. the German *Sachsenspiegel, Landrecht* I.62.7. Kelly, 'Audi alteram partem', 107 refers to similar inscriptions on some ancient buildings in Germany. The maxim *audite et alteram partem* appears in an inscription above the entrance of the old town hall of the Dutch city of Gouda: see the jacket of H. J. Snijders, *Inleiding Nederlands burgerlijk procesrecht* (1990).

[10] *Practijke civile* (Antwerp, 1573; reprint edited by Eg. I. Strubbe (Amsterdam, 1968)).

[11] See especially arts. 14, 15 and 16.

[12] See Motulsky, *Le Droit naturel dans la pratique jurisprudentielle*. On p. VII of the preface of the *Ecrits* the editors Cornu and Foyer write, speaking of Motulsky: 'On devine avec quelle élévation il a su, dès l'origine, faire rayonner sa pensée au sein des commissions qui ont préparé la réforme de la procédure civile et dont on peut espérer un code qui portera

In our modern western societies litigants are no longer the Crown's subjects who humbly and patiently accept the wisdom of the sovereign's courts. They require the state to render the necessary judicial service, for which, after all, they pay taxes. Consequently they expect the courts to do their job in a highly professional way. The binding force of the court's decision finds, I submit, its *raison d'être* not in the first place in the powers of the state, although the practice of having disputes settled by judges and not by arms and vendettas has everything to do with the state claiming a monopoly in respect of the actual enforcement of the law. It is in the court's objectivity and impartiality and in the cogency of the arguments by which the judges reach their decision that a judgment finds its intrinsic value and its justification, if not its right to exist. Therefore, it is simply every court's duty to render a judgment that convinces both parties that the court has, at least, done its job in a proper way, even if the decision does not satisfy the party whose case was dismissed. The result of the decision-making process may be unacceptable to that party, but the process itself should give him no cause for complaint.

This means that any party involved in a lawsuit should eventually have the feeling that he has had sufficient opportunity to bring forward all the facts and arguments necessary to convince the court of his view, and the court should have attained the conviction that it has been provided with all the elements necessary to reach a decision that would be satisfactory from a professional point of view.

It is for these reasons that the court has the obligation to hear all parties concerned, at least those who wish to be heard. They should have full opportunity to defend their interests in the case which, consequently, might be affected by the judgment that will be rendered. Only by respecting this right of all parties will the court be able to render an objective judgment, the result of carefully establishing the facts and weighing the rights and obligations as well as the interests at stake.

The principle of *audi et alteram partem* – in French *le droit de la défense* and in German the right to *rechtliches Gehör*[13] – to be taken in the broad sense, as I have just explained, has two aspects. On the one hand the court should conduct the procedure with impartiality and detachment in order to guarantee both parties their procedural rights and to see to it that both parties meet their procedural obligations. Thus the court should be free of bias and partiality not only as to the substance of the case but also in respect of the procedure. In particular the court has to bear in mind that any premature view on how the case should be decided might influence

---

sa marque et conservera sa mémoire.' The new code became operative in 1975. See also J. Héron, *Droit judiciaire privé* (1991), 182, no. 247.

[13] This right is guaranteed by art. 103 of the German *Grundgesetz*.

the conduct of the case to the effect that the *audi et alteram partem* principle would be violated, for instance because the court feels that there is no need to hear one of the parties any further on a specific point, although that party should have been given the opportunity to express a view on it. Bias need not be caused by any specific interest of the judge in the outcome of the dispute, but may very well be the result of his coming to premature conclusions.

On the other hand the litigants have a right to *equal* and *effective* access to the court. They should be considered by the court as *participants* in the machinery of the legal procedure, hence as equals before the court, entitled to equal treatment by the court and to equal procedural rights and equally bounded by procedural obligations. They should be guaranteed equality of arms, *Waffengleichheit*, as the Germans call it. It will be remembered that art. 14 of the International Convention on Civil and Political Rights of 1966 guarantees equality before the court.

To English members of the legal profession all this may seem unquestionable. For the system of English civil procedure is strongly adversarial, since the conduct of the proceedings is in the hands of the parties and the court is, in general, inactive as far as the procedure is concerned.[14] The parties have therefore little to fear with regard to their right to be heard.

On the continent, however, the principle of *audi et alteram partem*, taken in the wide sense of the right to defend one's interests in court, is much more liable to be neglected. In countries like France, Germany and the Netherlands, the court has a much more active role in the conduct of the proceedings. The character of the civil procedure in those countries may, it is true, not be as inquisitorial as is often thought in the world of the Common law – continental judges are not inquisitors. One may perhaps even maintain that the ordinary civil procedure is *basically* adversarial in so far as the parties have the ultimate control over the procedure and decide which questions are to be answered by the court. But given the more – and in some countries like France very – active role of the court especially with regard to fact-finding, the continental court should be especially aware of its obligation to hear both sides. This is the more so in those kinds of procedure that are basically of an 'inquisitorial' (as opposed to 'adversarial') character, such as proceedings with regard to

---

[14] See for the role of the English judge in civil proceedings Sir Jack I. H. Jacob, *The Fabric of English Civil Justice* (London, 1987), 9ff., where in nn. 11 and 12 it is explained that the English court is, in exceptional circumstances, 'under the duty or is empowered to act of its own motion and thus to be active and if necessary to ascertain "the truth"'.

certain matters of family law, in which the court may even of its own motion bring forward facts and evidence.[15]

The problem is, I submit, that when a judge is, or feels, free to conduct proceedings in order to discover the facts necessary to the decision – in other words, to find the 'truth' – he runs the risk of descending 'into the arena and is liable to have his vision clouded by the dust of the conflict'.[16] 'If he goes beyond this he drops the mantle of a judge and assumes the role of an advocate.'[17] This may be an overstatement, and that other rule of natural justice, namely that no man may be a judge in his own case (*nemo iudex in causa sua*[18]) does not, strictly speaking, apply to such a situation, because the judge has no particular interest of his own in the outcome of the suit, but there is some truth in it. We all know that first impressions may play a decisive role in the formation of our ideas of how things are or should be. Hence the judge, pursuing what he thinks might be the 'truth', could become interested only in facts or arguments which would fit in with his own ideas, losing his professional readiness to listen to such arguments and to consider such facts when they are put forward by one of the parties. Thus a judge would create his own 'truth', so to speak. By doing so, even though he acts without malice and because he thinks that he is acting purely for the benefit of justice, he leaves far behind his duty to decide the case as presented to him by the parties. In fact this judge has already decided the case and is only collecting facts and arguments to ground his decision.

These observations are not entirely academic. Apart from the more 'inquisitorial' forms of civil procedure that we have mentioned before, certain continental systems,[19] unlike the English system,[20] do not know orality and 'immediacy' as fundamental features in ordinary civil pro-

---

[15] The Germans use the term *Untersuchungsgrundsatz* or *Inquisitionsmaxime* to qualify the principle that underlies such proceedings, in contrast to the *Verhandlungs-* or *Beibringungsgrundsatz* as the principle of ordinary proceedings. See L. Rosenberg and K. H. Schwab, *Zivilprozessrecht* (Munich, 1986), §78. See for the proceedings regarding *matière gracieuse* in France, art. 25–9 of the new Code of Civil Procedure, which grants the court almost unlimited powers. Also in Dutch law the court has much more freedom of action in such matters of *voluntaire juridictie*: see arts. 429aff. of the Dutch Code of Civil Procedure. For England, see supra, n. 14.
[16] Lord Greene, M. R. in *Yuill* v. *Yuill* [1945] P. 15 at 20.
[17] Lord Denning, M. R. in *Jones* v. *National Coal Board* [1957] 2 Q.B. 55 at 64.
[18] See Marshall, *Natural Justice*, 5 and 25ff.; Jolowicz, 'Fundamental Guarantees', 150.
[19] Like the Netherlands, Belgium and France, although the French system has been changed to some extent by the new French Code.
[20] See in this respect Jacob, *English Civil Justice*, 19ff. Germany also has a system in which the case is heard in an oral *Haupttermin* (trial), which is preceded by a pre-trial which is either oral (*früher erster Verhandlungstermin*) or in writing (*schriftliches Vorverfahren*). Which kind of trial will take place is decided by the court. See *Zivilprozessordnung*, §§273ff.; Rosenberg and Schwab, *Zivilprozessrecht*, 642ff.

ceedings.[21] The fact-finding stage, which is fully controlled by the court itself, or rather by one of its members on its behalf,[22] is separated from the debates by an interlocutory judgment of the *court*.[23] This may involve the danger that the court, by developing in its interlocutory judgment a certain line of thought even before all the relevant facts have been proved and established, neglects the principle of *audi et alteram partem*, with the result I have indicated above. However, I would like to stress that the high degree of professionalism of the judges in many continental countries will minimise this danger.

Now when a court, and I am speaking of continental courts especially, is in search of the 'truth', whatever 'truth' it may envisage, it is so because it wishes to deliver a judgment which is in accordance not only with the law but also with such a wide concept as 'justice' – something which is, I would say, the result of a combination of law in the broadest sense, professional experience, judicial intuition and ordinary common sense. Since law and justice concern the society as a whole, the court will, rightly, I think, intend to try the case on a realistic basis. A trial should not be a mockery. Imaginary cases should not be heard.[24] This may be regarded as a matter of public interest. Perhaps the continental courts have in this respect a stronger tradition of being inquisitive, literally speaking, than the English courts. But apart from the fact that the tradition is, as it is, not contrary to *audi et alteram partem*, the idea that

---

[21] It should be pointed out that criminal proceedings on the continent are similar to the English system.

[22] In this respect the continental systems differ fundamentally from the English pre-trial machinery, in which the master gives directions and makes orders as to the preparation for trial but 'has no direct role or function to play in connection with the trial itself'; see Jacob, *English Civil Justice*, 112–13.

[23] This judgment should not be compared with an interlocutory order in the English pre-trial phase, by which the court often decides on the burden of proof, on what facts have to be proved, and by which it orders the measures concerning the taking of evidence such as the hearing of witnesses or experts. The interlocutory judgment may already contain judgments as to questions of fact and of law. In France the taking of evidence may also be introduced by a simple court order (art. 151 of the *Nouveau code de procédure civile*). Although such an order does not prejudge the main issue, the choice by the court of the way by which evidence should be taken (*le choix de la mesure d'instruction*), may, however, already reflect the ideas the court has with regard to the merits of the case. In this sense see H. Solus and R. Perrot, *Droit judiciaire privé*, vol. III (Paris, 1991), no. 738.

[24] Sometimes serious issues may underlie such actions. Some years ago people opposing Nato's deployment of cruise missiles in Holland, which had been approved by the Dutch Government and Parliament, started various civil actions on the basis of invented facts in order to get a judgment by which the Government's policy would be declared unconstitutional. These claims, based on a most ingenious contrivance, were of course recognised to be false, and were for that reason dismissed. The Dutch Hoge Raad, assessing the true cause of action, assumed that the claimant did not intend to have a genuine dispute with his opponent determined, but only to elicit a judgment from the court on the constitutionality of the deployment of cruise missiles. See HR 27 June 1986. Nederlandse Jurisprudentie, 1987, no. 354.

civil justice is, or at least should be, concerned with 'real' cases is undoubtedly also held in England, much as the proceedings are different.[25]

In this respect it is important to remember that it is generally accepted that the parties have the right to determine the issue at stake, that is to say the *facts* that are in dispute and those that are not. The court should not base its decision upon facts which have not been alleged by the parties or one of them and which cannot be found in any document produced by them.[26] However, this does not always mean that the court may only make use of facts to which the parties have expressly made reference.

This is the case in France, where art. 7 of the new Code of Civil Procedure allows the court to take into consideration facts which the parties have not particularly referred to in support of their claim or defence. It may occur, for instance, that facts can be found in documents or by examining witnesses,[27] without the parties having especially referred to that fact, although the court regards it as relevant or perhaps even decisive. In the English system of pleading this will not happen frequently, since it is the parties who, by pleading the material facts, decide which facts may be considered as such and which may not.

Now when a court finds such facts, the question arises whether it should confront the parties explicitly with such material, before basing a decision on it. This may be illustrated by the following example. A plaintiff claims payment of a commission of 10 per cent for bringing about a certain transaction. That claim is denied by the defendant, who alleges that there had been no transaction of that kind or any other transaction which could give ground for the claim. The court rules that there is evidence in the written contract, produced by the plaintiff, that the parties had agreed on a percentage of 7 per cent for the kind of transaction at issue. Since the defendant had neither admitted nor denied the alleged 10 per cent, the court felt free to sustain the claim to a maximum of 7 per cent, assuming that the plaintiff had made a mistake.

---

[25] Would not the English courts almost certainly strike out or dismiss claims of the sort mentioned in the preceding footnote as frivolous or an abuse of the process of the court? See D. B. Casson (ed.), *Odgers on High Court Pleading and Practice* (London, 1991), 187–8.

[26] One may find this rule in, for example, art. 7 of the French code and art. 176 of the Dutch Code. It is also recognised in German law: see Rosenberg and Schwab, *Zivilprozessrecht*, 455–6.

[27] It will be remembered that, contrary to the English system, in the Civil law systems of civil litigation it is the court itself that examines the witnesses, although the parties have the right either to invite the hearing judge to ask certain questions in addition (as, for example, by arts. 208 and 214 of the French *Nouveau code de procédure civile* and art. 938 of the Belgian Judicial Code) or to examine the witnesses themselves (as laid down in art. 205 of the Dutch Code of Civil Procedure and §397 of the German *Zivilprozessordnung*).

The question is whether the court was allowed to do so without previously confronting the parties with that fact and giving them an opportunity to give their views on it. The danger of a court following this line is that it might happen to be that the parties had actually agreed on 10 per cent and that the document was wrong or outdated by a later agreement. It is in fact a question of *audi et alteram partem*: the parties have the right to give their views on such facts as the court finds essential.[28] Similar situations arise where the court bases its judgment upon knowledge of its own. It may have acquired certain knowledge or technical know-how from similar cases in the past or particular knowledge with regard to the parties from earlier proceedings concerning them. In situations like this courts should be careful not to use such knowledge too readily without first hearing the parties on that particular point.

So far we have discussed the question to what extent the principle of *audi et alteram partem* sets a limit to the court's activities in the field of finding facts and the 'truth'. Another field where the principle should play a role is in what is traditionally regarded as the territory where the court has an exclusive competence: the field of the law. *Ius curia novit*, 'The court knows the law', is a well-known maxim which shows that it is the court's duty to 'find' the law applicable to the facts presented by the parties: *da mihi factum; tibi dabo ius* – 'Give me the facts and I shall give you the law' – is another famous maxim that says virtually the same.[29] Or, as art. 12 of the French *Nouveau code de procédure civile* provided, 'le juge tranche le litige conformément aux règles de droit qui lui sont applicables'.[30] Of course the parties will 'help' the court in finding the law. They are in no way excluded from presenting and discussing questions of law.[31] For how can they ever be sure that the court really knows the law? But in the end it is the court that will make clear what the law is: 'le juge doit rester maître de la règle de droit'.[32]

---

[28] See the discussion in France on art. 7 of the French Code; see Solus and Perrot, *Droit judiciaire privé*, nos. 95 and 96.

[29] Cf. *Odgers*, 131, with regard to Order 18, rule 7(1) of the Rules of the Supreme Court: 'it is for the court to declare the law arising on the facts proved before it'; and 132: 'He [i.e. the judge] knows the law, and can apply it to the facts of the case without its being stated in the pleadings.'

[30] The same principle is accepted in other countries. See, for example, art. 48 of the Dutch Code of Civil Procedure, requiring the court to supplement the legal grounds (*rechtsgronden*) advanced by the parties in their claim or defence; for Germany, Rosenberg and Schwab, *Zivilprozessrecht*, 838–9; and for Switzerland, W. J. Habscheid, *Droit judiciaire privé suisse* (Geneva, 1981), 365ff.

[31] See in this respect the remarks made by Solus and Perrot, *Droit judiciaire privé*, 166ff. on art. 12 of the new French Code of Civil Procedure. See also Jacob, *English Civil Justice*, 165, speaking of the parties, in trial, making submissions on the law applicable to the facts which each contend should be found by the judge.

[32] Solus and Perrot, *Droit judiciaire privé*, 57, no. 63.

Now one may ask whether this *ius curia novit* principle would allow the judge to base his judgment upon rules of law which the parties did not consider relevant and which, consequently, they did not discuss. Should they not be given the opportunity to do so before judgment is rendered on the basis of such rules of law? The question has significance in view of the principle of *audi et alteram partem*, especially since anyone who is familiar with the practice of law would admit that in many cases questions of fact cannot be separated neatly from questions of law, even, as I would say, in the English system of pleadings, where the pleader must know the applicable law before being able to discern which facts are material and which are not.[33] There cannot be any doubt that all proceedings are, in the end, concerned with the law, because the plaintiff does not start proceedings to obtain a verdict on the facts only, but to get a decision in respect of what he pretends to be entitled to according to the law. So the plaintiff, or rather counsel, will mould the mass, or sometimes chaos, of facts into a coherent body consisting of legally relevant facts which should enable him to win his case. This view is expressed clearly by the French authors Solus and Perrot in their manual on civil procedure:[34]

Lorsqu'un demandeur (ou même un défendeur) formule une prétention, il n'invoque pas seulement une masse de faits neutres: s'il saisit un juge, c'est pour lui demander, à partir des faits qu'il lui expose, la reconnaissance d'un droit dont il se prétend titulaire, en fonction précisément de la règle de droit ou d'un principe juridique qui lui paraît devoir justifier sa prétention: autrement, comment pourrait-il se découvrir un droit digne d'une protection judiciaire? Et inversement, la sélection des faits par le demandeur est souvent commandée par les présupposés de la règle de droit qu'il estime, à tort ou à raison, devoir s'appliquer au cas d'espèce; de telle sorte que le demandeur (ou le défendeur), en formulant ses prétentions, est inévitablement conduit à privilégier certains faits de préférence à d'autres, selon la règle de droit retenue par lui pour construire son argumentation.[35]

Therefore a judge should always realise that the facts presented by the plaintiff are relevant to the outcome envisaged by that party. The same applies to the facts which were put forward by the defendant. This sets a limit to the principle of *ius curia novit* and should restrain the court from choosing, *ex officio*, too readily a legal basis for sustaining or dismissing

---

[33] See *Odgers*, 135: 'The pleader must apply his knowledge of the law, and his common sense, to the facts stated in his instructions, and decide for himself which he must plead and which he may safely omit.'
[34] *Droit judiciaire privé*, 3.68–9.
[35] To this they add in a note (p. 69 n. 1) the following observation: 'Les avocats savent bien qui, dans la masse des faits que leurs clients déversent en vrac, doivent sélectionner ceux qui leur paraissent "concluants" ou "relevants". En fonction de quoi peuvent-ils opérer ce choix, si ce n'est par référence à une règle de droit sur laquelle ils envisagent de fonder la prétention de leur client?' See also 94–7, no. 92.

the claim which had not been envisaged by the parties. Such problems may occur, for instance, in cases of an international character, in which the parties may have impliedly based themselves on the law of one country, whereas the court finds that the facts, as qualified by the court, lead to the application of the law of another country or the provisions of a certain treaty. This may cause embarrassment on the side of the unsuccessful party, or even of both parties, since they might have wished to adapt their pleadings to that law if they had known that the court would think of applying it. Perhaps the court overlooked the fact that both parties, before starting proceedings, had agreed upon regarding the application of that treaty to be excluded, which is why they did not discuss it.

The Germans consider such an *Überraschungsentscheidung*, a decision by surprise, to be contrary to the right of *rechtliches Gehör*, the principle of *audi et alteram partem*, as laid down in art. 103 of the *Grundgesetz* and particularly in §278, section III of the *Zivilprozessordnung*,[36] which allows the judge to base his judgment on any point of law which has obviously been overlooked or regarded as irrelevant by a party, only when he has given the opportunity to comment upon that point. Besides that, the court should, in order to avoid surprises and in accordance with §139 of the *Zivilprozessordnung*, discuss with the parties the points which are raised by the court of its own motion in order to enable the parties to give their view.

Art. 16 of the new French Code of Civil Procedure explicitly forbids the judge to found a decision on a legal basis which the parties did not bring forward. Speaking of the judge, it provides:

Il ne peut fonder sa décision sur les moyens de droit qu'il a relevés d'office sans avoir au préalable invité les parties à présenter leurs observations.

I shall not go into the difficult question of the exact meaning of 'moyens de droit'.[37] One may roughly describe it as a rule of law, applicable to the facts that have been assessed as instrumental to the outcome of the suit. Here too the reason is that there should be no decision by surprise.[38] The parties should have the opportunity to give their view and to defend their interests as far as they are touched by the new finding.

The principle of *ius curia novit* and the limits set to it by the principle of *audi et alteram partem* lead us to a more delicate question relating to the continental institution of *cassation*.

This kind of review, which originates from France and which we find in

---

[36] See Rosenberg and Schwab, *Zivilprozessrecht*, 458–9.
[37] See Solus and Perrot, *Droit judiciaire privé*, 71–3, no. 73; J. Vincent and S. Guinchard, *Procédure civile* (Paris, 1991), no. 373.
[38] In this sense, see Solus and Perrot, *Droit judiciaire privé*, 129.

Belgium, the Netherlands and some other countries, is concerned with questions of law only. The duty of a Court of Cassation is to review findings of law, not of fact. It is the ultimate check whether the lower court (the *iudex facti*, as it is sometimes called) indeed knew the law and applied it in the way he should. It goes without saying that also in the proceedings before the Court of Cassation the *audi et alteram partem* principle applies. However, since the court does not review the case as such but only the findings of law by the lower court (in most cases a court of appeal), the court has a far more independent position towards the parties concerned. The Court of Cassation in those countries where it exists is assisted by legal officers who are not members of the court but who are attached to the court: the *procureur général* and his assistants, the advocates general. These officers give an opinion (submissions or 'conclusions') on the case to the court after argument has been closed.

Recently a case regarding the *audi et alteram partem* principle and the advice of those officers was decided by the European Court of Human Rights in Strasburg. On 30 October 1991 it rendered a quite remarkable judgment[39] concerning the way the proceedings before the Belgian Court of Cassation are conducted. It raises the question whether a party has the right to answer to the observations on the merits of the case made by the advocate general attached to the court.

Mr Borgers, a Belgian lawyer, politician and former substitute district judge, had been charged with a criminal offence. He was tried and found guilty by the Antwerp Court of Appeal. He appealed successfully to the Court of Cassation, which quashed the decision and remitted the case to the Ghent Court of Appeal (the Court of Cassation cannot decide the case itself). After being convicted once more Borgers again appealed to the Court of Cassation, which now dismissed the appeal.

Both times the Court of Cassation, at the hearing, had heard the submissions ('conclusions') of the advocate general of the Court of Cassation, who had also participated in the deliberations of the court, as allowed by art. 1109 of the Belgian Judicial Code.[40]

Borgers subsequently went to the Court of Human Rights at Strasburg. Alleging a violation of art. 6 §1 of the Convention, according to which, 'in the determination of ... any criminal charge against him, everyone is entitled to a fair ... hearing ... by an ... impartial tribunal', he complained:[41]

In the first place that, at the [second] hearing ... in the Court of Cassation ... he had been unable to reply to the submissions of the *avocat général* or to address the

---

[39] No. 39/1990/230/296, Publ. Series A, vol. 214-A.
[40] This provided that the *procureur général* or a member of his department is entitled to attend the deliberations of the court, though without a vote.
[41] I quote the judgment of the European Court, §22.

court last; secondly he objected to the fact that the *avocat général* had participated in the deliberations which took place immediately after the hearing. He argued that as ... the *ministère public* formed a single unit for institutional and disciplinary purposes, the official in question could indeed have been seen as his opponent. That official's presence at the deliberations had served only to aggravate the breach of the principle of equality of arms which had already occurred at the stage of argument.

The Commission shared this opinion in substance and declared the complaints admissible, finding a violation of art. 6 §1 of the Convention and inviting the court to reconsider the view taken in its judgment in the *Delcourt* case of 17 January 1970.[42]

Although the case is mainly of importance to those continental jurisdictions which have a system similar to the Belgian, it might be of some interest to the English judiciary as well, since the decision of the Strasburg court might, as *ad hoc* Judge Storme pointed out in his dissenting opinion in the *Borgers* decision,[43] also affect the position of a high judicial officer such as the English Lord Chancellor, who unites in himself executive, legislative and judicial powers.

For a better understanding of the decision we should make some remarks on the Belgian judiciary. Although the *procureur général* as well as the advocates general of the Court of Cassation of Belgium formally belong to the *ministère public*, a body answerable to the Minister of Justice and in charge of the prosecution of criminal offences and the execution of criminal judgments,[44] they have no prosecuting authority (except in those rare cases such as proceedings against ministers in which the decision falls to the Court of Cassation). Their task is to advise the court, not the Minister of Justice, who has no influence whatsoever on the proceedings before the Supreme Court. They do not receive any instructions from the Minister of Justice as to how to carry out their duties, which is, as the European Court has recognised,[45] to be the independent and impartial adjunct to and adviser of the court both in civil and in criminal cases. By doing so they might be regarded as 'extraordinary members' of the Court of Cassation, as Judge Martens describes them in his dissenting opinion in the *Borgers* case,[46] or as *amici curiae*, as *ad hoc* Judge Storme in his dissenting opinion prefers to call them.

In fact one may compare the *procureur général* and his advocates general with the advocates general of the Court of the European Commu-

[42] Publ. Series A, no. 11.   [43] See that opinion, no. 11.
[44] See arts. 400 and 414 of the Belgian Judicial Code, cited in the decision of the European Court, §18.
[45] Cf. the decisions in the *Delcourt* case (§§32–8) and the *Borgers* case (§§16 and 24).
[46] See §2.4. The same applies to the Dutch *procureur generaal* at the Hoge Raad and his advocates general; the position of the same officials in France is comparable.

nities,[47] whose impartiality and independence have never been questioned. There cannot be any doubt about the position of the *procureur général*'s department: together with the Court of Cassation it in fact makes up one body, which may be regarded as the Supreme Court.

The European Court in its decision in the *Borgers* case indeed did not impugn the position of the *procureur général*'s department as such. For it declared the findings in the *Delcourt* judgment on the question of the independence and impartiality of the Court of Cassation and its *procureur général*'s department entirely valid. Yet the court agreed, though not unanimously,[48] with the Commission that art. 6 §1 of the Convention had been violated. It ruled that it was 'necessary to consider whether *the proceedings*[49] before the Court of Cassation also respected the rights of the defence and the principle of the equality of arms, which', according to the court, 'are features of the wider concept of a fair trial' and have 'undergone a considerable evolution in the court's case-law, notably in respect of the importance attached to *appearances* and to the *increased sensitivity of the public*[50] to the fair administration of justice'. Then, after having confirmed that no one questions the objectivity with which the *procureur général*'s department discharges its function, the court continues (§26):

Nevertheless the opinion of the *procureur général*'s department cannot be regarded as neutral from the point of view of the parties to the cassation proceedings. By recommending that an accused's appeal be allowed or dismissed, the official of the *procureur général*'s department becomes objectively speaking his ally or his opponent. In the latter event, Article 6 §1 requires that the rights of the defence and the principle of the equality of arms be respected.

After having pointed out (in §27) that Mr Borgers could not reply to the unfavourable submissions of the advocate general, being prevented therefrom by art. 1107 of the Judicial Code, which prohibits even the lodging of written notes following the intervention of the advocate general,[51] the court considers that it cannot see the justification for such restrictions on the rights of the defence.

Once the *avocat général* had made submissions unfavourable to the applicant, the latter had a clear interest in being able to submit his observations on them before argument was closed. The fact that the Court of Cassation's jurisdiction is confined to questions of law makes no difference in this respect.

[47] See arts. 165 and 166 of the EEC Treaty.
[48] See the dissenting opinions of Judges Cremona, Thór Vilhjálmsson, Martens and Storme.
[49] My italics.   [50] My italics.
[51] In the Netherlands, however, this is, within strict limitations set out by the Hoge Raad, allowed according to art. 238 of the Code of Civil Procedure and art. 440 of the Code of Criminal Procedure; see also the dissenting opinion of Judge Martens in the present case, n. 2.

As to the advocate general's taking part in the deliberations of the court,[52] the court ruled that by this 'the inequality was increased even more' (see §28). From the assistance of the advocate general to the Court of Cassation in chambers it could, according to the European Court, *'reasonably be thought'*[53] that the deliberations afforded the *avocat général* an additional opportunity to 'promote, without fear of contradiction by the applicant, his submissions to the effect that the appeal should be dismissed.'

Apart from the fact that the decision shows how far the Strasburg Court would wish to go involving itself in questions of the judicial organisation of member states – which constitutes a problem of its own which I cannot discuss here[54] – one observes that it is not the position as such of the members of the *ministère public* at the Court of Cassation which is the key to the court's reasoning. It is not because one might confuse the advocate general with the public prosecutor and consequently regard him as the natural opponent of the defendant that the applicant is granted the right to reply to the former's submissions. The reason is rather the advocate general's *opinion* concerning the merits of the case, as laid down in his submissions. This makes him *objectively speaking* either an opponent or an ally of the applicant. It is the *appearance* and the general public's *sensitivity* which apparently are the keywords. However, one may wonder why the court, in this respect, uses the phrase 'objectively speaking', since appearance and sensitivity are not matters of objectivity but rather of subjective, personal perception.

I think that if one takes the principle of *audi et alteram partem* seriously and understands it as a rule which guarantees the parties the right to defend their interests in court, the decision of the court raises some other questions, especially with regard to the limits of the principle.

The issue in cassation is a question of law. As we have seen, the interests of the parties in civil litigation are mainly concerned with questions of fact. It is the parties who have the right and the duty to allege the relevant facts in order to decide the case according to the rules of law. Where the court has the duty to inform the parties of points of law which the court finds relevant or even decisive but which had not been discussed by the parties, this is because those points of law may throw a different light on the facts at stake, or may even make it necessary for the parties to adapt their factual allegations.

---

[52] The Dutch *procureur generaal* and advocates general are not admitted to the deliberations.
[53] My italics.
[54] See the remarks made by Judge Martens in his dissenting opinion under IV, where he recommends 'self-restraint' of the Strasburg Court where national procedural provisions are at stake.

In the system of cassation there is no room for discussing questions of fact. Therefore the role of the parties is a limited one, even if we admit that the outcome of the cassation proceedings may be decisive as to the concrete issues of the case and even when we consider that the parties may have a broader interest in the judgment of the Court of Cassation because they have brought up a test-case. The argument in cassation is about what the law should be and how it should be applied to the facts assessed by the lower courts. Therefore I would submit that, contrary to the consideration of the European Court, the fact that the Court of Cassation's jurisdiction is confined to questions of law indeed makes a great difference with regard to the right of being heard in court.

Moreover, the view of the Strasburg Court that, by giving his independent and impartial opinion of the case, the advocate general is making himself, at least in the perception of the parties, either an opponent or an ally of the party whose standpoint in cassation he rejects or supports, is not conclusive. The judge deciding against one of the parties is not making himself an opponent or an ally of the party concerned. The advocate general has no interest whatsoever in the outcome of the case. It is the lawfulness and consistency of the decision in the lower court, and in a wider context the unity, consistency and further development of the law in general that are his concern.

One might ask whether the European Court, by following its line of thought, did not overstretch the meaning of 'fair trial' and in particular of the 'rights of the defence', as guaranteed by art. 6 of the Convention. It may still[55] seem, I admit, questionable to those who are brought up in the Common law tradition that the Supreme Court is advised by a special judicial officer, who is not a member of the court, on how to decide the appeal without the parties being given the opportunity to discuss the opinion of that officer. However, one should bear in mind that when the case is placed in the hands of the *procureur général* in order to give his opinion on it, argument has been closed. The problem created by the Strasburg decision is that the proceedings may start all over again if the parties are granted an *a priori* right to give their view on the submissions of the *procureur général*. It would probably not add much to all that had already been said. The principle of *audi et alteram partem*, fundamental though it may be, does not guarantee endless debate: there must also be some limit to it.

---

[55] Cf. the proceedings before the European Court of Justice in Luxemburg, referred to above.

Index of sources

ROMAN LAW

LAY AUTHORS

Cicero, M. Tullius *Pro Milone* 11.30, 149
  Pro Lege Manilia, 132
  Ad Fam. VIII.8, 102
Festus *De Lingua Latina* 178
  (FIRA I.13), 44
Frontinus *De Aquis* 100–1, 104, 106, 108, 125, 127, 102
Aulus Gellius *Noctes Atticae* 11.18.13, 57, 62
11.18.20, 56
11.18.21, 56, 59
11.18.23, 56

JURISTIC SOURCES

Gaius, Institutes
2.20, 183
3.195, 57
3.202, 59, 60
3.211, 38
3.212, 20
3.214, 20, 25
3.219, 34, 39, 40, 41, 43

Collatio Legum Mosaicarum et Romanarum
12.7, 34, 40

Pauli Sententiae
2.31.35 (FIRA 2.356), 60, 67

Justinian, Institutes
Const. Imperatoriam Maiestatem, 206
1.2 *pr.*, 146
1.3.1, 136
1.3.2, 135
1.8, 156
1.13 *pr.*, 156
2.1.17, 124
2.1.27, 66
2.1.28, 66
2.1.41, 183
2.1.44, 194

2.20.23, 105
3.27.3, 161, 172
4.1.1, 57
4.3, 35
4.3.9, 20, 25
4.3.10, 20
4.3.16, 34, 39
4.6.19, 25
4.6.20, 161, 176
4.17.4,5, 161, 167, 176

Digesta
Const. Tanta 20a, 115
1.1.1.3, 146
1.1.3, 149
1.2.2, 105
1.2.2.47, 19
1.5.4 *pr.*, 136
2.5.4.1, 135
1.16.7–8, 131
1.18.10–11, 131
2.15.6, 108–9
2.41.5, 105
3.3.40.2, 86
4.3.7.7, 59
4.3.18.3, 61
4.4.27.4, 105
4.8.4, 132
5.1.37, 112
6.1.5 *pr.*, 66
7.1.37, 89
7.6.5 *pr.*, 87
8.6.6, 87
9.1.1.7, 41
9.2.5.1, 38
9.2.6.1, 149
9.2.7.2, 40
9.2.7.3, 41, 50
9.2.7.6, 40
9.2.7.7, 40, 41
9.2.9 *pr.*, 40, 44
9.2.9.1, 40, 44
9.2.9.3, 39, 40, 41
9.2.9.4, 40

Index of sources

9.2.9.7, 39
9.2.11 *pr.*, 41
9.2.11.1, 41
9.2.11.5, 41
9.2.13 *pr.*, 34
9.2.21.2, 21ff.
9.2.22 *pr.*, 23
9.2.23.2, 25
9.2.23.3, 21ff.
9.2.23.4, 15ff.
9.2.23.5, 21ff.
9.2.23.6, 21ff.
9.2.27.6–8, 34
9.2.27.13, 42
9.2.27.19, 40
9.2.27.20, 40
9.2.27.21, 59
9.2.27.22, 45
9.2.30.3, 34
9.2.31, 40
9.2.33 *pr.*, 23
9.2.39, 39
9.2.51 *pr.*, 41, 43
9.2.52.2, 40
9.2.52.7, 61
9.2.52.22, 61
9.2.55, 23
10.1.8.1, 83
10.2.55, 168
10.3.2.1, 167
10.3.3 *pr.*, 160
10.3.4.3, 160
10.3.6.2, 161
10.3.10 *pr.*, 161
10.3.12, 161
10.3.14.2, 160, 162, 173
10.3.14.3, 173
10.3.28, 164
11.3.3.1, 40
11.3.4, 40
12.6.53, 88
14.2.9, 131
14.6.7.12, 90
17.2.38.1, 161
18.1.19, 183
18.1.53, 183, 191
18.1.78.2, 189
18.3.1, 184, 193, 195
18.3.8, 184
18.4.22, 189
18.7.6.1, 113–14
18.7.7, 114
19.1.13.8, 189
19.1.25, 189
19.5.14.2, 59
19.5.23, 59
19.5.23, 59

20.6.14, 187
21.1.31.8, 189
21.1.57 *pr.*, 189
23.2.1, 111
23.2.28, 114
24.1.32.14, 68
26.7.43.1, 107
28.1.8.4, 111
29.2.59, 104
29.2.60, 104
29.3.1, 108
29.5.1.17, 44
30.1, 112
30.47.1, 66
32.3.16, 200
33.5.19, 105
33.7.12.9, 66
34.9.22, 82
35.2.38.2, 184
35.2.61, 113
36.2.13.4, 132
39.1.1.6, 89
39.1.5.10, 89
39.3.1.12, 201
41.1.5.1, 56
41.1.7.8, 66
41.1.44, 61
41.1.55, 59
41.2.1 *pr.*, 124
41.2.3.5, 82–4
41.2.3.6, 109
41.2.3.13, 84, 125
41.2.3.19, 88
41.2.6.1–7, 73–90
41.2.8, 80–1, 89, 109
41.2.31, 79
41.2.44.2, 80
41.2.46.8, 80
41.3.4.22, 87
41.3.4.27 (28), 87
41.3.33.2, 87
41.4.2.3, 184
43.16.1.18, 90
43.16.1.19, 90
43.16.3.6, 90
43.16.3.13, 84
43.17.3, 89
43.19.1.9, 90
43.24.5.5, 85
43.24.11.5, 86
44.2.15, 86
45.1.1.4, 65
45.1.23, 200
45.1.33, 200
46.3.80, 110
46.3.81, 89
47.2.1 *pr.*, 57

226 *Index of sources*

47.2.1.1, 60
47.2.1.3, 57
47.2.14.1, 189
47.2.17.1, 57
47.2.20.1, 57
47.2.21, 63ff.
47.2.21 *pr.*, 56
47.2.21.7, 60
47.2.22 *pr.*, 1, 57, 60, 67
47.2.25 *pr.*, 62
47.2.36 *pr.*, 59
47.2.37, 59,60
47.2.39 *pr.*, 60, 67
47.2.43.5, 60
47.2.50.4, 59
47.2.52.13, 59
47.2.52.19, 57
47.2.52.20, 59
47.2.52.22, 61
47.2.52.27, 57
47.2.53 (52), 90
47.2.54 (53), 90
47.2.54 (53) *pr.*, 67
47.2.56, 57
47.2.61, 57
47.2.66, 57
47.2.67.1, 57
47.2.67.2, 59
47.2.76, 60
47.2.91.1, 60
47.10.11 *pr.*, 39
47.14.1 *pr.*, 111
48.6.5.1, 112–13
48.17.1 *pr.*, 209
48.19.18, 112
49.15.5, 122
49.15.6, 122
49.15.19, 122
50.2.3.3, 111
50.4.7, 108
50.16.80, 112
50.16.88, 113
50.16.215, 156
50.17.153, 109
50.17.202, 54
50.17.203, 90

Codex Justinianus
1.3.37, 83
1.18.5, 194
1.22.6, 133
2.3.20, 192, 194
2.26.3, 132
2.42.2, 105
3.37.1–5, 176
3.37.1, 168

3.37.3.1, 160, 168
3.37.5, 160
4.23.4, 108–9
4.54.3, 184
4.54.4, 184
4.62.1, 112–13
5.2.1, 114
5.72.1, 105
7.32.4, 80
7.53.3, 105
8.4.11, 90
9.12.7, 112–13
10.32.26, 111
11.48 (47).14, 78, 90

Novellae
12.2, 153

MODERN CONTINENTAL EUROPEAN LEGISLATION

GERMANY

Grundgesetz art. 103, 211, 218
Bürgerliches Gesetzbuch 823 I, 32, 39
Zivilprozessordnung §139, 218
§273, 213
§278, 218
§397, 215

FRANCE

Code civil art. 1656, 195
Code of Civil Procedure art. 7, 215–16
 art. 7, 215–16
 art. 12, 216
 art. 14, 210
 art. 15, 210
 art. 16, 210, 218
 art. 25, 213
 art. 151, 214
 art. 208, 215
 art. 214, 215

THE NETHERLANDS

Code of Civil Procedure art. 48, 216
 art. 176, 215
 art. 176, 215
 art. 205, 215
 art. 238, 221
 art. 429a, 213
Code of Criminal Procedure art. 440, 221

BELGIUM

Judicial Code art. 400, 220
 art. 414, 220
 art. 1107, 221
 art. 1109, 219

Index of sources

COMMON LAW

ENGLISH LAW

Statutes

9 Edw. III c. 1, 128
13 Rich. II c. 5, 130, 133
15 Rich. II c. 3, 130, 133
2 Hen. IV c. 11, 130, 133
8 Eliz. I c. 5, 134
20 & 21 Vict. c. 77 (Court of Probate Act 1857), 207
20 & 21 Vict. c. 85 (Matrimonial Causes Act 1857), 207
22 & 23 Vict. c. 6 (High Court of Admiralty Act 1859), 207
Sale of Goods Act 1893, 182
Larceny Act 1916 s. 12 (1), 58
Police and Criminal Evidence Act 1984 s. 24 (4), (5), 70
Sexual Offences (Amendment) Act 1976 s. 1, 54
Theft Act 1968 s. 1 (1), 58, 61, 69
 s. 3 (1), 58, 69
 s. 9 (1) (b), 55
 s. 15 (1), 71
Sale of Goods Act 1979 s. 17, 198
 s. 62 (4), 198

Cases

Acton v. *Blundell* (1843) 12 M. & W. 324, 200–2
Anon. (1353) Y.B. 27 Lib. Ass. pl. 64, 51
Anon. (1368) Y.B. 42 Lib. Ass. pl. 9 (Essex Assizes), 51
Anon. (1374) Y.B. Mich. 48 Edw. III, fol. 25, pl. 8, 46
Anon. (1428) Y.B. Mich. 7 Hen. 6 pl. 36 (*recte* 16) fols. 10, 11, 199
Anstey v. *Dowsing* (1746) 2 Stra. 1253, 200
Att.-Gen. v. *Lady Downing* (1767) Wilmot 1, 200
Beaulieu v. *Fingham* (1401) Y.B. Pas. 2 Hen. IV, fol. 18, pl. 6, 47
Bourden v. *Alloway* (1708) 11 Mod. 180, 35
Browne v. *Best* (1747) 1 Wils. 174, 201
Browne v. *Davis* (1706) Baker and Milsom, *Sources*, 575, 48, 52
Cantrel v. *Churche* (1601) Cro.Eliz. 845, 36
Coggs v. *Bernard* (1703) Lord Raym. 909, 200
Cook v. *Hasard* (1387) 103 S.S. 404, 51
Dobson v. *General Accident Fire and Life Assurance Corporation plc* [1990] 1 Q.B. 274, 69, 71
Donoghue v. *Stevenson* [1932] A.C. 562, 37, 48
Doughty v. *Turner Manufacturing Co. Ltd.* [1941] 1 Q.B. 518, 33
D.P.P. v. *Morgan* [1976] A.C. 182, 54
Eason v. *Newman* (1596) Cro. Eliz. 495, 36
Eddy v. *Niman* (1981) 73 Cr.Ap.Rep. 237, 70
Ellis v. *Angwin* (1390) 103 S.S. 405, 52
The Farrier's Case (1372) Y.B. Trin. 46 Edw. III, fol. 19, pl. 19, 46
Gibbons v. *Pepper* (1695) 1 Lord Raym. 38, 49f.
Havent v. *Ward* (1364) 103 S.S. 402, 51
Indian Oil Corporation Ltd. v. *Greenstone Shipping S. A. (Panama)* [1987] 3 W.L.R. 869, 200
Isaack v. *Clarke* (1614) 1 Rolle Rep. 126, 36
Jason v. *Norton* (1653) Style 398, 46
Jones v. *National Coal Board* [1957] 2 Q.B. 55, 213
Lawrence v. *Metropolitan Police Commissioner* [1971] 1 Q.B. 373; [1972] A.C. 626, 69, 70, 72
Mason v. *Hill* (1833) 5 B. & Ald. 1, 201
Moreton v. *Hordern* (1825) 4 B. & C. 223, 36
Moses v. *Macferlan* (1760) 2 Burr. 1005, 208
Parker v. *British Airways Board* [1982] Q.B. 1004, 200
Pillans v. *van Mièrop* (1765) 3 Burr. 1663, 200
R v. *Burnside and Morris* [1984] A.C. 320, 58, 61, 69
R v. *Cabbage* (1815) R. & R. 292, 60
R v. *Figures* [1976] Crim.L.R. 744, 70
R v. *Fritschy* [1985] Crim.L.R. 745, 70
R v. *Gomez* [1991] 3 All E.R. 394; [1993] A.C. 442, 58, 61, 69–72
R v. *Hircock* (1978) 67 Cr.App.Rep. 278, 70
R v. *Holloway* (1848) 3 Cox 241, 60
R v. *Jones and Smith* [1976] 1 W.L.R. 672, 55
R v. *McPherson* [1973] Crim.L.R. 191, 70
R v. *Meech* [1974] Q.B. 549, 70
R v. *Monaghan* [1979] Crim.L.R. 673, 70
R v. *Morgan* [1985] Crim.L.R. 447, 596, 70
R v. *Rader* [1992] Crim.L.R. 663, 69, 72
R v. *Satnam* (1983) 78 Cr.App.Rep. 149, 54
R v. *Shuck* [1992] Crim.L.R. 209, 69, 72
R v. *Simson* (1664) Kel. 31, 58
R v. *Skipp* [1975] Crim.L.R. 114, 70

Index of sources

Cases *cont.*
R v. *Pitham and Hehl* (1976) 65 Cr.App.Rep. 45, 68
Reynolds v. *Clarke* (1625) Baker & Milsom, Sources 307 46
Reynolds v. *Clarke* (1725) Lord Raym. 1402; Stra. 635, 35
Savignac v. *Roome* (1794) 6 T.R. 125, 37
Scott v. *Shepherd* (1773) 2 W.Bl. 892, 34f., 49
Shury v. *Piggot* (1625) 3 Bulstr. 339, 201
Slade v. *Morley* (1602) 4 Co. Rep.; [1971] C.L.J. 51, 36
Slater v. *Baker* (1767) 2 Wils. 359, 49
Southern Centre for Theosophy Inc. v. *South Australia* [1982] 1 All E.R. 283, 200
Taylor v. *Caldwell* (1863) 3 B. & S. 826, 200
Tremaine v. *Pike* [1969] 3 All E.R. 1303, 33
Tucker v. *Smith* (1359) 103 S.S. 402, 51
Tyssen v. *Clarke* (1774) Lofft 496, 204
Weaver v. *Ward* (1616) Hobart 134, 46
Whitaker v. *Wisbey* (1852) 12 C. B., 44
Williams v. *Holland* (1833) 10 Bing. 112, 36f., 48
Windham v. *Chetwynd* (1757) 1 Burr. 414, 200
Yuill v. *Yuill* [1945] P. 15, 213

SCOTS LAW

Statutes
Statute of Commons 1695, 164, 167, 168
Sale of Goods Act 1893, 182
Sale of Goods Act 1979 s. 17, 197–8
s. 62 (4), 197–8

Cases
Anderson v. *Anderson* 1857, 19 D.701, 168, 171
Armour v. *Thyssen Edelstahlwerke A.G.* 1989 S.L.T. 182; 1990 S.L.T. 891, 189, 191–2, 197
Brandt & Co. v. *Dickson* 1876 3 R.375, 196
Brocke v. *Hamilton* 1852 19 D.701, 166, 168–71, 179, 181
Campbell v. *Murray* 1972 S.C. 310, 170, 176
Clarke & Co. v. *Miller & Son's Tr.* 1885 12 R.1035, 196–7
Cowan v. *Spence* 1824 3 S.42, 197
Cowie v. *Cowies* 1707–8 M.2453, 5362, 166, 178
Crathes Fishings Ltd v. *Bailey's Executors* 1990 S.L.T. 46; 1991 S.L.T. 747, 170, 173–4, 179–80
Cushney v. *Chrystie* 1676 M. 6237, 187–8
Denholm's Trustees v. *Denholm* 1984 S.L.T. 319, 177–8
Emerald Stainless Steel Ltd. v. *South Side Distribution Ltd.* 1982 S.c. 61, 192
Grant v. *Heriot's Trusts* 1906 8.F.647, 174–5
Hughes v. *Lord Advocate* [1963] A.C. 837, 33
MacCartney v. *Macredie's Creditors* (1799) M. App. s.v.Sale No. 1, 196
M'Neight v. *Lockhart* 1843 6 D.128, 169
Milligan v. *Barnhill* 1782 M. 2486, 167, 179
Morrison v. *Kirk* 1912 S.c. 44, 175
Murdoch & Co. Ltd. v. *Greig* 1889, 16 R.396, 189, 197
Parker v. *Law* (orse *Park* v. *Findlay*) 1621 Stair *Institutions*, 1.14.2; Hope, *Major Practicks* II.4.3, 185–6
Price v. *Watson* 1951 S.L.T. 226, 177
Prince v. *Pallat* 1680 M. 4932, 187
Provost Magistrates and Councillors of Banff v. *Ruthin Castle Ltd* 1944 S.L.T. 373, 172, 179
Robertsons v. *McIntyre* 1882 & R.772, 192
Scrimgeour v. *Scrimgeour* 1988 S.L.T. 590, 176–7, 179
Stewart v. *Feuars of Tillicoultry* 1739 M.2469, 167, 179
Stewart v. *Simpson* 1835 14 S.72, 168
Thom v. *MacBeth* 1875 3 R.161, 171
Thomsone v. *Chirnside* 1558 M.827, 192
Wright v. *Mitchell* 1871 9 M.516, 197

INTERNATIONAL LAW

International treaties
European Convention of Human Rights 1949 art. 6, 219, 221, 223
International Convention on Civil and Political Rights 1966 art. 14, 212
European Economic Community Treaty 1957 arts. 165, 166, 221

Cases
European Court of Human Rights
Delcourt (1970) 220, 221
Borgers (1991) no. 39 1990 Publ. Series A, vol. 214–A, 219–23

Index of names and subjects

Accursius 3, 104, 106, 111, 114–16
actio communi dividundo 159ff.
actio doli 19
actio ex empto 189
actio ex vendito 184n., 186
actio familiae erciscundae 159, 161, 166, 169, 170–1
actio furti 19, 60, 61n.
actio in factum 34, 60, 184n.
Admiralty, Court of 9, 119ff.
adtrectatio 56
Agustín, Antonio 5, 98ff.
Albanese, B. 56n., 63n., 64n.
Alciatus 5, 105
Allanbridge, Lord 173, 178
Althusius 144
America, discovery of 13
Andrews, N. 40
Ankum, H. 17, 19, 27
Anglo-Spanish peace treaty, 1604 122
Aquinas, St Thomas 7, 12
Aretio, F. de Accoltis de 133
Aristotle 153
Arminius, Jacobus 145
  Arminianism 143, 145–6
Arniston (Scots advocate) 169n.
Aulus Gellius 57
Austin, John xi, 208
Ayala, B. 121
Azo 3, 4, 12, 75, 77

Bacon, Francis 10
Backhaus, R. 65n.
bailee, liability of 10
Baker, J. H. 46n., 50, 52n., 57n.
Balduinus, Franciscus 106
Baldus de Ubaldis 13, 110, 133, 144
Balfour, *Practicks* 192
Bankton, Lord 163–5, 168, 190, 195
Bartolus da Sassoferato 73, 74, 106, 110, 144
Barrow, G. W. S. 154n.
Barton, J. L. 37n., 41n., 60n., 199n.

Bassianus, Johannes 3, 75
Bell 164–5, 190–3, 195, 197
Belleperche, Pierre de 73, 74
Bellus, Petrinus 121
Bembo, Pietro 98ff.
Bentham, Jeremy 13, 205
Beseler, G. 16–18, 21
Bezemer, C. H. 74
Birks, P. 208
Blackburn, Mr Justice 200n.
Blackstone, Sir William (Mr Justice) 35–6, 203, 205–6, 208
Bodin, Jean 144
Bologna 2, 3
bona materna 194
Borgers, Mr 219ff.
Bourges 116
Bracton xi, 4, 8, 9, 10, 12, 125n., 199, 200n., 203
Brutus, M. Junius 45
Buckland, W. W. 56n., 61, 67, 136, 173, 184n., 200n.
Budé 12
Bulgarus 2
burglary 55
Bynkershoek 117–18

Caelius Rufus 102
Caesar, Sir Julius 120ff.
Cairns, J. W. 136n.
Callistratus 112
Calvin, Jean 145n., 152
  Calvinism 138, 142–3, 148–9, 158
Campbell, A. H. 137–40
Campbell, W. M. 145n.
Canon law 120ff.
  'pontifical law' 122n.
Capranica, Camillo 99
Carey Miller, D. 192n., 197n.
case, action on the, *see* trespass on the case
Cassation, Court of 219ff.
Casson, D. B. 215n., 216n., 217n.
Castrensis, Paulus 110

229

caupo 9
Cecchelli, c. 100n.
Celsus 39n., 41, 113
Celtic custom 8
Challis, 118
Chancery, Court of 9, 131
Chevrier, G. 78
China 14
Church, Christian 2, 7
 church courts 9, 207
Cicero, Marcus Tullius 102, 132, 149
Cinus Pistorensis 198
city-states, mediaeval Italian 4, 5
Clyde, J. A. 161n., 162
Clyde, Lord 173–4
codification i, 11, 14
Coke, Sir Edward 205
commentators (*see also Ultramontani*) 4
conciliarism 12
consilia 4
Colonna, Ascanio 102
Colonna, Vittoria 102
Common Bench (or Common Pleas),
 Court of 131
Constantinople 2, 111
contract, Common law of 10
contrectatio, see furtum
Copper, Lord 172, 177
Coquille, G. 6, 204
Coquillette, D. R. 120
Corbet, John 144n.
Cotereus, Cl. 121n.
Covarruvias 7, 144
Cowell, John 10, 12, 203–5
Craig, *Ius Feudale* 161–2, 164, 167, 179
Crassus, Peter 3, 12
Crompton, Dr 125n., 127n., 128n.
Cujas 5, 107–9, 111n., 112, 114, 116
custom of the realm 9, 52
customary law 2, 4, 5, 11, 124
 see also Scotland, feudal law

Dagger, R. 141n.
damnum iniuria datum 59
Daube, D. 25n., 56n.
Deas, Lord 171
De Grey, C. J. 36
Delegates, High Court of 134
Denning, M. R., Lord 213n.
depositum 64
division, brieve of 164ff.
division, institutional 11, 202, 205
Doctors' Commons 119, 207n.
dominium 183, 192–3, 196–7
Donellus 5
Dort 143

Drago, Giovanni Pietro del 98–9, 100n.
Duck, A. 123n., 130
Dumoulin 6
Dun, Dr 125n., 126n., 127n.
Dunedin, Lord 174

Eden, W. 207n.
Egerton, Thomas 10
Emslie, Lord 176
England
 Anglo–Saxon 2, 8
 mediaeval 8, 9
 early modern 135
Entrèves, A. P. d' 139
Erskine, Lord 163–4, 169, 190, 192n., 195
Etablissements (of Louis IX) 4
European Communities, Court of Justice
 of the 220–1, 223n.
Exchequer, Court of the 131
Exchequer Chamber, Court of 201
exceptio non impleti contractus 189

Faber, Antony 106–7, 110
Faerno, Gabriele 103
Fearne, Charles 207n.
Feenstra, R. 73
Ferrary, J.-L. 89n.
Finch, Henry 205–6
fire, liability for 33, 47, 51–3
Flanders 210
Florentinus 135–6, 149, 151
Flume, W. 184
Four Doctors, The 2
France
 mediaeval 4
 Code civil (1804) 6
 modern 12, 14
Frangipani, Antonio 99
Frangipani, Curzio 98–8
Frangipani, Mario 99
Frier, B. W. 49
Frontinus, 102
Fuero Real 4
Fulbecke, W. 205
furtum 56ff.
 contrectatio 55ff.
 furtum manifestum 63

Gaius 20, 34n., 41, 43, 45, 60n., 108, 111, 149, 208
Gardner, S. 54n., 58n.
Gentili(s), Alberico 7, 13, 110ff., 119, 205
Gerke, Th. J. 17n., 20n.
Germany
 mediaeval 2, 4

Index of names and subjects 231

sixteenth century 5, 6
modern 12
Gifford, Lord 171
Gilbert, Sir Geoffrey 207n.
Glanvill, Rannulf de 4, 8, 199
Gloss, Great (*glossa ordinaria*) 3
Glossators xi, 3, 4, 104
Goldingham, Dr 125n.
Gordon, W. M. 135n., 149, 194
Gosford, Lord 188
Greek language 22, 115–16
Greene, M. R., Lord 213n.
Gregorovius, F. 99
Griew, E. 61n.
Grotius, Hugo de 4, 6, 7, 13, 14, 140–3, 145n., 146, 149
Gualteruzzi, Carlo 99, 100–1
Guidelinus, Petrus 135n., 155n.
Gulathingslov 4

Hale, Sir Matthew xi
Halpin, A. 69n.
Hammond, Dr 121n., 124n.
harmonistion of laws i, 5
Heineccius 107
Helmholz, R. H. 120, 199
Hill, L. M. 120n., 123n.
Hobbes, Thomas 13, 139–41, 143, 152, 154n.
Hohfeld, W. N. 143
Holt, Lord Chief Justice 200
Honoré, T. 68n.
Hope, *Major Practicks* 185–6
Hope, Lord 169n., 173
Hotman, François 107, 110, 114
Hove, Dr 126n.
Hugo 2
Hugolinus 12
Huls, Andrew 199
Human Rights, European Commission of 220
Human Rights, European Court of i, 219ff.
Huvelin, P. 56n.
hypothec 185–7, 190–2

Ibbetson, D. J. 36n.
Imola, Jason da 110
Indonesia 14
Inglis, Lord 197n.
iniuria 39, 59, 148
Inns of Court 9, 203, 206
interpolations 117
international law, *see ius gentium*
Investiture crisis 2, 4, 12
Ireland 131
Irnerius 3

Isidore of Seville 2
Islamic law 2
iudex 49
ius commune 122–6, 128–9
ius gentium 13, 119ff. 137
ius naturale (natural law) 7, 10, 137–8
ius postliminii 122–3

Jacob, Sir Jack 212n., 213n., 214n., 216n.
Jacobus 2
James I & VI, king 119, 121
James II & VII, king 137n.
Japan 14
Javolenus 104, 113
Johnston, Archibald 144
Jolowicz, H. F. 22, 68n.
Jolowicz, J. A. 209n., 213n.
Jones, Sir William 200n., 207n.
Julian 41, 43
jury 49
Justinian 1, 113, 153, 205
 Corpus Iuris Civilis 2, 3, 104–5 , 117, 121, 124n., 154, 167, 174, 177, 180–1, 188, 209
 Institutes 2, 3, 10, 135–6, 137, 157n., 161, 165, 172, 183, 204
 Digest 1, 2, 3, 10, 12, 21, 106, 117–18, 125n., 168, 177, 188, 193; *littera Fiorentina* 2, 98, 110; *Codex Secundus* 2
 Codex Justinianus 2, 3, 168
 Novels 2
'imperial law' 122n.

Kaser, M. 16n., 183n., 184n., 209n.
Keith, Lord 177, 178
Kelly, John 209
King's Bench, Court of 131, 204
Kinnear, Lord 175
Kolbert, C. F. 16n., 31
Kretzmer, D. 32n.

Labeo, Antistius 16ff., 44n., 104
Lambe, Dr 130
Lancelotti, G. P. 205
Latin 115–16, 204
Laudensis, Martinus 121n.
Lawson, F. H. 22
Leeuwen, van 6
legal autonomy 11
legal humanism xi, 5, 7
legal reasoning i, xi, 1, 4, 5, 6, 11, 12, 13, 54ff.
Lenel, O. 16, 39
Leonardi, M. de Blanchellis de 99
lex agraria (63 BC) 102

lex Aquilia 15, 25, 33, 38, 44, 45, 46n.
lex commissoria 183–5, 193n.
lex Cornelia de sicariis 41
lex Falcidia 112
Lignano, J. de 121n.
litis contestatio 210
Lobban, M. 206
Locke, John 13
Lombards 2
Longueil, Christopher de 101
longi temporis praescriptio 105
Louisiana 14
Lübeck, laws of 4

McCluskey, Lord 176–7
MacCormack, G. D. 56n., 63n.
MacCormick, D. N. 143n.
MacKay, Lord 172
MacKenzie, Sir George 137n., 157–8
M'Laren, Lord 175
MacQueen, H. L. 158n.
Magdeburg, laws of 4
Maitland, F. W. 15, 104, 118
mancipatio 183n.
Mansfield, Lord 200
Marcellus 201–2
Marcian 108, 112–13
Margani, Tiberio 98–9
Marshall, H. H. 209n., 213n.
Martens, Judge 220, 221n., 222n.
Martinus 2
Mason, R. A. 154n.
Matal, J. 98, 101, 102–3
Maule, Mr Justice 201–2
Maxwell, John 144–6, 152
Maynus, Jason 110
Medicus, D. 17–19, 23
mens rea 56
Meijers, E. M. 73, 74n.
Miquel, J. 64n.
Mitteis, L. 184n.
Modestinus 111, 200n.
Molina 7
Mommsen, Th. 2, 16, 56n., 63n.
Moncrieff, Lord 171
Monro, C. H. 19n., 65n.
Montaigne, M. de 99, 105
More, Sir Thomas 10
Mopha, Gribaldus 105n., 109–10
mos italicus 124, 129
Motulsky, H. 209n., 210
Mysingerius, J. 133

Natural law *see ius naturale*
Neratius 104
Netherlands, The 6, 14, 122

Nörr, D. 41–2, 44–5
Noodt 6
Numa, law of (Festus 178) 44n.

Ockham, William of 13
Odofredus 74
Ofilius 39n., 41–2, 48n., 50n., 56n.
Olivecrona, K. 63n.
Ormidale, Lord 171
Ouston, H. 158n.

Pacius 110
Padua 2
Paladino, Giovanbattista 99
Pandectists xi
Panvinio, Onofrio 99, 100n.
Papinian 1, 108, 113–14
papyri 1
parlements 5
Paul, Saint (the Apostle) 153
Paul(us) (Roman jurist) 23, 34n., 57, 59, 67n., 104, 107, 109, 184
Peckius, P. 132
Pedius, Sextus 23
Pernice, A. 19n.
Perrot, R. 214n., 216n., 217, 218n.
Peters, F. 184n.
Philippines, The 14
Phillimore, Sir Robert 207n.
Pillius 3
Placentinus 3, 105
Plautus 44
podestàs 5
political thought, western 12, 14
Pomponius 59n., 65, 104, 110
Popelinière, de La 121
Portugal 122, 135
Pothier 10, 172, 190, 195n., 197n., 200n.
Presbyterianism 138, 143, 145, 153, 156–8
Prest, W. 205n., 206
Prichard, M. J. 53
procedure
  Roman formulary 37
  Romano-canonical 6, 8, 9
  special pleading 49
Proclus 50n.
Prussian Code (1794) 6
Pufendorf, Samuel 13, 138–9
Pugsley, D. 57n.

quasi-delict 8, 165
Quebec 14
Quod legatorum 112
Quod quisque iuris 112

Rabelais 116

Index of names and subjects

Raber, F.   67n.
Ramism   206
rape   54
Ravenna   3
Rebuffus, Petrus   144, 153
reception   5, 14, 123
Regiam Maiestatem (3.3)   192n.
Reichskammergericht   6
res nec mancipi   183n.
Révigny, Jacques de   3, 73ff.
Rhodian sea law   123, 131–2
Rogerius   3, 75
Rome   i, 1, 111, 131, 182
Roman–Dutch law   6
Rosate, Albericus de   74
Roskill, Lord   69
Ross, Lord   192n.
roup, public   176
Rullo, Donato   102
Rullo, Quinto Fabio   98–9, 102
Rullo, Teofrasto   98–9, 102
Rullus, P. Servilius   102
Rutherford, S.   143–56
Rutherfurd, Lord   166, 168–70, 173, 176, 179–81

Sabinus   59n., 61, 63, 67, 113
Salvesen, Lord   175
Samson   38
San Marino   xi
Schiller, A. A.   28n.
Scotland   xi
  mediaeval   8
    Arbroath, Declaration of   154
  early modern   135
  universities   8
  feudal law   164–5, 167, 178
Scrutton, T. E.   199n.
Seipp, D. J.   199, 204n.
Senatus Consultum Silanianum (AD 10)   44
Servius Sulpicius Rufus   41n., 45, 48
Shuger, D. K.   152
Siete Partidas   4
Simpson, A. W. B.   207n.
Skinner, Q.   154
slavery   135ff.
Smart, I. M.   145n.
Smith, J. C.   58n., 63n.
Smith, T. B.   136n.
Solus, H.   214n., 216n., 217, 218n.
South Africa   14
South America   14
Spain
  mediaeval   4
  early modern   7, 135

Anglo–Saxon treaty 1604   122
modern   14
Squibb, G. D.   207n.
Sri Lanka   14
Stair, James Dalrymple, first Viscount   135ff., 162–6, 168–9, 185–8, 190–1, 193–5, 197n., 198
Staughton, Mr Justice   200n.
Stein, Peter   i, xi, 10, 14, 15, 32, 44n., 45n., 54, 57n., 61n., 138, 143, 154n., 158, 159, 182, 198, 200n., 204n., 208n., 209
Steward, Dr   128n.
Storme, Judge   220, 221n.
Stracca, B.   121
Strada, Jacopo   99
Stuart, R. R.   58n.
Styward, Dr   125n., 126n.
Switzerland, modern   12

Tartagnus, Alexander   110, 133
Terence   102–3
Texas   14
theft   55ff.
  appropriation   55ff.
Theodosian Code   13, 108
Thomas, J. A. C.   56n., 57n., 59n., 60n., 61n., 62n., 63n., 64n., 67n., 68n.
Thomasius   7
Tindal, C. J.   36n., 37n.
Torelli, Lelio   103
torts, Common law of   10, 32
traditio   183n., 186, 189, 192–7
Transylvanian tablets   1
Trebatius   56n., 61n.
trespass, action of   46ff.   52
trespass on the case   47ff.   52
Trevor, Dr   122–3
Tribonian   105–8, 110, 111n.
Truchsess, Otto   100
Tübingen, University Law Faculty   124n.
Tuck, R.   139, 140n., 147
Turkey   14
Turner, J. W. C.   58n.
Tyacke, N.   145n.

Ulpian   21–3, 25–6, 29–31, 34n., 41, 61n., 62–8, 111, 112, 184, 189, 195
Ultramontani   78
unde vi   77
universities, mediaeval   4, 5, 8, 9
usucapio   183n., 192–4, 196
usus modernus (pandectarum)   121, 129
uti possidetis   76–7

Valerius Flaccus   44

Vázquez (Vasquius), Fernando 121n., 144, 146
vindicatio 184, 186
Vinnius 6
Virgil 102–3
Vitelleschi, Giovanni 100
Voci, P. 16n.
Voet 6, 21, 190

Wales 131
Wark, Lord 172
Watson, W. A. (Alan) J. 40–1, 56n., 59n., 61n., 137, 157n., 158n.
West, William 10
Wieland, Philips 210

Williams, G. 68n.
Wilmot, Mr Justice 200
Windscheid 7, 22
Wirszubski, C. 154n.
Wolff 7
Wolff, H. J. 19, 21
Wood, Thomas 206
Wormald, J. 136n.

Young, Lord 197

Zasius, U. 6, 12, 133
Zimmermann, R. 21, 44n.
Zouch 119